STUDIES IN ECONOMICS AND RUSSIA

Also by Alec Nove

AN ECONOMIC HISTORY OF THE USSR
ECONOMICS OF FEASIBLE SOCIALISM
EFFICIENCY CRITERIA FOR NATIONALIZED INDUSTRIES
GLASNOST IN ACTION
SOCIALISM, ECONOMICS AND DEVELOPMENT
STALINISM AND AFTER
THE SOVIET ECONOMIC SYSTEM
WAS STALIN REALLY NECESSARY

Studies in Economics and Russia

Alec Nove

Professor Emeritus
University of Glasgow

St. Martin's Press New York

 For information, write:
Scholarly and Reference Division,
St. Martin's Press, Inc., 175 Fifth Avenue,
New York, N.Y. 10010

First published in the United States of America in 1990

Printed in Great Britain

ISBN 0–312–04509–3

Library of Congress Cataloging-in-Publication Data
Nove, Alec.
Studies in economics and Russia/Alec Nove.
p. cm.
ISBN 0–312–04509–3
1. Economics—Soviet Union—History. 2. Soviet Union—Economic conditions. 3. Soviet Union—Economic policy. I. Title.
HB113.A2N68 1990
338.947—dc20 89–70362
CIP

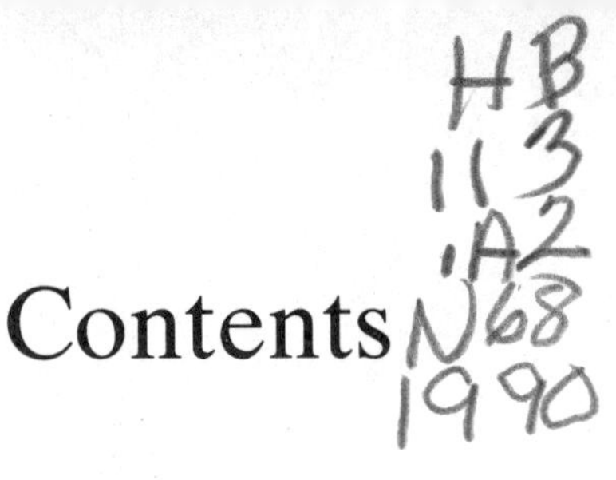

Contents

Preface vi

PART I HISTORY OF ECONOMIC IDEAS 1

1 Three Early Russian Economists 3
2 M. I. Tugan-Baranovsky (1865–1919) 24

PART II ECONOMIC HISTORY 41

3 War Communism 43
4 Lenin and the New Economic Policy 50
5 Trotsky, Markets and East European Reforms 71
6 The End of NEP 80
7 The Soviet Peasantry in the Second World War 90
8 Industry under Khrushchev 104
9 Russian Modernization 114

PART III ECONOMICS: EAST AND WEST 127

10 Planning 129
11 Markets? Yes but . . . 144
12 Friedman, Markets and Planning: A Comment 153
13 The Fragmentationist Disease 164
14 Marxism and 'Really Existing Socialism' 171
15 Planning and Markets 222
16 'Feasible Socialism' Revisited 232
17 Soviet Reforms and Western Neoclassical Economics 244

PART IV CONTEMPORARY USSR 263

18 Has Soviet Growth Ceased? 265
19 Labour Incentives in Soviet *Kolkhozy* 290
20 Soviet Agriculture 302
21 The Contribution of Imported Technology to Soviet Growth 312
22 The Defence Burden: Some General Observations 325
23 Is Within-system Reform Possible? 340
24 Soviet Economic Reform: Progress and Frustrations 355

Index 367

Preface

This collection reflects the rather wide range of my interests, from the history of Russian economic thought to the contemporary Soviet scene, as well as questions relating to socialism and the role and limitations of markets. Major changes are taking place in the Soviet Union and in a number of other communist-ruled countries, changes which involve decisive strengthening of market forces and abandonment of the attempt to plan everything from above. However the reformers are frequently unaware of how a real market functions in real capitalist countries, and indeed I have had three articles published in the Soviet Union in 1988 in which I tried to draw attention to 'market' problems, some of which beset (for example) Mrs Thatcher's Britain today. These are also the subject of some of the papers in the present collection. I would particularly draw to the reader's attention my critique of what I call 'fragmentationism', a disease that has actually become worse since I wrote the paper on the subject: to the disruption of urban transportation, the hospitals and school systems, electricity generation, London and the Post Office has now to be added the ambulance service. All this seems to link up with an ideological blind spot peculiar to Britain: the whole is seen as no more than the sum of its parts, and therefore any network can apparently be costlessly broken up. Conservative governments and municipalities in other countries behave quite differently.

Whenever it is relevant I have added a short introduction to the papers here published, if some recent events have rendered their contents significantly out of date. To cite just one example, the paper entitled 'Has Soviet Growth Ceased?' was written at a time when official Soviet publications were claiming a growth rate of around 3 per cent; now it is accepted that these have been years of stagnation, with growth close to zero. (I do *not* suggest that this is because Soviet statisticians had read my paper!)

There should be something here to interest a wide variety of readers, those who are concerned with political economy in its broadest sense.

Here and there the reader will find the same argument repeated. For example a brief critique of the psychological oversimplifications of so-called public choice theory occurs even three times. This seems to me excusable, as this occurs in the body of the argument in somewhat different contexts. Also inevitably some judgements have been overtaken by events. Thus in an analysis dated 1985 I did not anticipate the very great sharpening of the nationalities issues which occurred four or five years later. It may still be of interest to see how this critical observer viewed the situation at the beginning of Gorbachev's rule, so I did not 'update' the text.

ALEC NOVE

Part I
History of Economic Ideas

1 Three Early Russian Economists*

What sort of economics was there in Russia during the reign of Alexander I? The ideas of Adam Smith became known early: indeed one of our three subjects, Mordvinov, read the *Wealth of Nations* in the year of its publication while he was in England as a naval officer. By 1820 it was the 'in' thing to have at least a claim to know of his ideas. Thus Pushkin's fictional man-about-town, Evgeni Onegin was given by his author the following characteristic:

> Theocrites and Homer bored him,
> But Adam Smith he read right through.
> In economics he was learned,
> He knew how wealth of nations grew,
> And how they lived and why they need
> Just simple products and not gold;
> Advice his father would not heed,
> The family estates were sold.

(This is my attempt at translation. Actually the estates were mortgaged, but I failed to find the necessary rhyme.)

The three leading economists of the period were the first professor of economics of Moscow University, the first economist–member of the Imperial Academy of Sciences, and an influential policy adviser and prolific writer on economic questions who happened also to be an admiral. (The distinguished composer Borodin was also a successful professor of chemistry. There are some other examples of the pursuit of multiple careers.)

The ideas of these economists are of interest from several different angles. One is just to see what sort of economics was being taught in St Petersburg and Moscow in the first decades of the nineteenth century. The second is to observe how Adam Smith's ideas in-

* This was part of a project on the history of Russian economic thought, for which I had financial assistance from the Leverhulme Trust, which is gratefully acknowledged.

fluenced, and were modified by, those who lived and worked in circumstances so different from his. Finally, the ideas themselves are worthy of note for anyone interested in the history of economic thought. The issue of protection versus free trade, of productive and unproductive labour, of the validity of a labour theory of value, remarks on the causes and remedies of inflation, on human capital and even on the valuation of capital assets – all these matters are touched upon in ways which have original features, though there is no doubt as to the influence of Adam Smith and to a lesser extant of J.-B. Say (None of them seems to have become aware of Ricardo.)

The first two economists here presented both have German surnames, but both lived and worked in Russia, and are described as 'our fellow-countrymen' in Russian reference-books and publications.

CHRISTIAN SHLETSER

Christian SHLETSER (1774–1831) was the son of an eminent German historian, August-Ludwig von Schlözer, who settled in Russia in the reign of Catherine. Shletser attended the University of Göttingen, graduating in 1796. He was appointed to the University of Moscow in 1801. His ideas were fully expressed in his textbook, *Nachal'nye osnovaniya gosudarstvennogo khozyaistva* (Basic principles of the state economy).[1] It was regarded at the time as the first Russian book on the subject. Its author expressed pride in the fact that it was translated into German and used as a textbook in Würzburg and Landshut universities. A French translation also appeared.

After an account of mercantilist and physiocratic doctrines, he comes to Adam Smith, 'who was first able to base this [economic] science on true and solid principles'. Deeply influenced by Smith, he none the less was no blind follower.

He discusses welfare, stressing also mental welfare ('joy, clear conscience . . .') and then goes on to labour and capital. Production is the result of labour plus use of capital. Capital used in production (a hunter's knife, a machine and so on) is the product of surplus labour; that is, surplus to what is used to cover basic needs. Capital is also personal, in the form of acquired knowledge and skills.

Society's net gain (*chistyi vyigrysh*), or surplus product, is the amount in excess of what is required to maintain labour (that is, subsistence) and capital. 'Value' (*tsennost'*, *Wert*) arises in exchange. Men are motivated by egoism ('love of self'), by love of gain and by indolence. Men therefore seek to obtain what they desire through exchange, with the least effort necessary. The value of non-reproducible goods is determined by their scarcity in relation to the desire to acquire them. Reproducible goods acquire their exchange value by the interplay of the desire to acquire and the 'forces of production' needed to reproduce them, sometimes modified by the scarcity of the materials required.

> Few products are made solely by labour, that do not need various kinds of capital . . . Exchange values of goods can be related to labour only in the most primitive period . . . The concept of labour as the only source of goods is a totally abstract one, which has not existed in reality for thousands of years, since in our society the major part of commodities is none other than the complex product of material and personal capital. So if we wish to relate price only to labour we would have to carry on calculating for ever . . . So even the glorious Smith acted carelessly by utilizing too exclusively the concept of labour as expressing the forces of production.[2]

Variations in demand ('need', *nuzhda*) for labour and capital and for the product cause its price to fluctuate above and below the 'true or natural valuation', the latter being that which provides the equilibrium rate of return to labour and capital. Profit on capital tends to be lower in populous and more developed countries, because the more highly profitable opportunities of applying capital to land, mines and manufactures will already have been taken.

The rate of return (or income, *Rente*) of capital, its share in the net gain, is determined by the relative scarcity of capital in relation to its opportunity for use, demand, competition and risk (subject to availability of insurance). Similar principles apply in the case of human ('personal') capital, which requires to be compensated: the skilled craftsman or other specialist is seen as loaning out his personal capital to his employer, his return being an amount in excess of the subsistence wage.

Unskilled labour too may share in the net gain of society, by earning more than subsistence, depending on supply, demand and opportunity: thus in North America and in South Russia profits are high and labourers few, so wages are well above subsistence. In a country with slaves, a free worker 'can use his freedom as personal capital', and can thus obtain higher income.

Shletser distinguishes between 'natural' and 'artificial' (manufactured) products. In the case of silver, for example, 'the sum of forces of production required for extraction is not, as in the case of artificial products, the measure of their value; on the contrary, their value acts as the measure of the sum of productive forces that can be profitably applied . . .'.[3]

Land is treated as a variety of capital, for which people have to pay to gain access. This sort of capital earns a low return in land-abundant poorly-developed countries and rises to higher levels in 'societies approaching full development'. Demand and competition give to land an 'imagined valuation'. The value of land is not due to the amount requiring to be spent on it, rather the reverse: thus fertile virgin land is of high value. 'The sums payable for the use of a field have as their sole basis the introduction of private property and the resulting need for those who do not possess it to have access to it'.[4]

On *money*, after discussing the usefulness of precious metals and of prices, and variation in the value of gold and silver over time, he notes the effect of velocity of circulation on price levels: 'Circulation of money is not the same in all societies. In some it is slow, in others fast. The rapid circulation of money has the same effect on the rise of nominal prices as an increase in the total supply of money . . .'. Conversely, if money is hoarded ('kept in trunks') it is as if it did not exist. So one cannot deduce the general price level from the quantity of money, because of differences in velocity.[5]

There follows a discussion of interest on money capital, with stress placed on the fact that 'money capital is not real capital, but the right to acquire capital'. Interest rates will be a function of the relative profitability of capital in the given society. Of course the entrepreneur who borrows the capital does so to make a profit, so the loaner of money will get only part of the net gain. 'Money capital as such does not yield its own revenue. Interest can only exist when there is profit from real [physical] capital.'

The quantity of money in circulation will have no effect on interest rates, as distinct from nominal prices, including the prices of physical capital assets, which would rise along with other prices if money supply increased. But 'a sudden and large increase or decrease in the money in circulation can for a short period cause an excess or a shortage of capital and thereby lead to changed interest rates'. The value of real capital assets changes in the light of the expected profitability of its use. Thus, if a factory which made 10 000 roubles profit expects in future to make only 5000 roubles, its value will fall.[6]

Shletser then returns to human capital, and suggests the following formula to express a rate of return:

$$b = \frac{\frac{cq}{r}}{r - \left(\frac{r}{r+q}\right)i}$$

b = annual income of educated specialist;
c = capital; $\frac{q}{r}$ = rate of interest; i = expectation of life.

This is over and above costs of subsistence.[7]

Forces of production therefore consist of 'physical capital, human capital and simple (natural) labour'. The *wealth* of a nation is a function of its 'net product' (net gain) of society, being the amount left over after subsistence and capital replacement. This is available both for unnecessary luxury and enjoyment (*izlishniye naslazhdeniye*) and for investment ('the expansion of capitals').

Some nations are wealthier than others because of climate, soil, skill (including intelligent use of division of labour), minerals, convenient transport systems (such as navigable rivers and harbours), and also modesty in luxury, propensity to save, availability of credit and so on. *Credit* is of great use in organizing production and distribution. Credit notes (both private and state) must be seen as part of the supply of money, and can have the effect of forcing up prices to the disadvantage of holders of 'real' (that is, metallic) money.

Turning now to *state economic policies*, Shletser insists on the need to have flourishing agriculture, manufacture and trade – all three. A rich country has, in relation to the number of its inhabitants, a large 'net gain' and much capital. Government policy cannot directly increase net gain, it can do so only through increasing the forces of production: that is, the quantity and effectiveness of labour and capital. A large population as such could have negative effects: poverty, high taxes, even revolution. To support this contention, he cites Malthus.

To avoid social problems the government in an overpopulated

country should either set up industries or encourage emigration. 'In a country where industry has only just begun to develop' industry should be fostered with care and discrimination. Often agriculture provides the most profitable use of resources in such a country, though it could be obstructed by what he called 'feudal remnants' (a cautious reference to serfdom!). Too much development of manufacture can lead to a dangerous overdependence on imports of machinery. Also factories can only be profitably started if the return on them is at least as great as that foregone in agriculture, 'which cannot happen if the manufactured product is much dearer than an imported one'.[8] It paid North America to 'abandon manufacture', and Russia resembles America in having unused and fertile lands: 'A prosperous peasant is preferable to a poor factory worker.'

Some factories are set up in Russia with barriers against imports, plus monopoly. Yet despite these advantages some would not survive if the labour were not serf but free. All would benefit, he insists, if workers were free to go and cultivate unused and fertile land. Manufacturing should concentrate on 'simple necessities' and be small-scale and cooperative ('associations of labourers exercising their craft on a small scale and at their own expense'), using Russian materials. Exceptions include weapons, needed for national security, and necessary processing of minerals and timber to make them transportable for export.

As a country becomes more developed, state support may be needed to encourage 'capitalists', craftsmen and so on to set up new industries. The infant industry argument is duly made:[9] some manufactures, at first unprofitable, can become highly effective after the learning process. He cites woollens in England in the reign of Edward III, and, as a negative example, Germany: politically divided and open to British manufactures, private individuals lack capital to set up factories. A government should

> make greater effort to secure advantage over another country that has ample capital and other favourable circumstances. Germans are by nature just as efficient as the English, and do very well in London as well as St. Petersburg. Eliminate the division of Germany and the Germans could be raised to a level worthy of their industriousness.

To set up business one needs a low rate of interest. Direct government intervention is 'useless'. Government can set up credit institutions, but they should lend at the going rate. It can affect interest rates by reducing risk, as by strengthening legal rights of creditors, proper bankruptcy laws, publication of accounts and so on. Similarly, direct government intervention in pricing is wrong. But government can reduce costs (and so prices) by building good roads and canals, and encourage division of labour. When a government wishes to set up an industry, it is better to contract the task out to a private entrepreneur. A factory publicly owned always requires a vast number of administrators, inspectors and so on, as compared with one that belongs to a private citizen. Furthermore salaried officials who are charged with running the factory, seeing no advantage in increasing revenues, usually neglect their tasks.[10]

On *foreign trade*, Shletser warns against export subsidies, which benefit a few merchants 'and, worse still, the foreign consumer'. *Customs duties* are a useful form of protection, when capital and labour are abundant, but 'can frequently do more harm than good' in less developed countries, 'not only diverting productive resources from the more profitable and directing them to less profitable pursuits, but also creating harmful monopolies'. Tariffs should be used with care and discrimination.

The government should facilitate trade by improving roads and canals, imposing weights and measures standards, providing a postal service and maintaining order, encourage associations of traders and insurance, give preference to Russian shipping (Cromwell's navigation acts are here referred to) and negotiate trade treaties.

The author cites Adam Smith on balance of trade, and then goes on to try to identify relative advantage from trade. He sees greatest advantage in export of what he calls 'natural goods' and least in 'complex manufactures'. He advances two reasons for this. One is that 'natural goods' (raw materials and minerals) are usually in surplus in the exporting country, and so there is little opportunity cost. (Thus Russia has more timber and flax than it can use.) The other is that the element of gift of nature is greater, the specific contribution of labour and capital less than is the case in manufactures.

A final section deals with public finance. There is a warning about not issuing too many banknotes (*assignatsii*), which would lead to price rises. It is better to raise a loan than to print money. *Taxes* he sees as a necessary evil, which can be mitigated if paid by all in proportion to their wealth (or, presumably, income). Taxes should be levied on net gain, not on 'forces of production', should not discourage enterprise, should be simple and hard to evade and be spread across a wide range of activities. Budgets should be balanced. Export taxes make sense if one has a monopoly, as with Chinese tea and Russian caviar, but are harmful if one has to compete.

Shletser's course, therefore, has a 'cost-of-production' theory of value, with an emphasis on the role of human and material capital, and treats land as a form of capital (and rent as a consequence of private ownership and relative scarcity). He shows himself very conscious of dangers of inflation, and lays stress also on velocity of circulation of money of various kinds. He seems to be quite modern in his treatment of human capital, with a formula on a rate of return to education. He is ambiguous on the trade policy appropriate to a developing country, conscious both of the dangers of indiscriminate protectionism and of the need to foster industry to a degree appropriate to the level of development the given country had reached. He clearly prefers private to state enterprise (except that he insists that only the state should operate the postal service) but, interestingly, sees advantage in encouraging cooperative small-scale industry. In discussing gains from foreign trade, he claims that primary-producing countries are in a relatively favourable position (exporting *surpluses*, embodging gifts of nature). His practical recommendations, as well as many of his examples, relate specifically to Russia. He almost totally dodges the vexed problem of serfdom, which is not the case with his St Petersburg colleague, as we shall see. Both, however, do stress the desirability of encouraging the 'middle classes', as the foundation of national prosperity.

ALEXANDER KARLOVICH SHTORKH

Alexander Karlovich SHTORKH (Storch) was born in Riga in 1766 and died in 1835. He studied at Jena and Heidelberg, where, according to the Russian historian of economic thought, Vernadsky, he was offered a chair and refused it. He had a wide range of interests and was apparently trilingual, writing in Russian, French and German, on literature and history as well as economics. His *Historisch-statistische Gemälde der Russischen Reichs an ende des 18-ten Jahrhunderts*, published in Leipzig in nine parts between 1797 and 1803, was published in French and (according to Vernadsky) also in English (London, 1801) 'and it is said that it was translated into Russian' (!). His principal work was published in St Petersburg in 1815 in French:

Cours d'économie politique: une exposition des principes qui déterminent la prospérité des nations. A German translation in three parts appeared in 1816–20, and J.-B. Say published an unauthorised version in Paris. Shtorkh had several works published there: *Considérations sur la nature du revenu national* (1824) which he himself translated into German, in which he disputed with Say the question of 'the value of services' and *Examen des funestes effets d'un papier-monnaie déprécié* and *Réfutation d'une doctrine professée par M. de Sismondi concernant l'accroissement du capital d'une nation*.

He was made a member of the Imperial Academy of Sciences in St Petersburg in 1801, and his textbook was based on lectures given to the imperial family, including the future Tsar Nicholas I. He rose to be vice-president and for a time acting president of the Academy. He was described by McCulloch as 'the best continental writer' on political economy, and he rates half a page in Schumpeter's history of economic thought as a 'critical Smithian'.

References below are to the Russian version of the *Cours d'économie politique* (translated by Vernadsky in 1881) except where the original French edition is referred to; this was found in the Helsinki library.

Shtorkh begins by seeing political economy as a branch of sociology, concerned with 'laws' independent of the human will relating to wealth and education. He regretted having to write all this 'in a foreign language', without explaining why. Economics cannot be an exact science, because of the varieties of human behaviour: 'This shows the uselessness of applying algebraic formulae to economic phenomena, as some writers do.' Economic laws emerge from the nature of things. Those set in authority over others cannot breach them without suffering the consequences. But, even if the sovereign and his ministers understand the correct principles, their decisions will not be effective unless those whose duty it is to carry them out understand them too. So economic theory requires to be widely taught.

His *theory of value*, while recognising that values are produced by Man, is basically subjective. Goods are valued because they have the quality of satisfying need (*godnost'*). 'From this it can be concluded that value does not arise out of circumstances of production, but from the judgment of those who desire that the given product satisfy their needs.' After praising Adam Smith, he criticizes his value theory for attributing value to labour expended or commanded:

> Is this not to confuse the origins of the commodity which can have value with the origins of value? Nature and labour undoubtedly are the source of goods, but this does not make them the source of their value. Goods have value not because they contain a material or are made by labour, but because they are useful and their usefulness is recognised.[11]

While some items not produced by labour have value (for example, a growing forest), some that *are* produced by labour have none (for example, a book which no one wants to read, or a garment out of fashion). 'Labour in industry is productive not *because*, as Smith asserts, it produces values, but is productive *when* it produces values. It is not effort and sweat as such that produces value, but the usefulness of the products.' True, no one makes productive effort without expecting at least a commensurate return, in which case (he asks) does it matter whether the source of value is labour or subjective judgment (*mneniye*, opinion)? It does matter, he answers, because judgment is cause and labour effect. Besides, nature also contributes to value.

He goes on: 'As labour is not the *source* of the value of goods, neither is it its *measure*. A commodity costs more than another not because it requires more labour, but because of its higher cost of production, which, as we shall see, is not directly proportionate to labour.' Anyhow, 'how can we ever discover, even approximately, the total labour, i.e. physical and mental effort and trouble, expended in the process of production, how can we measure it, how can we relate it to price?'. Smith was much superior to his predecessors, but he too saw *goods* as values, seeing them as physical objects. Smith was a genius, but he did not appreciate 'internal [subjective] valuation' and non-material forms of value and welfare which are part of a civilized society.[12]

Shtorkh earlier discusses the *nature of exchange*, noting its advantages over two other ways of acquiring goods – violence and begging. Left to themselves, men will try to utilize their comparative advantages in skills and so on, and society will benefit. *Exchange value* depends on the views (preferences) of the purchaser and of the seller, but the purchaser's evaluation is primary. Prices will fluctuate, with variations of supply and demand, around *costs of production*; he defines as 'necessary costs' those that provide the normal reward to factors of production (of which more in a moment).

He insists on the importance of non-material values, such as knowledge, taste, art, freedom and the pleasure of ownership. Non-material services must be included, but so should 'internal [subjective] goods', by which he means, for instance, art appreciation, even though they cannot enter into exchange (though a teacher of art appreciation can, of course, sell his services). This led him into some argument with J.-B. Say. It is worth dwelling on this dispute, which can be studied in the 1824 Paris edition of *Cours d'économie politique*, by 'Henri Storch'. Say had earlier published and (partially) praised Shtorkh's book, and both men had criticized Adam Smith's treatment of non-material services as unproductive. However Shtorkh argued that, while 'I tried to show that personal services, treated by Smith as sterile, contribute *indirectly* to the formation of national income by producing *products*, mostly indispensable for material production', Say had a different view, that 'services create *values*, that this work is *directly* productive'. The difference between the two is illustrated by the example of medical services: what is the product, the work of the doctor (Say) or the health of the patient (Shtorkh)? 'It is the *services themselves* which M. Say calls product. But then what of their *results*, their effects?' Having criticized Smith for his omission of 'musicians, actors, judges, public administrators', how can Say now attack Shtorkh for assigning value to religious cults and public security ('*Le culte une valeur? La securité une valeur? C'est insoutenable!*' wrote Say). No, argues Shtorkh, 'though it may displease M. Say, I am still of the opinion that productive labour is not its own product, any more than the cause is its own effect'. Say's view leads him to deny that services contribute to wealth, only to consumption, because they cannot be accumulated: 'a nation with a mass of musicians, priests, officials, could be a nation well diverted, indoctrinated, admirably administered, but that is all. Its capital would show no increase'. Shtorkh disagrees: the results can be accumulated, services 'participate indirectly in the enrichment of nations'.[13] Presumably the best illustration of the difference would be education. If the 'product' is not the time spent teaching but the acquisition of knowledge by the pupil, this would contribute, indirectly, to the wealth of nations.

Shtorkh follows Smith in asserting that without personal freedom and property '*there can be neither riches nor enlightenment*' (his emphasis), an important point to make to a future tsar of a country with serfdom. 'In Russia society would grow quicker' if all classes in the empire were guaranteed property rights. He also follows Smith in analyzing the division of labour, the importance of capital and of the size of market, and cites Smith's views on the adverse effects of narrow specialization on the labourer.

A chapter is devoted to *accumulation*. Goods used for further production become capital. He treats all unearned income ('income not requiring work') as *rent*, whether this is obtained by allowing the use of capital or land. Some valuable goods are hoarded and fulfil no useful purpose: he states that Russian peasants hide valuables in holes in the ground, 'due to their lack of security' (serfs' property can be taken by their master).

'When government expenditures absorb so high a proportion of total incomes that private persons are compelled to dispose of capital', this is not conducive to the public good. In discussing *income distribution*, Shtorkh makes the important distinction between the income of the entrepreneur and income from ownership of capital. These can be combined in the same person, but often are not. If the owner chooses not to do entrepreneurial work, he must pay a salary to a manager.

He imagines a farmer borrows seed-corn, and then divides the product (corn) between workers' wages, rent to the owner of the land and interest on the borrowed capital, plus his own reward. The 'price' of land, labour and capital is determined by the interplay of supply and demand. However the lower limit of wage for unskilled work is subsistence, and this must include reproduction of the next generation (he assumes, in passing, that half the children will die in infancy). Heavy or dangerous work, or skilled work, will earn more. Incomes are also affected by a job's high or low social standing, and wages can be particularly low if the recipient has another source of income (examples: servants who knit in their spare time; soldiers who are part-time artisans; wives).

He then discusses *rent of talent*, which he regards as analagous to land rent, as it emerges from personal ownership. The talent could be anything from exceptional physical strength to high skills; the rarer the talents in relation to demand, the higher the rent. The quality of honesty, if rare, will be well rewarded in the job of cashier or jeweller.

The basic wage in any country will be high if labour is very scarce in relation to capital and land, as in the United States, or low if very abundant, as in Bengal. It is not the absolute amount of capital but its growth that makes higher wages possible. In Great Britain there is much capital, but, despite the country's riches, wages are far below American levels, and even Russian wages compare favourably. In countries that stagnate wages tend towards subsistence levels. Higher wages do not necessarily lead to higher costs and prices, if associated with more skill, better health or better morale.

Interest is treated simply as rent paid for the use of capital. It is Shtorkh's treatment of *land rent* that is interesting, and Russian critics considered it better than Ricardo's (of whose work Shtorkh seems to have been unaware in 1815). '*Primary rent*' (absolute rent) has to be paid because of private property and scarcity. 'No one, luckily, can say: "wind and rain are mine, so pay for their use".' Unlike the rate of interest, which influences the supply of capital, there is no 'necessary' level of rent, since land as such is a gift of nature, as is anything beneath it (minerals, for example). Rent – unlike wages, profit or interest – is a consequence of the prices of goods. If prices fall, rent falls. It can fall to zero, if there is no profit to be made in renting land. Marginal land may still be worth cultivating, if the proprietor cultivates it. More fertile land commands a higher rent, as does convenient location. Less fertile land is brought into cultivation when the price of the product rises. Improved land (irrigated or drained, for example) commands the primary rent plus a hiring charge for improvements, analagous to what would have to be paid for buildings on that land. The price of land does not determine its rent; the expected rent is a determinant of its price.[14]

The point is made that the 'feudal rent' charged for the right to fish leads to a loss to the consumer, since it can have no effect on production and simply increases costs. At least private ownership of land encourages land improvements and so can lead to increased yields. The *profit* of the entrepreneur is a reward for *work* and for *risk-taking*, and is usually not separately identifiable, because the entrepreneur may also be supplying his own capital, in whole or in part. Shtorkh then imagines a pharmacist who has had to learn skills and acquire a reputation for reliability. His income contains a lifetime's return on his expenses of education, plus a 'rent for his moral and mental qualities', plus a business profit.

In Shtorkh's discussion of *national income*, he divides it into two parts. The first covers the 'necessary' (subsistence) reward of labour, plus necessary interest and rent. The second part consists of 'net income or net profit of society', consisting of wages in excess of subsistence, excess rents of capital and land plus the net profit of entrepreneurs. This 'surplus' is the amount which can be taken away without reducing production. (There is an analogy with Marx's simple and expanded reproduction, or Baran's reinvestible surplus.)

He notes that 'growth of capital causes a fall in interest and profits, and a rise in wages and in land-rent'.[15] The rise in wages is also a consequence of higher productivity ('better tools, greater dexterity' and so on). On *money*, he stresses velocity. The monetary unit circulates much faster than do goods. As nations become richer, their need for money rises, but less than proportionately, as it tends to circulate faster. Credit instruments of many kinds (banknotes, and 'toutes sortes d'obligations particulières', such as bills of exchange, letters of credit and so on) supplement money proper. He then takes a line which would please Mrs Thatcher: 'While individuals usually seek to borrow in order to use funds productively, governments seek them to spend them without any return . . . All kinds of public loans have the defect of withdrawing capital from productive employments'; furthermore it forces up the rate of interest.[16]

Shtorkh favours borrowing from abroad for a developing country. A developed country's interest and profit rates tend to fall, so it tends to lend some capital to foreign countries, to their mutual benefit. 'If imports of goods exceed the value of exports, this can be due either to excess consumption or to shortage of [physical] capital. In the first case the country incurs debt and is on the road to ruin, in the second it can be enriching itself.' The apparent Russian export surplus he sees as fictional, owing to massive unrecorded smuggling.

On the *value of money and prices*, he notes the effects on prices of 'excess' issue of paper money, especially if it ceases to be convertible. While privately-owned credit documents are also a kind of money, private individuals and banks, in their own interest, will limit their number. This, however, cannot be said of governments. While a limited issue of paper money has advantages, the possibility of printing money causes 'des dangers si graves et si difficiles a éviter, que cette invention funeste peut être regardée comme le plus grand fléau des nations'.[17] Governments spend 'to operate enterprises which seem useful to them, but which the general interest would never have supported', or to make war, often encouraging 'luxury, prodigality and idleness'.

> Even the wisest government, once it creates paper-money, is in danger of dissipation, without knowing or wishing it. It is not for its own glory that it multiplies these fictional units of value: it is to revive industry, to extend enlightenment, to beautify cities, to erect useful monuments . . . Sums are advanced to traders and manufacturers to create new enterprises, and they are lost in a

> country where neither capital nor industry are yet at the necessary level . . . Capital which the infallible [*sic*] instinct of private gain would have utilized in the most fruitful manner is in part diverted to less productive use, and partly just consumed.

It is an 'irresistible' temptation to issue more paper, especially as earlier issues have already forced up prices and caused additional deficits to appear. 'Beyond a certain point the disease becomes incurable.' Metallic currency disappears from circulation. Incomes are unjustly redistributed. 'The productive work of the trader is replaced by speculation' (*agiotage*). It has a deplorable effect on 'public morale', by enabling some to pay their debts legally in depreciated currency 'while pretending to repay the total'.

Public enterprises are often monopolies which overcharge the public. 'Government cannot economise costs as well as can private individuals, who are stimulated by personal gain.'

On *foreign trade* Shtorkh is basically for free trade. The whole world should be seen as if it was one trading nation: 'If commerce was wholly free, everyone would gain.' Some, it is true, would gain more than others; *maybe* the rich nations gain more than the poor, but the poor nation would become even poorer if it refrained from trading. 'It is not in the interest of an agricultural nation to sacrifice its advantage merely to deprive another of a greater advantage.' If Russian flax worth two days' work exchanges for British cloth containing one day's work, while it would take three days' work to produce the cloth in Russia, then both nations gain by trade and specialization. A wise Russian government would only set up or encourage those industries which could effectively sustain foreign competition.

Finally, a section is devoted to *slavery*. The basic argument follows that of Adam Smith. Slave labour is inefficient and costly, bearing in mind the cost of managing slaves and organizing their consumption, as well as their low productivity. In Russia 'servitude prevents the people from going where it would be most advantageous'. The least harmful variety of serfdom is quit-rent, which at least gives partial free-worker status. In Russia as a rule only the gentry estate was allowed to own serfs, and entrepreneurs who sought to hire them (and some hired them as slaves, others via quit-rent) preferred a situation where there were free workers available. While some slave-owners could become entrepreneurs themselves, most of the gentry do not do so, preferring a life of unproductive luxury. The system is utterly 'pernicious'. Peasants must be given personal freedom, security and property rights. (A pity that Nicholas I did not follow the advice of his teacher!)

Shtorkh is distinguished, then, by a militantly *subjective* theory of value, a well-developed theory of rent, and emphasis on the value of non-material 'goods', a deep suspicion of government expenditure, a profound belief in sound money and in the disastrous consequences of printing too much of it. He tries to distinguish entrepreneurial reward from unearned income of the provider of capital and land. He is an almost total free trader. Finally, he uses Smithian principles to denounce slavery/serfdom in its Russian manifestation. Is this, one wonders, why he was compelled to publish the work (in St Petersburg) in French?

N. S. MORDVINOV

Mordvinov was the son of an admiral; the family were rich landowners, of the gentry (*dvoryanski*) estate. He was born near Novgorod in 1754. Intended for a naval career, he was given a good education and was sent to England at the age of 20. He read the *Wealth of Nations* in England when it first appeared. He then sailed the oceans, visiting America several times, as well as Germany, France and Italy. He spoke five languages. In Russia he undertook a variety of duties: in the navy, where he became an admiral, like his father, he headed the imperial admiralty; he was also made a member of the ministerial committee on finance in 1820; his many writings and memoranda on matters economic caused him to become president of the Free Economics Society in 1823; he was also active in business, was a co-founder of Russia's first insurance society and chairman of the Russian American company, which was particularly active in the fur trade. He died in 1845, in his ninety-first year.

His works include *Nekotorye soobrazheniya po predmetu manufaktur v Rossii i o tarifakh* (Some considerations on the subject of manufactures in Russia and on tariffs), first published in 1815, with later re-editions. Shorter books or papers concerned the setting-up of banks in the provinces (1816, then several editions) and why Russia has poor harvests (1839); and a long memorandum, *Mneniya admirala Mordvinova* (The views of Admiral Mordvinov), was addressed to Tsar Alexander I in the last year of his reign, 1825, setting out particularly clearly his ideas on economic policy. Finally, there is a multi-volume set of the family archives of the Mordvinovs, published in 1901–3, which contains still more of his memoranda, notes, correspondence and so on.

Before summarizing the ideas which he expressed, it is useful to situate Mordvinov within what could be called the Russian economic policy school. By this I mean those who had relatively little interest in abstract theory, who hardly ever paid any attention to the law of value, for instance, but who sought to devise a development strategy for the Russia of their time. They sought answers to questions such as: why is our country backward, or what is to be done to encourage industry, enterprise, trade, financial stability? Their ideas sometimes took the form of giving advice to monarchs. This was true of I. Pososhkov, who sought in vain to influence Peter the Great, and of M. Chulkov in the reign of Catherine. It was partly true also of Mordvinov's ideological opponent, Shtorkh, who acted as tutor to the future Tsar Nicholas I, though, as we have seen, Shtorkh was also a considerable theoretician. In more recent times the same can be said of Mendeleyev (that eminent scientist wrote much about an economic development strategy for Russia), Chuprov and Witte (the last-named's main work was also intended to instruct members of the Tsar's family). This does not mean that all these writers were unaware of economic theories or of their authors. As we have seen, Mordvinov was among Adam Smith's earliest readers. But their interest was primarily in the area that the Germans call *Nazionalökonomie*. In this respect, Mordvinov could be described as a sort of Russian List, but he arrived at his conclusions quite independently, as can be seen from the dates of his writings.

Soviet analysts such as F. Morozov place Mordvinov in the camp of 'liberal landlords', and correctly note a contradiction in his approach to the Russian reality of his time. He knew well, from his reading of Adam Smith and from looking around him, that serfdom was a major obstacle to Russia's development. He stressed repeatedly that 'labour' is the principal source of wealth, deplored the high level of infant mortality, desired the extension of the division of labour and greater mobility of goods and people. Indeed he went so far as to say that 'the brains and hands of slaves are incapable of generating wealth'. Yet, unlike his contemporary, Shtorkh, he did not conclude or advise that serfdom be abolished. It seems reasonable to interpret this omission in the light of his commitment to the nobility (or gentry) estate, the *dvoryanstvo*, which he plainly regarded as the very foundation of Russian society, and whose economic activities he sought in every way to encourage. Its economic basis could be shattered by too hasty an elimination of serf labour; there were also considerations of public order in rural areas. The nobility required capital for investment and enterprise, and he saw one source of such capital in payments made by serfs to purchase their freedom. Private profit he saw as a major motive force for economic progress, so he advocated (subject to the above condition) individual freedom and legal order. Also he saw the vital importance of banking and insurance, as can be seen from his writings and indeed his personal activities in these fields. But even there one notes his concern for the *dvoryanstvo* estate: the provincial banks, the creation of which he advocated were to make special provision for the *dvoryane*. However, he saw the importance of banks for encouraging enterprise by the merchant estate, and also wished that the peasant communities (*obshchestva*) should keep bank accounts – though this would hardly make sense if the peasant members had quasi-slave status. He was among the first to note and indeed stress the importance of peasant communal institutions, which most writers of his period tended to ignore.

Mordvinov's particular concern is the power of Russia, its political and economic independence. Agricultural production he recognises as of vital importance, but it is none the less essential to bring Russia out of its over-dependence on agriculture and developed 'handicrafts and manufactures'. This is all the more necessary in Russia because of the climate: for half the year the peasants have little or nothing to do. Manufacturing can also provide the tools needed for the improvement of agriculture. For Russia the doctrines of free trade advocated by Adam Smith, and by some contemporary economists such as Shtorkh, are inapplicable or dangerous. Mordvinov cites the example of Spain and Portugal, whose industries were (he argues) ruined by free trade, and who therefore became militarily weak and helpless.

Arguments for protection are then skilfully deployed. Experience argues for prohibiting certain imports, rather than charging high import duties, because of the problem of combating smuggling: if the mere presence of a prohibited foreign good is evidence of an offence, enforcement is made easier. He cites examples of past success: under Catherine II factories making hats, beer, carriages, furniture, kitchenware 'and many other items' were duly set up, and the needed capital duly appeared, when such imports were prohibited. He admits that Russian consumers tend to prefer foreign manufactures, and that Russian capitalists find it more profitable to use their capital for buying foreign goods rather than investing in factories in Russia.

In principle he favours non-interference with profit-making business, but in this instance he deploys the 'infant industry' argument: following a learning process, Russian manufactures can become competitive. English manufactures were originally of mediocre quality, and only gradually reached the high levels of that day. If foreign goods were freely available (he also argues), and imports increase sharply, the effect would be to devalue the rouble, which would lead to a subsequent rise in price of imports. Universal free trade might be a blessing, but many other countries impose import restrictions. 'To give free access to foreign goods in Russia, at a time when others have restrictions and prohibitions, would this not mean that our own industry, handicrafts, internal trade, would be in the power of alien peoples and would be snuffed out?' All this is by reference to the relatively liberal tariff of 1816, adopted under free-trade influences.

Mordvinov specifically attacked Shtorkh's free-trade arguments, without actually naming him, and it is interesting to note that a later Soviet commentator chooses to stress that Shtorkh was German, not Russian (he was from Riga; other Russian sources describe him as a 'Russian economist' or 'our fellow-countrymen'). Here is a taste of Mordvinov's polemics on this point:

> Russia is not so poor as some describe her, borrowing their judgments from French books. The Russian language cannot handle such statements as 'Russia is poor; the work of the Russian yields no profit; it is to Russia's advantage to grant rights of manufacture and trade to richer powers; Russia in her present state should not and cannot cease to be dependent on foreign countries'. All this can be said in French; it is incomprehensible in Russian.[18]

An editorial note refers to a handwritten remark made later by Mordvinov, indicating that he took the phrases which he attacks from Storkh's *Economie politique*, which, as noted above, was published in St Petersburg in 1815 in French. Reiterating the infant industry argument, Mordvinov asserts that, while Russian manufactures will indeed be dearer and of poorer quality at first, prices and costs will fall as skills are acquired and output rises.

In advocating a sound banking and financial policy, he does not fall into mercantilist fallacies: 'the science of national economy clearly states that money forms the smallest part (*maleishuyu chast'*) of the nation's wealth; it is not its quantity but its circulation, the freedom and velocity of its movements, which nourish and strengthen private and social power'. He points to the advantages of having banks in which citizens can keep their money, for then it can circulate and be used, which is much to be preferred to keeping it in a trunk under the bed. His proposed 'provincial banks' (*gubernskiye banki*) would pay 4 per cent interest on deposits. He drafted an elaborate set of rules for their operation.

In his memorandum to Alexander I, Mordvinov stresses the damage done by government interference with private trade, 'the excessive efforts to direct private advantage by orders and regulations'. He deplored internal trade barriers, excessive imports, lack of credits for expanding factories and workshops, 'the failure to take measures to attract foreign capital', failure to have a stable currency, and also inadequate measures to increase population and combat disease. He devotes several pages to explaining that private enterprise should be the basis of industrial growth, but that the government can and should help by 'the spread of technical and other information, publicizing new inventions, enlarging education in agriculture, botany, mineralogy, metallurgy, technology, physics, chemistry . . . the introduction of new machines and best instruments, the multiplication and improvement of means of transport . . .'. He recommended that government officials in embassies abroad should seek out and send back the latest technological information. The growth of towns should be encouraged, and the right to trade should be granted much more freely, and not limited to members of merchant guilds. When he heard later of the value of railways, he urged that they be built on a large scale. (This was opposed during much of Nicholas I's reign, since his exceptionally reactionary ministers imagined that they would menace public order because people would find it easier to move about!) He also pointed to the value of steamboats, 'which in England and America are numbered in thousands'.

So Mordvinov was a competent and eloquent *nazionalökonom*, and the claim in some Soviet sources that he used many of List's arguments before List does have some foundation.

NOTES

1. Shletser, Co., *Nachal'nye osnovaniya gosudastvennogo Khozyaistva*, published in 1805, second edition 1821. All pages references are to second edition.
2. Ibid., p. 71.

3. Ibid., p. 82.
4. Ibid., p. 99.
5. Ibid., p. 116–18.
6. Ibid., p. 145.
7. Ibid., p. 152.
8. Ibid., p. 89.
9. Ibid., p. 111.
10. Ibid., p. 130.
11. Shtorkh (Vernadsky translation), p. 55.
12. Ibid., p. 57.
13. Cited from vol. 5, 1824 Paris edition, preface, pp. iii, xxxix, emphasis in the original, my translation.
14. Shtorkh, (Vernadsky translation), pp. 202 ff.
15. Ibid., pp. 153–4, (St Petersburg French edition).
16. Ibid., pp. 154–5, (St Petersburg French edition).
17. Ibid., p. 2, vol. 4.
18. Mordvinov, *Izbrannye proizvedeniya*, M. 1945, p. 109.

2 M. I. Tugan-Baranovsky (1865–1919)*

The fiftieth anniversary of the death of a major scholar has passed unnoticed, or at least without comment, in his own country. Yet arguably his was one of the great minds among economists of the first quarter of the present century, and certainly he was the first Russian to be given international recognition, his work being particularly well known in Germany and Austria. To many British or American readers he is either a joke name ('two-gun Baranovsky') or only the author of a work on trade cycles in England. It may therefore be worthwhile to take belated advantage of the anniversary to introduce him to English-speaking readers.

TUGAN-BARANOVSKY'S CAREER

First, some particulars of the man. Mikhail Ivanovich Tugan-Baranovsky was born in 1865 in Kharkov Province, of a family half Ukrainian and part Tartar. He was educated in Kharkov University, graduating in 1888. He went to Moscow University and began his research on industrial cycles, which took him to London for six months in 1892. Using materials gathered there, he obtained his master's degree with a dissertation on economic crises. Its publication won him a very high reputation and with it a position as *privatdozent* at the University of St Petersburg. His active interest in Marxist socialism led to his dismissal by the minister of education in 1899 for political unreliability. He had meanwhile published his second magnum opus and doctoral dissertation, *The Russian Factory, Past and Present*. He was reinstated in St Petersburg University in 1905, but his election to the chair of political economy there in 1913 was vetoed by the minister. He resigned in 1915 and was re-elected to the chair after the February revolution of 1917. He never took up his appointment, leaving instead for his native Ukraine. There he be-

* From *History of Political Economy*, 1970.

came academician, dean of the Faculty of Law at Kiev, chairman of the Cooperatives of the Ukraine and chairman of the Ukrainian Economic Association. For a short while he acted as the head of the Ministry of Finance of the Ukrainian Rada (a short-lived national government). He seems to have become a latter-day Ukrainian nationalist, but amid confusion and collapse he apparently decided to leave. He died on the train taking him from Kiev to Odessa, en route for France, in 1919.

In an obituary article another famous Russian economist, Kondratiev, described him as an emotional, uneven, erratic, brilliant man and a fine stylist: 'Many pages written by him, and relating to what might seem prosaic and dull economic issues, achieve classical quality in their brilliance and passion.'[1] He was, said Kondratiev, a man imbued with ethical principles, a believer, sometimes intuitive, sometimes 'childishly naïve' in matters social and political, too often convinced that his virtues were not appreciated by his contemporaries. But Tugan, Kondratiev insisted, was a top-drawer economist.

EARLY WRITINGS

By the time he graduated, Tugan found himself in a milieu impregnated with Marxism. The very first translation of *Das Kapital* had been into Russian. The Marxists were engaged, on the whole successfully, in combating the Populist notion that Russia could avoid Western capitalism. In the context of the Russian intellectual life of the time, Marxism was (*inter alia*) an industrializing ideology, and many of its advocates were arguing for capitalism's progressive (and inevitable) role even while denouncing its abuses and preaching its replacement by socialism. Tugan-Baranovsky was clearly influenced by socialist ideas and by Marxist economics. But he also read Menger, Jevons, and Walras and took them very seriously. His first published work, an article in *Yuridicheski Vestnik* written as early as 1890, was an attempt to find some synthesis between labour theory and marginalist economics. He was to go very much further in this direction in later years, as we shall see. Meanwhile he showed great interest in Utopian socialism, writing a monograph on Proudhon (1891); this was followed by one on John Stuart Mill (1892). None of these was a major work.

'INDUSTRIAL CRISES IN ENGLAND'

Tugan's first major work was undoubtedly the astonishing master's dissertation, published in 1894, on crises in England. Its maturity and level of argument dazzled his colleagues. In my opinion it remains a work of power and relevance. The book divides itself into two parts. The first 370 pages consist of high-level empirical analysis. There is a survey of English economic history, with a wealth of statistics organized to show the trade cycles to which Britain was subject, their extent, duration, content and consequences. While this was a first-rate piece of research, the chief interest for us is to be found in the second part, where the author analyzes various theories of crisis and seeks to develop his own ideas.

Part II begins with a discussion of the views of Say, Ricardo, Sismondi, J. S. Mill and Chalmers. Tugan examines critically but seriously Malthus's argument to the effect that too much saving can reduce the market for finished goods and Moffat's point that, if capitalists invest, the additional purchasing power may be insufficient to absorb the additional output. He is particularly severe on the crude under-consumption theories of such as Sismondi. This is the more understandable if we appreciate that Sismondi's Russian followers happened to be anti-industrializing Populists. Such men as Vasily Vorontsov ('V. V.') and Nikolai Danielson ('Nikolai-on') argued that for capitalism to exist it must export its unsalable surpluses, and since Russia cannot export manufactures, capitalism cannot come to Russia! On their view profits always tend to exceed the value of the goods which the capitalists wish to buy; so overproduction is chronic and inevitable. Nonsense, says Tugan-Baranovsky. Capitalists' income is not all spent on consumers' goods; some of it is turned into capital for the expansion of production. Citing Marx's two-sector 'expanded reproduction' model, he emphasized that the expansion of investment requires a change in the pattern of production and creates demand for producers' goods. (Lenin made the same point at about the same time.) 'The process of production creates its own market and needs no other markets. If output can be increased, if the productive forces make this possible, then demand can be expanded too, since, with the appropriate distribution of productive resources, every newly produced commodity is a newly created purchasing power for the purchase of other commodities.' Demand is, of course, not only for consumers' goods.

Indeed 'demand for consumers' goods could decline while total demand for commodities could rise.'[2]

This seems to be a defence of Say against the doubters. Underconsumption is not built into the model, even if saving by capitalists is so great that demand for consumers' goods declines. (Tugan does not assert that this *is* so; he does not adopt Marx's 'immiseration' thesis.) However he then reminds us of the over-simplifications on which such a model is based. It assumes that 'the entrepreneur, before beginning production, has a wholly correct and accurate knowledge of the requirements of the market and of the output of every branch of industry'. It assumes capital mobility. It abstracts from foreign trade. Above all, no one knows *the future relationship between consumption and savings*. Tugan quotes from Moffat a sentence about the 'continuous struggle between the requirements of unknown demand and the fluctuations of unknown supply' and goes on: Suppose there is 'an increased propensity to save' (*stremlenie k sberezheniiu*). Output can expand if the necessary means of production exist, but this requires the use of the new capital in the right proportions. If it is not so used, then 'capital will not in fact be accumulated'. In other words, if increased savings lead to an increased demand for types of capital goods which, through imperfect information, have not been made and cannot be provided, this investment demand is at least temporarily frustrated.

Furthermore many savings (for example, those arising from rents and fixed interest) are made whether or not there exists an opportunity to invest them and regardless of the current rate of profit. Tugan used the much-quoted parable of the steam engine, in which steam (savings) accumulates, creates pressure, and then pushes out strongly. This causes a kind of cyclical irregularity in the demand for investment goods. His empirical researches led him in particular to note the correlation between trade cycles and the price of pig iron, this being most directly affected by demand for capital goods and the volume of investment. When savings are made and not invested, demand for some consumers' goods falls off, while that for producers' goods does not rise or also falls. The resultant reductions in demand and incomes are cumulative and reduce other demand and other incomes. In any case, as Moffat also said, the logic of competition causes entrepreneurs to create excess capacity, and lack of information facilitates misinvestment. In so far as Marx and Engels stressed 'the anarchy of the market' or 'planlessness' (*Planlosigkeit*),

Tugan agrees with their explanation, though he also roundly asserts that 'the difficulties of expanding production do not depend at all on the shares of each social class in the national income'.[3]

Tugan dismisses other theories rapidly and effectively. Harvest variations do not, as a statistical fact, explain crises. Jevons and his sunspots get short shrift. Nor can stock-exchange speculation be anything but a surface symptom. Credit policy may be more significant, but at this stage of his development Tugan regarded it as of secondary importance; critics of the Bank of England (he said) have contradicted themselves. (However in Tugan's later works the unevenness of capital creation, facilitated by credits, is given a much larger place.)

Tugan tried to interpret the trade cycle in relation to savings, investment and the structure of the productive process, basing his work on a mass of empirical data. He used such concepts as the multiplier and propensity to save. True, one can find precedents for all his ideas. In the words of Alvin Hansen, 'It has been said that there is not a new idea in Adam Smith; yet his book turned economic thinking upside down. In some measure the same can be said about Tugan-Baranovsky with respect to business-cycle theory. He began a new way of thinking about the problem.'[4] The vigour and clarity of the language and the wealth of empirical data in the first part of the book placed the author in the very front rank among Russian economists of the period.

'THE RUSSIAN FACTORY'

Tugan's next major work, *The Russian Factory*, was another and very different masterpiece published in 1898. There had been very little research on the history of Russian industry. Tugan succeeded in bringing to light fascinating material on early manufacturing under conditions in which serf villagers were forcibly turned into factory workers, as well as in tracing the growth of modern factories in the nineteenth century. He described how factories functioned and the relations of masters and men and between the masters and the state, which was often the principal sponsor and customer. The book was reprinted in Moscow in 1934, despite Tugan's status as a banned 'bourgeois' author, for it was still an irreplaceable source of historical information. Because it is about to appear in an English translation, no detailed analysis of this work will be given here.

Tugan made a pungent and witty attack on some of the then fashionable doctrines touching Russian industrial development and centring on the misuse of the terms 'natural' and 'artificial'. In the West, as Marx also said, bourgeois economists tend to treat *laissez-faire* as natural and all remnants of the feudal order as artificial. In contrast to the backward economists of the West, as Tugan puts it, the backward economists of backward Russia take the reverse view: 'Natural institutions are the remnants of our "ancien régime": the field commune (*obshchina*), the work gang (*artel'*), handicrafts; it is capitalist, bourgeois institutions which are artificial'.[5]

All this is apropos of a view widespread among Russian economists and historians with regard to Tsar Peter's actions in setting up factories, instead of relying on traditional handicrafts. Tugan shows that Russian merchants had already accumulated considerable capital, but that it seemed to them most profitable to buy from widely scattered craftsmen, many of them in rural areas, rather than invest in manufacturing. It might have been easier to expand production by encouraging the handicrafts sector, as Peter's critics maintained, but Peter happened to need metal, guns, broadcloth and sailcloth. In any case, as Tugan skilfully argued, in a semi-barbarous country like eighteenth-century Russia

> new branches of industry could arise only in the form of large factories. The small craftsman had neither the capital nor the knowledge required. True, the merchant who set up a factory was almost as ignorant as the craftsmen. However, possessing capital, he could hire foreign experts . . . One can accept as a general rule that in culturally backward countries like Peter's Russia the transfer or introduction of new branches of industry can take the form only of large-scale industry. Peter could hardly have set up technical schools for craftsmen . . . How many years would this path have taken him . . . ?.[6]

So the government set up or subsidized the setting-up of factories, the products of which were bought chiefly by the government. Tugan notes the importance of merchants in the role of factory owners. It was often the merchants to whom the government handed over the factories which it set up. 'Artificial'? But why more so than any other act? Serfdom, which affected labour recruitment for the new factories, was no more and no less artificial than its abolition. Governments everywhere play an important part in economic affairs.

Was Peter therefore responsible for the birth of Russian industry? Tugan points to the importance, along with Peter, of the role and magnitude of merchant capital. This capital needed support to get labour, and in 1721 Peter issued a decree allowing merchants to buy villages so long as their inhabitants worked in factories. But some years later, as Tugan shows in fascinating quotations, the gentry and merchant estates were in conflict, both trying to persuade the monarch to give sole rights to operate factories to their particular estate. He also showed that under Catherine II industry made great strides even though she, unlike Peter, took few steps to encourage it and declared her support for handicrafts. However by then a trained industrial labour force was beginning to emerge. In the 1840s, that is, twenty years before the end of serfdom, the so-called possessional factories, using serf labour, had been found in many cases to be unprofitable, and the owners themselves were sending petitions to the crown asking it to allow them to operate with freely hired and therefore more productive and skilled workers. This evolution, in all its complexity, is admirably described. Tugan's book was truly a major contribution to industrial history.

'FUNDAMENTALS OF POLITICAL ECONOMY'

Tugan wrote books and pamphlets on socialism and also on cooperation, a subject which greatly interested him. He gradually moved farther away from orthodox Marxism under the influence of German revisionism (Bernstein), but continued to consider himself a Marxist, at least in respect of his social analysis. The only work of his so far translated into English is *Modern Socialism in Its Historical Development*, published in 1910.

The evolution of Tugan's thought and his whole concept of economics show best in successive editions of his *Osnovy politicheskoi ekonomii* (Fundamentals of political economy). The pages that follow are based on the fourth edition, which appeared in March 1917.

Among the virtues of the book are, beyond doubt, its style and clarity. It begins with a methodological introduction, but, unlike some of his Russian and (especially) German contemporaries, Tugan does not get bogged down in quasi-philosophical considerations. Very quickly he makes clear his ethical position. Unlike medicine or biology, the social sciences are clearly affected by conflicts of interest between human beings. These must occur in any 'freely developing exchange economy'. Class or interest does affect outlook: thus from the worker's point of view wages are income; from the capitalist's, expenditure. An extra effort by labourers may represent disutility to the labourer, but for the employer it is a gain. From an employer's standpoint, worker, horse, plough and field are all factors of production. But, argues Tugan, here one can and should interpose an ethical principle that goes beyond a class-centred view. A man is different, and not just a factor of production. Economics should be concerned with *human* welfare. A man is not a horse or a plough or an instrument. In this sense, the labour of man has a special relationship to production. Tugan thus supports an ethically based labour theory of value (though we shall see how he modifies it). Marx too is ethical. After all, Tugan argues, he and Engels were not proletarians. Above the class war must stand the higher principle of an ultimately equal society. He added that, if a horse society could be imagined, horse-economists would undoubtedly devise a horse theory of value. The ancient Greeks would deny the legitimacy of putting free men, barbarians and slaves on the same plane of analysis.

What is value (*tsennost'*, the German *Wert*)? It has both a subjective and an objective aspect. The marginal-utility theory is elegantly and clearly presented by Tugan, and its discovery is attributed to Gossen (*Entwicklung der Gesetzte des menschlichen Verkehrs*, 1853), if not indeed to Aristotle. Gossen was ignored. Menger, Jevons, and Walras rediscovered these principles. Their importance is beyond doubt, but, argues Tugan, they are one-sided in virtually ignoring the conditions of production. The marginal-utility and labour-in-production theories are 'opposites but not contradictory'. Ricardo and Menger looked at the same process from two different angles, both legitimate. The Marxists were wrong to denounce or ignore marginal utility. Objective factors and subjective valuations coexist. An infinite variety of products can be made which require 'the most varied expenditure of human effort. The labor cost of production cannot but be one of the determinants . . . of the distribution of human labor between different branches of production'. By decreasing or increasing output one can vary marginal utility. The latter therefore cannot have an existence independent of supply and of the conditions of production. Labour cost is objectively given. So, ' in the language of mathematics, marginal utility must be a function of labor cost'.[7] At the margin, in equilibrium, labour cost and marginal utility should be proportional to each other, though this relation may be modified by indivisibilities. In the last analysis 'the objective conditions of production determine the economic valuation (*rastsenka*) of products', and these conditions do not depend on subjective valuations.[8] Ricardo's theory does not contradict marginal utility, though Marx is in some respects inconsistent with it.

Marx 'illegitimately mixed up two different theories: to the correct idea that goods may be regarded as products of human labor only was added the totally incorrect idea that labor is the only source of the product's value (*tsennost'*)'. It is clear that one cannot ignore the role of valuation (utility) in arriving at exchange value. Tugan disagrees with Marx's notion that labour provides the very essence and substance of value and maintains that this creates logical difficulties for Marx in volume 3 of *Das Kapital*, when even in equilibrium there is no connection between relative prices and relative values.

Marxists, he asserts, make matters worse by confusing two terms used rather ambiguously by Marx: *Wert* (value, *tsennost'*) and *Kosten* (cost, *stoimost'*); indeed the two have long been used interchangeably in Russian, though Tugan lays great stress on the distinction between them. (He points out that Marx used the 'emigrant-German' word *Kost*, obviously taken from English, instead of the correct *Kosten*.) When Marx writes 'wirkliche Kost der Ware', he refers to cost and not value in the sense of *Wert*. Cost here evidently relates to expenditure, of means used up to attain a given end. Value has to do with utility, satisfaction of demand, human choice and welfare. These are different aspects of the same thing.

Tugan accepts the concept of surplus value; it is absurd, he writes, to imagine that capital earns its own interest and profit. The exploitation relationship is disguised by commodity-money fetishism. Man is turned into a commodity. Agreeing with Marx in these respects, he claims that 'my theory of value and cost as two independent categories' – representing respectively subjective valuation and objective conditions of production – 'makes possible the preservation of the social content of Marx's value theory'.[9]

So, for Tugan, goods are the products of labour, and their equilibrium price is a function of cost (that is, conditions in which labour is applied) and of marginal utility, demand. Marshall is quoted in support. Market prices in the short run are determined by supply and demand, and it is supply which fluctuates most and is the more important element in price changes. But the level around which the price fluctuates is determined, in Tugan's view, by costs of production, these being affected by technical progress. Of course, all kinds of immobilities and frictions cause many departures from this level in practice. Orthodox price theory assumes perfect knowledge, perfect mobility and rational behaviour. In reality there are forces of custom, routine and inertia.

Tugan's consciousness of immobilities, frictions and indivisibilities affects his view of marginal cost. Yes, he agrees, price will tend to equal marginal cost, but will not necessarily be at this level. Thus the cost of the *average* producer may determine the price, the others having rates of profits above or below average. What happens depends on the productive capacity available at various levels of cost; a major low-cost producer can force others down to his price level, and owing to immobility of capital assets this situation can last for a considerable time.

Tugan has good, if unoriginal, chapters on monopoly, credit, rent, insurance and free trade versus protection ('a tariff is a form of tribute imposed on users'; high tariffs can delay growth and technical progress). Descriptive chapters deal with the firm, cooperatives, transport. He then goes on to devote a whole section of the book to distribution.[10] He deplores the fact that many economists (J. B. Clark, Wieser and others) had taken to omitting any separate discussion of this phase. It cannot be treated as just part of a general theory of value and price. The 'prices' of labour, capital and land are interlinked. The marginalist approach ignores the inequality of the parties to the bargain. Marx's value theory, based (said Tugan) on an unsound 'absolute labor value', led him to an equally unsound view of wages tending to subsistence levels. The division of the national product is affected by 'power and dependence' relationships. Labour's bargaining power varies. Labour cannot be analyzed as just another commodity or one factor of production among others, not only for reasons of ethics but also because the supply of labour is affected mainly by population growth (which shows no straightforward response to 'price') and also because of the importance of bargaining power between classes. Tugan notes the importance of the force of custom as a factor making for wage stickiness.

The supply-and-demand theory of wages and the wages-fund theory both err by treating labour and capital as independent variables. One creates the other. 'The working class itself creates its own subsistence fund and the means of production'.[11] Taussig is criticized for in effect saying, in his *Wages and Capital*, that the average wage is the average wage. In general, Tugan accepts that what the thinkers of the marginal school say is true as far as it goes, but repeatedly taxes them with one-sidedness and superficiality and sometimes tautology.

J. B. Clark's 'factor productivity' argument is well summarized and then attacked. Why should wages not be below the marginal product? Competition between capitalists? But why should they use their capital to pay labour up to its full marginal product, whereas they purchase materials and equipment only if it provides them with a profit over and above *their* respective marginal products (p. 390)? Clark, argues Tugan, failed to see this, even though for him labour is just one factor of production among others, because he failed to see the wages fund as part of capital, in respect of which profits cannot be nil.

So, according to Tugan, the distribution of the social product is the result of struggle between classes and groups. Equality of bargaining power cannot be assumed. There is indeed a connection between labour productivity and wages, in so far as higher productivity means a bigger cake to divide. But labour's share in this cake is not determined by labour productivity. Indeed labour alone, or capital alone, would produce very little. It is all a matter of bargaining, between the limits set by minimum subsistence and zero profits.

This whole distribution doctrine attracted a vigorous criticism by Schumpeter in the *Archiv für Sozialwissenschaft* (1915). Tugan, in the 1917 edition of his *Osnovy*, rejects this criticism.

Tugan has some interesting thoughts on the position of the managers – salaried, yet dependent on profits and perhaps themselves shareholders. He also remarks in passing that all parliamentary labour and trade-union parties are bound to be reformist. The large increase in the middle class was a fact and was not foreseen by Marx. Marx was also wrong about the disappearance of the individual peasantry.

'Surplus value' is viewed by Tugan in a way rather different from Marx's. He agrees with Marx's concept of 'exploitation'. The alleged necessity of profit is due to 'confusing capital with capitalist'.[12] Profits arise as a consequence of a given, historically conditioned system of property relations. But Marx, writes Tugan, is wrong in trying to squeeze profit determination into his value theory. Marx included surplus value in the value of goods, while Tugan envisages it as the surplus *product*, this surplus being equal to the value of goods used (consumed) by capitalists. This view worried Kondratiev: in his already cited obituary article he said that it left the relationship between profit and value unclear; does value rise if profits rise? How does one identify the products which are surplus products? Peter B. Struve, himself a former Marxist, also attacked Tugan's idea of 'a kind of physical surplus product separate from value'. His whole theory (argued Struve) is based on unprovable assumptions concerning labour value. Ethics are not economics. 'Expenditures of labor are economically comparable . . . only through valuations . . . or (what is the same from the strictly empirical point of view) as prices.'[13] However Tugan stuck to his guns. His idea does enjoy one evident advantage over Marx's: if one takes the ethical view that labour is the source of all value and that therefore the recipients of profits and interest do not really earn what they get, then it is surely best to measure their share by the goods they *consume*; Marxists have repeatedly confused this with the total surplus, regardless of its use. But of course this whole approach is wide open to criticism.

Tugan then returns to some of his ideas of 1894. Capitalist growth creates its own market; not all products are consumed or distributed between classes. The fact that there are exports (and imports) clearly does not prove that there is overproduction. Here he quotes Lenin's early work in support. After high praise for Quesnay and Marx, he develops a simple three-sector model of his own:

I Production of means of production
II Production of workers' consumers' goods
III Production of goods for capitalists' consumption

Tugan then goes in some detail into theories of crises. As in his early work, he lays stress on anarchy and planlessness, with resultant disproportions. He imagines a model in which the over-production of one item, through error, leads to a cumulative fall in prices and demand. To a greater extent than in his early work, he attributes imbalance to credits which are freely available in a period of upswing and inflate its scale.

There is much else in this volume. It includes a well-argued critique of Malthus ('not only poverty but also riches limit births'). Nearly a hundred pages are devoted to a historical survey of development in general, the development of Russia especially. In analyzing the features peculiar to Russia, he identifies two in particular. The first was the smallness and weakness of towns, with little manufacturing, few free urban craftsmen and no effective guilds ('Die städtische Luft macht frei,' he quotes). The second was the survival until modern times of forced labour. A discussion of serfdom leads to a most succinct analysis of the causes of its abolition. There is well-documented sense about the peasant commune (*obshchina*), agricultural

Table 2.1 Factory industry, 1900

	Russia	USA
Value of output (billion roubles)	3 005	25 296
Number of workers (millions)	2 373	5 321
Average wage (roubles)	200	850
Output per worker (roubles)	1 266	4 754

reform policies and lopsided industrial development of Russia (large modern factories and a big handicrafts sector, with little in between). He quotes a statistical comparison with the United States, from the calculations of one Sergovsky (Table 2.1).

Tugan's predecessors in Russia, with few exceptions, wrote textbooks which were either historical–descriptive only (under the influence of the German historical school) or reproduced uncritically the ideas either of the Austrians or of Marx. Tugan's *Fundamentals* provided, it seems to me, a very rich and varied intellectual diet for students. Its excellent Russian style makes it a pleasure to read. His last work was a new version of this book, published in Kiev during his brief career as a Ukrainian academician–politician.

'LAND REFORM AND COOPERATIVES'

Both as a socialist and believer in cooperatives and as an economist passionately concerned with the development of his own country, Tugan had much to say on agriculture. His last work before leaving for Kiev, a short booklet written (judging from internal evidence) at the end of 1917, was published by an obscure cooperative publisher in Tver (Kalinin) early in 1918. In view of subsequent history, his prescience was remarkable (and rare among academic economists in any country). Since the booklet is a bibliographical rarity, it may be worth citing his argument at some length.

The transfer of land from big to small holders is as logical in Russia as it was in Ireland, except that the scale and violence of the process in Russia is obviously much greater. The peasants in Russia still in the main believe in equal distribution of the land. But this creates a contradiction between 'the sense of social fairness and the development of productive forces'. Statistics that Tugan quotes for the period 1861–1910 show clearly not only that landlords achieved higher harvest yields than peasants but that the difference between them was greater in 1910 than in 1861. The landlords were destroyed, not by their economic inefficiency, but by the peasants' moral indignation and land hunger. The peasant sense of property is still different from that of the West. It involves an idea that everyone has the right to land. But obviously someone has to work in towns. Not everyone can be a cultivator. Therefore those who do cultivate have, by the very principle of universal right to land, the duty to supply their fellow-countrymen who are engaged in other work.

But the prewar agricultural surplus was based both on landlord production and on peasant poverty: 'the *muzhik* went short of food'. The land settlement of the Revolution would enable him to eat better. Present (end of 1917) shortages may seem due to the war, but 'even when peace comes not only will we lack grain for export, but food supplies for our towns will be very difficult'.[14] The elimination of the landlords and land reform, places before Russia a vast and terrible (*groznyi*) problem. Production must rise, yet the division of the estates reduces production. Among diseconomies of small scale, Tugan emphasizes particularly the greater number of tools and implements required by smallholders.

How, then, can productivity be raised? The answer, as 'our socialist parties' believe, is producers' cooperatives.

> It is evident that the peasant would not agree to abandon his independence and go and work on some sort of state farm. A producers' cooperative [*artel'*] is another matter. The peasant then does not part with his holding but enlarges it by including his fellow villagers. Joint work in the cooperative does not prevent the peasant from feeling himself to be an independent proprietor.[15]

As an old cooperator, nothing would please Tugan better. Yet he has little hope that this solution will be practicable. 'Producers' cooperatives will attract not the masses but a few of the select, men standing above the crowd and seeking to make a new world.' A few such cooperatives will be set up and will be worshipped by intellectuals. The bulk of the peasants will stay out.

What, then, is to be done? The answer is patiently to develop partial forms of cooperation, relying not on officials but on the peasants themselves, with help – not direction, but advice – from outside. There could be joint utilization of equipment, joint selling, possibly joint ownership of livestock, though this would probably be impracticable. In sugar-beet areas the peasants might jointly own collecting centres and processing plants, as peasants do in the Czech lands. It will be difficult, but indispensable, to achieve technical progress through some degree of joint operation of peasant small holdings. In the West, peasants and workers are hostile. 'We do not have this situation yet, and that is why the revolution seems so powerful. But will this continue? The land reform can break up the revolutionary united front.' Cooperation could save the situation.

Tugan showed that he saw, even before the dawn of 1918, both the future conflict with the peasants and the key role of agricultural surpluses in the relationship between the government and the towns on the one hand and the peasants on the other. As he foretold, the producers' cooperatives (*arteli*, *kolkhozy*) attracted few peasants. What he did not and could not foretell was that Stalin would ultimately try to solve the problem by forcible collectivization.

TUGAN-BARANOVSKY AND SOVIET ORTHODOXY

Tugan's influence on his contemporaries in Russia was at least as great as that of Marshall on English economists. Many disagreed with him, of course, but his greatness was appreciated by all but a handful of extremists. Kondratiev testified to his outstanding abilities as a teacher. Unfortunately for his posthumous influence, party ideologists had no patience with those who departed from orthodox Marxism, and Lenin had attacked him. Although in fact Tugan's ideas evolved very differently from those of, say, Struve, it became simplest to lump them and others together under the pejorative headings of 'legal-Marxists', revisionists, or even renegades. Tugan's brief association with Ukrainian nationalism in 1918–19 did not help. In the first decade after the Revolution some associates and pupils still held academic positions, but after 1927 the remnants of the non-Marxist schools were squeezed out and were soon, like Kondratiev, to vanish into concentration camps. It became impossible to debate Marxism any more or to discuss the correctness of any of the economic (or other) theories advanced by the Founding Fathers. In such an atmosphere the spirit of Tugan had no place. He was ignored, or remembered only in the context of adverse epithets. In 1966 he re-emerged into the public eye in his own country when the series on the history of Russian economic thought, edited in Moscow, reached the twentieth century.[16] Here he was indeed taken seriously and some of his doctrines were expounded, but in a very critical spirit; and the Soviet reader gets only a garbled story.

Yes, Tugan is truly an economist worth remembering.

NOTES

1. N. D. Kondratiev, *M. I. Tugan-Baranovsky* (Petrograd, 1923) p. 25.
2. *Promyshlennye krizisy v sovremennoi Anglii* [Industrial crises in contemporary England] (St Petersburg, 1894) pp. 416–17. German and French translations appeared in 1901 and 1913 respectively.
3. *Promyshlennye krizisy*, p. 478.
4. *Business Cycles and National Income* (New York, 1951) p. 281.
5. M. I. Tugan–Baranovsky, *The Russian Factory*, 1934 edition, p. 10.
6. Ibid., p. 19.
7. M. I. Tugan–Baranovsky, *Osnovy politicheskoi ekonomii* [Fundamentals of political economy], fourth edition, 1917, p. 50.
8. Ibid., p. 54.
9. Ibid., pp. 72 ff.
10. His ideas on this subject were also published separately and were translated into German as *Soziale Theorie der Verteilung* in 1913.
11. *Osnovy*, p. 386.
12. Ibid., p. 447.
13. Peter B. Struve, *Khoziaistvo i tsena* [The economy and prices] (Moscow, 1913) pt 2. pp. 375–8.
14. *Zemel'naia reforma i kooperatsiia* [Land reform and cooperatives] (Tver, 1918) p. 9.
15. Ibid., p. 11.
16. *Istoriya Russkoi ekonomicheskoi mysli* (Moscow, 1966) vol. 3, pt 1.

Part II
Economic History

3 War Communism*

This term is used to describe and define the period roughly from mid-1918 until March 1921, when the Soviet government, under Lenin's leadership, adopted a policy of requisitioning farm produce (the so-called *prodrazvestka*), sought to ban all private trade, nationalized almost all industrial establishments and tried to achieve central control over production and allocation of goods, partially replacing money (which was rapidly depreciating) by accounting in kind. The words 'sought' and 'tried' in the above sentence are essential, because real life at no time conformed fully to the government's intentions. Thus Kritsman, in his pamphlet on 'The Heroic period of the Russian revolution', described the economic system then prevailing as 'the most complete form of proletarian natural-anarchistic economy', and also claimed that in world history there was never a time when so large a proportion of the people had engaged in trade (though it was illegal). Controls were confused and contradictory, reliable and efficient controllers extremely scarce, the official distribution network frequently broke down and various official bodies duplicated each other. Local soviets and party officials often acted independently, disregarding Moscow's instructions. Lenin on many occasions deplored the tendency to issue orders that were in fact not carried out.

It is none the less possible to speak of a system which may be labelled 'war communism'. It profoundly influenced, and was influenced by, the civil war. It formed the behaviour patterns of thousands of Bolshevik officials, as they struggled to create some sort of order out of chaos, and found ruthless methods to be the only way. Life became cheap. To shoot someone was to 'waste' him (*v raskhod*). The Cheka, forerunner of the KGB, was the effective sword of the revolution. For a few months the Bolsheviks shared power with the left socialist-revolutionaries, but the latter walked out, and even (ineffectually) rebelled in July 1918. The Mensheviks (moderate social-democrats) survived, despite some arbitrary arrests and

---

* Reprinted from Blackwell's *Encyclopedia of the Russian Revolution* (ed. H. Shukman) 1988.

harassment, until 1921, but to all intents and purposes the one-party state was established by mid-1918.

Was all this the consequence of the ideas and policies with which the Bolsheviks had come to power in the October revolution? This conclusion could be challenged by reference to the policies propounded prior to that date. Thus, for example, before October there was nothing to suggest that the Bolsheviks believed in a one-party state, and indeed several Bolsheviks (including Rykov and Nogin) actually resigned in protest when Lenin announced that they would try to rule without the participation of other socialist parties. The Bolsheviks (along with other left-wing groups) had been on record as opposing the death penalty. As for economic policy and doctrine, this had been a mixture of demagogic slogans and short-term expedients. Marxist doctrine on economics of socialism had been little developed, in Russia or elsewhere, beyond vague and utopian notions on an undefined sort of socialist planning for the good of society. In his most utopian work, *State and revolution*, Lenin wrote:

> We, the workers, shall organize industrial production on the basis of what capitalism has already created . . . We shall reduce the role of state officials to that of simply carrying out instructions as responsible, revocable, modestly paid 'foremen and accountants', of course with the help of technicians of all sorts . . . The function of control and accountancy, becoming more and more simple, will be performed by each [citizen] in turn, will become a habit and finally die out as a *special* function of a special section of the population . . . To organize the *whole* economy on the lines of the postal service, so that foremen, technicians and accountants, as well as *all* officials, shall receive salaries no higher than workers' wages, all under the leadership of the armed proletariat, that is our immediate task. (Emphases in the original.)[1]

Again, in his 'Can the Bolsheviks retain state power?', written on the eve of the revolution, we have such statements as: 'Capitalism has simplified the work of accounting and control, has reduced it to a comparatively simple process of bookkeeping, which any literate person can do.' But in the same work he wrote that 'the important thing will not be even the confiscation of the capitalists' property, but . . . workers' control', plus 'a fair tax'.[3] Indeed Lenin had also written: 'Everyone agrees that the immediate introduction of socialism in Russia is impossible',[4] and also that 'there was not and could not be a definite plan for the organization of economic life'.[5]

After war communism had been abandoned, Bogdanov said, 'they had tried to act cautiously, but military–revolutionary necessity . . . compelled them, life compelled them, to act as they did'.[6] It could thus be argued that Lenin and his comrades had no blueprint corresponding to the war communism model, that they were driven into it by circumstances. This view can be sustained only if the 'circumstances' can be made to include the consequences of the Bolsheviks' own attitudes and policies. Thus, for example, while their original programme, in its vagueness, might appear to be compatible with a mixed economy, with nationalization confined to 'banks and syndicates', the Bolsheviks' own slogans ensured that the remaining capitalists, private managers and traders, were placed in an impossible position. 'Workers' control' was an ambiguous term, which could mean merely the power to inspect the accounts, but in practice there were many instances of crude seizure of factories, and many employers were driven out or just fled. Indeed there were decrees trying to stop unauthorized nationalization 'from below'.

In the case of the peasants the situation was more complicated. It must be recalled that the exigencies of war had driven the Tsarist government in 1916 to introduce a state monopoly of grain purchases, and in fact peasant unwillingness to sell at the officially-fixed prices contributed to the food shortages which touched off the riots that brought down Tsarism. The provisional government also tried, ineffectually, to secure enough produce to feed the towns. Bolshevik ideology did not prescribe confiscating or requisitioning: it prescribed some sort of 'product exchange'. But the collapse of the economy meant that there was little to offer. There were strong pressures to keep prices of food from rising, and, as in other warring countries, free-market sales came to be seen as black market 'speculation' even by many non-Bolsheviks. Lenin at first believed that he could count on support from the poor peasants in fomenting 'class war in the villages', and that this would help in obtaining food. But peasant solidarity was too strong, and the *kombedy* (committees of poor peasants) were soon abandoned.

It might seem inappropriate to blame the Bolsheviks for the civil war, since after all it was launched by their enemies. Yet it was a Bolshevik slogan to 'turn imperialist war into civil war'. They adopted, quite deliberately, policies which rendered civil war inevitable. Even before it began, under the Treaty of Brest-Litovsk the Soviets were forced to abandon large territories of the former Empire, including the Ukraine. The armies of Denikin, Kolchak, Yudenich, the Czech legion, plus foreign interventionists, occupied large areas, and destroyed railway lines and bridges when they retreated. Supplies of fuel, materials and food were highly irregular and precarious. To save Bolshevik rule it was plainly necessary to mobilize and to centralize, to impose on a country already exhausted after nearly four years of war the priority of supplies to the Red Army. So there were strong, urgent purely practical reasons for extending central control over production and allocation, and for the extension of requisitioning. Similarly, the Cheka's activities and powers, and the increasing use of the death penalty seemed to be justified by the emergency, given the precariousness of the Bolsheviks' hold on power.

It may therefore be seen that war communism had two interrelated and mutually reinforcing causes: a set of ideological presuppositions (anti-employer, anti-trader, belief in planning, a negative view of the market) and war emergency. Furthermore the war emergency gave additional impetus to, and appeared to justify, the more extreme manifestations of the ideology. For example, hyper-inflation occurred in many countries under anti-marxist regimes, as for instance in Germany and Hungary, but in Soviet Russia zealot Bolsheviks such as Preobrazhensky and Larin saw in the rapid devaluation of money a stage in the progress towards communism, when money would disappear. There were anti-black market measures in other countries, in wartime, but no one else tried to outlaw *all* trade. The Hungarian historian L. Szamuely argues with reason that 'the state deliberately aimed at eliminating every element of market relations from economic activity'.[7] Then, as already mentioned, the state monopoly of grain purchases was inherited from pre-revolutionary wartime legislation, and Lenin favoured some ill-defined form of barter, with the state paying the peasants in industrial goods. It was civil war and ruin which turned 'produce exchange' into requisitioning. Similarly, while Bolshevik theory did incline its believers towards labour conscription, under the slogan 'who does not work shall not eat', material incentives were lacking under conditions of hunger and economic disruption, and this, plus the fact of breakdown and emergency, led to theories about 'militarization of labour', propagated in 1920 by both Trotsky and Bukharin, but which both tried quickly to forget once 'war-communism' had been abandoned.

It is also appropriate to add that the ideologically-inspired methods used by the Bolsheviks during this period contributed significantly to economic disruption and chaos, which seemed to justify these very methods.

Lenin himself several times stated that mistakes had been made; Bukharin spoke of 'illusions'; excesses were admitted, with the ready excuse that this 'was forced on us by extreme want, ruin and war'.

By 1920 most workers received their meagre rations free of charge, paid no rent and travelled free on the over-crowded tramcars. State enterprises were subject to detailed orders from above about what to produce and to whom to deliver, and no money passed. Side by side with this the state continued to print enormous quantities of rapidly depreciating roubles (to avoid the monetary designation, they came to be known as *sovznaki*, ('soviet tokens')), which helped to fuel a flourishing illegal market, described as *Sukharevka*, after the name of a Moscow square in which sales were made. There was a big expansion of barter deals, especially barter of clothing, furniture, samovars or anything else for food brought in illegally from the countryside. The peasants resisted requisitioning and hid their produce from the squads sent to seize it, but in the last resort many were prepared to support or tolerate the Bolsheviks for fear of the victory of the Whites, who would (they feared) bring back the landlords. Lenin was wise enough to leave land redistribution in peasant hands. Even though he would have preferred to set up state or collective farms, he knew that this was quite impracticable in the circumstances. This contrasted with policies pursued by more dogmatic communists during the revolution in (for instance) the Baltic states and in Hungary, when they failed to support peasant demands for land and suffered the consequences.

By May 1920 only one White army, that of Wrangel in the Crimea, remained in the field. In that month the Poles chose to attack. After successfully counter-attacking, the Red Army was itself defeated in front of Warsaw. When that war ended and Wrangel was driven out of the Crimea (at the end of 1920) the 'war' justification of war communism was ended too. The people were hungry, cold and exhausted. Most urban residents had fled to the countryside. Disease was rampant. Most industries had stopped, for lack of materials, fuel and labour. The peasants were unwilling to produce for the requisition squads and, now that the Whites no longer threatened, rebellions broke out, and the shock of the sailors' revolt in Kronstadt, which took place during the tenth congress of the Party (in March

1921) was the last nail in the coffin of war communism. Yet Lenin and the bulk of his comrades had intended to continue with the methods of war communism during the period of reconstruction. In October 1920 he was telling the Soviet authorities in the Ukraine to confiscate money and implements from so-called *kulaks* (richer peasants) and to collect all grain surpluses over and above basic needs.[8] Even as late as December 1920 Lenin was still advocating the continuation of requisitioning, and his government set up so-called 'sowing committees' (*posevkomy*) intending to compel the peasant households to sow and to harvest. But by March 1921 he had seen the necessity of relaxing pressure, substituting a tax in kind for requisitioning, and allowing peasants to keep or freely to sell the remainder. Thus was born the New Economic Policy (NEP). He had a hard time persuading the party to accept this. But for the shock of the Kronstadt rebellion, he might not have succeeded.

So what *was* war communism? Lenin himself was ambivalent. On the one hand, it had been all-out assault, like the first attack of the Japanese on the fortress of Port Arthur; that attack too had failed, but it was a necessary learning process, so that success would come when the attack was resumed. NEP was then to be seen as a necessary but painful retreat (*reculer pour mieux sauter*). But on the other hand Lenin also and repeatedly spoke of NEP as the right road, one which would have been followed in 1918 for the exigencies of war. It would be followed 'seriously and for a long time'.

The two interpretations of war communism are not only of interest to historians today. They played an important role in explaining what followed. Those among the Bolsheviks who believed (or, like Bukharin, came eventually to believe) that war communism had been an error, that NEP was after all the right road, would try to follow Lenin's injunction to cling to NEP 'seriously and for a long time'. Those for whom war communism was a glorious period, an all-out offensive against the class enemy, who saw NEP as a forced and hateful retreat, would try to resume the offensive and smash the market-based compromise on which NEP rested. By 1929, this second group, under Stalin, was in the ascendant. We know the consequences.

NOTES

1. Lenin, *Works*, vol. 25, pp. 426–7.
2. *Ibid.*, vol. 27, pp. 212–14.
3. Ibid., *Works*, vol. 26, pp. 105, 107.
4. Ibid., vol. 25, p. 69.
5. Ibid., vol. 26, p. 365.
6. *Vestnik sotsialisticheskoi akademii*, no. 1 (1922) pp. 148–9.
7. L. Szamuely, *First models of socialist economic systems* (Budapest, 1974).
8. Lenin, *Sochineniya*, vol. 40, pp. 337–9.

REFERENCES

Dobb, M. (1951) *Russian economic development since 1917* (London: 1929) (1951 edition).

Gimpelson, E. and the best Russian Book. (1977) *Voyenny kommunizm* (Moscow).

Malle, Silvana (1985) *The economic organization of war communism* (Cambridge: CUP).

Nove, A. (1972) *An economic history of the USSR* (Harmondsworth Per: given Books: Pelican) 1972. 1982(?)

Szamuely, L. (1974) *First models of socialist economic systems* (Budapest: Akadémiai Kiado).

4 Lenin and the New Economic Policy*

The New Economic Policy, initiated in 1921, was a response to a number of circumstances and forces, understood by the politicians of the time in mutually inconsistent ways. In this chapter, I shall be arguing that Lenin's own views were to some extent internally inconsistent. Among the factors involved were: revolutionary emergency, ideological preconceptions, political tactics, and just harsh overriding necessity, all of which tended to interact. Thus it is extraordinary how often the most cogent ideological reasons are found for doing what must be done. It would be wrong to present a clear but superficial picture.

WAR COMMUNISM

NEP replaced 'war communism'. What did Lenin think war communism was? To this question too there are several answers, and a brief look at the problems involved is essential if we are to understand how he saw NEP.

Lenin's picture of the transition to socialism was never fully or consistently worked out. He was, after all, primarily a politician. To seize power seemed, even as late as 1916, a rather distant prospect. His past works on the development of capitalism in Russia, on imperialism, on the present question, were doubtless both interesting and important, but they did not, and could not, come to grips with the question of what actually to do. Full communism was a vision indicated by Marx, and doubtless Lenin saw that same vision. But

---

* This paper appeared in *Lenin and Leninism*, edited by Bernard W. Eisenstadt, Lexington, 1971, and was presented at a conference held in Stillwater, Oklahoma. The whole question of Lenin and NEP is now (1989) very much at the centre of historians' attention in the Soviet Union, as part of the discussion on the nature of NEP and of the alternatives to stalinism. Did Lenin, by the time he was struck down by disease, have a coherent 'gradualist' alternative? Or was it just a matter of *reculer pour mieux sauter*?

nowhere could such a state of affairs arise without a period of transition of unknown duration. Evidently such a period could be particularly long in a country such as Russia, predominantly peasant, industrially semi-developed, culturally backward, even if revolutionary governments in Western Europe were to come to her aid, even if times were normal.

But of course in 1917 times were anything but normal. The war exhausted Russia, and its necessities had created numerous organs of state control, of material allocation and of rationing. Even so controversial a decree as the state of monopoly of trade in grain, at fixed prices, dates from well before the seizure of power by the Bolsheviks, as a consequence of wartime emergencies.

During the last months before October, Lenin did express some views about economic policy, and these have often been quoted. For example:

> In addition to the chiefly 'oppressive' apparatus – the standing army, the police and the bureaucracy – the modern state possesses an apparatus which has extremely close connections with the banks and syndicates, an apparatus which performs an enormous amount of accounting and registration work, if it may be expressed this way. This apparatus must not, and should not, be smashed. It must be wrested from the control of the capitalists; the capitalists and the wires they pull must be *cut off, lopped off, chopped away from* this apparatus; it must be subordinate to the proletarian Soviets; it must be expanded, made more comprehensive, and nation-wide. And this *can* be done by utilizing the achievements already made by large-scale capitalism (in the same way as the proletarian revolution can, in general, reach its goal only by utilizing these achievements).
>
> Capitalism has created an accounting apparatus in the shape of the banks, syndicates, postal service, consumers' societies, and office employees' unions. *Without big banks socialism would be impossible*.
>
> The big banks are the state apparatus which we *need* to bring about socialism, and which we *take* ready-made from capitalism; our task here is merely to *lop off* what *capitalistically mutilates* this excellent apparatus, to make it even *bigger*, even more democratic, even more comprehensive. Quantity will be transformed into quality. A single State Bank, the biggest of the big, with branches in every rural district, in every factory, will constitute as much as

> nine-tenths of the *socialist* apparatus. This will be country wide *bookkeeping*, country wide *accounting* of the production and distribution of goods, this will be, so to speak, something in the nature of the *skeleton* of socialist society.
>
> We can *lay hold of* and *set in motion* this *state apparatus* (which is not fully a state apparatus under capitalism, but which will be so with us, under socialism) at one stroke, by a single decree, because the actual work of bookkeeping, control, registering, accounting and counting is performed by *employees*, the majority of whom themselves lead a proletarian or semi-proletarian existence.
>
> By a single decree of the proletarian government these employees can and must be transferred to the status of state employees, in the same way as the watchdogs of capitalism, like Briand and other bourgeois ministers, by a single decree transfer railwaymen on strike to the status of state employees. We shall need many more state employees of this kind, and more *can* be obtained, because capitalism has simplified the work of accounting and control, has reduced it to a comparatively simple system of bookkeeping, which any literate person can do.[1]

This is followed by the oddly ambiguous statement: 'The important thing will not be even the confiscation of the capitalists' property, but country-wide, all-embracing workers' control over the capitalists and their possible supporters. Confiscation alone leads nowhere, as it does not contain the element of organization, of accounting for proper distribution. Instead of confiscation, we could easily impose a *fair* tax. . . .'[2]

These ideas, naturally, had little to do with the realities of this or perhaps any other time. However, it must be noted that Lenin did not advocate total nationalization and expropriation. 'The capitalists and the wires they pull' suggests that the wires of control be snapped or taken over, rather than the capitalists expropriated. Nor did he demand their total expropriation on the morrow of the seizure of power. In the spring of 1918 he was still talking of 'state capitalism', of control over employers. VSNKh was issuing instructions forbidding local authorities to nationalize industries without their specific authorization. Aware of the appalling state of the economy, Lenin gave especial emphasis to the establishment of order out of chaos, to the restoration of production, causing intense chagrin among those comrades who wished to preserve the forms and methods of 'workers' control'. Thus some Soviet authors assert that Lenin intended all along speedily to expropriate the private industrialists and producers,[3] but the balance of the evidence seems not to support this view.

However, Brest-Litovsk was followed by the slide into civil war, and with it went the slide into war communism. I have described and documented this process elsewhere.[4] There are many factors involved, including the interaction of ideological enthusiasm and desperate necessity. Kritsman asserted, in describing this period, that 'were it not for external factors, the expropriation of capital would not have taken place in June 1918'.[5] Lenin at times put things rather differently, but he was not by any means always consistent in his view, which must be examined more closely.

In looking back, he several times returned to the theme of a would-be gradualism disrupted by events. Speaking to the second congress of political educators (*politprosvetov*) in October 1921, Lenin said of NEP that it was a 'new' policy by contrast to the one that preceded it, but that

> in essentials it was older than the preceding economic policy. Why so? Because our previous policy was calculated – though in the then situation we did not really calculate, rather asserted – that the old Russian economy could be directly converted into state production and distribution on a Communist basis. Yet if we recall our own economic literature, if we recall what the Communists wrote before taking power . . . and in the first period after taking power, for instance at the beginning of 1918 . . . we then spoke much more cautiously and circumspectly than in the second half of 1918 and during all of 1919 and all of 1920.[6]

Reminding his audience of his own, more gradualist, position, he said that he had hopes that Brest-Litovsk would be followed by 'peaceful construction'. He blamed the 'mistake of trying directly to pass to communist production and distribution' on 'the overwhelming military problems and the desperate situation in which the republic found itself'.[7] Returning to the same theme at the Moscow provincial party conference in October 1921, in a speech devoted wholly to NEP he said with even greater emphasis that, by the spring of 1918, 'We had expropriated more than we could control and administer', and that 'we should pass from expropriation . . . to the tasks of accountancy and inspection (*kontrol'*).' (This under conditions in which a large private sector continued to exist in industry.) Earlier illusions about direct and immediate construction of socialism were already becoming modified. 'Already then, in a number of respects, it was necessary to move backwards.' He went on: 'We assumed that the two systems – the systems of state production and distribution and of private commodity-production and distribution – would be in conflict with one another under conditions in which we would build up state production and distribution, capturing it step by step from the hostile system',[8] and that this was already the building of a new system, though there was at first no conception as to the relationship of the state's economy to the market and to trade. He cited as an example the 'nationalization of advertising', a fairly futile measure, but one indicating that they expected a large private sector to exist and to advertise. He then pointed out, as also did Trotsky on an earlier occasion,[9] that another vital factor was the behaviour of the bourgeoisie, and said:

> The state power, the proletariat, attempted to move towards new social relations with, so to speak, the maximum adaptation to the then existing conditions, as far as possible gradually and without extremes. The enemy, i.e., the bourgeois class, tried everything to push us into the most extreme and desperate struggle. Strategically, from the point of view of the enemy, was this correct? Certainly, since why should the bourgeoisie, without having tried out its forces in direct conflict, suddenly accept us and obey?[10]

And again, 'the bourgeoisie could not . . . accept those partial concessions which Soviet power was giving it in the interests of a more gradual transition to the new order. "No part of transition, to be part of a new order", that was how the bourgeoisie replied.'[11] (It matters little in the present context whether this is a fair picture of the then situation.)

Relations with the peasants were, of course, a key element in war communism as they were *the* key element in NEP. Here it is well to appreciate that neither Lenin, nor any sane man, ever imagined that such relations could be built on confiscations, other than in an emergency. It may be, indeed, that some Bolsheviks thought of *produkto-obmen* (products exchange, or barter, not *trade*) between a socialist industrial sector and a predominantly private petty-bourgeois peasantry. Lenin, as we shall see, aimed at this in the very first stages of NEP. But in 1918 the problem was that the towns were threatened with starvation, and the 'class struggle in the villages' and compulsory deliveries were means of getting food. As the civil war progressed and economic disruption deepened, it was increasingly found that there was nothing to pay the peasants with. No doubt ideological prejudice against trade and its association with 'black marketeering' played its role, but no one should imagine that Lenin was *ideologically* devoted to the principle of confiscation of surpluses, which was the essence of the hated *prodrazverstka*, for its own sake.

So in a sense Lenin took the view that war communism was a response to desperate necessity. But he over and over again said that 'we committed errors'. To that extent the return of what (he alleged) had been the original policy was a return to the right path. A return to the right path is the right thing to do, and cannot be described either as a defeat or a retreat. But Lenin also and repeatedly spoke both of defeat and retreat. The Bolsheviks deliberately tried to march directly into socialism and they had failed; they had lost a battle. At this same Moscow Party conference of October 1921, he developed at length his parallel with Port Arthur, and the related concept of necessary or positive mistakes. This argument, advanced with NEP in full swing, gives us an interesting insight into his mind at this time, and is worth dwelling on.

> The capture [by the Japanese] of Port Arthur went through two completely different stages. The first consisted of violent attacks which were all unsuccessful and cost the famous Japanese general [Nogi] a great number of casualties. The second stage, when it proved necessary to undertake an extremely burdensome, complex and slow siege of the fortress . . ., led in due course to the solution of the problem of capturing the fortress. If we look at these facts, then naturally the question arises: in what sense should we judge the first method adopted by the Japanese general against Port Arthur as a mistake? And if it was a mistake, then under what conditions had the Japanese army, in order to solve its problems, to speak of it and be conscious of it?[12]

On the face of it, he went on, the evident and bloody failure of the initial attacks meant they were a mistake. Yet, given the information available to General Nogi, he could not know the best way to proceed; there were great advantages to be gained from a speedy capture of the fortress, and he was therefore right to try. The 'mistake' was therefore 'necessary and valuable', and without it the Japanese army would not have gained the experience which led to victory, though at a very much later date.[13]

This was Lenin's parallel with the assault on bourgeois commercial relations launched unsuccessfully in 1918–20. (In the discussion that followed, one man suggested that *they*, Bolsheviks, were besieged in Port Arthur!) This was Lenin's way of reconciling the propositions that they had committed many errors, had all (he did not ever exclude himself) suffered from illusions, about what was possible, yet in the given revolutionary–military emergency they were, so to speak, constructive or necessary mistakes. As General Nogi did after his futile early assaults, one must retire, dig in and plan a more systematic offensive, to be launched much more cautiously and thoroughly prepared.

Retreat how far? Lenin devoted much eloquence to this topic since morale of retreating troops is apt to break, and at the date he was speaking (October 1921) the retreat was continuing. But more of that later on.

THE TRANSITION TO NEP

It is not part of the present chapter to trace the evolution of Lenin's actual policies in 1918–21. It is, however, important to note his obstinate commitment to the essential features of war communism. He knew of course, and frequently said, that the peasants were against *prodrazverstka*. He knew all too well the strength of the will to trade, the vast black market, the *meshochniki*. Yet, along with the vast majority of his colleagues, he was committed to a fight against these things as manifestations of 'petty-bourgeois *stikhiya*'. While his own statements were not among the more extreme, at least he did not object when others announced the imminent abolition of money, the substitution of rations in kind for wages, the provision of various services (tramcars, housing and so on) free of charge, as part of the construction of communism today. Of course, the economy was ruined, industry was either producing for war or at a standstill and half of the urban population had fled the hungry and cold cities. While the war continued, his attitude would perhaps be accounted for by the need to concentrate all resources for the fighting forces and the (widespread) association of wartime free trade with illegitimate black marketeering. Voices were raised early in 1920 in favour of abandoning *prodrazverstka*, allowing some freedom of private trade. Trotsky saw arguments in favour of this course, which was, as is known, urged by the surviving Mensheviks too. But Lenin said, in April 1920: ‘peasants must give their surplus grain to the workers, because under present-day conditions the sale of these surpluses would be a crime’.[14] Why a crime? In many speeches at this period, both Lenin and his party comrades repeatedly showed themselves to be emotionally committed to the bitter and cruel struggle against the very concept of freedom of trade. Food was desperately short, industrial consumers' goods equally so, fuel and raw materials seldom available, and transport was so disorganized that they in any case could seldom be moved. Any goods which could be sold would command (did, in the black market, command) very high barter prices. The regime depended on what was left as a ration. It seemed to Lenin that, even with the civil war won, those other enemies *golod*, *kholod* and *razrukha* (hunger, cold and ruin) were to be fought by the same method of coercion and control. The restoration of industry required food, yet peasant producers were unwilling to provide food without payment in industrial goods. Thus the peasants must be persuaded, and if not persuaded then compelled, to give food to the state, the workers and the army on credit. ‘We admit,’ said Lenin, ‘that we are despots to the peasants.’ The task of breaking out of the vicious circle must be ‘by military methods, with absolute ruthlessness and by absolute suppression of all other interests’. However, ‘when we restore our industry we will make every effort to satisfy the peasants’ needs for urban manufactures’.[15] But it is quite clear that in 1920 he was not yet thinking of NEP. Indeed, the most extreme economic decrees of the war communism period were adopted in November–December 1920, after the end of hostilities with Poland, presumably with Lenin's approval. The two decrees were: the nationalization of small-scale industry (most of which had been nationalized already) and the so-called *Posevkomy*, or committees, which were to make peasants sow and harvest as ordered. As late as 27 December 1920 he could still insist on the harshest *prodrazverstka* measures.[16] He may still, during this year, have harboured illusions about weaning the peasants from their traditional attitudes, persuading them to see virtues in the collective approach. In his more sober moments he must have known that this was a matter for the future, as when he imagined that an abundance of tractors would convince the peasants of the virtues of communism. Yet in his famous interview with H. G. Wells, Lenin left the following impression:

> 'Even now' said Lenin, 'not all the agricultural production of Russia is peasant production. We have in places large-scale agriculture. The government is already running big estates with workers instead of peasants where conditions are favourable. That can spread, it can be extended first to one province, then another. The peasants of the other provinces, selfish and illiterate, will not know what is happening until their turn comes!' It may be difficult to defeat the Russian peasant en masse; but in detail there is no difficulty at all. At the mention of peasant, Lenin's head came nearer mine; his manner became confidential. As if after all the peasant *might* overhear.[17]

In relation to the peasants, or the abolition of money, or repressing free trade, or in harbouring illusions about leaps into communism, it is therefore clear that Lenin stuck obstinately to the extreme views held by the vast majority of his party comrades right through 1920. When could he be said to have begun to change his mind? My own view is that the first signs of a new approach could be dimly discerned on 27 December 1920, for on the very day he was insisting on maintaining *prodrazverstka* he also proposed encouraging peasants to produce more by issuing bonuses in kind to those who did so. 'We have twenty million separate households, which are individually run and cannot be run otherwise. Not to reward them for increasing productivity would be basically wrong', he exclaimed.[18] Yet he failed to convince his comrades, who wanted to make the bonuses available only to peasant associations. While of course Lenin had not yet reached the stage of advocating NEP, he at least showed himself more willing than a majority of his friends to provide peasants with incentives. By then he could be in no possible doubt that *prodrazverstka* itself was, literally, counterproductive.

It is widely believed that it was the Kronstadt rising which was decisive. This is not really so, since the proposal to abolish *prodrazverstka* was put forward before Kronstadt. However, it is certainly true that peasant resistance and risings of so-called 'Kulaks' were leading to a situation so catastrophic that the survival of the regime came ever more clearly to depend on the relaxation of the rigours of war communism. Members of the party leadership began to sense the inevitable. According to the notes of the fifth edition of Lenin's works, Obolensky presented a report to the central committee on 8 February 1921, and in the discussion the view was expressed that *prodrazverstka* be ended and replaced by a tax. Lenin, according to the same source, made a 'preliminary draft' of a resolution on these lines for the use of a special commission which was set up on that day to look into this question.[19] Open discussion of this question began in *Pravda* on 17 February, the plenum of the central committee agreed to 'replace *prodrazverstka* by tax in kind' (*prodnalog*) on 24 February. The Kronstadt rising broke out on 28 February, before the Party congress had met to adopt the new policy.

Lenin admitted freely that he did not expect the retreat to be as far-reaching as it in fact became. Typical of his views at the time was a short amendment to the draft resolution, which he wrote on 3 March, which included a sentence about ensuring that 'products-exchange should not degenerate into speculation'.[20] Later he explained what had been intended:

> A whole number of decrees . . . all propaganda and legal enactments in the spring of 1921 were related to the growth of products-exchange. In what did this concept consist? . . . It was assumed that, in a more or less socialist manner, we would exchange [barter] on a nation-wide scale the products of state industry for the products of agriculture, and through this products-exchange restore large-scale industry. . . . What happened? What happened was, as you all know . . . product-exchange collapsed: it collapsed in the sense that it became purchase-and-sale. . . . The retreat had to continue . . . product-exchange was a failure, the private market proved stronger than us, and we had instead ordinary purchase and sale, trade.[21]

Therefore the measure which passed effortlessly through the Tenth Congress of the Party in March 1921 was very rapidly followed by a rather different policy, mostly spontaneously, though it was 'legalized' by later decrees. Private trade, small-scale manufacture, foreign concessions, even projects for mixed companies with the participation of Russian private capital, the abandonment of free distribution, the turning of state trusts into commercial enterprises – all this followed. To quote Lenin again, 'We are now [October 1921] in such a situation that we must retreat further yet, not only towards state capitalism but to state regulation of trade and monetary circulation.'

Having gradually, under force of circumstances, appreciated the overwhelming necessity of accepting this policy, Lenin quickly became its most eloquent propagandist. He showed very little patience with those who had ideological doubts or quoted the Founding Fathers or party resolutions against him. Preobrazhensky, for example, suggested that state capitalism was a form of capitalism: no, thundered Lenin, rubbish, scholasticism, there is no precedent in Marxist literature for a proletarian state to use (*inter alia*) capitalist and bourgeois elements to build up productive forces. He also criticizes Bukharin on the same issue: state capitalism is 'a capitalism which we are able to limit, the boundaries of which we are able to limit, the boundaries of which we are able to determine'.[22]

He spoke on this whole subject with passion and eloquence to the Eleventh Party Congress (March 1922), when he was able to assert that 'the retreat was over'. By this he meant that no further institutional–legal charges favouring the capitalists and Nepmen would be made. In this speech we see the clearest evidence of how he then saw NEP.

LENIN AND NEP: POLITICAL TACTICS AND AIMS

Undoubtedly Lenin was actuated by a sense of political self-preservation. 'If we had not begun to build [NEP] we would have been totally defeated.' Economic relaxation *had* to come in the spring of 1921 (if not earlier), otherwise he and his comrades would have been swept away. Lenin freely admitted this. Politically, his aim was to cling to power, so as to be able to resume the advance towards communism (just how, and when, is a complex question, to which we will return). In this connection, it is worth citing his notes: '1794 versus 1921', he wrote, twice.[23] Robespierre had been swept away by the French bourgeoisie. He, Lenin, would avoid his fate by bowing to the most urgent economic demands of the peasants.

For the party this represented a retreat, albeit a necessary one. Retreats are painful. They need particularly severe discipline, or panic can set in. Hence he insisted on the need to repress party factions such as the 'workers' opposition'. (It was obviously no accident that the Tenth Congress which adopted NEP also banned factions.) At the Eleventh Congress Lenin also expressed quite ruthless thoughts about other parties. 'When a Menshevik says "you are now retreating, I was always for retreat, I agree with you, I am with you, let us retreat together," then we say in reply: "for public manifestations of menshevism our revolutionary courts will shoot you. . . ."'[24] And again: '[if they say] "the revolution went too far; we always said what you now say; permit us yet again to repeat it." To this we reply: "Permit us to stand you up against the wall."'[25]

Therefore the maximum political control and *political* police repression was to be accompanied by economic flexibility and free trade. The bourgeoisie was being allowed to spread its wings, up to a point.

Not that Lenin was playing down the element of class struggle. On the contrary, within NEP he saw 'a desperate life-and-death struggle between capitalism and communism'.[26] But the forms of this struggle were to be primarily economic, within the general *political* limitations upon capitalism, made possible by the party monopoly of power. 'We all know,' he said, 'how in 1918 we got the bourgeoisie to work for us.' Now 'we do it by other means'.[27] The idea was that they should do so voluntarily, while acting in pursuit of their own interests. It would be a form of 'building communism with non-communist hands'. But no more retreat. We know, in principle, how to work with the capitalists and the bourgeoisie. Of course, he insisted over and over again, Communists are much better at making speeches and passing resolutions than at being business-like. 'Learn to trade.' Right now, he insisted, there is endless talk of the necessity of *Smychka*, of the link–alliance with the peasantry, but can the Communists satisfy peasant needs? The capitalist–Nepman may be a profiteer, but the peasants can see he delivers the goods. 'As for you, your principles are communistic, your ideals are excellent, you look like saints capable of instant transfer to Paradise, but can you run a business?'[28] Again, 'we must prove that the ruined, hungry small peasant can receive effective help from the communists. Either we will prove this, or he will send us to all the devils.' He may be prepared to wait and see. But before long the peasant might say: 'if you cannot run the economy, get out!'[29]

In what form, then, can an advance be planned? Whether he was using the 'Port Arthur' parallel or referring to the ending of the retreat, Lenin naturally thought of ultimate victory, of a resumption of the advance. Many later arguments centred upon what kind of timetable, what kind of advance, was intended. NEP, he insisted, was intended 'seriously and for a long time'. This means *competition*.

> It is necessary to prove in practice that you work no worse than the capitalists, [he told the Eleventh Congress]. The capitalists forge a

> link (*smychka*) commercially with the peasants so as to get rich. You must forge a link with the peasant economy to strengthen the economic power of our proletarian state. You have the advantage over the capitalists because power is in your hands, only you cannot utilize them properly. See things more soberly, throw off solemn communist robes, simply learn simple business, and then we will defeat the private capitalists.
>
> If we defeat the capitalists and establish the *smychka* with the peasantry, then this will give us invincible strength. Then the building of socialism will not be the job of that drop in the ocean, the Communist party, but of all the toiling mass. Then the ordinary peasant will say that they help me, then he will follow us, and then what if our steps will be a hundred times slower, they will be a million times more solid and strong.[30]

Lenin appeared to be saying that victory will come from *within* NEP and through NEP as and when the needs of the predominantly peasant society will be met out of the socialist sector of the economy. Therefore to learn to trade, to produce efficiently, was the form in which the class struggle was taking place. The Nepmen will retreat under the impact of competition, under rules and limits made by the 'proletarian' (i.e., Communist-controlled) state.

Lenin was concerned with the political danger to the Party and within the Party represented by such a course. He cited Ustryalov and the *smenovekhovtsy*. Is the Party's policy over NEP a tactic, or is it evidence of the Party's evolution or degeneration? The Party might sink into a 'bourgeois morass, waving little red flags the while'. Lenin admitted that the danger of such a development was real and had to be guarded against. He never grappled, however, with the problem of how to guard against it in the long run. He spoke again of the Party's determination to keep power, of the need to be efficient and businesslike, not to be led by the nose by bourgeois specialists and traders.[31] But what if the spirit which he feared penetrated into the party? For just such an accusation would later be made regarding the Bukharin–Rykov line. What would Lenin have said? But more of this in a moment.

LENIN'S VIEW OF THE PEASANTS DURING NEP

The key to everything was the relation of the Party and the socialized sector to the peasantry. Lenin saw this clearly, and from the spring of

1921 we hear no more about any rapid move of the peasants towards socialist forms and attitudes. Of course he saw the peasants in a differentiated way. Some are *kulaks*, some poor, most of them are in-between. But in 1922, in the aftermath of a terrible famine, he emphasized 'the overwhelming importance of the recovery of agriculture and of an increase in its output'. Therefore 'at the present time in relation to the Kulaks and the better-off peasants the policy of the proletariat should be directed particularly to the limitation of their exploiting tendencies'.[32] (The kulaks and the potential danger they represented were seldom mentioned by Lenin after NEP began.) In the same notes Lenin criticized Preobrazhensky for referring to 'directives in the form of decrees' in relation to peasants, though he did also write that the crude 'committees-of-the-poor' (*Kombedorskie*) methods might have to be reviewed if there was another war.

Addressing the Fourth Congress of the Comintern in November 1922, Lenin could claim with some pride that 'the peasants are pleased with their present situation', unlike their feelings in February 1921, when, as Lenin also admitted, 'huge masses of the peasants' were against the regime.[33] He deplored the still very poor condition of heavy industry and referred to urgent steps which were needed to see it on its feet. But here, as elsewhere, he proceeded on the clear assumption that the needs and wishes of the peasant masses, for trade and for goods, were the basis of Soviet economic policy, of the *smychka*, of the stability of the state.

Being busy, and stricken with ill-health, he had little to say about the future development of the peasants, until the much-misquoted and misunderstood article, 'On Cooperation', one of his very last works, written in January 1923, was published in *Pravda* on 26 and 27 May of that year.

Under NEP, he wrote, with private trade legal, cooperation is of great and vital importance. 'We overdid things in adopting NEP, not because we gave too much room for the principle of free industry and trade, but because we did not think of cooperation.' Cooperatives should be encouraged, should be given credits on favourable terms. Peasants should benefit from participation in cooperatives (Lenin had in view most of all consumer-cooperatives, since he referred repeatedly to 'shops'). The whole population should become so 'civilized' that they all participate in cooperatives and learn to count and calculate. That is 'all' that is needed to move on to socialism, and Lenin put 'all' in inverted commas, because of the low level of culture and mass ignorance. 'To achieve through NEP the participation of the whole people in cooperatives will require a whole historical epoch. We might with luck go through this epoch in ten or twenty years.' It is necessary to be a 'literate trader' (*gramotnym torgashom*). At present most Russians 'trade in the Asian manner', but they must learn to trade as Europeans.[34]

Cooperatives, then, are a means of ensuring the participation of the people in retail distribution, and so can be seen as a way of limiting private trade. State control over most of industry and state ownership of land would ensure that soviet cooperatives would be unlike those which exist in capitalist countries. Peasants should become increasingly involved in cooperation. But of course, Lenin insisted, this requires a 'cultural revolution', a real change in peasant awareness and education; this is 'necessary to become a fully socialist country', but it is also 'immeasurably difficult'.[35]

Years later, these arguments were alleged to be the 'Leninist' basis of collectivization. This is plainly nonsense. Lenin was mainly concerned with consumer-cooperation anyhow, and even here, in the context of a long-term cultural revolution, as in some other of his later works, he shows himself acutely conscious of abysmal Russian inefficiency and ignorance, not least among his own comrades. In so far as peasant producers' cooperation is concerned, he said nothing definite, and seems to have not gone further than some very moderate thinkers. The notes of the fifth edition of his works show him to have asked to read, *inter alia*, Chayanov and Tugan-Baranovsky. The latter, in a work published early in 1918, also spoke of slow and gradual cooperation, extending from joint marketing and purchasing very cautiously to the common ownership of scarce equipment and possibly beyond, one day, later.[36] There is nothing in Lenin's 'On Cooperation' which suggests any more drastic solution than this.

His 1922–3 policy was clearly one of gradualism.

BUKHARIN AND LENIN

It is then right to agree with Bukharin's policy of the middle twenties as being in line with the latter-day Lenin?

A good case can be made for this by comparing Bukharin's declaration of, say, 1925–6 with Lenin's views of 1922–3. In my view this can best be seen by examining his *Put'k sotsializmu i raboche-krestyanski soyuz*.

Bukharin soon dismisses his own ultra-left past. '*Prodrazverstka* and the ban on (private) trade were quite unsuitable for the time when it was necessary to go over to rebuilding productive forces. . . .'[37] Now there is a union of workers and peasants under the leadership of the working class and of its 'conscious vanguard'. But the peasants are burdened with taxes, and charged high prices for urban goods. There is taking place 'a struggle for an economic and business *smychka* with the peasantry. . . . This struggle is waged by our state industry and state trade against private capital, private traders . . . who try to make *their smychka* with the peasantry. . . .' It is essential to show 'that the state economy is better able to satisfy the needs of the peasants than the private trader, capitalist or middleman'. If these people gain economic influence over the peasants, this will be politically dangerous.[38] Of course, the peasants want higher food prices, the workers want lower food prices. But their unity will hold none the less, with the growing size and efficiency of large-scale socialist industry, which will oust the privateer gradually. While agriculture must expand, 'we must increasingly achieve a state of affairs in which all industry will be linked together by a single plan . . . However, such a planned industry is unthinkable by itself: our industry produces to a great extent for the *peasant market*' (emphasis his).[39] If the peasant economy is to grow (went on Bukharin) it must become more organized. 'It is self-evident that we cannot think that we can, or even should, persuade the peasants suddenly all to unify their land-holdings. Old habits . . . have such deep roots that to break them suddenly is just not possible. Yet none the less . . . the peasants will move in the direction of unification (*obyedineniye*).' How? Through cooperation.[40] Of course, the peasants are not a homogeneous class; there are kulaks, they must be limited, the poorer peasants must be supported. The poorest peasants might find it paid them to form *kolkhozy*, though even for them this would represent a sharp break with old habits of thought. Of course, the kulaks would form cooperatives too, and strive to gain influence over other peasants through the cooperatives. But all of them, including the kulak ones, will operate within an economy dominated by the state, and in some degree would 'grow into the system' (*vrastat' v sistemu*), for example, by having to keep their savings in the State bank. The cooperatives will initially be for marketing and joint purchases, perhaps also credit. They will extend, and thereby further strengthen socialism. Within the village and the cooperatives there will be a species of class war. But no longer will it take the form of 'requisitioning the kulak's goods to give to the poor'; rather the middle peasant will become better off, using more productive methods, and will 'overtake the kulaks'.[41] No more must we have 'administrative pressure and repeated confiscations and requisitions', some of which continued even after 1921. Against the village money-lender and petty trader we need not 'direct coercion' but credit cooperatives and efficient retail distribution.

Bukharin insisted on the dependence of socialist industry on peasant demand, and therefore on the need to increase effective monetary demand among peasants. 'Accumulation in one industry will increase the faster if accumulation in our peasant economy increases fast.'[42] If industry overcharges, and so impoverishes the peasants, it will harm itself by becoming 'deprived of its market in the villages'.[43] He ended by asserting that, far from eliminating market relations, as was once thought, 'we will reach socialism through market relations.' Large-scale industry, in the hands of the state, will squeeze out the small men 'through competition in the market'. 'NEP is not a betrayal of the proletarian line, it is the only correct proletarian policy.'[44]

What can we say in comparing all this with Lenin? Clearly, the two lines have much in common. Bukharin spelt out the 'market' logic of Lenin's Eleventh Congress speech. Both saw logic in peasant cooperation, but both could see that it was to be a slow process, given objective difficulties and peasant opinion and habits. But Lenin did pay at least lip-service to the special urgency of restoring and developing heavy industry too. Above all, Lenin was a *Realpolitiker* to his finger tips. He was very well able to persuade his comrades that whatever was needed at the given moment corresponded to eternal verities, or at least was 'correct' in some fundamental way. Convinced of the rightness of the logic of NEP, he lambasted his verbose and slogan-mongering colleagues, and strove to convince them that NEP and its logic were in the highest interests of the Revolution. But suppose in 1927 he saw that an administrative solution could be made to work? He was not averse to resolving social contradictions by shooting, as his record abundantly shows. I will return to this point in the conclusion.

LENIN AND SOCIALIST ECONOMICS

A Soviet economist, in private conversation, once said the following: 'Lenin did intend to resume the offensive on the bourgeoisie, to drive them out. But he did not want the Stalin type of command economy and expected socialist trusts and enterprises to operate autonomously by reference to a socialist market. He learned from the failure of centralization in 1918–1920.' Several Soviet reformers have recently been quoting the Lenin of 1922 in support of their proposals to introduce elements of a market economy in the USSR of today. Are they right?

It is hard to say. Lenin presumably believed in the ultimate establishment of full communism. But he did believe in the relative longevity of NEP and had no patience at all with the grandiose all-inclusive plans. Thus in the middle of 1921 we find him reacting as follows in a letter to Krzhizhanovski: 'We are hungry, ruined, beggars. A complete, overall total plan for us now is a bureaucratic utopia.'[45] Quite clearly there was no real way of organizing centralized planning in 1922 or 1923, and Lenin was far more concerned to urge the comrades to 'learn to trade'. He was still for electrification, of course, but he no longer spoke of the GOELRO plan, which so occupied him in 1920. In this same year he approved a measure which abolished all money taxes, but by mid-1921 he was a convinced partisan both of the restoration of taxes and of sound finance. We find him writing repeatedly to and about Sokol'nikov, urging the stabilization of the currency and even 'the free circulation of gold'. And indeed there was adopted by the government on 4 April 1922, a decree 'on the circulation of gold, silver, platinum, precious stones and foreign currency', and not too long after that the new Soviet *chervonets* acquired international respectability and dealings in gold and *valuta* were a common occurrence in Moscow.[46] Only at one point did Lenin remain obstinate: he rejected any easing of the state monopoly of foreign trade.

Yes, Lenin in 1922 was a partisan of the market economy, of efficiency, of competition. But this is not to say that he would have remained so, that his GOELRO enthusiasm had vanished for all time. The situation required the most rapid restoration of the productive forces of Russia, with the help of the bourgeoisie; the market-and-money mechanism was needed to compel the fantastically inefficient state enterprises to cut out waste and to produce what above all the peasants wanted, since NEP *was* the *smychka*. But Lenin would surely resume his advocacy of the priority of heavy industry (which he theoretically established in the nineties), of electrification and of nation-wide planning as, and when, this seemed practicable. In what form the economy would function in this new period was still unknown.

CONCLUSION

As the official Soviet histories assert, NEP was indispensable, necessary, right, though we need not agree with them in accepting that the need for NEP was seen by Lenin at just the right time. He was far better able than his colleagues to see the logic of NEP as well as its necessity. Most Communists were incapable of dealing with practical affairs, they must learn to do business from men of business, they must prove to the peasants their ability to supply their needs. So the proper conclusions must be drawn. Hold on to political power, hold on to the economic 'commanding heights', and in due course the socialist offensive will be resumed. At first he was hopeful of a revolution in Germany or some other advanced country coming to the aid of backward Russia. By the end of his days he must have known that this was, for a long time, a vain hope, but also that Soviet Russia had survived its crisis and would continue to exist.

But where would they go from there? In the debate which was to follow Lenin's name was invoked by all sides, and this debate, and the real issues involved, have yet to be seriously and honestly described, in works published in the Soviet Union. The 'Bukharin' argument has already been put. It was indeed in line with many things Lenin said and wrote in 1922. But experience would show that the socialist advance faced many obstacles. Large-scale state industry and state trade grew, sure enough, but the private sector grew also, until administrative measures inconsistent with NEP were taken against it after 1926. If genuine competition proved the viability of the 'privateer', would Lenin have had no recourse to police methods to ensure the advance of the state sector? He was fearful enough of the kulaks before 1921. Might he not have hearkened to the warnings of Preobrazhensky about the kulak danger, warnings discounted by Bukharin? What about the scale of accumulation, the urgency of heavy-industrial investment, the problem of agricultural marketings? Trotsky, who had supported NEP, was by 1925–6 attacking the Stalin–Bukharin leadership for dilatoriness in launching plans for industrial development. Lenin was removed by his disease from the political arena at a time when he was advocating policies wholly within the context and the bounds of NEP. But who knows, who can ever know, whether that other Lenin who advocated and practised economic–social coercion might not have come back, faced with the problems which faced Stalin at the end of the twenties. I am not arguing that he would have carried out Stalinist policies, only that his writings and attitudes in his last two years of political life cannot be sufficient proof as to what he would in fact have done.

NOTES

1. V. I. Lenin, *Sochineniia*, 5th edn (Moscow, 1955–65) v. 27, pp. 105–7; here and hereafter, unless otherwise stated, my own translation from the Russian edition.
2. Ibid., p. 107.
3. See notably A. Venediktov, *Organizatsiya gosunderstvennoi promyshlennosti v SSSR* (Leningrad, 1967).
4. *An Economic History of the USSR*, pp. 52 ff.
5. *Vestnik kommunisticheskoi Akademii*, no. 19 (1924), p. 26. For other similar views, see my *Economic History*, pp. 79–80.
6. V. I. Lenin, *Sochineniia*, v. 44, p. 156.
7. Ibid., p. 157.
8. Ibid., pp. 198–9.
9. *The Defence of Terrorism* (London) pp. 94–5.
10. Lenin, v. 44, p. 203.
11. Ibid.
12. Ibid., pp. 194–7.
13. Ibid.
14. V. I. Lenin, *Collected Works*, 4th edn (Moscow, 1960–70) p. 121. Hereafter cited as Lenin (English).
15. Lenin, v. 40, p. 329; v. 30 (English) p. 332.
16. Lenin, v. 42, p. 193.
17. H. G. Wells, *Russia in the Shadows* (London, 1921) p. 137.
18. Lenin, *Sochineniia*, v. 42, p. 185.
19. Ibid., v. 43, p. 433 (editorial notes).
20. Ibid., p. 365.
21. Ibid., v. 44, p. 208.
22. Ibid., v. 45, pp. 84–5, 117.
23. Ibid., v. 43, pp. 385–87.
24. Ibid., v. 45, p. 89.
25. Ibid., p. 90.
26. Ibid., p. 95.
27. Ibid., p. 97.
28. Ibid., p. 79.
29. Ibid., pp. 77, 98.
30. Ibid., p. 92.
31. It is interesting that Bukharin, speaking on 5 February 1923, outlined with prescient clarity a different danger: that ex-workers would turn into a ruling caste (see his *Proletarskaia revoliutsiia i Kul'tura* (Petrograd, 1932) pp. 42–7).
32. Ibid., pp. 44–5.
33. Ibid., p. 285.

34. Ibid., pp. 371–2.
35. Ibid., pp. 37, 76.
36. See A. Nove, 'M. I. Tugan-Baranovsky', in this volume.
37. N. Bukharin, *Put'k sotsializmu i raboche-krestyanski soyuz*, 3rd edn (Moscow, 1926) p. 11.
38. Ibid., pp. 25–6.
39. Ibid., p. 30.
40. Ibid.
41. Ibid., pp. 46 ff.
42. Ibid., p. 41.
43. Ibid., p. 44.
44. Ibid., pp. 64–6.
45. Lenin, *Sochineniia*, v. 52, p. 76.
46. Ibid., v. 54, pp. 90, 139, 606, *et passim*.

5 Trotsky, Markets, and East European Reforms*

The typical Western Trotskyist is apt to criticize reforms of the Hungarian or Chinese type as a step backwards, if not a betrayal. A Trotskyist such as Ernest Mandel is not against the temporary use of money and commodity relations, indeed would warn against trying to abolish them prematurely. None the less, they envisage the transition as a period in which markets are gradually replaced by planning, planning which functions democratically, which conforms to Marx's vision of control 'by the direct producers' of the means of production and the product. This they believe was Trotsky's own position. Not only they believe it. True, Stephen Cohen is on record expressing his belief that Trotsky was 'a Nepist'. Also, Hungarian work on Preobrazhensky stressed, correctly, that the bitterness of the factional struggle of the twenties should not blind us to the fact that the protagonists shared many common assumptions and common views.[1] None the less, it is quite widely believed that Trotsky was unhappy with the NEP compromise, and that Bukharin was the spiritual father of present-day economic reformism; Moshe Lewin wrote a whole book on these lines.[2] When I read *his* book I recalled a senior Soviet professor, who recalled the controversies, saying 'Bukharin and Preobrazhensky *both* believed that socialism and the market are incompatible, and both were wrong.' Bukharin was committed to NEP 'seriously and for a long time', but NEP was a mixed economy, not socialism. For him, and for Trotsky, too, socialism was a future society corresponding, more or less, to Marx's vision of at least the first stage of communism. Bukharin and Trotsky clashed, but not on whether markets were necessary under NEP, or on whether NEP was necessary. I shall argue that a good case can be made for making Trotsky an 'ancestor' of East European reform, or that, if the case be less than watertight, it would be equally so for Bukharin.

Let us look first of all at Trotsky's view of NEP. I have already written on this theme, and those who have read my earlier work are owed an apology for repetition.[3]

---

* Paper presented at AAASS conference, 1985.

Trotsky had claimed, in his autobiography, that he had proposed the essence of NEP, i.e., the end of food requisitioning, a year before Lenin adopted it. True, he had made no public statement about it at the time, and Deutscher in his biography has to explain why, after this proposal had been rejected, Trotsky went very far in advocating extreme forms of war communism, of which militarization of labour is but one example. None the less, there is no evidence that he did not welcome NEP when it came. In 1923 it fell to him to present the economic report to the twelfth party congress. He had, in the previous year spoken to the Fourth Congress of the Communist International:

> In the course of the transitional epoch each enterprise and each set of enterprises must to a greater or lesser degree orient itself independently in the market and test itself through the market. It is necessary for each state-owned factory with its technical director to be subject not only to control from the top – by state organs – but also from below, through the market, which will remain the regulator of the state economy for a long time to come.

He spoke on similar lines to the party congress, acting as a responsible member of the politbureau and wholly within the assumptions of the mixed economy based on market relations. He agreed with those who deplored some of the cruder manifestations of NEP, such as carousing in the *Yar* cabaret, but said that they had to accept this as a necessary cost of accepting the market, even 'the market devil'. His personal dislike of buying and selling was clear enough, but so was his advocacy, and acceptance of the logic, of NEP. He also advocated planning, deplored the lack of coherence in ecomonic policy, but, as he put it in his letter of the central committee of 24 October 1923, he wanted 'overall guidance in planning, i.e., the systematic coordination of the basic sectors of the state economy *in the process of adapting them to the peasant market*'.[4] He certainly did not have in mind an all-embracing plan of the directive type, quite impracticable in 1923. A reasonable interpretation of his ideas at that time would be as follows. State industry, recovering from the paralysis of 1921, is growing in an unbalanced way, without adequate direction, and furthermore is hampered by an inflexible financial strait-jacket being imposed by Sokol'nikov, the commissar of finance (in his efforts to stabilize the currency and end hyper-inflation). Priority should be given to industrial recovery, so that the market, especially the peasant market, be supplied. Indeed this finds support in his pamphlet, *The New Course*, also written in 1923:

> For the next period we shall have a planned economy allying itself more and more with the market, and as a result, adapting itself to the market in the course of its growth . . . By means of exact knowledge of market conditions and correct economic forecasts we must harmonize state industry and agriculture according to a definite plan . . . The different parts of our state industry (coal, metals, machinery, cloth) do not match with each other. The present selling crisis is a harsh warning the peasant market is giving us. The rational way of approaching successfully the solution of questions relating to the *smychka* is not by suppressing the market but on the basis of the market.

(*Smychka* is the 'link' with the peasantry.) 1923 was the year of the 'scissors crisis', a term Trotsky himself coined, to represent the excessive gap between industrial and agricultural prices, a gap which could discourage peasant marketings, and which Trotsky (and, of course, Bukharin) believed should be corrected by cutting the costs and increasing the output and efficiency of state industry. (Yet it is precisely at this period that Preobrazhensky formulated his notion of primitive socialist accumulation, with its stress on 'exploiting' the peasant through the price mechanism, which helps to explain Bukharin's strongly negative reaction.)

Trotsky, in his approach to the needs of agriculture, saw the urgent need to provide material stimuli for higher output, and therefore said (to the twelfth congress) that the peasant should feel able to 'get richer' (*stal bogache*),[5] and this two years before Bukharin's notorious slogan *obogashchaites*' ('get rich'). In later years Trotsky himself seems to have forgotten this, when he cast Bukharin in the role of a right-wing pro-kulak ideologue.

The evidence is strong. Stephen Cohen's characterization of Trotsky as a 'Nepist' is certainly correct when referring to Trotsky's position before his expulsion from the politbureau. This emphatically does not mean that Trotsky (or Bukharin, or any Bolshevik) actually loved the market or NEP as such. It merely shows that they shared a commitment to a market-based policy at this period.

Trotsky's views and declarations changed in tone and substance when he became an oppositionist, as is indeed a common feature of politicians the world over. Richard Day has had much of interest to say about the evolution of Trotsky's views on 'socialism in one country' and on the role of foreign trade, and I will not pursue these themes here. Let us look instead at Trotsky's views of markets and of NEP, first of all in the period between 1925 and 1928, that is, before his exile.

Here I have some disagreement with Day. In his introduction to his valuable collection of translations of Bukharin, he argues that Trotsky had a coherent and logical economic policy at this time.[6] This may seem irrelevant to the theme of this paper, but it is not unimportant to see whether Trotsky's views were in fact consistent with the continuance of NEP and the minimum of market equilibrium which that continuance required. It is also important to note the context of the argument: 1926, and still more 1927, saw the beginning of the crumbling of the NEP edifice. The young Novozhilov warned, in a prescient article published in *Vestnik finansov* in 1926 (No. 3), that 'goods famine' was the consequence of the (still relatively small) increase in investments and the rise in personal incomes in town and village, accompanied by efforts to hold down prices. By 1927 shortages had become more serious, with a growing gap between official and free-market prices, especially for agricultural products. An ill-judged policy of reducing purchase prices of grain led, by the end of 1927, to the procurement crisis and to 'extraordinary measures' inconsistent with NEP and the *smychka*.

In *this* context, what did Trotsky and his ally Zinoviev actually propose? A harsher line towards the richer peasants, more investment, higher wages and opposition to price increases. When Stalin countered that the Dnieper dam would be as useful as would be a gramophone to a peasant with no cow, Trotsky mocked him for excessive caution. True, by the standards of the following years it is absurd to see Trotsky as a 'super-industrializer', since Stalin adopted policies far more extreme than any that Trotsky had advocated. But this was when Stalin was destroying the entire basis of NEP.

Day argued that Trotsky's policies of 1926–7, if adopted, would have helped to overcome the crisis of NEP, because the higher investment he advocated would have increased the flow of goods. To this one can reply: firstly, that Trotsky's investment programme included large heavy-industry projects (like the Dnieper dam) which, whatever their other merits, would not provide a flow of consumer goods, and, secondly, that *any* investment takes a number of years to generate a flow of output, and that meanwhile the necessary savings must be made. The point is that the adoption of the left opposition's programme at this time would have worsened the already serious disequilibria which were about to contribute to the collapse of NEP. It is noteworthy that Trotsky's temporary ally, Preobrazhensky, showed himself fully conscious of the dilemma, in his challenging article 'Economic equilibrium in the system of the USSR',[7] and could indicate no way out other than the end of isolation, that is, revolutions in advanced countries. It is my contention that Preobrazhensky was more hostile to the market and less tolerant of the NEP compromise, than was Trotsky, a hypothesis that finds some confirmation in the fact that, when Stalin 'turned left', attacked the petty bourgeoisie and closed markets, Preobrazhensky deserted Trotsky and begged to be readmitted to the party.

Trotsky seems to have been mesmerized by what he conceived of as the 'right danger', casting Bukharin and Rykov in the role of agents of the Nepmen and kulaks in the party, and Stalin as a 'centrist' in alliance with them. This was a gross misunderstanding of the real situation, and of the respective positions of Bukharin and Stalin. But it helps to explain Trotsky's negative attitudes at this period to measures needed to re-establish the conditions in which the market could effectively operate, even while he had no coherent alternative.

I see no evidence that Trotsky actually believed in scrapping NEP and substituting directive planning plus forcible collectivization. He, like Day, seems to have believed that the adoption of his policies would have been possible *within* NEP.

In exile Trotsky was handicapped by lack of information and increasing difficulty (in due course impossibility) of communicating with his supporters inside the Soviet Union. I have cited elsewhere a number of his ambivalent and contradictory statements about collectivization and the five-year plans (see note 3). On the one hand, 'The successes in the sphere of industrialization and collectivization became possible only because the Stalinist bureaucracy came up against the resistance of its protégé [*sic!*] the *kulak*, who refused to surrender grain to the state, and thus the bureaucracy were compelled to take over and carry out the policy of the left opposition.'[8] This was said in an interview for the *New York Times* as late as 1932. In the same year, he wrote:

> grandiose enterprises have been created, new industries, entire branches of industry. The capacity of the proletariat organized into a state to direct the economy by new methods and to create

> material values in tempos previously unheard of has been demonstrated in life . . . Socialism as a system for the first time demonstrated its title to historic victory, not on the pages of *Capital* but by the Praxis of hydroelectric plants and blast-furnaces.[9]

Evidence of Trotsky's enthusiasm for Stalinist centralized planning plus collectivization? No, evidence perhaps of ignorance, certainly of inconsistency, since he was also writing quite different things on these very topics.

Numerous were his published criticisms of what he called 'prize-gallop industrialization', excessive tempos, quality deterioration, arbitrariness, falling living standards and excessive autarky. As for collectivization, while he had nothing to say about the barbarous methods used in the countryside (perhaps he simply did not know how bad they were), in the same year, 1932, he was also reasserting the virtues of NEP, which 'created economic links between town and village . . . Nationalized industry must provide the peasantry with products of such quantity and at such prices as would entirely eliminate or reduce to a minimum in the relation between the state and the peasant the factor of extraeconomic force.'[10] The state should be 'not forced to resort to administrative measures of compulsion against the majority of the peasantry in order to obtain agricultural products'. What ought to be 'a simple and profitable exchange for both sides' has become a 'campaign'.

> Collectivization becomes a viable factor only to the extent to which it involves the personal interest of members of collective farms, by shaping the relations between the collective farms and the outside world on the basis of commercial calculation. This means that correct and economically sound collectivization at this stage should lead not to the elimination of NEP but to a gradual reorganization of its methods.[11]

Again, as in the case of his policies in 1926–7, one can accuse Trotsky of advocating an unrealistic policy; voluntary market-based collectivization was simply not a feasible proposition. However, this *is* what he was advocating.

But the clearest and most vivid statement from Trotsky on the relationship between plan and market is to be found in his article published in November 1932 (and which he reasserted in *The Rev-*

olution Betrayed, so that it was no passing thought). It has been quoted often, but can bear being reproduced in full:

> If there existed a universal brain, registering simultaneously all the processes of nature in society, measuring their dynamics, forecasting the results of their interactions, then such a brain would no doubt concoct a faultless and complete state plan. True the bureaucracy sometimes considers that it has just such a brain. That is why it so easily frees itself from the supervision of the market and of Soviet democracy. The innumerable live participants in the economy, state collective and private, must make known their needs and their relative intensity not only through statistical compilations of planning commissions but directly to the pressure of demand and supply. The plan is checked and to a considerable extent realized through the market. The regulation of the market itself must base itself on the tendencies showing themselves in it. The drafts made in offices must prove their economic rationality through commercial calculation. The economy of the transition period is unthinkable without control by the rouble.

A key sentence follows: 'Only through the interaction of three elements: state planning, the market, and Soviet democracy, can the economy be correctly controlled in the transition epoch.'[12]

The coupling, twice, of 'market' and 'democracy' is, to put it mildly, very interesting, especially bearing in mind the typical attitude of most so-called Trotskyists. At a conference I attended a few years ago, one such produced the following piece of naiveté: 'Behind the plan – the proletariat. Behind the market – the bourgeoisie.' Trotsky could well have approved of my reply: 'Behind the plan – the planners, i.e. bureaucrats. Behind the market – housewives waiting for potatoes.' Not the whole story, of course, but nearer to reality.

Let us look carefully at the content of the above quotation from Trotsky. Firstly, although clearly referring to the 'transition epoch', that is, still having in mind a communist future without a market, the argument about 'a universal brain' would seem to be applicable to any society in the foreseeable future, so that, in this respect at least, the 'transition epoch' would be a very long period indeed. Secondly, it seems clear that Trotsky did understand that the market provides a vital counterforce to bureaucratic arbitrariness, and to this extent is not only compatible with 'Soviet democracy' but actually reinforces it. Thirdly, he seemed to appreciate that the plan, whatever its content might be, requires to be checked through the market. Indeed, there is a gap in Marx's vision: he imagined plans that ensured *ex ante* that labour applied in production was 'directly social', that is, that it was applied to satisfy needs which were known in advance to the 'associated producers'. Yet how can one know *ex ante* if the decisions made, howsoever and by whomsoever made, were correct, other than by some sort of *ex post* verification? And why should this be the case only during 'the transitional epoch'?

Ah, a Trotskyist might reply, Trotsky's strictures related only to bureaucratic planning. All would be well if there were 'democratic planning'. However, since no model of such marketless democratic planning is ever provided, the unbeliever is left with nothing coherent to criticize.

Indeed in 1933 Trotsky argued that 'the function of money in the Soviet economy' should be *expanded*, that there must be 'an accurate measuring rod, freely penetrating to every nook and cranny of the economy, i.e., a stable monetary unit'.[13]

To repeat, Trotsky's analysis was at times confused and contradictory, his policy prescriptions impracticable, and it is no part of my task, nor is it my desire, to defend him. But it can be argued that, if the Soviet reformers found it politic to do so, they could cite Trotsky to justify their programme. So could the Chinese, though no doubt Trotsky's ghost would warn them about letting loose what he once called 'the market devil'. It is one thing to use the market (his ghost might argue), it is another if the market takes command. Trotsky was an intensely political man, and on many occasions in the first half of the 1920s he warned of the need for the party to retain control and to prevent alien class forces from penetrating it; for example, at the thirteenth party congress he spoke of the danger of party democracy becoming 'a channel for petty-bourgeois influences'. Clearly, if only one party is allowed, anyone desirous of exerting influence might be tempted to join it. Trotsky in 1905 attacked Lenin's concept of the party, forecasting correctly what it might lead to. However he subsequently adopted this concept himself, and while in Russia never advocated freedom to form opposition parties, as distinct from groupings *within* the one party (and this only when he found himself 'the prophet disarmed'). I asked his former secretary, van Heijenoort, whether Trotsky ever, to his knowledge, drew from his bitter experience the conclusion that he had been right in 1905 after all ('The party organization substitutes for the party, the central committee substitutes itself for the organization, and finally a dictator substitutes himself for the central committee.') He replied in the negative.

However Trotsky's political theories, so well discussed in Baruch Knei-Paz's book,[14] are not my subject.

NOTES

1. János Mátyas Kovács, 'The Other Preobrazhensky' (mimeo).
2. Moshe Lewin, *Political Undercurrents in Soviet Economic Debates: From Bukharin to the Modern Reformers* (Princeton, NJ.: Princeton University Press, 1974).
3. 'New Light on Trotsky's Economic Views', *American Slavic Review* (March 1981); 'A note on Trotsky and the Left Opposition', *Soviet Studies* (October 1977); and 'Trotsky, Collectivization and the Five-Year Plan', reprinted in *Socialism, Economics and Development* (London: Allen & Unwin, 1986).
4. *The Challenge of the Left Opposition* (New York: Pathfinder Press, 1975) p. 59 (emphasis mine).
5. Twelfth Party Congress, stenographic report, p. 322.
6. Richard Day's introduction to N. I. Bukharin, *Selected Writings on the State and the Transition to Socialism*, translated, edited and introduced by Richard B. Day (Armonk, NY: M. E. Sharpe, 1982) p. lv, and *Leon Trotsky and the Politics of Economic Isolation* (Cambridge: Cambridge University Press, 1973).
7. See a good translation in E. A. Preobrazhensky, *The Crisis of Soviet Industrialization*, edited by Donald Filtzer (White Plains, NY: M. E. Sharpe, 1979).
8. *Writings of Leon Trotsky, 1932* (London: The Harvester Press 1975) p. 48.
9. Ibid., p. 26.
10. Ibid., p. 89.
11. Ibid., pp. 270–5.
12. *Byulleten' oppozitsii*, 1932, no. 31, p. 8.
13. Ibid., 1933, no. 34, pp. 5–6.
14. Baruch Knei-Paz, *The Social and Political Thought of Leon Trotsky* (Oxford: Clarendon Press, 1978).

6 The End of NEP*

'That which Lenin introduced "seriously and for a long time" did not last at all long. Stalin liquidated NEP, while pretending to be following Lenin's precepts.' This is how Anatoli Rybakov summarizes a view also widely held by Western scholars.[2] There is another view, also widely held, that, on the contrary, NEP was seen all along as a temporary manoeuvre, and that Stalin, in ending it, was continuing Lenin's work. Then there is what could be called the 'Bukharinist-alternative' school, which speculates on what could have happened if there were a Bukharin–Rykov leadership, which would have pursued a (slower tempo) industrialization strategy on the basis of a continuing NEP. One must also look to Trotsky and the 'Left Opposition': did they have an alternative policy, and is it correct to see Stalin, in 1928, stealing their clothes? Finally, there is what could be called the pragmatic view: that Stalin was driven into ending NEP by a series of unforeseen crises, which rendered its continuance increasingly difficult. This last view approximates to that of E. H. Carr.

Much hangs on the answer to the question: was there a crisis of NEP in 1927? If so, what was its cause? On this there is some disagreement. Thus it has been roundly asserted that there was no crisis, which is going too far. One has only to look at the evidence of *tovarnyi golod*, increasing market disequilibrium, which was to culminate by the end of the year in the grain-procurements crisis and in emergency measures to deal with it. But, if there were indeed difficulties, what were their causes? Were they inherent in NEP, or were they the consequence of the adoption of policies inconsistent with NEP? If the latter, then why and when were such policies adopted? In the pages that follow I will endeavour to discuss these questions.

---

* This was my contribution to the *Festschrift* for Professor Olga Crisp. Since it was written the discussions on the subject in the Soviet Union have ranged far and wide. Thus the view that Stalin's 'revolution from above' was a *coup d'état* (*perevorot*) was challenged in a remarkable set of articles by A. Tsipko:[1] stalinism, he asserts, 'is above all the tragedy of the Bolshevik old-guard, its pain and its historic guilt'. NEP ended because its basis was not really accepted by or acceptable to the bulk of the party. The debate continues.

Back, first, to Lenin. If it is true that he spoke of NEP being intended 'seriously and for a long time', it is also true that his last work, 'On cooperation', far from being consistent with Stalin's policy of forcible collectivization, was an extremely moderate and cautious document, gradualist in its approach to voluntary cooperation. In *Deti Arbata*, Rybakov puts into Stalin's mind (he soliloquises) the following description of the contrast:

> Tactically Lenin's NEP was a correct manoeuvre, but 'seriously and for a long time' was already an error. The manoeuvre was the temporary deal with the peasants to get the grain . . . [He then cited Lenin]: 'To achieve through NEP the total participation of the entire population in cooperatives . . . will need a whole historical epoch . . . Without total literacy, without sufficient good sense (*tolkovosti*), without accustoming the population to the use of books, without a material basis . . . we will be unable to reach our goal.' He closed the book and put it on the shelf. This would mean inoculating the peasant with the alien philosophy of the farmer. And a farmer does not need the dictatorship of the proletariat. The farmer, the property-owner, the individualist, must be throttled in the Russian *muzhik* at birth. Cooperatives? Yes, but such that the peasant will be a simple labourer . . . Yes, we need books and science, and the struggle against poor harvests. All this is needed. But not prior to collectivization, but on the basis of collectivization.[3]

Yet it is not quite so straightforward. Lenin was ambiguous in his treatment of NEP. 'Seriously and for a long time' could be interpreted as his estimate of the length of time necessary before renewing the offensive. One part of him must have hated the Nepmen, regarded the forced compromise, the 'retreat', as unavoidable but to be reversed as soon as practicable. War communism he described as an error, forced by circumstances and by 'illusions' about a direct leap into communism. NEP, then, was a return to the right road, where they should have been all along. But the right road is not a 'retreat'. Let me imagine a parallel. Lenin signed treaties which recognized the independence of the so-called *limitrofy*, Estonia, Latvia and Lithuania. This too was serious, and for a long time, since there was no likelihood of their reincorporation. Yet would Lenin have disapproved of their 'joining' the USSR in 1939–40?

There is no way of settling this sort of debate. More to the point is how Lenin's views were understood by party activists. If the majority saw NEP as a hateful retreat, and looked forward to the day when they would be strong enough to resume the advance, then Stalin's 'left turn' of 1928, and the measures inconsistent with NEP already taken before that year, represented a sort of consensus, with Bukharin and the 'rights' genuinely in a minority.

NEP was a *market*-based compromise. The destruction of market equilibrium, the refusal to accept that it is important to maintain it, all this was a gradual process, which can be dated from 1926. It was speedily noted by the then young economist V. Novozhilov. In an article in *Vestnik finansov*,[4] he showed that the (still modest) increase in new investment, together with the increase in personal incomes and a policy of price reductions, was bound to lead to shortages, had already begun to do so. In my *Economic History*,[5] I cited a decree of unique economic illiteracy: 'the reduction by 10% in the prices of goods in short supply', issued on 2 July 1926. Then there were a series of discriminatory measures aimed at limiting private activities, e.g. surcharges on rail freight, higher taxes, etc.[6] These measures were increasingly due to the growing gap between official and free prices: the private sector then appears to be profiteering, and supply to it (at fixed prices) of anything from state sources begins to look like an illegitimate source of enrichment. Pressure against the private sector could be seen as a natural consequence of this species of price-scissors (See Table 6.1.)

Why was such a price policy followed? I recall putting this question in Moscow to Albert L. Vainshtein, who had been deputy head of the conjuncture institute of *Narkomfin* at that time, and who survived many years of camp, prison and exile after his arrest in 1930. He spoke of political commitment to cut prices, which seemed important in the struggle against critics from the left; it will be recalled that Preobrazhensky had advocated unequal exchange ('exploitation') to pump resources out of the predominantly private peasantry. If so, Bukharin could be partly to blame, though he should have known the importance of market equilibrium to the survival of NEP. Paradoxically, the effect of such a price policy was not to benefit the peasantry, a point well made by Novozhilov in his article: when goods are in short supply, the townspeople, being nearer the place of manufacture, are able to obtain a disproportionate share of what is officially distributed, while the peasants, last in the queue, have to rely on the higher-priced free market. No doubt this contributed to peasant

Table 6.1

Price index	*(1913 = 100) (Manufactures)* *Official*	*Private*
Dec. 1926	208	251
Dec. 1927	188	240
Dec. 1928	190	253

SOURCE: Malafeyev, *Istoriya tsenoobrazovaniya v SSSR* (Moscow, 1964) pp. 384–5.

unwillingness to sell to the state at official purchase prices, and so to the procurement crisis of 1927–8.

It so happens that an uncle of mine, Yu. Novakovsky, was a high official of the *Tsentrosoyuz* (cooperative) organization at the end of the 1920s. I obtained from his widow a pamphlet he wrote, which may help to establish the atmosphere of the time (the more so because he was subsequently criticised for being too moderate, and was probably lucky to die a natural death before the Great Purge). Let me quote from a pamphlet he wrote:

> Retail cooperatives, squeezing out the private trader, cooperating and organizing the consumer masses, thus builds a first line of trenches around the socialist fortress of Soviet state industry . . . Private commercial capital is deprived of the means of pressing upon socialist industry, of increasing prices for raw materials through the fluctuations of supply and demand. Therefore both in disposing of industrial production and in supplying raw materials to industry, consumer cooperatives create a necessary second line of trenches, protecting access to socialist industry . . . Removing the mass of commodities from spontaneous market forces [*rynochnoi stikhii*], from private-trading speculation, creating inventories of food and raw materials in its shops and storehouses, the consumer cooperatives build around socialist industry a third line of trenches.

1927 was a year of growing disequilibrium, growing shortages, with private activities showing, for the first time since 1921, an absolute decline. It was also the year in which Trotsky and his comrades were exiled, and Great Britain broke off diplomatic relations, contributing to a war scare, part contrived, part genuinely felt (though in fact neither Baldwin nor Poincaré had the slightest intention of taking military action, and Japanese aggression in the Far East was yet to come). It was also the year of the fifteenth party congress. If I may cite again a conversation with Vainshtein: when I asked him whether he could put a date to a decisive change in atmosphere, he replied without hesitation: 'December 1927. Before that date, I and my non-party expert colleagues were listened to, our opinions were taken seriously, whether or not our advice was accepted. After that date, we were regarded as an alien and hostile element, soon to be pushed out and soon to be arrested.'

The fifteenth congress appears in Stalinist historiography as 'the congress of collectivization'. This, of course, is misleading. The congress did indeed favour collectivization, but stressed that it should be voluntary and on the basis of high technique. Since both these conditions were known to be absent, Bukharin and Rykov could and did vote in favour. What Bolshevik could be against? The problem with the Bukharin–Rykov position was that they had been forced to retreat from the 1925 slogan of *obogashchaites*', and now favoured 'limiting the exploitative tendencies of the *kulak*'. That ill-defined category could include every successful peasant who develops what Stalin (in the reconstruction of his thoughts by Rybakov quoted earlier) would call 'farmer' tendencies, that is, commercial production for the market. He could have two horses or three cows, or both, and maybe hire a labourer to help with the harvest, and then he becomes a class enemy. Yet what sense is there in basing agriculture on the 'middle peasant', who is *defined* as one who has only a modest amount to sell over and above his family's subsistence? Bukharin also saw nothing wrong with the price-cutting policy, both in respect of state-produced manufactures and (in 1926) in purchase-prices for grain. It is true that subsequently he urged an increase in the latter, but the damage was done. All this must be seen in the context of the debate on growth tempos, the successive drafts of the first five-year plan. Even in its more moderate versions, this plan envisaged a substantial rise in investments, and a rise also in the import bill. So there were urgent reasons for a larger off-farm surplus, especially of grain. Would this be forthcoming on a voluntary basis, through the market, save at a cost which would either reduce accumulation or cut the modest living standards of the urban workers, or both at once?

Preobrazhensky summed up the dilemmas in his unfinished work, 'Economic equilibrium in the system of the USSR', recently republished in English by Don Filtzer. He there listed the contradictions, and saw no solution other than a revolution in advanced countries. A very different observer, the Menshevik P. Garvi, wrote a pamphlet entitled *Bolshevizm v tupike* (Bolshevism is in a cul-de-sac).

And where, in all this, should one put the Left Opposition? According to Richard Day (in his *Leon Trotsky and the Politics of Economic Isolation*) they had the answer: higher investment would have provided more goods, and so would greater reliance on foreign trade. However a strong case for a contrary view can be made. Trotsky, in alliance with Zinoviev and Kamenev, had many political points to make: about errors in Comintern policy, or bureaucratization, or lack of inner-party democracy. But their *economic* policy posture was internally inconsistent. On the one hand they criticized the leadership for too modest an investment programme. But on the other, if it had been speeded up the strains and shortages would have been greater. Shortages could not have been made good by imports without a sizeable increase in exports, primarily of agricultural produce, as there were no big unused sources of credits or loans. Yet the 'left' was persistently attacking the government for being soft on *kulaks*. Indeed Trotsky had developed a whole theory ('Thermidor') based on the notion that the Bukharin–Rykov group were representing the petty-bourgeoisie, and that Stalin was a 'centrist', vacillating between the line represented by Bukharin and the correct class line, advocated by the Left Opposition. Too late, Bukharin realized that he in fact had more in common with such men as Kamenev than he had with the ruthless Stalin, when the latter suddenly changed course in 1928. Trotsky had mocked Bukharin's notion of building socialism 'at the pace of a tortoise' (*cherepashyimi shagami*) within the confines of NEP. Yet his own investment plans, which included the expansion of heavy industry, would necessarily have taken several years to complete, and meanwhile belts would have to be tightened. The opposition also claimed that wages were too low. When, late in the day (in 1928) it was proposed that grain procurement prices be raised, the 'left' opposed this. Some members of the 'left', for instance Preobrazhensky, felt that Stalin's left turn did indeed mean that they were adopting the 'left's' policies. Even Trotsky, who split with Preobrazhensky when the latter sought to make peace with Stalin, insisted that Stalin's left turn was due in some part to 'our pressure'. So, while neither Trotsky nor any of his allies advocated the destruction of NEP, the policies they advocated were surely inconsistent with its continuance.

Let us return to the question of whether an economic crisis was developing in the second half of 1927. It could be argued that, in comparison with the years that followed, especially 1931–3, the disequilibrium and shortages were mild, as indeed they were, and that they were to a considerable extent due to incorrect or wrong-headed price policies, and thus remediable. The point about prices is well taken. Thus the grain procurement crisis of the winter 1927–8 was *not* due to *kulak* sabotage or a desire on the part of the peasants to combat Soviet power: they simply found the grain price too low and expected it to be raised. The violence of the government's response, which greatly upset Bukharin and his friends, was a devastating blow to the principles upon which NEP was built. Interestingly, Stalin found it politic to continue to claim that NEP would be preserved, even while he set about throttling it.

Again, one has to return to the five-year plan: if even the modest rise in new investment in 1926–7 placed so great a strain on the NEP structure, how could it possibly bear the burden of even the first, let alone the even higher second, version of this plan? Many previously middle-of-the-road Bolsheviks must have concluded that the 'market' strait-jacket had to be shed. Of course this did not mean that the plans had to be so hugely over-ambitious, take the form of what Trotsky called 'price-gallop industrialization'. Of course Bukharin was right in this 'Notes of an economist': one cannot build today's factories with tomorrow's bricks. There *were* fortresses the Bolsheviks could not take, the impossible remained impossible. In no way should the argument be taken as justifying the Stalinist strategy with all its brutalities, economic waste and human suffering. This note simply discusses some of the major causes for the abandonment of NEP.

Then, some more general queries. One relates to the relative role, in the Soviet situation, of fear, of the perception of military danger. In some way this probably affected both the chosen tempos and the priority of heavy industry, and both of these were inconsistent with NEP policies. Bukharin's views of the mid-1920s logically gave priority to those industries serving the needs of the peasantry. However the Bolsheviks also faced an internal security or political dilemma: how long could they rule in an overwhelmingly peasant country unless they undertook some version of rapid industrialization, a revolution from above? One returns to Stalin's soliloquy, imagined by Anatoli Rybakov: it was essential to prevent the emergence of commercially-minded 'farmers'. This concern was not directly related to a sense of external danger.

Another question is raised by considering the relevance of the NEP experience in the context of Soviet economic reform today. Interestingly, one advocate of 'trade in means of production' cited Dzerzhinsky in support of his opposition to bureaucratic material allocation, regretting the fact that the flexible supply system of the mid-1920s was later abandoned.[7] And this in turn raises the whole question of NEP as a mixed economy with strong market elements, as a 'transition' stage. Transition to what? Is the onward march towards some sort of real socialism synonymous with a reduction in the role of 'commodity-money relations', the growth of all-embracing planning? All the Bolsheviks in the 1920s thought this was so, including Bukharin, differing only about the timing ('seriously and for a long time' never meant for ever). This is now being challenged, the more so as this would be quite inconsistent with Gorbachev's reform programme. The same question is now being asked in China. In the USSR in the 1920s, and in China in the 1980s, the widespread use of the market mechanism was justified by, *inter alia* the low level of economic development. In the USSR in the 1980s it is argued that centralized planning of the 'Stalin' type must be abandoned and the role of markets enhanced, because of the *high* level of economic development.

The whole issue of NEP, its significance, the causes and legitimacy (or illegitimacy) of its abolition, all this has come into the area of public and published discussion as part of *glasnost'*. This has involved the rehabilitation of such political figures as Bukharin, and economists committed to peasant family production and genuine market-related cooperatives, such as Chayanov, Chelintsev, Makarov and Kondratiev, the last of them well known in the West for his 'long-wave' theory of crises.

Opinions vary. Thus N. Shmelev[8] argued that the suspension of NEP was a gross error with painful consequences. A Nuikin[9] supports this, speaks of the 'catastrophe' of forcible collectivization, and cites approvingly an article in *Znanie-sila* which treats Stalin's achievement of supreme power in 1928–9 as a *coup d'état* (*perevorot*), and a counter-revolutionary one at that. A. Nikonov,[10] praising Chayanov, declares that forcible collectivization was a disastrous departure from Leninist principles. It is wrong (says N. Shmelev) to justify Stalin's policy of that time by reference to war danger, since

Hitler and the Nazis were still insignificant. The causes of the procurement crisis of 1928 were the low prices offered to peasants.

Against this there is the argument of Klyamkin.[11] On the one hand he rightly 'defends' Trotsky and the Left Opposition from the charge of being indirectly responsible for the 'ultra-left excesses' (*levatskiye peregiby*) of collectivization. In doing this he criticizes the writer Belov, and he could also have added Mozhaev;[12] the latter even managed to attach blame to three named persons, Trotsky, Kamenev and Kaganovich, two of whom have perfect alibis (but all of whom share the characteristic of being Jews). Klyamkin pointed out that Trotsky's extreme statements about militarization of labour dated from 1920, at a time when Lenin too envisaged a considerable degree of militarization ('it was *war* communism!'). As for Trotsky and his friends, they had presented their left-wing criticism within the policy confines of NEP. Therefore Stalin, in launching his collectivization drive, was 'far to the left of the left opposition'. So far, so good. But then, rather surprisingly, Klyamkin takes the line that, given the exigencies of the time, the crash programme of heavy-industry investment was logical, and so, then, was collectivization, though he deplores its excesses and considers the fate of the peasantry to be a major injustice – though they were victims of necessity. This is not altogether unlike Gorbachev's anniversary speech of 2 November 1987.

In a challenging article, G. Shmelev[13] makes a devastating attack on the myth that Stalin was attacking the *kulaks*. No, he insists, the real target was the middle peasant. So the debate is rapidly extending. Its relevance for the present day is evident, and indeed is spelt out by Nuikin in the second of his two articles cited above. Some of today's supporters of *perestroika* state that they have in mind something other than NEP. He asks: why? If it is because under NEP there were some private speculators and corrupt elements, surely there is plenty of evidence of just such phenomena in much more recent times. Furthermore under NEP these were marginal phenomena, with most private activity genuinely productive, whereas in the centralized planning system the illegal activities were mainly redistributive.

One awaits the formal rehabilitation of other major figures in NEP economics, such as Bazarov, Groman, Falkner and Yurovsky. One awaits Danilov's two-volume history of collectivization, begun over twenty years ago and then suspended. There is every possibility of a major Soviet contribution to the economic and intellectual history of the period, for which we would and should be profoundly grateful. Better late than never.

NOTES

1. *Nauka i zhizn*, nos. 11 and 12, 1988 and nos. 1 and 2, 1989.
2. Rybakov, Anatoli, *Druzhba narodov*, no. 4, 1987, p. 107.
3. *Ibid*., p. 112.
4. Novozhilov, V. in *Vestnik finansov*, no. 3, 1926.
5. See Nove, A., *Economic History*, p. 140.
6. Ibid., pp. 136–7.
7. Latsis, O., *Kommunist*, no. 13, 1986, p. 35.
8. 'Avansy i dolgi', *Novyi mir*, no. 6, 1987.
9. *Novyi mir*, nos. 1, 2, 1988.
10. *Voprosy ekonomiki*, no. 2, 1988, pp. 5–7.
11. *Novyi mir*, no. 11, 1987.
12. *Don*, no. 3, 1987 (the postface).
13. *Oktyabr*, no. 2, 1988 (not to be confused with N. Shmelev).

7 The Soviet Peasantry in the Second World War*

INTRODUCTION: SOURCES

The books and articles on the peasantry in the war published in the Soviet Union are by now very numerous indeed, and indeed it is now possible for a Soviet author, V. T. Aniskov, to publish a volume devoted to analyzing the historiography of the subject.[1] The disasters and other negative aspects of the war are now being played down, and Aniskov's book is in fact part of this: the more critical works which will be used extensively here are regarded by him as too critical, though he does also say that some earlier publications had been insufficiently so. The very title of Aniskov's book reflects the official line: in the face of immense obstacles, with much self-sacrifice and hardship, and with occasional policy errors, the Soviet peasantry did its patriotic duty, 'though only 10–12 years previously, through collectivization, this class joined with (*priobsbchilsya*) the socialist order. Indeed, this is said to prove the durability and sound foundation of the *kolkhoz* system and peasant loyalty to it' (Aniskov, pp. 3–4).

However, in the period stretching roughly from 1961 to 1971, the emphasis was rather different, and one sees this also in the much franker and more critical approach to other sensitive historical questions, including collectivization as well as the war. The principal sources used here will be the books by Yu. V. Arutunyan with some references to other works.[2] Time did not permit a careful perusal of all possible sources, and more research on this topic would seem to be both desirable and possible.

Also desirable is some picture of what happened to the peasantry in the very large areas under German occupation. However if any statistics exist I have been unable to find them. Unfortunately, the head of the German agricultural administration of occupied territories, Otto Schiller, seems to have left no account of his experiences.

* From Susan Linz ed., *The Impact of World War II on the Soviet Union* (Totowa, N.J. Rowan & Allanheld, 1985).

The only book he wrote after the war was a short history of Soviet collective farming, published at Tübingen in 1954 (at any rate neither I nor a German colleague have been able to find another). I had a long talk with Schiller in Stuttgart in the 1950s, and he told of experiences of spontaneous decollectivization in those areas free of Soviet *and* German control, how he welcomed this, and how his advice was overruled by the Nazi authorities, who wished to preserve *kolkhozy* so as to maximize procurements for Germany, until it was much too late. No Soviet published work seems to exist on this aspect of the subject,[3] and Dallin's *German rule in Russia* naturally concentrates on other matters. Here is another area for original research, for those who could use German archive material. Meanwhile we should never forget that all Soviet statistics on wartime production relate (and could only relate) to territories under their control, and that millions of the most fertile hectares (and millions of peasants, and of urban consumers) were for several years behind the German lines.

It must be emphasized that, given the losses of vitally important agricultural areas, the mobilization of manpower for the armed forces and shortages of haulage power, equipment and fuel, the performance of agriculture in wartime has to be regarded as impressive. In the first important postwar work on the war economy, N. Vosnesensky[4] the contrasts this with the critical food situation in 1916–17. This is not altogether fair: the shortages and hardships of 1941–5 in town and village were in fact far greater than those which contributed to the collapse of the Tsarist regime, which underlines the role of imposed discipline (in fact, terror) in maintaining order in the years of disaster and hardship (one must also recall that losses of territory and the scale of defeats in 1941–2 far exceeded those of 1915–17). Yet when all is said, the army and the population were fed, with only a marginal (though not insignificant) contribution from abroad through Lend–Lease, and not only ruthlessness and coercion but also genuine patriotic commitment can explain the very impressive achievements of the Soviet war economy.

THE AGRICULTURAL LABOUR FORCE

The village lost men to the armed forces, of which 'over 60% were rural residents'[5] and also for work in industry. Yet the mobilization of many tractors and horses for the army, and the virtual cessation of

Table 7.1 Agricultural labour force (1 January, thousands)

	Working age			*Juveniles (12–16)*	*Aged and sick*	*Total*	*Per cent of 1941*
	Men	*Women*	*Total*				
1941	8 657	9 532	18 169	3 848	2 360	24 368	100.0
1942	5 890	9 533	15 423	3 779	2 369	21 572	88.5
1943	3 605	9 591	13 196	4 035	2 379	19 600*	80.5
1944	2 341	9 094	11 432	3 821	2 388	17 644	72.4
1945	2 770	8 661	11 440	3 124	2 390	17 346	71.2

*The printed table gives 12 609, which is evidently an error.
SOURCE: Arutunyan, p. 75, quoting *Istoricheski arkhiv*.

deliveries of new tractors, placed additional burdens on the labour force. Women, juveniles and old people were utilized on a large scale, but as Table 7.1 shows, numbers went down.

The table relates to what is called 'rear areas', that is, those behind the front. It is not made clear whether these vary with military retreats and advances, but the implication seems to be that they refer to the *same* areas; this follows from data for the whole country cited by Arutunyan[6] which explicitly refers to unoccupied territory: the fall in numbers between the end of 1940 and the end of 1943, and the rise to 1945, are much greater than in the above table. A further difficulty was that, precisely in those areas into which industry was concentrated, and where foods needs rose sharply, a large proportion of the peasantry migrated to work in war industry. Thus in many areas of the Urals and West Siberia the agricultural labour force fell by 45 per cent.[7] According to the same source, in 1942 no less than 96 per cent of 'aged and sick' and 95 per cent of juveniles (12–16-year-olds) 'took part in kolkhoz production'.

These numbers were quite insufficient to cope with seasonal peaks, and there was also a mobilization of 'millions' of urban citizens, students and school children. In 1943 they 'earned' 12 per cent of all *trudodni* in *kolkhozy*, as against only 4 per cent in 1940.

The compulsory minimum of *trudodni* which had to be worked by adult *kolkhozniki* was raised in 1942 to 150 in cotton-growing areas, to 100–120 in others; juveniles had a 50-*trudodni* minimum.[8] Minima within this total were laid down for the period of sowing, cultivation and harvesting. This was substantially over-fulfilled on average, and there is little doubt that wartime coercive measures would be taken to enforce extra work if it was thought necessary, with very long hours. However, in some areas the minimum proved too high, there not being enough *collective* work, whereas in others it was easily over-fulfilled, for example where there was a great number of labour-intensive tasks in livestock and vegetable production. The law-enforcement agencies ignored this, and 'did not take into account either what the imposed minimum was, or the objective possibilities of fulfilling it'.[9] According to Arutunyan, the law was in fact not imposed with its full severity, but the law was severe: for the first offence 'compulsory labour' in their Kolkhoz or Machine Tractor Station (MTS) for up to six months, with a 25 per cent deduction from the value of *trudodni* earned; or, if at that time no work was available for them, they were to be sent to a period of forced labour by the local NKVD. Also those failing to carry out the minimum number of *trudodni* could be deprived of their private plots, though this seems not to have been a much-used penalty. Chairmen of *kolkhozy* and brigade-leaders who failed to report breaches of rules were themselves subject to criminal penalties. The same source cites instances where the law was not applied, and others when it was applied too rigorously by *kolkhoz* chairmen and other officials who feared to be accused of leniency. Citing archives, Arutunyan stated that, for instance, in Kazakhstan 78 500 *kolkhozniki* did not work the minimum number of *trudodni* (many with extenuating circumstances); 5180 cases were brought before the courts, 4100 of them were found guilty and condemned. In the whole of 1944, only 3 per cent of all those who did not work the obligatory minimum were condemned by the courts. In 1944, in the entire 'rear areas' of the USSR, 11 per cent of *kolkhozniki* did not work the prescribed minimum.[10] Cases were usually brought in respect of the most barefaced work avoiders. However fear of being punished was real, the more so as repetition of the offence was quite severely dealt with: forced labour *outside* the place of work, that is, in a camp run by the NKVD.[11]

Factory workers during this period were under even sterner discipline, and there is nothing surprising about such rules as these. Most peasants doubtless felt it was their duty to work hard. The actual average number of *trudodni* worked has been calculated by Arutunyan as follows, using archive materials:

	1940	*1943*
Men of working age	312	338
Women of working age	193	244
Aged	132	135
Juveniles	74	100

These are, of course, *trudodni* (workday *units*), *not* days worked. Scattered evidence suggests that on average each represented roughly one and a half actual days in peace-time. It *may* be that the 'valuation' of each *trudodni* in terms of the time and effort required altered in wartime.

In any case, one must agree with Arutunyan that the fact that the highest number of *trudodni* tended to be worked in areas where the compulsory minimum was lowest showed that this form of compulsion could not be the decisive factor. Indeed he criticizes the regulations as 'one of the stupid (*nelepyi*) products of the bureaucratic system of control over agriculture.[12] We shall see that he has other examples of this.

Sovkhozy were able to maintain numbers, despite the mobilization of men for the army, by mobilizing all persons living on their territory and by hiring seasonal workers, mostly women and juveniles. According to archive data used by zelenin,[13] and relating to 'comparable' (i.e. non-occupied) territory, the total *sovkhoz* labour force changed as follows:

	Numbers (000s)	*Average per 100 ha. sown area*
1940	712	86.1
1943	639	89.7
1944	636	88.7

This clearly shows some fall in area sown. It should be stressed that *sovkhozy* in 1940 were responsible for only 6.9 per cent of area sown to grain, 4.5 per cent of cattle, and the main burden fell on *kolkhozy* throughout the war.

Bare statistics do not begin to show how hard life was. Mechanical aids of all kinds became scarce or non-existent, borses were mobilized, manual labour predominated. In areas over which war had raged many villages were destroyed, people lived in holes in the ground, used cows for ploughing, or even put themselves into harness and pulled the plough or harrow. Arutunyan (p. 156) cites memoirs: 'We had to haul the plough. Eight to ten women harnessed themselves and hauled; we used a wider harness than the horses. We hauled a big stick to which the plough was attached. Behind the plough we had another woman, or young lad.'

Remarkable stories are told of the evacuation of people and animals as the Germans advanced. A literary description can be found in Maksimov's novel *Sem' dnei tvoreniya*, and also in contemporary publications. This, for instance, is a brief extract from *Novyi mir*, nos. 9–10, 1941:

> "Vast flocks of sheep, cows, goats, make their way through our little town, exhausted, hardly able to move their legs; some are then loaded onto carts and are moved further. By the river, wherever you look there are shepherds resting under carts, milkmaids, sick sheep, freshly-slaughtered flesh, hides. A milkmaid says: 'We have been on the way for a month and four days . . . We have to deliver the livestock to its destination, but our animals are not used to long walks, they move slowly, and then what about being machine-gunned from the air? Frightened sheep gather in a tight circle, so the bullets get them . . . We lie in ditches, the cows scatter in the forest, almost all the sheep were killed. We had good sheep!'"

Arutunyan cites harrowing stories. Many thousands of peasants, livestock and tractors, made their way to the Dnieper in July 1941, and the few bridges were overwhelmed; pontoon bridges and boats partially relieved the pressure, and 600 000 head of livestock were moved to the eastern bank, along with 4500 tractors, but 'many were killed, and much machinery and livestock were lost . . . The Germans reached the river before the move was completed'.[14] We must imagine the scenes at the bridges and ferries, used also by retreating troops, those evacuating industrial equipment, civilian refugees. In the entire evacuation procedures, it was laid down that the extremely scarce transport was reserved for industry: peasants and animals had to walk. Citing the research work of M. Pogrebinsky, Arutunyan claims that 59.3 per cent of all cattle, 82 per cent of sheep, 26.7 per cent of pigs and 14 per cent of the horses that were in the Ukraine at the outbreak of war were evacuated, as were most tractors not requisitioned by the army. But many tractors were abandoned for lack of fuel and spare parts. Zelenin cites data on the evacuation of *sovkhozy*: while the larger part of the livestock was evacuated, many never arrived. Thus 'from the Ukraine, Belorussia and the Western regions of the RSFSR (Russian republic) the major proportion of livestock was evacuated: 83.4% of cattle, 97.7% of sheep and goats, 66.2% of pigs. However, few reached their destination: about 50% of cattle, 20% of sheep . . . Between 17 and 23% of evacuated livestock were delivered to units of the Red Army for meat'.[15] According to

Arutunyan, lack of fodder and of shelter led to the slaughter of the bulk of the 'evacuees': by 1 January 1942 very few of them could have been left alive.[16] Many of those that *did* reach their destination (for example, the North Caucasus) were overrun by the Germans in their 1942 summer offensive. A mass of human and animal misery is contained in such stories and such statistics.

MACHINERY AND EQUIPMENT

All sources agree that most horses and tractors were mobilized for the army, and that until 1944 hardly any tractors, spare parts or other machines were supplied to agriculture. Even the favoured *sovkhozy* got nothing. The commissar of sovkhozy, P. Lobanov, stated to his colleagues in 1941: 'It is clear that we will get no new tractors this year or next.' An order from the commissariat of *sovkhozy* envisaged even the use of cows (though not pedigree cows) for ploughing.[17] Bottlenecks then arose in supply of bridles, harness and ropes, which had somehow to be made on the farms. Spare parts for the remaining tractors had to be improvised, too, or made in local industrial workshops. Only in the second half of 1943 were supplies of tractors resumed, and many were sent to the ruined newly-liberated areas. All sources agree that 1943 was an exceptionally hard and difficult year, in these and in most other respects. *Sovkhozy* suffered least, but they too suffered, as the following figures show:

	Total, USSR			*Comparable territories*		
	1940	*1943*	*1944*	*1940*	*1943*	*1944*
Tractors (thousands)	74 278	37 901	40 257	42 474	26 994	23 993
Combine-harvesters (")	27 397	18 819	19 526	15 668	13 112	12 553

However, 18 per cent of the tractors and 30 per cent of combine-harvesters were unable to function at all, presumably because of shortage of fuel and spares (Zelenin, p. 24). The MTS were even worse off. Thus in 1942 as much as 79 per cent of all *kolkhoz* grain had to be harvested with horses or by hand.[18] Much of the sowing was also by hand. With the lack of machines and lack of manpower, it was not surprising that harvest yields fell: average harvests of grain in *kolkhozy* were 7–8 centner per hectare in 1938–41, but only 4.6 centner in 1942, despite favourable weather. There was not enough left for seed, which further complicated the situation in 1943.

Women drove many tractors and combine-harvesters in wartime, and tried to repair them in cold and ill-equipped workshops or out in the fields. Soviet tractors were (indeed many still are) very difficult for women to handle.

Payment in kind by *kolkhozy* for the work done by the MTS remained a major source of state procurements of grain and a major burden for *kolkhozy*, especially as these payments were based on the greatly exaggerated 'biological' yield, and not the much lower real harvest.

> The biological [*vidovoi*] harvest was very roughly estimated . . . Some directors of MTS and regional officials increased it without even bothering to visit the fields . . . At the end of 1942, when food shortages were particularly grave, the collection of any information about the harvest other than the biological yield was altogether forbidden. Even the drafting of a food and fodder balance using data on the actual threshed harvest was seen as a breach of this rule.

Kolkhoz chairmen tried to avoid excessive procurements by fair means and foul, and some were sentenced to long prison terms for 'sabotaging grain procurements'. Party officials were threatened with punishment too, and then had to be warned: 'do not overdo things, do not remove seed grain and beat up [kolkhoz] officials'. There were 'arrests and searches by the NKVD organs' in the course of grain procurements, with all sorts of excesses, 'so that many *kolkhozy* in almost every area were left without enough seed'.[19]

In occupied territories most of the remaining tractors and other machines were taken or destroyed by the German army, which, along with military damage of all kinds, greatly complicated the task of reviving agriculture after the reconquest of these areas by the Red Army.

POLITICAL CONTROL

At the beginning of the war (November 1941) the 'political departments' in the MTS were reconstituted, and acted as a species of party watchdogs over *kolkhoz* agriculture. Their task included both encouragement and, where necessary, coercion. Thus it was their task to watch over the enforcement of the minimum number of *trudodni* and of delivery plans. Very great difficulties were faced in reoccupied areas. For example, in Belorussia and Ukraine 'there were anti-*kolkhoz*, private-property and anti-state attitudes', and some peasants joined Ukrainian nationalist armed bands. In the Kursk *oblast* it was alleged that former *kulaks* had returned to their villages. Some formerly collective horses had been taken and hidden by peasants, and altogether there was much to do 'to restore collective land utilisation'.[20] In fact, we must suppose that in many places it was necessary to recollectivize.

The author cites statistical data about the political officers of the MTS and *sovkhozy*: it is noteworthy that 96.2 per cent of them were male, nearly all of military age.[21] The political departments were abolished in May 1943 as unnecessary, but as 1943 was a particularly unsuccessful year, Aniskov wonders if this abolition was not premature.[22]

Only harsh controls could extracted so much of the reduced output from the village. Voznesensky[23] contrasts the total procurements of grain in 1918–21 – 920 million poods – with the 1941–4 figure: 4264 million poods, 'despite the German occupation of the richest farming areas of the USSR'. And despite, he could have added, the food shortages this created in the villages.

PEASANT INCOMES AND WELFARE

All Soviet sources agree that life was exceedingly hard, both in terms of physical conditions of work and in levels of consumption.

Sovkhoz workers and permanent staff of the MTS, as well as rural officials, were paid predominantly in money, and fairly well paid by the Soviet standards of the time: engineer-technicians in *sovkhozy* received 700 (old) roubles per month, tractor-drivers 200–270, truck-drivers 320–30, and 'MTS pay was similar'.[24] *Kolkhoz* members were paid very little in comparison. However manufactured goods were practically unobtainable, and free market food prices were astronomic: thus in the RSFSR in 1942 the *average* price of a kilogram of grain was 53.80 roubles (1.88 roubles in 1940), a litre of milk 38 roubles, a kilogram of pork 261 roubles.[25] Many refused to sell for money, preferring barter. Therefore payments in kind were widespread, including bonuses in kind; thus in one region a tractor-driver who over-fulfilled his ploughing norm received a piglet, or a beehive.

Regular issue of grain and potatoes in part payment, and/or the right to purchase at the official (ration) price, became the rule.

It was always the rule for *kolkhoz* members, and along with the produce of their private plots, it was decisive in their survival. But low production and high state procurements left them very little. The price paid by the state for compulsory deliveries was quite negligible, indeed Arutunyan calls it 'symbolic', 3 kopeks for a kilogram of potatoes being an example. 'In 1942–3 the Kolkhozy issued per *trudoden* only about 800 grams of grain, 200–400 grams of potatoes, or about half of the amount issued in 1940'.[26] But, given the acute shortage and the huge free-market prices, these smaller amounts were greatly valued. Indeed, according to a speech by a party leader (A. S. Shcherbakov), some 'sold' the *trudodni* they earned for large sums. The amounts paid in this way to *kolkhoz* members even on average represented starvation rations. The following was the 'value' of the *trudoden* on average:

	1940	*1941*	*1942*	*1943*	*1944*	*1945*
Grain (kg)	1.60	1.40	0.80	0.65	n.a.	0.70
Potatoes (Kg)	0.98	0.33	0.22	0.40	n.a.	0.26
Money (old roubles)	0.98	1.07	1.03	1.24	1.12	0.85

Source: Arutunyan, p. 339.

This actually overstates the amount of produce because, according to the source, it represents the quantities 'allocated'. But in fact part of the amount formally 'allocated' as payment to the peasants was taken away as compulsory deliveries: thus 4.4 million tons was supposed to be allocated in 1942, but only 2.9 million was issued. Source estimates that on a per capita basis this was less than 200 grams of grain and one potato per day, and this had to feed a family whose head was probably away in the army. Survival depended on the private plot. But this too was subject to compulsory deliveries to the state (for example, 456 litres of milk per cow). As if this was not enough, there was a five-fold increase in 'agricultural tax' on notional income from private plots and livestock. Other burdens on private animals included mobilization of surviving private cows to haul carts filled with grain to the procurement centres; in 1944 there were 60 000 cows engaged in such work in the Kuban' alone![27] Taxes, delivery quotas and shortage of fodder led to a steep decline in the number of private livestock in the 'rear areas'.

It might be thought that the peasant household could make a great deal of money out of the very high free market prices. But only a few could benefit from this, because of transport problems and lack of time, and in any case there was little that could be bought for money. Some were able to engage in barter trade with urban residents who came to nearby villages: thus near Barnaul (Altai) a metal bucket was exchanged for six kilograms of flour. The *kolkhoz* markets even of such towns as Moscow sold little in 1942–3, despite the huge prices (the prices were huge because so few peasants were selling). True, some made a small fortune in paper roubles, but most were in dire poverty.

It must again be stressed that there were great variations. Thus in one Uzbek region 30 per cent of *kolkhozy* issued no money or grain whatever in 'payment' for *trudodni* (Arutunyan, p. 29) and in the USSR as a whole 5.4 per cent paid *no* grain, 37.5 per cent less than 300 grams per *trudoden*, 75 per cent issued no potatoes in 1945.[28]

OUTPUT

During the war and during the first postwar years, the false 'biological' harvest statistics were the basis of claims that, despite all the difficulties, harvests compared well with the prewar situation. This very bright picture is to be found, for instance, in the third volume of Lyashchenko's economic history, published as late as 1956.

Yet losses were immense (about a third), owing to orders to increase sown area under conditions in which labour and equipment were desperately lacking both for sowing and harvesting, plus all the other problems already referred to. The difference between real and official yields can be illustrated as follows; the figures are for Kazakhstan (centners per hectare):

	1940	*1941*	*1942*	*1943*
Biological	6.4	10.9	9.1	5.6
Real	4.8	7.2	3.9	2.6

Source: Arutunyan, p. 200, citing archives.

Note the *increase* in official overestimates, on which payment for MTS services was based.

The areas under Soviet control produced 24.9 million tons of grain in 1942 on 58 million hectares of sown area, with the low yield of only

5 centners per hectare. 1943 was climatically a much less favourable year, and it was also one in which all the disasters of the war bore particularly heavily: thus although several major liberated areas (such as Krasmodar, Rostov and Stavropn) were 'in' the 1943 area and not in the 1942 one, only 56.6 million hectares could be sown (52.5 million harvested) and the total grain harvested was only 20.6 million tons. No wonder both Zelenin and Arutunyan argue that 1943 was an appalling agricultural year, the low point of all the wartime miseries. Thus Zelenin[29] gives data as follows:

	Grain yields (centners per hectare)			
	1940	*1943*	*1944*	*1945*
Sovkhozy	8.9	3.8	7.0	6.7
Kolkhozy	8.5	3.9	5.7	5.1

In 1944 it was possible to deliver more equipment, tractors and fuel to agriculture, and to start recovery in the reconquered regions, and so there was a notable improvement over the dreadful year 1943.

In his survey of Soviet historiography of the period, Aniskov takes Arutunyan to task for being over-critical with regard to the policy of increasing sowings in rear areas. He insists that it was a 'necessary' consequence of the heavy losses of territory to the invaders. But the point of the criticism is that the extra areas could not be properly sown, cultivated or harvested, and consequently this was wasteful.

Data on livestock show, as might be expected, very heavy losses of horses and pigs, but a surprisingly high proportion of cattle and sheep in the rear areas survived. Meat and milk production fell steeply (after an initial upsurge in slaughtering), because of critical shortages of fodder. Table 7.2 tells the basic tale.

By 1 January 1945, when almost the whole prewar territory was back under Soviet rule, total livestock numbers, as a percentage of

Table 7.2 Livestock numbers ('rear areas') (end year, millions), kolkhozy

	1940	*1941*	*1942*	*1943*
Cattle	22.7	21.6	22.5	22.9
Sheep & goats	56.4	59.7	61.2	63.7
Pigs	6.1	6.5	5.6	3.6
Horses	14.8	12.2	10.7	9.8

SOURCE: Arutunyan, p. 188.

1941 levels, were: cattle 81 (cows 77), pigs 32, sheep and goats 47 (all categories of owners).[30] Extremely heavy losses occurred in occupied areas, owing to attempted evacuation during the Soviet retreat, requisitioning by the Germans and destruction during their retreat. It took many years to repair the damage, to rebuild villages and farm buildings.

Milk yields per cow fell from 949 kilograms (1940) to 751 in the worst year, 1943, in *kolkhozy*.[31] In *sovkhozy* the fall was from 1803 kilograms to 1138 in the same period.[32] There are regional and other data in profusion, including other crops than grain, but this chapter must not be further lengthened.

CONCLUSION

One must agree with Arutunyan's judgment: a realistic picture of the appalling situation, the desperate shortages, the errors of policy (for example on sown areas), the hardships suffered, do not detract from, but on the contrary magnify, the achievement of the Soviet peasantry. He rightly points out that the *prodrazverstka* (requisitionings) of war communism took a far smaller share of the harvest than did the procurement agencies in 1941–5; the peasants in 1918–20 rebelled, those in the 'Great Patriotic War' did not. He asserts that this shows their commitment to the system and their sense of patriotism. We may reasonably point out that their patriotism overrode their hatred of the system, and that the organs of Soviet power were much more strong in the villages in 1941–5 than in 1918–20. Yet we should (in my view) accept that there was much that was genuinely heroic in the conduct of millions of overworked and underfed peasants, mostly women, who somehow kept the towns and the soldiers fed under conditions which we have difficulty in even imagining. Recovery after the war was impeded by anti-peasant policies, as evidenced by the decrees of 1946 and the continuation of heavy taxes on private plots, ever-increasing compulsory delivery quotas and extremely low procurement prices; Khrushchev had much to say about this after Stalin's death. But the postwar period falls outside the scope of this chapter.

I will end by drawing attention again to the very extensive Soviet literature on the war years, much of which is conveniently listed in Aniskov's book on historiography. Only a few sources have been utilized in this paper, and even these could have provided data for a chapter three times the present length. Anyone looking for a research topic need look no further.

NOTES

1. V. . Aniskov *Bodvig sovetskego Krestyanstva v velikoi ot echestveppei voine*, 'Mysl', Moscow, 1979.
2. Yu V. Arutunyan, *Sovetskoe Krestyvanstvo y gody velikoi otechestvennoi voiny*, Nauka, and I. E. Zelenin Sovkhozy SSSR 1941–50, 'Nauka', Moscow, 1969.
3. See ibid., pp. 220–42.
4. N. Vosnesensky, *Voyennaya ekonomika SSSR*, Moscow, 1948.
5. Aniskov, p. 4.
6. Arutunyan, p. 398.
7. Ibid., p. 75, citing archive material.
8. Ya. Chadayev, *Ekonomika SSSR 1941–5*, p. 359.
9. Arutunyan, p. 91.
10. Ibid., p. 92.
11. Ibid., p. 90.
12. Ibid., p. 96.
13. Zelenin, p. 35.
14. Arutunyan, p. 50.
15. Zelenin, p. 110.
16. Arutunyan, p. 53.
17. Zelenin, pp. 26–7.
18. Arutunyan, p. 164.
19. Ibid., pp. 200–4.
20. Ibid., pp. 250–2.
21. Ibid., p. 399.
22. Aniskov, p. 107.
23. Voznesensky, p. 90.
24. Arutunyan, p. 83.
25. Ibid., p. 352.
26. Ibid., p. 79.
27. Ibid., p. 263.
28. Ibid., p. 351.
29. Zelenin, p. 83.
30. Chadayev, p. 359.
31. Ibid., p. 443.
32. Zelenin, p. 96.

8 Industry under Khrushchev*

THE SITUATION AT STALIN'S DEATH AND THE MALENKOV INTERREGNUM

Stalin spoke to an 'election' meeting in Moscow on 9 February 1946. The country had been exhausted by war, conditions were exceedingly tough, and industrial output in 1946 was inevitably adversely affected by reconversion to peacetime industry and by the need to repair war damage, as well as by shortage of food. So when Stalin set out some targets, to be achieved in three quinquennia, that is, by 1960, they must have seemed over-ambitious. And yet consider the achievements:

millions of tons	*1945*	*1960 (Stalin target)*	*1960 (actual)*
Steel	12.25	60	65
Coal	149.3	500	513
Oil	19.4	60	148

By 1950, even allowing for statistical exaggeration, the 1940 level had been substantially exceeded, especially for the priority producer's goods sectors. While neither cotton cloth nor footwear had reached target (or 1940 levels), the output of coal, steel, oil and tractors, was above expectations. The great Dnieper dam, blown up in the retreat of 1941, was operational again as early as the spring of 1947. So when the nineteenth congress met in 1952, and Malenkov (in Stalin's presence) made the keynote speech, presenting (two years late) the five-year plan for 1951–5, there seemed to be some very solid achievement to boast of, and on which to build future growth. However, the high growth rates of these years were partly the consequence of postwar recovery, which were also achieved in West Germany and Italy in these years. Agriculture remained in the

* Reprinted from McCauley, M. (ed), *Khrushchev and Khrushchevism* (Basingstoke: Macmillan, 1987).

doldrums. Industry's recovery was not accompanied by technological advance, apart from such sectors as nuclear weapons and military aircraft. This was a time of cold war, when Soviet science was purposefully isolated from contact with Western science; we were told that everything Soviet was best, that Russians had invented everything from radio to the steam engine. Traditional methods and patterns of production were retained: steam locomotives were favoured, while natural gas was neglected and the chemical industry languished.

Centralization of industrial planning was strengthened, and new ideas in economic theory, whether on capitalist countries (Varga) or economic rationality at home (e.g. Novozhilov) were suppressed. No one dared mention input–output techniques. Kantorovich's ideas, originally devised in 1939, were also ignored, their author having to 'retire' into pure mathematics. The energetic and talented chief planner, Voznesensky, was arrested and executed. Finally, Stalin himself, in his last work, warned economists not to interfere: 'The rational organization of the productive forces, economic planning, etc., are not problems of political economy, but of the economic policy of the directing bodies.'

Economic policy and performance in Stalin's last years were doubtless affected by the re-switching of resources into armaments, and a sharp rise in numbers in the armed forces (the published military budget in 1952 was 45 per cent above the level of 1950). There is evidence that war was regarded as a serious possibility on both sides of the Iron Curtain.

Soon after Stalin died, Malenkov was edged out of the top position in the party, retaining the post of prime minister. Khrushchev was at this point only the senior of several party secretaries, but lost no time in consolidating his position (acquiring by the end of 1953 the title of first secretary). He must therefore have had an influence – though not yet a decisive one – on policy also in the period that can be called the Malenkov interregnum.

The new leadership speedily took steps to decompress the atmosphere: agriculture, consumers' goods industries and housing were given higher priority. In October 1953 there was announced an accelerated programme of consumers' goods production, cutting back on investment, while also cutting prices. This proved to be unsound economically, in that all this could not be done at once without causing shortages and overstrain. When, in February 1955, Malenkov finally fell, this was accompanied by criticism of his pro-consumer-goods policy; some so-called 'woebegone economists' (*gore-ekonomisty*) were charged with having fallen for the heresy that consumers' goods output could rise faster than that of producers' goods. It therefore appears that Khrushchev rode to power with the help of the heavy industry lobby. However his subsequent actions suggest that his own priorities were also pro-consumer, though with greater relative emphasis on agriculture.

THE ABORTIVE SIXTH FIVE-YEAR PLAN AND THE POLITICAL CRISIS OF 1956–7

The fifth plan fulfilment record was a fairly successful one, even if one allows for a degree of 'inflation' in the global indices (the 'Malenkov' accelerated programme is ignored in Table 8.1). It is on this basis that the twentieth party congress adopted the sixth plan, of which the principal targets are given in the table.

In the process of drafting the new plan, stress was laid on the need to study foreign techniques (Khrushchev remarked acidly that some Soviet 'inventions' reproduced rather imperfectly what had been long ago introduced in the West), and a State Committee on new techniques was created in 1955. A number of measures were also adopted to streamline and coordinate the planning process and to enlarge the role of management, to combat bureaucracy, and so on.

Yet this plan was still-born. At a plenum of the central committee held in December 1956 it was decided that the investment plan was out of line with available resources, that the plan was over-taut. It was to be revised. At the same time, Pervukhin was appointed to the job of a sort of economic overlord. In fact the plan was never revised. It was abandoned. Evidently, the 'anti-party group' (to use the label Khrushchev subsequently attached to it) was in the business of reducing the economic powers of the first secretary. Khrushchev's counter-attack eventually succeeded in getting rid of his opponents, who at that moment were in a majority in the politbureau. In the process he pushed through the drastic remedy of abolishing virtually all the industrial ministries, substituting regional councils (*sovnarkhozy*), who were to be coordinated by Gosplan.

Table 8.1 The sixth five-year plan

	1950	*1955 plan*	*1955 actual*	*1960 plan*
National income (1950 = 100)	100	160	171	160*
Gross industrial production	100	170	185	165*
Producer's goods	100	180	191	170*
Consumer's goods	100	165	175	160*
Coal (million tons)	261.1	373.4	389.9	592
Oil (million tons)	37.9	70.9	70.8	135
Electricity (milliard kWh)	91.2	164.2	170.2	320
Pig iron (million tons)	19.2	33.8	33.3	53
Steel (million tons)	27.3	44.2	45.3	68.3
Tractors (15 h.p. units)	246.1	292.9	314.0	—
Mineral fertiliser (million tons)	5.5	10.3	9.7	20
Cement (million tons)	10.2	22.4	22.5	55
Commercial timber (million cubic metres)	161.0	251.2	212.1	301
Cotton fabrics (million metres)	3 899	6 277	5 905	—
Wool fabrics (million metres)	155.2	239.0	252.3	—
Leather footwear (million pairs)	203	315	271	—
Sugar (thousand tons)	2 523	4 491	3 419	—
Fish (thousand tons)	1 755	2 773	2 737	—

*1955 = 100

NOTE: I am aware that, since 70 per cent of industrial output consisted of producers' goods, the 1960 plan indices for gross industrial production are inconsistent. But that is how they appeared in the plan.

SOURCES: *Nar.khoz.*, 1965, pp. 130–9, 557; *Promyshlennost' SSSR* (1957) p. 43; *Direktivy XIX S'ezda Partii po pyatletnemu planu razvitiya SSSR na 1951–5 gody* (1952) pp. 3–4, 25; *Direktivy XX S'ezda KPSS po Shestomu pyatletnenu planu razvitiya norodnogo khozyaistva SSSR na 1956–60 gg*; *XX S'ezda KPSS stenotchet*, vol. II (1956).

THE SOVNARKHOZY AND THE SEVEN-YEAR PLAN

It is hard to disentangle the political from the economic motives for this reform. There certainly was (and still is) a tendency for ministries to form self-contained, self-supplying 'empires', with the result of needless duplication of component production, wasteful cross-hauls, waste of by-products, plus all the familiar problems of departmental boundary-lines (*Vedomstvennye baryery*). At the same time, Khrushchev may well have been influenced by his desire to attack the ministries for political reasons, as part of his counter-attack on what came to be known (after its final defeat) as the 'anti-party group'. The effect of basing industrial planning on *regional* economic councils, almost all of which coincided with the boundaries of *oblasti* and republics, represented a transfer of power towards local and republican *party* organs, since these were dominant *vis-à-vis* any state institutions operating within 'their' territories. At this stage in his career, Khrushchev was apparently relying on the party machine – though this changed a few years later, as we shall see.

However, given the centralizing logic of a modern industrial economy of a non-market type, the *sovnarkhozy* (105 initially) represented a step in the wrong direction. While decentralization to management, already being proposed by reform-minded economists in 1955–6, might have represented a viable alternative to the 'traditional' system, *sovnarkhozy* were inevitably subject to the disease known as *mestnichestvo* or 'localism'. An authority with power over the resources of a given area is bound to direct them to the needs of the area which is its area of knowledge and responsibility, unless prevented from doing so by orders from some superior authority. (I pointed this out at the time in an article in *Problems of communism*, November–December 1957). Precisely this began to happen, as was attested by numerous complaints in the press. Also it is an evident weakness of regionalization that the common problems of each industry became no one's central responsibility, except the overworked Gosplan, which, in this scheme, emerged as the supreme coordinator. If Khrushchev thought that the local party secretaries would ensure the priority of central as against local needs, he was sadly mistaken, as can be seen from the wording of a decree of 4 August 1958, denouncing *mestnichestvo*.

An exception had to be made at once for the armaments industry, which quite plainly required a central 'overlord'. This was followed by the creation of numerous State Committees, which replaced some of the functions of the ministries, but without the power to issue orders.

So the stage was set for recentralization, but still without the resurrection of the economic ministries (these did not return until after Khrushchev's fall). There was also a bewildering series of changes affecting the power of Gosplan, which was split and relabelled (thus *Gosekonansovet* was set up in 1960, with the task of perspective planning, and in 1962 there came into being the *Sovnarkhoz of the USSR*, with the function of implementing plans drafted by Gosplan. But this is running ahead. Suffice it to say that there was

Table 8.2 Seven-year plan

	1958	*1965 plan*	*1965 actual*
National income (1958 = 100)	100	162–5	158
Gross industrial output (index)	100	180	184
Producers' goods	100	185–8	196
Consumers' goods	100	162–5	160
Iron ore (million tons)	88.8	150–60	153.4
Pig ore (million tons)	39.6	65–70	66.2
Steel (million tons)	54.9	86–91	91.0
Coal (million tons)	493	600–12	578
Oil (million tons)	113	230–40	242.9
Gas (milliard cubic metres)	29.9	150	129.3
Electricity (milliard kWh)	235	500–20	507
Mineral fertilizer (million tons)	12	35	31.6
Synthetic fibres (thousand tons)	166	666	407
Machine tools (thousands)	138	190–200	185
Tractors (thousands)	220	—	355
Commercial timber (million cubic metres)	251	275–80	273
Cement (million tons)	33.3	75–81	72.4
Cotton fabrics (million square metres)	5.79	7.7–8.0	7.08
Wool fabrics (million square metres)	303	485	365
Leather footwear (million pairs)	356.4	515	486

SOURCES: *Nar.khoz.*, 1960, pp. 210–12; *Nar.khoz.*, 1965, pp. 136–9, 262, 557, 609; seven-year plan, 1959–65.

much administrative confusion and crossed wires. Formally speaking, the enterprises' immediate superior was 'their' *sovnarkhoz*. In practice, production tasks and material allocation were progressively recentralized, which in fact meant that enterprises were subject to many masters, none of whom had direct responsibility for the totality of the enterprises' functioning. *Sovnarkhozy* lost what power they had: in 1962 the head of the Estonian *sovnarkhoz* complained that it controlled only 0.2 per cent of that republic's output.[1]

But let us return to the actual drafting of plans. 1957 and 1958 could be described as 'orphan' years, in that no long-term plan covered them after the abandonment of the 1956–60 plan. A *seven*-year plan was drafted in 1957–8, and Table 8.2 gives details of this plan and also its fulfilment (the period ended in the year following Khrushchev's fall).

The usual caveat concerning aggregate growth indices is needed, but performance was reasonably good in physical terms, too, even though the rapidly-expanding chemical and gas industries were well below target, as was also the case with textiles. Khrushchev was well aware of the backwardness of the chemical industry (especially in providing synthetics, and also mineral fertilizer) and pressed extremely ambitious projects to overcome this backwardness more quickly than was strictly feasible. Similarly, he correctly observed the over-dependence of the USSR on solid fuels, with natural gas neglected, and once again the plans outstripped practical possibilities. He also demanded (and obtained) a very big increase in cement, which he believed to be superior to bricks as a building material. Subsequent criticism rightly pointed to the tendency to overdo things. A favourite phrase of Khrushchev's was that 'in the next two to three years' various ambitious targets were to be reached in industry and in agriculture. The effort to do so was not seldom disorganizing in its effects. Thus 'campaigning' to produce more cement and natural gas had as one consequence shortages of coal and bricks.[2] Similarly, his attack on so-called 'steel-eaters', who use and plan for too much steel, contributed to a shortage of metal – since no effective measures to stimulate economy were taken.

The 1958–9 period could be said to mark the high point of Khrushchev's confidence and relative political and economic success. The successful launch of the world' first *sputnik*, followed by Gagarin's flight into space, highlighted what seemed to be the USSR's technological achievement. Growth rates were impressive. Khrushchev's travels in third-world countries, and Soviet aid, seemed to promise substantial political dividends. The Western book markets soon saw many works on 'Soviet economic warfare'. This feeling of confidence was widely shared among the citizenry (though foreign aid was and is unpopular): living standards were rising, consumer durables of many kinds became widely available, housing improved (from very low levels, to be sure), there were significant social reforms (pensions, maternity leave and minimum wages, for example, were increased in 1956–7), and optimism seemed justified. It is on this basis that Khrushchev began confidently to forecast the date at which the USSR would overtake America in per capita production, and he also announced that the first steps towards 'communism' – the provision of some goods and services free – would be taken by the early 1980s. Needless to say, these things are not now spoken of. There have been disappointments. But we should not forget that the future seemed much brighter, to Khrushchev as well as to ordinary people, when the seven-year plan was launched.

DECLINE AND FALL: WHAT WENT WRONG?

Some of the reasons for Khrushchev's fall relate to matters unconnected with industry (for example, agricultural failures and the Cuban missile crisis). However industrial problems certainly made their contribution. One cause has already been touched upon: too many reorganizations, leading to disorganization. In 1962–3 a series of changes affected the role of local party officials and their relationship with industrial management (and agriculture too). The party was split into industrial and agricultural parts, an unprecedented and shocking decision. Furthermore the number of *sovnarkhozy* was sharply reduced, from over 100 to 47, so that they no longer corresponded to the boundaries of *obkom* secretaries' powers. This was a puzzling set of measures: on the one hand, the division of the party seemed to be aimed at strengthening their controlling and supervising functions; on the other, the lack of correspondence between the boundaries of the *oblasti* and those of the enlarged *sovnarkhozy* made such supervision difficult, and plainly reduced the powers of the secretaries. Since something similar was being done in rural areas, it seems that Khrushchev was dissatisfied with the party officials' 'localist' deviations and meant to cut down their functions. Apart from any practical consequence of such measures, they had the political effect of uniting the local party secretariats against him and so contributed very directly to his overthrow – after which all these measures were speedily reversed.

The last years of Khrushchev's reign saw a notable slowdown in growth throughout the economy. It is by no means easy to explain the reasons, or to give adequate weight to each. The reasons were overwhelmingly internal: foreign trade was expanding (it expanded much faster after Khrushchev's fall), and so industry's troubles cannot be explained by external factors.

One reason could well have been the impact of the *sovnarkhozy* and the confused *ad hoc* recentralization of these years. But a deeper-lying one concerned the nature of the planning system itself. Khrushchev inherited a highly centralized system, created under Stalin to transform an under-developed society into a great military power quickly. New problems were bound to arise, not only because of greater complexity, but also through what could be called the dilution of priorities: under Stalin's successors great efforts were made to modernize agriculture, to build more houses, to increase the supply and assortment of consumers' goods and services. No longer was it possible to give top priority to heavy industry and let all errors and shortages be absorbed by the rest of the civilian economy. The Soviet press, and economic literature, began to express numerous criticisms, highlighting the often wasteful inefficiency of the system. Liberman's articles attracted attention, as did the ideas of Kantorovich, Novozhilov, Nemchinov and many others. Leontief wrote a piece on 'The fall and rise of Soviet economics'; this was the period which saw a notable rise.

When Khrushchev and his comrades became aware that something was amiss, resolutions were adopted to encourage managerial initiative, to cut down the number of compulsory plan indicators. The largely abortive *sovnarkhoz* reform was also an attempt to cope with overcentralization (in and through the economic ministries). But the basic problem remained: the essence of the Soviet economic model was (and still is) the issuance of administrative orders (compulsory plans) as to who should produce what, with resources allocated by the planning agencies; 'commodity–money relations' and the profit motive play a secondary role. Since prices do not, either in theory or practice, reflect relative scarcity or supply-and-demand relationships, this is hardly surprising. Under Khrushchev there were many organizational changes, but the basic principles remained unaltered, and indeed have remained unaltered under his successors.

A further source of strain was the arms programme. The official arms expenditure figure, which must be seen as only a very partial reflection of reality, showed a sharp rise in the budget of 1961. The crushing superiority of the United States in nuclear weaponry emerged clearly in the Cuban missile crisis. So Khrushchev – and even more his successors – increased military spending, a direct competitor for resources needed for industrial investment.

A sharp fall in the rate of increase of investment was a feature of the period: increases of 16 and 13 per cent were recorded in 1958 and 1959 respectively. In 1961–3 the increases ranged from 4 to 5 per cent. In these years, owing no doubt to shortage of material means, there was a cutback in decentralized investment and also in private house-building.

Khrushchev was removed in October 1964. An ungrateful public seems to have forgotten him. In retrospect, one can see him not only as a reorganizer–disorganizer, but also one under whom supplies of foodstuffs and consumer durables increased impressively; life became more tolerable for ordinary citizens. And if he was unable fully to comprehend, let alone solve, the problems which stood in the way of industrial efficiency, the same can be said of those who followed him.

An economic or political historian in the next century is, in my view, bound to evaluate Khrushchev's record positively, but will distinguish the period of his rise, 1953–8, as the most fruitful and positive. After Stalin's grim remoteness, his much more approachable, human, folksy style was a welcome contrast (except for those of his fellow-countrymen who believed that rulers should be remote and dignified). He did devote much attention to sectors neglected under Stalin, and he has a good record on social welfare. His first years saw not only high growth rates but also better harvests, and much greater freedom of discussion, including discussion of economic shortcomings, as well as the publication of a wide range of previously secret statistics. But he was a child of the Stalin era, he was inconsistent, he blustered; after getting rid of his enemies he became more unpredictable, given to 'hare-brained schemes' and campaign methods, reorganization and exhortation. He thought he could correct defects through the party machine, and then correct the party machine itself, but that was a fatal error: the machine was able to get rid of him.

NOTES

1. *Ekonomicheskaya gazeta*, 10 November 1962, p. 8.
2. For evidence see, for instance, A. Birman in *Novyi mir*, no. 1, 1987.

9 Russian Modernization*

THE BACKGROUND: 'BARBAROUS EUROPEANIZATION'

The Soviet novelist Vasili Grossman, echoing a tradition in Russian historical interpretation, referred to 'the curse of Russia, the association between its development and unfreedom, serfdom'.[1] The examples he clearly had in mind were Peter the Great and Stalin, but he brought Lenin, too, into his equation. Not because Lenin was guilty of the gross barbarities of his despotic successor, but because of his own fanatical intolerance and its totalitarian implications (though this word was not used by Grossman).

Take Peter first. Inheriting a backward, ignorant and traditionalist society, he determined to bring it kicking and screaming into the eighteenth century. Serfdom, justified by *raison d'etat*, that is, to provide an economic basis for the tsar's civil and military servants, had been established much earlier, and had become one of the mainstays of the traditional society which Peter was detemined to alter. But the effect of his 'revolution from above' could be described as a universal enserfment. The older aristocratic boyar families were merged along with the service gentry (*dvoryanstvo*) into a unified class of civil and military servants, in full-time service to the state for life. No one had any rights *vis-à-vis* the monarch: sons of the aristocracy and gentry could be, were, ordered to study prescribed subjects, shave off their beards, dress in 'German' clothes, effectively forbidden to choose their occupations or to travel without permission. As for the serfs, though Peter was aware that serfdom had adverse effects, his ambitious military and social policies had the effect of tightening the noose even closer around the necks of the peasantry, many of whom were arbitrarily conscripted into huge forced-labour gangs to build the new capital of St Petersburg ('on the bones of Russian peasants'), or to work as virtual slaves in factories and mines for purposes determined by the state, or to serve in the army. Peter

* This was a conference paper presented in Turin in December 1987 under the auspices of the Fondazione Feltrinelli. Were I writing this today I would say more about the frustrations and problems attending the process of change, and end on a gloomier note.

did introduce manufactures, foreign customs and influences, and sent many Russian gentlemen to study in Europe (he himself had gone to Holland and England to learn about shipbuilding). He is called 'the Great' in tsarist and Soviet historiography, because he was a great modernizer. He was brutal, had his son tortured to death in prison, used forced labour on a vast scale, established the closest equivalent (before Stalin) of what could be called the universal-service state. Indeed, in one of my own earliest historical essays I developed the parallel between Peter's *tabel o rangakh* – the list of civil and military ranks into which the service gentry were divided by him – and the Soviet *nomenklatura*.[2] Both plainly believed that a revolution from above was required, that they had the duty to enforce the necessary measures by ruthless methods, and that those defending the traditional ways (of Muscovy, or of the original Bolshevik revolution) had to be destroyed.

I follow the idea of Alexander Gerschenkron in seeing the major role of the state in Russia's development as a consequence of the absence of 'natural' preconditions for economic development. By 'natural' he meant the existence of social and economic institutions, plus infrastructure, which could form the basis of a spontaneous social–economic transformation, of an industrial revolution, that did not require to be imposed from above. The weakness of spontaneous social forces in Russia could be seen as the cause, but also as a consequence, of the very large role of the tsarist state.

Forty years after Peter, the empress Catherine did much to press ahead with the modernization of society. She corresponded with Diderot and Voltaire, encouraged the arts and sciences, and the use of the French language. Indeed the gentry were now freed of obligatory service (though the only alternative to serving the state was for them to moulder aimlessly in their country estates). She too carried through a vigorous foreign policy, using a modern European-style army with effect, defeating the Turks and annexing a large part of Poland. Yet under her the residual rights of serfs were eliminated (one such right was an appeal to the sovereign), and the enlightened absolutist who exchanged civilized letters with Voltaire and Diderot turned serfdom into slavery for a large part of her people. She also gave away hundreds of thousands of *state* serfs to her lovers, thereby worsening their condition. There is an interesting contrast here between my old friend and colleague the late Leonard Schapiro and the great poet Alexander Pushkin. Schapiro had a portrait of Catherine in his office, and justified this by pointing to her role in providing freedom for the gentry. For him legal rights were an essential feature of modernization, and he had a sort of trickle-down theory: after all, Magna Carta began by giving rights to the barons, *not* to the common people, but they too eventually benefited. Pushkin hated Catherine, and denounced her for what she did to the peasants. I took his side in the 'argument', pointing out that the gentry acquired greater freedom to oppress their serfs. Also that from the date of Magna Carta (1215) to the time when ordinary workers in England acquired rights and the vote did require a certain lapse of time, such as six hundred and fifty years!

In the first decades of the nineteenth century the majority of the peasantry was thus virtually slaves, while Russian industry was partially slave (or serf) too. Some factories, workshops and mines were 'possessional'. This meant that they worked for and were regulated by the state, with most of their labour force tied to their jobs for life, that is, as slaves, though the state imposed some minimal welfare benefits. Others, mainly working for the market, were unregulated and used hired labour. However some of this labour consisted of serfs who paid quit-rent to their masters, which has led to varying estimates of the proportion of free and serf labour in Russian industry at this period: thus Ivanov could have the formal status of a serf, belonging to Count Bobrinsky, but in fact was working as a wage-earner in a textile factory, paying annual quit-rent to the count. To complicate matters still further, he may well have been employed by a serf entrepreneur who paid a much higher quit-rent to this or some other master, until he could buy himself out (there were a number of serf millionaires!).[3]

Russia was late in coming to terms with industrial revolution for a number of reasons, of which serfdom was one, lack of a native entrepreneurial class another. An important element was the indifference or opposition of the tsarist regime itself, especially under Nicholas I (1825–55). Thus at his death there were only two railway lines in the entire empire (St Petersburg–Moscow, and St Petersburg–Warsaw), and not a single iron steamboat was available to oppose the British and French navies in the Crimean War.

The next 'modernization' period is usually dated from the abolition of serfdom, decreed by Alexander II in 1861. However the initial motivation of the designers of this vitally important measure could hardly have been economic development: far from acquiring freedom of movement or individual land ownership, the freed serfs were to stay in their villages, and the peasants' land was, as a rule, reassigned by the commune and could not be sold. After centuries of serfdom, the tsarist government had no doubt some reason to regard the peasants as being incapable of being wholly free. But by the end of the century circumstances were changing rapidly, and Russia was well on the way towards a 'European' style of capitalism, as Lenin indeed noted in his first major work, *The Development of Capitalism in Russia*. Foreign capital and state sponsorship played important roles, but there was now arising a Russian bourgeoisie, a more modern trading class, a banking system, cooperatives and some major large-scale industries. Under the Stolypin reforms of 1906–11 several million peasants were able to leave the commune and set up as property-owners. A sizeable class of professional men, teachers, judges and lawyers, plus a flourishing literary and artistic life, all contributed to the Westernization. Indeed Western Europe was becoming conscious of the importance of Russia's cultural contribution, with Tolstoy, Dostoevsky, ballet and music. True, development was very uneven, the majority of the population were still peasants, living standards of the masses were low, and the political system was still autocractic, despite the existence, since 1906, of an elected legislature. But Russia could be seen as the least developed industrial power, or alternatively as a developing country well on the road to 'capitalist' modernization.

THE IMPACT OF REVOLUTION AND OF STALINISM

Another interesting thought is that one motive of those who supported the Bolshevik revolution was fundamentally reactionary, *anti*-modernizing. Thus the bulk of the peasantry took the opportunity offered by the breakdown of authority to undo much of the Stolypin reform, actually strengthening the traditional communal institutions. Workers resented capitalist entrepreneurs. Many intellectuals, both of the slavophile and of the Marxist persuasion, were opposed to the 'mercantile' spirit and to capitalism.

Anyhow, the immediate impact of the revolution was in a real sense to set back the modernization clock. Much was destroyed in the civil war, but the human loss was perhaps more important. A large part of the Westernized strata – professional men, capitalists, landlords, managers, bankers, lawyers, merchants and officers – emigrated or were killed. The role of the state in economic development was vastly enhanced, since there were now no private investors, no capitalists, no landlords. The debate on '*primitive socialist accumulation*' in the 1920s centred on how the state could mobilize the needed capital to resume the industrialization process interrupted by war and revolution. After the interregnum of the New Economic Policy (a mixed market-oriented economy), Stalin launched, at the end of the 1920s, his 'revolution from above'.

This is not the place for yet another essay on Stalinism, but clearly his regime, his economic strategy, fits well under the rubric of barbarous modernization, mobilizing all of society to catch up the more developed West. His was indeed a universal service state, with the new 'gentry' – party and state officialdom, the *nomenklatura* – in full-time service to the despotic ruler and, at the bottom of the heap, a peasantry once more attached to the land, subject to compulsory deliveries of produce and mass mobilizations, in a kind of new serfdom. Forced labour was used on a massive scale. At the same time there were big strides in the mass education, and modern industry was expanded at breakneck speed. A Russian poet, Voloshin, had written that: 'Peter the Great was the first Bolshevik' and the philosopher Berdyayev that 'Peter's methods were purely Bolshevik'. Gerschenkron took the same view: 'the resemblance between Soviet and Petrine Russia was striking indeed'. Stalin himself ordered Russian history to be rewritten to make Peter great again, and showed himself aware of his place within the Russian political tradition. (And if someone says he was not a Russian but a Georgian, one can reply that Catherine II was German, Nicholas II was a cousin of George V, Napoleon was not French, and so on.)

Under Stalin the party was turned into an instrument of despotic rule, together with the so-called secret police. As Gorbachev was recently to say, 'for well-known reasons' original ideas could no longer be expressed, everyone had to accept official myths about society.[4] The economy was highly centralized, enabling the ruling group to impose its priorities. In terms of the situation as they then perceived it, this must have seemed rational. The more so because, in the 1930s, 'modernization' was largely concerned with the creation of a heavy-industrial base for national security and the modernization of the Soviet armed forces. (Here too there is a close parallel with Peter.) Stalin did say, prohetically, that they had just ten years to catch up, 'otherwise we will be crushed', and he said it in 1931. True, he failed to identify the enemy, whom he then saw to be Britain and France. He did, however, get the date right.

The Polish marxist Oskar Lange once described the Soviet economic system as 'a war economy *sui generis*', that is, its logic was that of a war economy. Indeed during an actual war all countries tend to centralize resource allocation, impose the state's priorities, mobilize people, determine prices and ration many goods, as can be seen if one studies (say) the British or German economies in 1943. In the USSR in Stalin's time even the everyday language was military: 'campaigns', 'fronts', 'bridgeheads', 'advance-guard', and of course there were also heroes, traitors and spies.

Despotism and terror were integral parts of the system, in that the non-priority sectors included consumers' goods and services, which, together with housing, were in very poor shape. But of course potential public protests were silenced through fear.

Was Stalinism really conducive to modernization at all? Heavy losses of scarce skills through mass arrests, paralysis of initiative through terror, the shooting of the large majority of generals and other staff officers on the eve of war and very great damage to agriculture have to be set against the very rapid expansion of production of steel, energy, machinery and armaments. The system performed very well in making possible Soviet military recovery after the initial disasters of the war. It served well also in the process of reconstruction (in effect until the death of Stalin) except that his anti-peasant policies actually halted the recovery of agriculture.

His successors inherited this ultra-centralized system, as near the totalitarian model as one can get in the real world (pure totalitarianism is as impossible as perfect competition and perfect markets!). They speedily abandoned mass terror, and priorities were modified in the direction of the formerly neglected sectors: consumers' goods, agriculture, housing and services. This led to a number of consequences, which, along with the growth of the size of complexity of the economy, presented the leadership and the economics profession with new challenges.

Thus, firstly, the multiplication of priorities was in itself a source of strain for a planning system designed to impose a few key priorities at the cost of neglecting other needs.

Secondly, technical progress came to depend more and more upon decentralized initiative, while well-meant central initiatives which had technical progress as their objective came up against the obstruction of management, who found it easier to earn bonuses by fulfilling quantitative plans, while not being rewarded for the risk-taking involved in any innovation.

Thirdly, higher incomes and more diversified output of goods and services came into conflict with the planning system, which was poor at reflecting user requirements. There was no *economic* link between consumer demand and the producing enterprises.

Fourthly, the entire material allocation system, organically linked with the 'directive' output-planning procedures, placed an intolerable burden on the planning and allocation staffs, necessarily creating contradictions and imbalances.

Fifthly, in their endeavours to cope with their task, planning organs had to aggregate, issue plan-orders in roubles, tons, millions of units and so on. This had a whole number of negative consequences, such as the following:

(a) Management was directly interested in concealing potential in order to have an easy plan to fulfil. It hoarded labour and materials.
(b) Production, and the product mix, were adjusted to fit into plan-fulfilment indicators, to the detriment of quality and the customer. These indicators often actually rewarded waste, as for example when, to fulfil a plan in tons, goods were made unnecessarily heavy, while plans in roubles rewarded extravagance. Conversely, economy of metal would result in penalties.
(c) As anomalies and undesirable consequences were observed, plan-indicators multiplied, to cover cost reduction, economy of materials, labour productivity, numbers of clerical staffs and so on, creating new contradictions and further interfering with managerial initiative (though in fact these very contradictions gave them some room for manoeuvre, as was pointed out by Zaslavskaya and others).

In theory, the plans which management has to obey were supposed to incorporate the needs of society. They, so to speak, contained use-value *ex ante*, reflecting the old Marxist notion that, whereas under capitalism production is for the market, and thus only valued *ex post*, under socialism 'society' will know in advance how to produce directly to satisfy needs. However, as a large number of Soviet economists have been pointing out, in practice the planners cannot know the detailed requirements of hundreds of thousands of enterprises and hundreds of millions of citizens. There is neither the time nor the information to assign use-value to millions of product variants.

The economic system was intimately linked with the political hierarchy. The politbureau could be seen as the board of directors of the huge firm USSR Inc. Party officials at all levels interfered with the economy. Plans and contracts were frequently arbitrarily changed. Some Western and some Soviet analysts used the word 'feudal' to characterise the system of human relationships based upon domination–subjection. Without a despotic ruler, without terror, the political machine itself became corrupt. Under Brezhnev and his gerontocracy there were clear signs of petrification, of inertia. The system lacked built-in dynamism, as it lacked also any direct link, through prices, between supply and demand. There was a realization even at the highest levels that (to cite Brezhnev himself) 'in this age of scientific–technical revolution basic change in our methods of management is essential'. Minor and partial reform measures abounded. But they left unaltered the centralized and hierarchical nature of the planning mechanism and the dominant role of the party apparatus. Growth declined, the technological gap showed signs of widening. When, finally, Gorbachev became party leader, he faced what he himself has called a 'pre-crisis situation', calling for 'radical reform' and even 'revolutionary change'. There is a recognition that the sort of 'modernization' associated with Peter and Stalin, and the centralized planning system itself, are now obstacles on the road, have become 'fetters on the forces of production', to use a familiar Marxist phrase.

The *glasnost'* associated with Gorbachev's cultural policy has led to a proliferation of extremely frank criticisms of the present situation in the Soviet press. Many of them are as radical and far-reaching as any criticisms published in the West.

THE 'GORBACHEV' MODERNIZATION

What Gorbachev and his advisers are seeking is an effective combination of plan and market. Strategic decisions, major investment, income policies, plus basic infrastructure and the bulk of social services, will remain the responsibility of the political organs and the central planners. The reformers reject the notion of a pure free 'socialist' market. They accept, indeed stress, the need for the micro-adjustments between demand and supply, the detailed product mix, to express themselves via market relations: contract, purchase-and-sale, with choice of supplier. The administrative material-allocation system is to be replaced by trade in means of production. Current output is to be determined through negotiations with customers, undistorted by the need to fulfil aggregate plans in tons or roubles. Stricter financial discipline is to replace 'soft' credits and subsidies. Prices are to be no longer of the cost-plus type, and many will be subject to negotiation. In agriculture, within the unwieldy state and collective farms, labour is being organized in small contract groups, many of them family groups, with responsibility for organizing their own work. Cooperatives and individual (family) enterprises are being legalized urban areas. Party and state organs are being told not to interfere with management. Even foreign trade is being freed of the grip of the monopolist Ministry of Foreign Trade: many enterprises are to have direct access to foreign markets. Economists point to the need to make the rouble a real currency: enterprises have little interest in acquiring monetary assets if they cannot freely spend them (because of the allocation system), and monetary labour incentives are also weakened by shortages of goods and services to buy.

This broad outline of a radical reform programme has yet to 'translate' itself into reality. The Soviet press is full of reports to the effect that managerial autonomy is not respected, that output plans are still imposed from above in the usual way, that the material allocation system survives, that prices remain unreformed, that contracts are too often not observed, private enterprise obstructed – the list could be prolonged. In the words of one Soviet journal, officials 'will seek to turn the hurricane [of change] into a storm in a teacup'.

This is not the place for an analysis of obstacles to radical reform. Residual ideology, vested interest of party and state bureaucrats, reluctance to take responsibility, the genuine difficulty of devising and implementing an alternative model, the contradictions which necessarily complicate step-by-step reform, the very real problem of finding a workable balance between plan and market, all play a role. So does fear of the consequences of relaxing control under conditions of shortage – though Gorbachev himself remarked that the allocation system itself generates shortage, and so, if one were to wait for the overcoming of shortage before going over to trade in means of production, one might have to wait for ever. Then there is the complex question of labour relations: workers are accustomed to job security and general slackness, also to highly subsidized rents, utilities and basic foodstuffs. A more rational pricing policy, and the closing of hopelessly inefficient enterprises, could lead to social tensions or even to disorders. So one can scarcely blame Gorbachev for calling for careful preparation, and it may be that the full scope of the intended changes will not become clear until 1990, if then.

Can there be economic reform of this kind without political reform? Interestingly, the answer given by Gorbachev is an emphatic NO. The *perestroika* must go far beyond the economic if it is to be effective. Cynicism, indifference, drunkenness, abuse of authority, widespread injustices, alienation, corruption at all levels, all these are seen as obstacles to necessary change. Hence much talk of *glasnost'* and (limited but meaningful) *demokratizatsia*: more circulation of information, in the media and by statistical offices, open discussion of real and painful issues, open criticism, genuine elections of some officials in the party and of managers – all these are being much talked about and referred to in decrees. Competition for customers is to be accompanied by competition for office and (again, subject to limits) between alternative reform measures. The Soviet media have come to life, publishing not only controversial material on today's problems, but also forthright criticisms of the Stalin era (and also protests from those who believe that this is going too far). Much is also being said about the need for greater freedom for science, and also for the need for radical reform of law and justice.

This last point is worth dwelling on. The Soviet press has had much to say in the past year both on abuses of legal norms and procedures in general, and on such abuses in the economic realm in particular: that the property of enterprises can be arbitrarily taken away; contractual obligations to customers or to employees (including the small contract groups in agriculture and in construction) are too frequently ignored. A new economic legal code is being introduced. Gorbachev, let us remember, has a degree in law. He must surely be conscious of the fact that the reform he has in mind is inconsistent with arbitrariness. He must also know that party officials have in fact been exercising their authority arbitrarily, in the economy and also in criminal cases (they tell manager and judges what they should do). They also, through the so-called *nomenklatura* system, decide on appointments, including the appointment of those who are supposedly elected. How are these well-ingrained habits of exercising power to be reconciled with the needs of modernization? Several Soviet authors have publicly advocated the end of 'feudalism', of the key role of domination–subjection, throughout society.

It may be useful at this point to refer to two Soviet Marxist legal theorists of the early 1930s, Pashukanis and Reisner. Following what they thought was orthodox Marxist doctrine, they regarded law as a sort of by-product of market and commercial contract; as and when these are replaced by all-embracing planning, law (like the state) will wither away. They were wrong, but also right: wrong to suppose that there would come a socialism which would not need markets, contracts or laws; right, however, to see that there is indeed a connection between the downgrading of legal norms and the role of contract in the economy and the weakening of legal restraints in civil society in general. Arbitrariness in the economic realm was accompanied by arbitrariness in the administration of justice, and a low status for judges and lawyers. So it is not a coincidence that, today, advocacy of raising the status of contract and market transactions in the economy is accompanied by the advocacy of a legal order and a genuinely independent judiciary. This too is part of the struggle for modernization.

CONCLUSION

Soviet modernization requires a total break from what could be called the 'Peter–Stalin despotic modernization' tradition. It requires also a break with, or a radical reinterpretation of, the Marxist tradition of viewing the onward march to socialism/communism as requiring the elimination of 'commodity–money relations', the creation of an all-embracing planning mechanism. The radical reform currently under consideration also requires a fundamental change in the way that political–economic power is exercised, a redefinition and limitation of the role of the full-time party functionary and a transfer of authority to management (managers are also, as a rule, party members). The expanded role of the market has as its corollary the extension of competition, with winners and losers, and so the possibility of bankruptcies and (limited) unemployment. Millions of officials, managers and technologists, will have to learn how to work in an unfamiliar environment, in new ways. A truly formidable task. Gorbachev and his principal advisers know this well. It can cause serious upsets and conflicts in society. Yet, if the USSR is to maintain its place as a superpower in the modern world, there is no alternative. Hence Gorbachev's frequent speeches on this theme: 'the fate of our country, the future of socialism in the world, depend in large measure on how we tackle this task', he said soon after his accession. In the way of progress stands what Alexander Bovin called "home-grown bureaucratic soviet socialist conservatism'. It is still too soon to say just how radical will be the measures finally adopted, let alone the likelihood of success. But a few years ago it was widely believed that they could not or would not even be tried.

NOTES

1. See his *Vsyo techyot*, published in the West (Posser: Frankfurt, 1970), and later in the USSR, 1989.
2. See Alec Nove, 'History, hierarchy and Soviet socialism' in *Soviet Studies*, July 1969, reprinted in *Political Economy and Soviet socialism*, London, 1979.
3. Interested readers are referred to Tugan-Baranovsky's excellent book *The Russian Factory*.
4. *Pravda*, 28 January 1987.

Part III
Economics: East and West

10 Planning*

'Planning; planned: Intended, in accordance with, or achieved by, a careful plan made beforehand.' This is the Chambers dictionary definition. Of course in this sense we all plan, whenever we think carefully of what we might do in the future. All economic decision-making relates to the future, since all transactions take time, and in the course of time some circumstances might have changed, and so plans are frequently unfulfilled, or have results different from the original intention.

However we will have in mind the deliberate actions of *public* authorities, primarily the state, while referring from time to time also to plans made in the private sector. Plans can be of many kinds. The Soviet version is '*directive* planning' or command planning. The authorities issue binding instructions to subordinate management, telling it what goods and services to provide, from whom to obtain the required inputs, and, as we shall see, much else besides. Then there is *indicative* planning, when the state uses influence, subsidies, grants and taxes, but does not compel. There is also *sectoral* planning, which concerns, for instance, a road network, urban rapid-transit, the coal industry and the national health service. This need not be related to any overall plan for the economy as a whole

Then there are differences in purpose, reason or objectives. One is to impose the centre's priorities, to replace or combat spontaneous market forces, that is, deliberately to achieve what would not otherwise occur. This applies most evidently to a war economy, but also to Stalin's economic strategy of the 1930s, with its mass mobilization of material and human resources to create a heavy-industrial base in the shortest possible time. On a less drastic scale these considerations

* This was my contribution to the *New Palgrave*, an encyclopaedia of economics. Had it been written today, I would have devoted some space to the very grave difficulties being encountered in the USSR and in China in implementing reforms designed to combine plan and market. It is intended that the authorities will no longer 'issue binding instructions to subordinate management', while inputs are to be freely purchased and not administratively allocated – though this has not yet happened. I would also have referred to the ideologically-inspired privatization even of water in Great Britain.

also apply to programmes of rapid development in some third-world countries, that is, to conscious attempts to transform a country's political economy. In such cases the market is seen as an enemy, to be limited or combated (as in Preobrazhensky's phrase about the battle between 'primitive socialist accumulation and the law of value'), and the same was at least partly true in war economies in the West: prices were fixed, materials allocated, free-market deals in controlled commodities were treated as black market criminal offences.

However other kinds of public-sector planning have, or need have, no such hostility to the market, and can and do coexist with it. The motive relates partly to what are called public goods (such as the road network, street lighting or rubbish collection), and partly to externality-generating sectors, where the profit-and-loss account of the enterprises concerned constitutes a misleading criterion even on narrowly economic grounds, and/or where private and the more general interests conflict. Examples are many: thus urban public transport, docks and airports, are in the public sector in the United States (a point which escapes the attention of the '*laissez-faire*' fanatics currently advising Mrs Thatcher's government). Environmental protection is another important factor: thus in a number of countries deforestation threatens ecological disaster, while in the North Sea it is essential to act to preserve fish stocks, while short-term private profit dictates the cutting of trees and over-fishing respectively. There are also natural monopolies, where competition is unnecessary or wasteful: electricity, water, post, until recently also telephones, are examples; the choice here lies between a regulated private monopoly and state ownership and control. The choice may be influenced also by considerations of public policy. Thus, if it is desired to provide a comprehensive postal or telephone service, to supply all houses with pure water, and even remote Scottish islands with electricity, then clearly the public-service aspects must be given some priority: it has always been evident that some of the above activities cannot be profitable.

Some confusion is engendered by the inability to distinguish between *responsibility* for provision of a good or service and the way in which it is provided. Thus, to cite an example, the public authorities must ensure that city rubbish is collected and disposed of, but this no more requires the rubbish collectors to be public employees than responsibility for road-building requires those who build the roads to be civil servants!

Then there are sectors to which economic profitability considerations may be held not to apply at all: education, health and pensions are widely held to be the proper subject of planning and provision by public authorities.

Finally, there is the species of planning designed to facilitate and encourage the operation of market-orientated private enterprise. This ranges from infrastructural investment to what is usually called indicative planning, which is not compulsory or imposed, but which helps to fill a most evident gap in the pure free-market doctrine, which is concerned with large-scale investment. Long ago G. B. Richardson pointed out that, on the assumptions of perfect competition and perfect markets, it is hard to imagine how or why investment should take place, since the profitable opportunity is, by definition, equally visible to all the competitors. Therefore imperfect knowledge and/or collusion, neither of which are in the model, are preconditions for investment. The important role of the state in the success of the South Korean and Japanese export-orientated strategies is inexcusably ignored by the *laissez-faire* ideologists, who can see the success and attribute it wholly to free-market entrepreneurship. Indicative planning of this sort, reinforced by unofficial pressures and fiscal incentives, could be described as a form of state-organized collusion. In addition there is the role of the state in ensuring macrobalance, or taking countercyclical action, which used to be accepted quasi-universally as necessary, though this is now vigorously questioned by the revived *laissez-faire* school, which considers that the economy is basically self-righting.

So only in one of its versions is planning to be seen as in inherent contradiction with the market; in all the others they supplement each other, or plans are actually made operational *through* the market.

Socialist planning has a long history. Generations of socialist thinkers, including Marx and his followers, contrasted the deliberate planning that would occur under socialism with the 'anarchy' of capitalism, in which production was for profit, not for the use. The 'associated producers' would join together to discuss what is needed and how best it could be provided. As Engels put it, they would compare the useful effect of products with time necessary to produce them.

Some, for example Kautsky and Lenin, saw a socialist society of the future as if it were one giant enterprise, a single all-embracing factory or office. There would be no 'commodity production', that is, production would be for use, not for exchange. Labour would, when applied, be 'directly social', that is, its use would be validated not *ex post*, through the market, but *ex ante*, by the all-embracing plan, which would express society's needs. Costs would be measured in terms of what was seen as the one ultimately scarce resource, human effort.

Critics, such as Barone and L. von Mises, pointed out some major weaknesses in this approach to socialist planning: the number of calculations required would be enormous and the economic criteria for decision-making would be lacking without meaningful prices. Yet, with but few exceptions, socialists in the marxist tradition persisted in their belief that such planning would be 'simple and transparent' (Marx); that 'everything would be simple without the so-called value' (Engels); 'capitalism had so simplified the task of accounting and control . . . that any literate person can do it' (Lenin); 'The society of the future will do what is called for by simple statistical data' (Bukharin).

Planning in practice proved to be very complicated indeed. It must be emphasized that it did serve its purpose when that purpose was analagous to that of a war economy: to concentrate resources for the priority objectives determined by the central political authority. When the war did break out, the USSR's survival, after initial military disasters, was in no small degree made possible by the ruthlessly-imposed priority of military requirements. In Western countries too, though in lesser degree, central controls were tight, resources were allocated, and the resultant bureaucratic deformations had much in common with Soviet-type planning. Yet these must be seen as a cost, in the circumstances a necessary cost, of imposing the priorities of war. It was Lange who once likened the Soviet planning system to a war economy, *sui generis*.

In normal times, the priorities become more diffuse, also more numerous. The growth of the economy itself presents new problems and challenges. A Soviet scholar remarked that, if the size of the economy grows six-fold, the number of links to be planned grows to the square of that (or any other) number, that is, 36-fold, and indeed this can be seen as one expands the number of items included in an input–output table.

The Soviet economy today contains several hundreds of thousands of enterprises, in mining, manufacturing, agriculture, construction, transport, distribution, catering and services. The large number is not due to their excessively small size. On the contrary, it has been argued that Soviet agricultural and industrial establishments are too large, certainly much larger than is the case on average in Western capitalism. Because neither production nor the supply of inputs is based on horizontal, market-type relations, each of these hundreds of thousands of enterprises needs to receive, from some unit in the planning hierarchy, specific instructions as to what to produce, what materials to obtain and from whom, and other plan targets relate to labour productivity, wages, costs, material utilization, investment, technical progress, fuel economy and much else besides. The number of identifiably different products and services, fully disaggregated, has been estimated as upwards of twelve million. The sheer scale of the task of the planners is probably *the* most important source of inefficiency and imbalance. Though Soviet experience shows that a planned economy of this type can function, this same experience strongly supports Barone's conclusion, arrived at in 1908, before there was any practical example to study: it would be difficult but not quite impossible to arrive at a 'technically' balanced plan, that is, one where the needed inputs match the intended output, but *quite* impossible to see how one could approach an *economic* optimum. Thus it is indeed very hard for those institutions responsible for material allocation to ensure that the needed inputs are provided, but they seldom have the practical possibility or the information to ensure that the inputs are those which are most economical.

This is but one of the difficulties attributable to the sheer scale of the required coordination between multi-million plan-instructions. Academician Fedorenko quipped that next year's plan, if fully checked and balanced, might be ready in approximately 30 000 years' time.

It is necessary to distinguish between *long-term* and *current* planning. The long (or medium-term) plan looks forward to the end of a quinquennium, or in some instances as much as fifteen years; thus in 1985 some targets were published relating to the year 2000. These plans are necessarily highly aggregated, and contain broad objectives relating primarily to productive capacity (and so to investment), rather than to the product mix, which will be adapted to requirements which cannot be foreseen in advance in detail. A long-term plan must be balanced in an input–output sense, and planners proceed by so-called material balances for major products, ensuring that planned availability matches planned utilization. These plans are not yet operational; that is, they have no 'addressee': no specific enterprise is instructed to act. Or rather the addressee is the planning and administrative mechanism itself. It is true that there have been proposals, and even decisions, about the need to incorporate enterprises' own quinquennial plans into this process, and indeed to make these plans stable and to relate various norms and incentives to them. However, this has not been possible in practice. Indeed, stable 'micro' plans for five years ahead are surely an impossibility, when even annual plans are notoriously unstable, being altered repeatedly during the period of their currency to cope with the unexpected or to correct errors belatedly identified.

The drafting of the relatively aggregated 'unaddressed' longer-term plans does not present an impossible task, there being only several hundred items. It is the operational annual plan, broken down by quarters and by months, which presents formidable problems. It is drafted in the last few months of the previous year. According to one Soviet source, output plans are made for about 48 000 products, which implies that on average each will contain about 210–300 sub-products or varieties. To go into greater detail would cause inordinate delay. But since each of the 48 000 requires numerous inputs, which must be provided through the allocation mechanism, and since every enterprise must receive specific plan-instructions relating to output and inputs, even in relatively aggregated form the burden on the planners is huge. The essential task of coordination is rendered the more complicated by the fact that responsibility is necessarily shared by numerous separate planning departments and economic ministries.

The centralized planning model is based upon the supposition that 'society' (in practice, the planning agencies, under the authority of the political leadership) knows or can discover what is needed, and can issue orders incorporating these needs, while allocating the required means of production so that the needs are economically met. It is worth noting that in some sectors this supposition is close to reality. Thus electricity is a homogenous product, power stations are interlinked into a grid and information on present and estimated future needs is best assessed at the centre, as it is also in many Western countries. The centre is also the obvious place for decision-making on armaments production. However a very wide range of goods and services, both producers' goods and consumers' goods, are supplied in a wide variety of types, models and sizes, to serve specific needs. Choice of technique, decisions on new products and possible alternative uses of agricutural land are also matters on which the centre has little relevant information which could serve as a basis for microcommands. Also it is an evident fact that management possesses vital information as to the production potential of the enterprise, and the planners must rely on an upward flow of proposals and suggestions if they are to issue the correct orders. 'Many if not most commands in a command economy are written by those who receive them', remarked a wise Hungarian.

Devolution of authority is thus not only necessary, but inevitably occurs, since plans are frequently late, contradictory, aggregated, and their implementation requires much managerial ingenuity, which frequently has to stretch the boundaries of legality. But the system lacks any criterion for managerial decision-making other than the plan-targets to which management's bonuses and promotion prospects are related. Since prices do not, in either theory or practice, reflect supply-and-demand relationships, relative scarcities, demand intensity and profitability cannot serve as a rational criterion for micro decision-making. Furthermore, because of lack of time and imperfect knowledge, the planners are compelled to proceed on the basis of past performance, introducing the so-called ratchet effect: output targets in the next plan period will be a little higher, costs a little lower, than in the previous period, and indeed all concerned proceed on the assumption that no major changes in past supply or delivery arrangements are likely to occur. It is this which enables the system to function, but Soviet sources understandably criticize these methods, since they are not only conservative, but stimulate undesirable bahaviour by management. The latter, judged by plan-fulfilment, seeks a plan which is easy to fulfil and avoids doing too well in case the following year's target is set too high. Fears of supplies not arriving, and of arbitrary plan changes, also stimulate hoarding of labour and materials, and over-application for inputs.

Attempts to fulfil aggregate plan targets, in roubles, tons, square metres or whatever it might be, engender some familiar distortions, when management produces not for the customer but for plan-fulfilment statistics. This can generate the sort of waste which is typified by the building industry (whose plan is in roubles spent) trying to use the dearest possible materials, and metal goods which are unnecessarily heavy to 'clock up' the necessary plan tonnage. It proves to be remarkably difficult to express a plan for heterogenous products in any unit of measure which does not result in unintended distortions. The weak position of the customer has two causes: the supplier is a *de facto* monopolist, and there is a chronic tendency for shortages to occur, which finds expression in a 'take-it-leave-it' attitude on the part of the supplier. But perhaps the most fundamental cause is the one already mentioned: the model requires the centre's plans to incorporate requirements in a degree of detail which is impossible in the complex multi-product real world, and yet it is these necessarily aggregated plan targets which serve as the basis for microeconomic activity of enterprises, since they are judged by their fulfilment of these targets.

Initiative is likewise (unintentionally frustrated. It is not only that management is risk-averse, since risk-taking is not, as such, rewarded. It is that any new action requires not only motivation but also information and means. Thus innovation, whether in product design or in production methods, is frequently rendered impossible because the required machines or materials are not obtainable, these being allocated by remote bureaucratic offices.

While enterprises are supposed to operate on so-called 'economic accounting', in fact money and prices generally play a passive role, priority being given to plan-fulfilment indicators. The absence of any built-in incentive to economize has meant the proliferation of compulsory cost-cutting and material-economy plans, which can conflict with the objective of providing what the customer requires. While citizens are free to spend their wages on goods in state shops at state-fixed prices, there is no direct economic link or feedback from these prices to the wholesale prices received by the producing enterprises.

Such a planning system as this becomes increasingly unable to cope with the challenges of what has to be known as 'intensive growth': that is, growth based on the more efficient use of scarce resources. However this same system, does give to the political authorities – party and state officials – a high degree of control over material and human resources. There also has developed a kind of informal social contract with the masses: security of employment, toleration of slackness at work and prices of necessities and rents kept low. The major changes, towards some species of 'market socialism', would thus encounter considerable resistance at all levels of society.

The *Hungarian* New Economic Mechanism (NEM), introduced in 1968, sought to overcome the deficiencies of the Soviet model by the limited use of the market mechanism as the basis of current enterprise operations. That is to say, enterprises made their own output plans, based upon negotiated contracts with customers, and purchased their inputs without having to apply for an administered allocation. The 'addressed' current obligatory plan was eliminated. State plans were now to be concerned mainly with investment, that is, with the creation of new capacity and structural change. Prices, markets forces and profitability were to play a major role in guiding the actions of managements. However state-owned enterprises remained under the ultimate authority of economic ministries and, as also in the Soviet Union, party officials can issue orders on almost any subject.

Hungarian experience can only be seen as a partial test of the viability and effectiveness of the 'market-socialist' model, and this for a number of reasons. One of these has little to do with the model itself: Hungary was hard hit by adverse terms of trade in the 1970s, and the resultant strains led to adverse effects on living standards and to the imposition of tighter controls than was envisaged within the logic of the model, and this included controls over prices. Another 'external' factor was that Hungary trades mainly with other communist-ruled countries, and this trade is predominantly based on annual inter-governmental bilateral deals, a procedure inconsistent with the 'market' logic of the NEM. But there were other problems, which may highlight some contradictions inherent in 'marrying' the principles of market and of socialism. Thus the market requires competition, but there is little competition in Hungarian industry, partly because it is a small country with few producers, but also because of mergers. Competition in turn generates winners and losers, but the commitment to full employment and the pressures from the unsuccesful result in there being no bankruptcies: the loss-makers receive a subsidy, while extra taxes are levied on those judged to be too successful. For all these reasons, the microeconomic logic of the NEM's 'mix' of plan and market has had only limited success.

The success is particularly visible in two sectors: agriculture and distribution (trade, catering and many services). In agriculture cooperative (collective) farms are freed from compulsory delivery quotas and freed also from the need to apply to the planners for authority to purchase their inputs (usually they are able to buy them without any permits). There is much more autonomy, much less outside interference, than in the USSR, and also greater flexibility in providing incentives for peasants, and in allowing scope for peasants' private activities as well as for non-agricultural activities of the farms themselves. Since agriculture is notoriously unsuitable as an object of central planning, this is indeed a sector which benefits from reliance on decentralization and the market. Trade and catering benefited both from realistic pricing (persistent shortages of many goods in the

USSR were at least in part due to the tendency to underprice them), and also from the legalization of a sizeable private sector: thus many shops and restaurants in Hungarian cities are either privately owned or leased from the state by private operators. Competition has a visible effect on quality and service. Private ('second economy') activities are legal also in construction, repairs, transport (private taxis are allowed) and a range of small-scale manufacturing. In the USSR most of these activities would be illegal, but a sizeable underground second economy exists there also. Thus in Hungary one can observe both the advantages and difficulties which arise when plan and market are allowed to coexist – though of course the particular 'mix' that exists in Hungary is not the only possible one.

It is noteworthy that Poland and China have formally adopted a model which resembles the Hungarian NEM, though one difference concerns agriculture: in Poland the bulk of the peasantry have remained private smallholders, while in China the 'household responsibility system' introduced after 1979 has effectively decollectivized the peasantry. In the Polish case the serious economic difficulties which persist have been an obstacle to the implementation of these reforms. In China the resolution adopted in October 1984 explicitly asserts the need to recognize the role of market forces as well as of state planning and, apart from greater freedom for peasant agriculture, petty private trade and ownership have been legalized. This is a 'mix' reminiscent of NEP in the Soviet Union in the early 1920s. However it is too soon to conclude that the Chinese have a new and durable plan model. One of their leaders remarked that, while managers must be allowed to show enterprise and spread their wings, they had been confined to too small a cage, but insisted that there must be a cage: 'otherwise the bird will fly away'. There appears to be considerable differences of opinion among Chinese party leaders as to the meaning of present policies. Is the use of the market, and the opening to foreign capital, a temporary phase, as NEP was in Russia, with some sort of real socialist planning to follow? Or is the mix between plan and market a long-term model of socialist planning? The rapid growth of income inequalities, the corruption of many officials and a speed-up in inflation could lead to a counterattack, to the reimposition of more central planning. This is not the place to speculate on such matters, only to note that the Chinese are still seeking their own model.

Yugoslavia's combination of plan and self-management was also based in principle on the use of the market mechanism. The microeconomy was to function on the basis of contractual relations between self-managed enterprises, guided by material advantage and by realistic free-market type prices. Yugoslavia's economy has run into serious difficulties, not least because the necessary minimum degree of central planning was absent. Tinbergen wisely remarked that 'It is highly improbable that the proponents of "*laissez-faire*" theory of management are right. It can be convincingly shown that in an optimum order some tasks must be performed in a centralised way . . .'

Part of the problem was republic–regional fragmentation, complicated by a long history of local nationalisms, so that each republic tended to make its own investments, to keep its own earnings from exports and to run its own finances, which helped to disintegrate the economy of what is, after all, a small country. There is a moral here of wider application about regional planning powers; a regional authority will tend to divert resources for the use of its own region, even if it harms others, if it has the power to do so. But this is but one aspect of a more general problem: the interests of the parts do not necessarily add up to the interests of the whole. There are economies (and diseconomies) of scale, and externalities, which cannot be ignored. Furthermore the self-management model itself tends to encourage excessive income distribution and discourage labour-intensive investments, a situation which can and did give rise to serious unemployment combined with accelerating inflation. The latter was also due to lack of adequate control over credits issued by the (numerous) banks, and to what for several years was a negative real rate of interest.

Yugoslav experience does not prove that either self-management or the market mechanism were wrong. It does strongly point to the need of economic powers at the center, not only to ensure macro-economic balance but also to devise and enforce the 'rules of the game' for the microeconomy. It also demonstrates the limitations and dangers of 'socialist laissez-faire'. If the USSR's economy is stifled by all-embracing central controls, then Yugoslavia shows the consequences of having no central controls at all.

This criticism can be extended to some early models of a decentralized socialist economy, such as that of Oskar Lange and Abba Lerner. These do contain a Central Planning Board, but it is imagined as functioning only via the fixing of parametric prices, to which management is supposed to react in accordance with the best neoclassical principles. Intended to show, in reply to critics (notably

Mises), that socialist planners do not require to solve innumerable simultaneous equations, Lange's counter-model contained neither growth nor indeed any plan at all. Nor, of course, did the world of Mises. What was shown was that equilibrium with efficient allocation would be possible, on the abstract assumptions common to both protagonists. It is worth reminding oneself of Kornai's dictum: few indeed are those who take decisions on the basis only of information about price (especially when, in taking investment decisions, the relevant prices are those of the future).

Those critics of socialist planning who emphasized the alleged impossibility of solving too many simultaneous equations had grounds for alarm when the computer, programming and input–output techniques appeared to make the impossible possible. After all, whereas in a capitalist planless society there was and could be no operational objective function, a centrally planned economy could – it might be supposed – use the new techniques to arrive at the most economically efficient way of achieving the objectives defined by the supreme political authority, which is simultaneously in command of the economy. Indeed some members of the Soviet mathematical school explored in very interesting ways how this might be attempted, and Kantorovich, who received the Nobel prize for his pioneering work on linear programming, proposed a system of plan-valuations which could be used in calculations designed to achieve optimal allocation (and had to defend these valuations against criticism from dogmatic defenders of the labour theory of value).

It turned out that progress along this route was disappointingly slow. We can now see more clearly why. Firstly, the 'objective function' proved to be operationally indefinable, despite efforts by able mathematical economists to define it. What could be the objective basis for optimal plan; what could be the criterion by which to judge if any given plan were optimal? The objectives of the political leadership cannot serve as such a criterion, since (as one Soviet economist remarked) it seeks advice as to what the plan objectives should be, and would not thank those economists who replied that its wishes were their criterion. Any real society generates numerous inconsistent objectives, and in a one-party state these are also present, and find expression within the one party. Then the 'curse of scale' must again be emphasized. Botvinnik, the former world chess champion, estimated that the number of possible moves in a chess game exceed substantially the number of words spoken by all human beings since the Pyramids were built. A chessboard has only 64 squares, and rules of the rules of the game are known. An economy or a society has many more, and the human 'pieces' play different games and dispute about the rules. So even if one day a chess grandmaster might have trouble beating a chess-playing computer, the idea that computers could replace markets and make Soviet-type centralized planning 'efficient' is surely a chimera. Computers can aid the centre in making calculations, it is true. They have numerous uses at micro, that is, decentralized levels, as a source of data, or in design bureaux and so on. However one can scarcely imagine that the centre can administer through a computerized programme a fully disaggregated microplan for millions of products, distributed among hundreds of thousands of enterprises. Not only would there be too much information to handle (and check), but decisions involving quality, or judgment as to uncertain outcomes, can hardly be left for computers. Scale is also a hindrance to the use in practice of prices based on central computerized programmes (the 'objectively determined valuations' of Kantorovich). At operational disaggregated level there is no such thing as *the* price of 'agricultural machinery' or 'ball-bearings,' or 'footwear': there are hundreds or thousands of different products under each of these heads, which need to be provided, and priced, for different requirements or preferences.

Plan and market have been seen as incompatible opposites, both by dogmatic socialists and by dogmatic anti-socialists. However a strong case can be made for the proposition that a mix of the two is essential in any modern society. True enough, a long list can be made of distortions and deficiencies directly attributable to planning. Disastrous indeed have been some comprehensive redevelopment schemes devised by well-meaning urban planners, and some of the housing has later had to be dynamited. Planning foreign trade in a number of countries, especially in the third world, has been a means of personal enrichment for those entitled to issue import licences. Development plans have sometimes been grandiose and wasteful. From these and similar experiences some have drawn the conclusion that planning is 'bad', that reliance on the market mechanism will provide the right answers to all economic problems, and that state intervention should confine itself to controlling the money supply and to providing a minimum range of so-called public goods, such as defence and lighthouses. Conversely, socialists see that the operation of the free market generates excessive income inequalities and gives rise to monopolistic abuses, to trade-cycles, to unemployment. The market inspires acquisitiveness, substitutes conflict (between classes, and also between competitors) for the desired harmonious cooperation.

Yet both sets of dogmatists appear to be mistaken. The evils which they have noted do indeed exist, and require to be explicitly recognized and combated. The difficulties faced by centralized marketless socialism have already been discussed at length, and it is hard to see how decentralization could be envisaged without some sort of market mechanism which would link the parts together. *Laissez-faire*, the belief that virtually all public-sector planning or provision is either harmful or unnecessary, ignores much of what did or does happen in the real non-textbook world.

Investment is clearly one relevant sector. Given the degree of uncertainty facing private investors, their understandable desire for security, the attraction of high interest rates (and the negative effect of such high rates on would-be borrowers), it would seem to be a remarkable act of faith to imagine investments, especially in the longer term, as rational, let alone optimal. Various forms of indicative planning, reinforced by the state's own investment plans (in infrastructure, for example), become an important contribution to guiding private investment decisions. The South Korean government played a key role in the process of developing highly successful exporting sectors. If interest rates are (say) 15 per cent, whose private concern should it be to think about (for instance) the consequences for Great Britain of the exhaustion of North Sea oil or gas supplies by the end of the century? It requires ideological obstinacy of a high order not to think that an energy plan might be desirable, in the national interest. The devotees of 'methodological individualism' go so far as to assert that there *is* no national interest, distinct from the individual interests of the citizens. Even on so extreme an assumption it must still be recognized that individual or sectoral interests can conflict with one another; the elementary example of many people wishing to park cars in a narrow street is but one of many instances when people literally get in each others' way, and public authority has to sort out the mess. One returns, too, to examples cited earlier concerning external effects. Docks, airports and rapid-transit systems have wide spreading effects – on industrial profitability, property values, congestion and so on – which do not show up in their respective profit-and-loss accounts. It does seem absurd to assert that the Washington or Montreal (or Moscow, or Munich, or Budapest) metros should not be part of a transport plan for their respective cities, or should not be provided because – as is the fact – they do not 'pay'. But the 'methodological individualists' are plainly mistaken. In virtually any institution, from the state to a firm or a university, it is frequently possible for the perceived interest of the part to conflict with that of the whole. While it is too complex and time-consuming to attempt to 'internalize' all externalities, it is essential to try to identify contradictions and conflicts of interest when these are important, and not to evade the issue by pretending that – with appropriate legal and institutional arrangements – they will not exist. State intervention is one form of dealing with these problems, in the general interest.

Some extreme anti-planners need reminding of the fact that trade-cycles existed even when trade-union powers were minimal, that chronic unemployment may be as irrational a waste of resources as anything that happens in a centrally planned economy. The notion that labour markets 'clear' but for remediable imperfections is surely a myth derived from general-equilibrium analysis. Real competition *requires* unused capacity and necessarily involves winners and losers, otherwise how could competition actually proceed? This is apart from the serious danger of technologically-induced long-term unemployment, which may pose a major threat to overall stability. Yet to combat unemployment by an expansionary policy can engender accelerating inflation unless consideration is given to an incomes policy, itself part of a plan.

It is true that, in the effort to plan and control, major errors have been and could be committed. However, to take one last example, the fact that dreadful mistakes in town-planning have occurred does not prove that no town-planning powers should reside in public authorities.

The whole subject remains highly controversial, and ideologies of both left and right heavily influence both policies and theoretical formulations. At present in many Western and third-world countries it is the advocates of planning that are fighting a rearguard battle.

11 Markets? Yes, but . . .*

Historians of economic ideas, and of economic policy, will have some difficulty in understanding or explaining the way the most influential members of the profession thought in the 1980s. Their perplexity will have a number of aspects: 'naive monetarism' combined with 'rational expectations' will make little sense to them, especially when they observe the high rates of unemployment of material and human resources, the misuse (or non-use) of windfall oil revenues, the zigzag and unpredictable (and unpredicted) course of material and energy prices, the behaviour of foreign exchanges and of interest rates. They will puzzle about the resurrection of nineteenth-century *laissez-faire*, the emphasis in university courses on general-equilibrium theories based upon 'perfect competition', at a time of market-dominating giants. They will be surprised at the overwhelming success of mathematical and econometric models, despite the total irrelevance of most of them to the real world. They will learn also of efforts of some of the best minds of the profession to challenge these trends, and will puzzle over their relative failure to make much headway against the current.

Consider what has happened to oil revenues. Future generations may well say: surely such a windfall could have been utilized, at least in part, to modernize Britain's productive capacity, infrastructure, the quality of life? How was it possible that *nothing* was earmarked for any of these purposes? And this at a time when resources, material and human, were rather drastically underemployed, and when state policy was directed towards limiting or cutting public investment expenditures. Oil revenues pushed up the value of the pound, contributed to falling competitiveness and to the reduction of manufacturing output, and to a balance of payments surplus. It was known to all that oil revenues would probably begin to taper off in a decade or so. Meanwhile there was a massive outflow of funds into investment abroad, while British productive capacity contracted.

---

* Reprinted from *Economic Affairs*, January–March 1985.

EXAMINE HEADS

Obviously, investments abroad have their advantages and do provide for a flow of future revenue which could offset a predictable worsening of the visible trade balance. It is the very modest scale of investments at home that is the problem. Some fashionable economists, Tim Congdon, for example, seem remarkably complacent about what future generations might well view as supremely irrational behaviour. Suppose a large corporation obtained a windfall profit and considered it appropriate to use it to invest in developing the productive capacity of its competitors. Surely we would consider that its managing director needed his head examining? It might have to be explained that these species of economists (like some IEA authors?) believe, in an extreme form, in 'methodological individualism' ('the nation ultimately consists of individuals and *nothing* else', to cite Congdon – my emphasis), *and* in the self-evident coincidence of the general interest with the short-term interest of individuals. It seems not to be appreciated by such economists that such a coincidence is not guaranteed at any time, but common sense suggests that it is scarcely consistent with the existing degree of uncertainty and historically very high real interest rates, which shorten the time-horizon of profit-seeking businessmen. There is no reason for a rational individual businessman to worry about Britain's longer-term productive capacity – but surely a government must. True, it might be objected that the time-horizon of politicians can also be short ('to win the next election'), but is it not our duty to look ahead, and not blithely assume that market forces will take care of all our problems. Myopia is neither a private nor a public good.

Incidentally, would Congdon and those who think like him assert that a *firm* 'ultimately consists of individuals and *nothing* else', and that therefore the pursuit of their own short-term advantage by each of the firm's employees is necessarily and always consistent wih the interest of the firm as a whole? *Reductio ad absurdum*, is it not, outside an imaginary textbook world? (Why is it that firms exist at all?)

In their 'monetarist' perspective, such economists seem unable to distinguish different species of state expenditures, as is illustrated by the accepted current definition of the Public Sector Borrowing Requirement (PSBR). Both in its causes and in its effects it seems somewhat self-evident that investment expenditure by the electricity or gas industry is different from borrowing to cover social security or civil service salaries, and in most countries they are treated quite separately; why should a productive investment which is economically justifiable be cut in order to get the PSBR to some desired figure? Would a private firm treat similarly borrowing to modernize the plant and an overdraft to cover current operating losses?

'NAIVE' MONETARISM

There is, of course, no necessary connection between a consciousness of the importance of money supply and *laissez-faire* ideology. Several Soviet works have recently expressed alarm about the excessive creation of money (via rapidly-expanding bank credits) in the Soviet economy. One can believe (or not) in a major economic role for the state, and be equally concerned to combat inflation. That inflation and the expansion of the money supply are intimately related has, of course, been known for hundreds of years. 'Naive monetarism' I would define as, firstly, a willingness to be satisfied with superficial explanations, a lack of concern for causes. To 'explain' inflation by the increase in money supply is to attribute the failure of a firm to the (undeniable) fact that its revenues were exceeded by its expenditure. There is also the dubious assumption, not made by past generations of monetary theorists, that velocity of circulation remains constant in the short run, which is important in the context of trying to control the quantity of money. Very relevant here is what has come to be known as 'Goodhart's Law': when something is controlled or becomes a target, it ceases to be a good measure.

The other aspect of 'naive monetarism' is connected with the belief of its main proponents in elementary *laissez-faire*, in the magic powers of market-clearing prices, in an automatic equilibrating mechanism which is supposed to operate satisfactorily if the supply of money could be controlled and various artificial restrictions removed. This goes with such phrases (in editorials in *The Times*) as 'discredited Keynesian notions of stimulating demand'. One should leave well alone, and then all will come right, as I heard Professor Minford tell the French. On two occasions Tim Congdon took so-called Keynesians to task for their alleged belief that one cannot get out of recession/depression without government intervention, which is more than a little unfair: generations of trade-cycle theorists were concerned with mitigating the ill-effects of down-turns, which can (did, do) have very unfortunate consequences for millions of people of all classes and in many countries, before they were followed by up-turns. How can such economists take on board the fact that American recovery has been accompanied (preceded) by a budget deficit that is an all-time record? How is it possible not to see that a substantial state-financed investment programme can have cumulative effects for the private sector, stimulate private investment, private spending and employment? Is it really necessary to argue against the notion of 'crowding out', meaningless in the context of an under-employed real economy? There is, of course, the problem of the inflationary effects of economic recovery, given the possible response of organized labour. But this would be true of any recovery, howsoever generated.

In this context, too, future generations will be puzzled (and perhaps amused) by that cousin of naive monetarism-cum-*laissez-faire*, 'rational expectations'. We would all accept, needless to say, that expectations affect outcomes, and particularly inflationary expectations. But we are surrounded today by an ocean of uncertainties: possible variations in the size of the US budget deficit, interest rates, exchange rates, prices of energy and materials, all are of sufficient importance to have effects on the macroeconomy – national income, expenditure, investment, etc. Rational people can and do have different expectations (and different theories about the effects of expectations!), which is indeed why there are buyers *and* sellers in currency and stock markets. We do not all operate on the same theoretical assumptions; we all have only partial knowledge. Not all share the associated belief in the magic properties of market-clearing prices for factors of production. It makes no sense to assert that government cannot affect outcomes 'unless it takes people by surprise', if by 'outcomes' is meant the real economy. A decision to modernize Britain's roads, docks and railways, whether right or wrong, whether anticipated or unanticipated, would have quite considerable effects on output and employment. Unless, that is, we assume we are already at a 'natural' rate of employment and unemployment, or have donned a monetarist strait-jacket and are thereby compelled to assume that any expenditures on anything must be at the expense of something else (probably more rational), within a given money supply (whether the economy is operating at 99 per cent or 55 per cent of capacity).

I wonder how those who believe in the self-righting nature of disequilibria can analyze regional problems which resolutely resist 'automatic' correction: in Italy, say, or Mexico, or Yugoslavia, or nearer home. The collapse of British ship-building has profound effects on the economy of Clydeside and Tyneside, which are doubtless expressing themselves in a reduction in demand for money by both individuals and businesses in these regions. Needless to say, *if* money supply in these areas did not fall, then one could assume that the 'slack' will have been taken up. But this would be an argument of meaningless circularity.

True, a sovereign state with its own central bank is not a region. Yet, in the absence of exchange controls, a small or medium-sized country shares some of the characteristics of a region. For one thing, as recent critics of Friedman have pointed out, price changes are to some considerable extent due to events outside that country's borders, just as today's interest rates in Britain, France and Italy are a consequence of policy decisions in the US and the size of the US budget deficit. The collapse of key industries can and does have macro effects, as is also obvious in countries which depend heavily on the export of one or two commodities. To regard any disequilibria so occasioned as inherently self-righting is all the odder when we observe what has been happening to the dollar exchange rate.

THEORY BEYOND REASON?

Reasonable and theoretically sustainable ideas can be pushed beyond the bounds of reason:

(a) Rent control has some deplorable effects on the housing market. Agreed – but to imply that the decay of inner cities, slums and over-crowding would all disappear if the free market were allowed to operate flies in the face of experience: there were and are slums where rent control did not and does not exist.
(b) Some who are now unemployed would be working if there were no minimum wage legislation and trade union obstruction. True – but a far cry from treating all unemployment as 'voluntary', or 'full-time job search', as is asserted or implied by many of the 'Chicago' school.
(c) Expectations are an important influence on behaviour and on outcomes, but the 'rational expectation' hypothesis is baseless. 'Real world decision-makers are not trapped as are your "rationally expecting" choosers in a world of pre-ordained equilibrium'.[1]

(d) Money supply matters. Yes – but to say that is all that matters, as policy or as explanation, is another story.
(e) Very high marginal tax returns have disincentive effects and encourage avoidance. True – but even at less high rates tax avoidance flourishes, and it is unfounded assertion to imagine that lower taxes will yield higher revenues, as American experience during the Reagan administration abundantly proves.
(f) Free markets are of real value. Very true – the attempt to replace them by 'planning' is a frequent cause of waste and inefficiency. This is not in dispute. Nor is the proposition that, *prima facie*, a loss-making activity suggests an irrational use of resources. But the IEA 'philosophy' takes these inherently sensible propositions to extremes, by applying them in the 'wrong' situations.

NATURAL MONOPOLIES?

Take the Serpell report on the railways. In virtually every country, it is understood that suburban rapid-transit is vitally important as a means of combating congestion, that the existence of a public transport system benefits also those who do not use it (for otherwise they could not get to their destination in their cars and it affects property values, too); and so there should be a subsidy – though its size is open to discussion. Most transport authorities try to attract the regular traveller by offering big discounts on season tickets. (This device also has the merit of saving time and staff on ticket-issuing.) The point was quite lost on the authors of the Serpell report. They recommended a sharp increase in the already very high charges at peak periods in the London area, at times when people have to go to work, the times at which they need to be attracted away from cars and into public transport. The very object of having a transport system was ignored, and 'efficiency' separated from purpose, that is, from the question 'efficiency for what?' (Imagine a firm judging the performance of its transport department, or of a sub-contractor, without taking into account how its goods were transported!) Inappropriate marginal theory leads to a disregard of 'systemic' elements, a downgrading of externalities, wasteful complexity of the fare structure. In discussing 'hiving off' there seems an inability to distinguish between competition and complementarity. Complementarity and network are ignored, for instance, in the proposal to disrupt urban transport systems which is now before Parliament.

In British Telecom the issue is not essentially one of privatization, but of breaking up what was always regarded as a natural monopoly and a public-service *system*. This is also the case for the postal service. A system with quasi-total coverage based upon standard charges necessarily involves a considerable amount of cross-subsidization: letters and telephone links to Thurso, Caernarfon, Penzance, doubtless cost several times more than those between (say) London, Birmingham and Manchester. Competition will naturally concentrate on undercutting Telecom on the profitable services, with predictable consequences – which can be studied in vivid detail in America, following the ideologically-motivated break-up of the Bell telephone network. Apart from complicating the directories, the billing and much else, it is already leading to a sharp rise in domestic telephone charges, threatening smaller communities with very large increases in costs, in the name of what the president of AT&T called 'the basic rule of competitive pricing: you charge the customer an amount which reflects the costs of providing him with your product or service'.[2] I met only one American who did not express strong disapproval of the break-up of this efficiently-functioning natural monopoly in the name of 'Chicago' economics. How far can one go in disregarding the public-service aspect of public services? What about policy questions with regard to location of population and business outside the largest conurbations? Do we wish to penalize rural areas? (Apparently we do, since by government order there is a policy to close rural post offices if they do not 'pay'.)

Underlying these and other errors of thought is a view of economic theory, a view which rests on a number of simplifying assumptions, legitimate in a textbook, which are improperly applied to the real world. In a textbook world, externalities can be relegated to footnotes, there are innumerable competitors who are price-takers, products are homogenous, entrepreneurs operate with quasi-perfect knowledge, indivisibilities and complementarities can be forgotten, prices play the role assigned to them in theory. Therefore the pursuit of 'profit maximization' leads inescapably to the most rational use of resources and to their full utilization, if only economic forces are allowed to function unhindered by various institutional frictions and imperfections – though this same theory leads to the conclusion that profits fall to zero in equilibrium. As many critics have pointed out (Shackle is perhaps the most pertinacious of them), usually in vain, this is a timeless world of quasi-instantaneous adjustment.

In this world of unreality not only are the uncertainties of everday life absent, but no reason is given that firms should exist at all. Indeed, it is odd that some Marxists still regard the orthodox general-equilibrium theory as 'apologetics for capitalism', when there is in this theory no role for entrepreneurs (which is why their profits become zero), and in effect no competition either, as all capacity is already fully utilized.

IMPERFECT INFORMATION NECESSARY

In vain did G. B. Richardson point out, in a book which was unanswerable,[3] that entrepreneurial action in the real world is rendered possible by *imperfect* information: if all one's competitors were deemed to have exactly the same knowledge as oneself, how could any decision to do or produce anything new ever be profitable? Who would invest on the assumption that the same opportunity is perceived and acted upon by all one's competitors? Richardson, and O. E. Williamson also, asked the question implied by the title of the latter's book, *Markets and Hierarchies*:[4] why in the real world, are some things handled through the market mechanism and others through hierarchical, administered decisions? The question cannot even be posed on the assumptions underlying most microeconomic models.

Uncertainty and indivisibility or lumpiness play the key role in any major investment decision; yet, when discussing investment criteria, we teach our students to pay particular attention to the distinction between internal rates of return and discounted cash-flow, as if there has been a single recorded instance of an investment whose rightness or wrongness could be attributed to this sort of cause. Our textbooks also almost always conflate two very different kinds of investment decisions: those that deal with the question 'what?' (shall we do this) and the question 'how?' (what is the most economical way to achieve a given objective). This is linked with the issue of complementarity, and with efficiency criteria too. Thus, having decided to develop an oilfield, a firm cannot decide not to invest in transport facilities, and its evaluation of alternatives (tankers, pipelines, etc.) is made in the context of the project as a whole. The profit-and-loss account of the transport taken in isolation simply makes no sense.

Which, at long last, brings me to mathematics, or to 'taking the con out of econometrics', to cite the title of an admirable and witty assault on current fashion by Edward E. Leamer.[5] Econometrics, like monetarism, has no necessary connection with *laissez-faire* (though it can be used to sustain *laissez-faire* arguments). In far too many econometric models, hidden assumptions or specifications predetermine the result, whether the model is devised by the Treasury or by its 'Cambridge' critics. Attacks on irrelevant abstract models come from many quarters: Leontief, Meade, Phelps Brown, Bauer. Hayek, too, surely opposes such excessive abstraction from the real world. (If perfect markets, why not perfect planning? Both are equally impossible!) He, and most readers of *Economic Affairs*, would probably agree with Keynes in at least this respect:

> Too large a proportion of recent 'mathematical' economics are mere concoctions, as imprecise as the initial assumptions they rest on, which allow the author to lose sight of the complexities and interdependencies of the real world in a maze of pretentions and unhelpful symbols.

NOTES

1. Peter Earl, *The Economic Imagination* (New York: M. E. Sharpe, 1983) p. 74. This is required reading for believers in orthodoxy.
2. *New York Times*, 12 February 1984.
3. *Information and Investment* (Oxford: Oxford University Press, 1960).
4. The Free Press, New York, 1975.
5. *American Economic Review*, March 1983.

12 Friedman, Markets and Planning: A Comment*

After reading Milton and Rose Friedman's latest book, *The Tyranny of the Status Quo*, the *New York Times* reviewer remarked: 'for Milton Friedman the world is a simple place; if only a robot controlled the money supply . . . the economy would prosper', so long as the government did not interfere. It is this belief in *laissez-faire* which Friedman takes to an extreme. While he is prepared to recognize that 'the market is simply incapable of doing some things', that there are what he calls 'neighbourhood effects' or 'externalities', he at once warns us that 'government attempts to deal with such externalities typically turned out to do more harm than good'. 'Every system', writes Friedman, 'is something of a mixed system', of commands and voluntary cooperation, 'the problem is one of proportion', but he firmly believes in 'keeping commands to a minimum'. As can be seen from the preceding quotation, that minimum is really minimal. National defence is the one exception that he quotes. He is on public record as opposing even the Food and Drug administration. The market will take care of (almost) everything. If one were to accept his assumptions, then indeed deregulation should be the name of the game, and state planning will appear an unnecessary and harmful interference with natural economic laws, whose untrammelled working leads almost by definition to the best of all possible worlds.

What is wrong with his argument? In putting the case against, I am not for one moment counterposing the imperfections that exist in our society with some imaginary perfect planning system, and of course I am well aware of the deficiencies, both of the centralized system of the Soviet type and of self-management *à la* Yugoslavia. Indeed, I have devoted much of my academic life to analyzing the limitations of, and the distortions and inefficiencies engendered by, would-be all-encompassing centralized planning. I agree entirely with Friedman that the attempt to plan all things fails, for the reasons that he advances and a few others too. Informational blockages not only

* Reprinted from Centre for Research in Communist Economies (CRCE), 'Market or Plan', occasional paper, 1984.

prevent the centre from knowing what in terms of its own model it must know; the centre is also frequently incapable of formulating its orders in a comprehensible and unambiguous fashion. At enterprise level orders arrive which are aggregated and contradictory. Aggregated because a fully disaggregated plan would take far too long to formulate ('thousands of years', according to one Soviet academician), contradictory because 'the plan' issues from a large number of different government offices, and therefore the operational microplans for production, material allocation, labour, investment, costs, profits and so on are often mutually inconsistent.

While it is possible to devise a system of material incentives to motivate management, in many instances the incentives have a perverse effect: thus a manager with a plan to fulfil expressed in tons will avoid using light and econometric materials; road transport undertakings with a plan in ton-kilometres will try to send lorries on long journeys with heavy loads. Plans in roubles motivate managers to use dear materials and shift to dearer product variants, and so on. The user (whether an enterprise or a citizen) has far too little influence on what is produced and distributed. The attempt to eliminate the market, which Marx and Engels thought would be a simple matter, has proved to be either impracticable or highly inefficient, or both at once.

Friedman would probably agree with me that some sectors are more amenable to central planning than others. One example is the national electricity grid which exists in many countries. But most of the economy is not in this category. Areas of particular weakness include the diffusion of innovation and also agriculture (though Friedman should not repeat the fallacy about private agricultural plots in Russia: yes, they do occupy only 3 per cent of arable land, and yes, they produce 26 per cent of the output, but two-thirds of it is livestock products, and the livestock is not fed from these plots). The substantial strengthening of the market mechanism is an essential feature of any effective reform in the communist-ruled world.

My problem with Friedman is that he implicitly compares the deficiencies of the Soviet or Yugoslav model with a quasi-perfect market. If indeed it were a fact that externalities were minor exceptions, if oligopoly was only encountered occasionally, if investment decisions were not liable to large and expensive errors, if unemployment was due only to labour-market imperfections, if economies of scale (informational, organizational, technological) did not lead to the emergence of large and economically powerful corporations with powers over prices, if the distribution of property bore any recognizable relationship to present or even past economic merit, then his case would be cast-iron. Yet he well knows that in the real world, to take but one example, would-be investors in the creation of new productive capacity have to make a guess at the future prices of and demand for their product and of their material input, not to mention interest rates, exchange rates, labour costs, other countries' tariff policies . . . To say that there is, or can be, a futures market adequate for this purpose is surely absurd. The number of thousands of bankruptcies which occur each year, involving the dismissal of many more thousands of workers, the closure in Britain of much of the capacity for making steel, aluminium, lorries, paper and ships, can be seen as evidence of resource misallocation in the past. The institution of bankruptcy is indeed a method for dealing with misallocation and inefficiency, and its virtual absence in 'eastern' countries is a source of weakness. But to invest massively in capacity which is consigned to the scrapyard soon after it becomes operational is not quite what we mean by efficient use of resources either. Perfect foresight is an unreal and unreasonable assumption, as is 'actuarial' or insurable uncertainty. Of course, the existence of risk is recognized by Friedman, and so is the fact that risk involves the possibility of failure. But orthodox textbooks tend silently to assume 'perfect competition' in the sense that the entrepreneurs are price-takers, that errors made by a multitude of producers in some sense cancel out. This is not quite what we see if, to take an example from Britain today, a large part of total capacity to produce lorries and buses is closed down, with disastrous consequences for towns and families, and perhaps also for the future balance of payments. The decisive factors could well be quite beyond the control (and rational expectations) of management and workforce alike.

Friedman naturally recognizes that markets are far from perfect, that there are distortions due to monopoly, inflation and huge budget deficits. In his sort of world these things would not be, and prices and interest rates would play the equilibrating role assigned to them by theory. In his (and his wife's) latest book the idea was mooted of a constitutional amendment to outlaw (literally) excessive money creation and deficits, though it is hard to see how, in a democracy, one can prevent by law a majority vote in favour of policies of which Friedman disapproves. Nor is it a matter of right versus left: record deficits have been achieved under some right wing administrations, while Soviet and Chinese policy-makers, whatever their other deficiencies, seek monetary and fiscal balance, even if they do not achieve it. The point is: are the so-called imperfections avoidable in the real world, and, secondly, are they 'imperfections' anyway, or are they necessary for the functioning of the system? For example, G. B. Richardson argued that imperfect information, or collusion, are preconditions for making investment decisions. If everyone was equally well informed of the opportunity, it would not seem profitable for anyone to take it. It is arguable, of course, that the various deficiencies of a free-enterprise system are a price well worth paying for securing the advantages which it gives. Such a cost-benefit analysis may indeed work out in a way favourable to Friedman's conclusions. But cost as well as benefit must be counted.

Let me look more closely at a few of Friedman's propositions, beginning with his view of freedom. He makes the parallel between a command economy and an army. He seems to regard only government commands as commands. Labour contracts freely entered into he sees as 'voluntary co-operation'. Freely-negotiated contracts cannot be a zero-sum game but must benefit both parties. All these propositions have merit, but some of their implications can be questioned, so let me question them.

First of all, *most* people have to obey orders. This is particularly obvious in the army; even in a volunteer army the soldier voluntarily undertakes to obey commands. One obeys also in hierarchically structured corporations. It is clearly of importance to stress that in our society people have choice as between different employers, that is, they can choose within limits *whom* to obey, while in the Soviet system virtually everyone has to work for the state (with some limited choice as to which of a large number of state enterprises he or she works in). But must we not recognize that we cannot confine the term 'command' to government commands? Employees of a Soviet and of a Western factory have to obey those placed over them. The similarity dismays idealistic socialists who thought it would be otherwise, but that is another story. Milton Friedman and I, in our different ways, are among the fortunate few who need obey only themselves.

Secondly, yes, freely-negotiated contracts are not to be seen as a zero-sum game, but must clearly benefit both parties. But one can easily imagine institutional and legal settings in which a contract could be seen by all the readers of this page, including Friedman, to be none the less quite improper and inequitable.

In the days of serfdom in Russia, for instance, it is recorded that serfs who succeeded in business bought their freedom for up to

40 000 gold roubles. This clearly benefited both the owner and the former serf and was thus not a zero-sum game. Yet the legal situation which made the deal possible would still be condemned by us as ethically intolerable. In the British Army until 1870 officers *bought* their commissions: you could become a major by purchasing the vacancy from the major that occupied it. Again, we have a voluntary contract benefiting both parties, but Friedman and I would doubtless agree that it was right to end the purchase of commissions. If it is true (as Beaumarchais and others claimed) that in the eighteenth century lords of the manor could assert the *jus primae noctis*, then payment to the lord by the prospective husband to persuade him to forego that right was a mutually beneficial transaction. If there were a law requiring junior staff in our universities to hand over half of their earnings from publication to their heads of department, then, within such a law, junior lecturers would still be voluntarily entering into mutually beneficial contracts with publishers.

It may be objected that these are fantastical examples, relating to circumstances that do not exist. Yes, but I imagined them to illustrate the proposition that it is not enough just to say that, within a given institutional setting, a contract voluntarily entered into benefits both parties. The given institutional and legal setting *may* be one which gives rise to incomes which bear no relation to any significant productive contribution of some individuals or groups, and open to challenge also on grounds of principle.

A much more realistic example may be cited. Suppose that most of the land in Great Britain (or a Latin-American country) belongs to great landlords, whose families acquired this land centuries ago, either by conquest or by performing valued services (sometimes in bed) to long-dead monarchs. Anyone desiring to use this land must pay them for so doing. They become exceedingly rich, by doing nothing at all. Given existing laws and property distribution, this may seem perfectly rational, yet cannot Friedman appreciate that those who have not inherited thousands of acres of valuable land might not see it that way? All this is not an argument against charging rent or having a market for land. It rather relates to the consequences of initially highly unequal property distribution.

It *was* a fact of history that Scottish landlords ordered their crofter-tenants off the land they have lived on for centuries in the rightly infamous Highland clearances. Given the system of tenure, it was a procedure seen (by the landlords and most contemporary economists) as both rational and efficient. The landlords found that sheep were more profitable than clansmen. Yet it could be argued that forcible expulsion and forcible collectivization are forms of coercion, one in the name of the rights of private property and the other in the name of its elimination. One can be justifiably indignant about both, even if one believes in the necessity of a market mechanism, as I most certainly do.

Situations of this kind can still arise in the third world, and can justify government intervention with the rights of private property. Surely one can and should recognize that human freedom and enterprise are highly limited if one is a labourer on a big estate, rather than a land-owning peasant. Also in industry and in retail distribution the decline of the small independent entrepreneur, his replacement by big corporations, has effects both on human freedom (a larger proportion of the population is 'under command') and on the applicability of conventional theory (more of the economy and of prices are administered). This is not a disguised or indirect apologia for what happens in the USSR. Far from it, the more so as they quite ruthlessly eliminated the property-owning peasant and small businesses by police measures. It serves only to remind us that any system, or indeed any major decision, contains costs as well as benefits, and it behoves us all to be conscious of this, and not see only the one or the other as it suits us.

However, let us now pass to considering workers' cooperatives as a form of economic organization. That 'self-management' in Yugoslavia suffers from grave defects of many kinds is not here in dispute, certainly not by me. But let me try to explain why the standard economic arguments against the self-management *model* may be less powerful than might appear. Let us assume that self-managed enterprises operate under conditions of (real) competition and that there is freedom of entry, that is, new enterprises can be set up.

It is true that each worker receives what Friedman calls 'a share of the property income accruing to the enterprise', instead of this being appropriated by the owner. It is also true that, if the enterprise is successful, the workers would be reluctant to recruit additional labour, under conditions in which it would pay a capitalist employer to do so. In Ward's 'Illyrian' model, when the price goes up it might seem that it would 'pay' the worker-managed enterprise to shed labour and reduce output, but this would hardly happen under real, as distinct from 'perfect', competitive conditions: customers once lost might not be regained; prices that go up can in due course come down! (Friedman does show that he is aware of the importance of 'consumer goodwill'). None the less he, and other analysts, see labour-managed cooperatives as inherently inefficient. Maybe, but let us make a not too far-fetched parallel.

Suppose that there were, in Chicago today, a successful cooperative of (say) ten lawyers or ten business consultants. They enjoy high incomes. Maybe it is true that, if each business were owned by one man, who employed the rest on fixed salaries, he would expand the business more readily by employing more lawyers or consultants. But let us introduce the notions of producer preference, or producer goodwill. It may well be that the quality of the work benefits from the fact that the partners are real partners, that they participate in running the business, and this has effects also on efficiency. Would Friedman condemn the partnership on grounds of formal principle, as inherently inefficient? Of course, the success of the enterprises in question may be due not only to the scarce talent of the consultants or lawyers, it may be a quasi-rent arising from the temporary scarcity of legal or consultancy firms. In the latter case, surely others would seek to set up similar firms, and by their competition bring down earnings to more normal levels? I acknowledge that I am deliberately strengthening my case by choosing the type of firm that needs relatively modest amounts of capital, but it does illustrate a principle which ought to have some appeal to a real libertarian: we should try to aim at a social order in which there is not only freedom to buy and sell in a market, but also one in which we can exercise some influence on our work and environment. Whatever may be the failings of the Yugoslav model and of Yugoslav experience – and there are many failings – a real libertarian ought not lightly to reject participation, whether in the affairs of one's community or the workplace, even though it does sometimes obscure lines of responsibility and present problems of rewarding risk-taking and penalizing failure.

One point is also worth making in this connection. Friedman correctly points out that 'older workers' would not favour investments that would not pay off for ten or fifteen years, preferring 'current benefits', since they cannot carry any capital assets away with them when they retire. This is indeed a problem in Yugoslavia. But I learn (and perhaps Friedman has also learned) that the average American corporation executive stays with his corporation for little over five years (unlike his Japanese equivalent, whose commitment to his firm is virtually for life). So, unless the executive has a sizeable shareholding in his corporation, his time-horizon may also not extend to ten or fifteen years. He may be preferring a spectacular short-term profit strategy, which will result in an offer from another corporation. Is this necessarily 'efficient'? Have there not been some studies, for instance by Seymour Mellman, suggesting rather strongly that, in their obsession with short-term profits, many American executives have failed as *managers*? Salaried managers and executives do have some considerable influence on corporate decision-making, and it may be useful to see their status, with regard to a frequently remote headquarters, as having some similarity with that of a manager in a communist country in relation to *his* frequently remote headquarters. The manager of a supermarket in Chicago is no more an owner than is the manager of a supermarket in Kiev. He is, admittedly, running a much more efficient operation, but this may have some causes unconnected directly with ownership, such as competition. The point of this and of so many other of my comments relates to the need to compare the imperfections of the USSR or Yugoslavia (which are indeed many) with the real societies of the West or 'South' and not with the model of a smoothly-functioning free-market economy of the textbook imagination.

Similarly, there appears to be a silent assumption that only *public* waste is waste. What of vastly expensive *private* follies? Or would he regard the latter as, by definition, the legitimate and proper manifestation of individual consumer preference, whatever it might be? It is a point of view that will not necessarily commend itself to the poor in a country with very unequal property distribution.

The 'functions of prices' do indeed include vitally important transmission of information. The price mechanism is a 'must'. Yet was not Janos Kornai right in asserting, in his challenging *Anti-equilibrium*, that few decision-makers can act on the basis of price information alone, and this is evidently true of major investment decisions? A brief reference by Friedman to the existence of futures markets is surely a quite inadequate way of taking care of the vital factor of uncertainty. Decisions taken today relate to the future, and freedom of choice is inherently inconsistent with perfect foresight. We live in a world in which prices of basic commodities and energy, interest rates and the rate of exchange have varied abruptly and unpredictably, and seem likely to do so in the future. A country – let us call it the United States – might be running a huge foreign-trade deficit and by far the largest budget deficit known in human peace-time history and the government may or may not follow sound advice (e.g. from Friedman) and do something about it, thereby affecting thousands of decisions on resource allocation around the globe, which in turn affect the livelihood of maybe millions of people.

Of course Friedman is aware that mistakes can be made, by 'capitalists' as well as by planners. But to repeat a point made earlier, the degree and nature of the uncertainty which faces a would-be investor today are on a scale which renders correct or rational decisions less than probable.

But let us return to our main theme. Is a democratic kind of 'market socialism' feasible? Would it necessarily have the defects seen in models of the Lange–Lerner kind? Would these defects be graver than those which affect us today? Certainly the existing centralized systems are notably less efficient than our own, in that they are demonstrably more wasteful in achieving their own objectives (while we seem to be much more efficient in achieving objectives which are sometimes wasteful). Furthermore, centralization of economic planning leads to a dangerous concentration of power at the centre, with consequences which I deplore as much as Friedman does. In my book, *Economics of Feasible Socialism*, I imagine the existence of five kinds of producer: a few centralized state enterprises where there is monopoly power combined with economies of scale (e.g. electricity, telephones), self-managed enterprises in a competitive market situation (socially-owned with an elected management), co-operative enterprises (owned by the members), and small owner-managed private enterprise, plus individuals (writers, craftsmen, artists, consultants, etc.). In the case of the centralized monopolies, it would not be correct, *pace* Friedman, merely to set them 'generalized targets in profits or money' since they could achieve these targets at the expense of the customer; there would have to be duties, that is, they would be called upon to carry out specific tasks or purposes with limits on prices. (One of my first jobs after graduation, as research assistant to Robert E. Cushman, who was writing a book entitled *Independent Regulatory Commissions*, taught me about regulation of privately-owned public utilities in the United States which was introduced when *laissez-faire* was dominant; and the same need to regulate arises if the utilities are nationalized and told to aim at profits.)

But the larger part of the provision of goods and services would be the task of enterprises operating in the market under competition, with material incentives linked to the satisfaction of demand at least cost. It should be possible to link the long-term interests of the employees with the longer-term future of a 'self-managed' enterprise by some sort of lump-sum payments related to length of service and to the appreciation of the enterprise's assets, analogous to the 'with-profits' policies offered by insurance companies. Opportunities for small-scale entrepreneurship would exist, on a scale equal if not superior to those that exist today. The last chapter of my book is devoted to a rough sketch of such an economy.

Friedman would probably concentrate his critical fire on the problem of risk capital, but perhaps our most serious disagreement would relate to those areas of human activity which would be wholly or partly excluded from the market. How far should 'deregulation' go? When drafting this paper, I read in the *New York Times* (25 February 1984), the following report of an oil pipeline explosion in a shanty-town in Brazil:

> Cubatao, just off the Sao Paulo–Santos highway, is one of the world's most polluted cities . . . Twenty-three factories, many producing petro-chemicals, belch fumes into clouds over the town. Thousands of trees stand bare over the surrounding hills, and occasional pools of waste in the area smoke. Birth defects and other health problems among the population, estimated at 90 000, are abnormally high.

I am aware that pollution has not been effectively combated in many communist-ruled countries, but my point is simple: that crusades for deregulation, against government interference, strengthen the hands of those who, in Brazil and elsewhere, prefer to let such scandalous conditions continue and profit by their continuance.

Likewise, what of parks and recreational facilities? To take another comparatively recent example: before the Second World War empty moorland near some of Britain's industrial cities was barred to walkers because the landowners wished to use it for grouse-shooting. (I recall as a student being chased off a hill near Sheffield by a gamekeeper.) Now much of this land is the equivalent of a national park, with free access for the public. Is this to be seen as unwarranted government interference, a step on the road to serfdom? Would this apply also to America's rightly famous national parks? Would Friedman say that America's welfare would increase if they were sold to private individuals? In his terms, why not? And what of urban transport, education, health? At a recent conference on health economies held in Italy, there was a noticeable split between Europeans (East *and* West) and Americans on the issue of the role of the profit motive in what we sometimes call 'the caring professions'.

This raises a point of fundamental substance. It was Schumpeter who wrote: 'No social system can work which is based exclusively upon a network of free contract between (legally) equal contracting parties, and in which everyone is supposed to be guided by nothing except his own short-term utilitarian interest.' The key words are 'nothing except'. Doctors, and also actors, editors, playwrights, economists, chemists, and for that matter skilled workers, do seek material rewards and are right to do so. But there are other qualities: integrity, pride in a job well done. It may be profitable to become a prostitute, literally or figuratively; a corrupt judge or police officer may be better off than his honest colleague; the pornographer makes more money than the poet. The aim cannot always be only profit maximization. In some activities these distinctions matter more than in others. It is entirely reasonable for a tailor or butcher to measure his professional efficiency and success in terms of profit. But we would expect a doctor to come to the aid of a distressed child without first inquiring into the income of its parents. It is also worth noting that the 'market' for medical services is inevitably distorted by two other factors: the relative ignorance of the purchasers about the effectiveness of alternative treatments, and the fact that an error may have drastic consequences ('death is so permanent'). This is very different to the situation of a would-be purchaser of trousers or of meat, where the assumption of quasi-perfect knowledge on the part of the consumer is a reasonable one to make.

Needless to say, I am aware that much is amiss in many of these respects in Eastern Europe. Doctors are poorly paid and accept what amount to bribes, conformist authors make thousands of roubles out of literary prostitution, managers and workers are frustrated because of over-centralization or material shortages, and so on. This is *not* an essay in comparative economic systems. My aim is only to challenge what appears to me to be Friedman's complacency, as a theoretician and as purveyor of advice. 'Markets clear' only on far-fetched assumptions not satisfied in the real world. A market economy may be a necessary condition for human freedom, but it is certainly not a sufficient condition. In many countries its maintenance seems to require military dictatorship or even death squads. A free market provides some irreplaceable advantages, but does not solve all problems. State intervention can and sometimes does have negative consequences, but universal deregulation is no panacea.

13 The Fragmentationist Disease

While public attention has been focussed on the issue of privatization, another aspect of government policy has not received the attention it deserves. This is its tendency to fragment. One sees this in a variety of areas: public transport, local government, the BBC, schools, the electricity grid. This is partially explicable by the desire to stimulate competition, and/or by consciousness that there are dangers in turning public monopoly into private monopoly. However there seems to be a marked tendency to ignore the costs of such a solution, a neglect of the importance of system, network, interdependencies and complementarities. At the same time, an over-simplified theory of monopoly is combined with a downgrading of the concept of public service, of the external effects inherent in infrastructure, and of the relationship between efficiency and purpose. What could be called 'myopic marginalism' in combination with extremes of methodological individualism can lead to policy errors which it is the purpose of this chapter to examine.

Arthur Koestler, in his *Janus*, warned of two philosophical extremes: one sees the part only as a unit within a whole, which can lead to totalitarianism; the other regards the whole as only the sum of its parts, which leads to failure to see the wood for the trees. When this is accompanied by the delusion that firms in the real world undertake only activities and transactions which are *as such* profitable, the stage is set for ideologically-motivated errors which are not encountered in other conservative-ruled countries, where ultra-'liberal' think-tanks either do not exist or are not listened to.

Textbooks' oversimplifications are partly to blame. Models are built around firms that are one-dimensional in two senses. Firstly, they make one clearly-defined product of a given quality. Secondly, as Leijonhufvud has pointed out, the neoclassical production function 'does not describe production as a process, that is as an ordered sequence of operations'.[1] Real firms usually make many products (or variants of the same product), through time, in stages, which can include storage, transportation and after-sales service, with dimensions additional to quantity and price, such as punctuality, reliability, durability, sharpness, accuracy, freshness or other quality aspects. Firms' operations react upon each other in a variety of ways, either directly during the process of production, or indirectly through goodwill, reputation, and/or what I once analyzed under the heading of 'internal economies'.[2] This repeatedly causes firms to undertake some activities which, if costed separately and isolated from other transactions, would seem to be loss-making and thus 'cross-subsidized'. The analytical gap was well analyzed by Brian Loasby: 'Highly complex sub-systems, such as firms or even whole sectors of the economy, containing within themselves many layers of great complexity, are regularly treated as simple elements, while components of a complex system are analyzed as isolated units'.[3] Peter Earl made the same point even more succinctly: 'The neo-classical theorist sees aggregated concepts as if they are simply the sum of their component elements.'[4]

Goodwill is seldom even mentioned in microeconomic textbooks. This could be due to its irrelevance both under perfect competition (when, at the given price, one can sell anything one produces) and under pure monopoly. Also to recognize its existence could confuse the presentation of conventional marginal analysis by suggesting that the very word 'margin' needs to be discussed, qualified, seen as multi-level, not one-dimensional. Indeed, to a hierarchy of function in a firm corresponds a hierarchy of margins. It is *because* the interests of the part and the interests of the whole may diverge that there *is* a hierarchy; it is this, and not just 'transaction costs', which explains why firms exist. But to acquire and maintain goodwill involves a *cost*, that is, undertaking actions which would otherwise *not* be profitable, and therefore would not be undertaken by a profit-orientated undertaking which did not fear the consequences: possible loss of business to a competitor. This is (*inter alia*) why after-sales service, never profitable in itself, is notoriously lacking in the USSR.

Other examples of 'internalities', or of complementarities, abound in real life. A supermarket may have a free or a subsidized car-park. A railway may provide free or 'loss-making' lavatories. A hotel located on an island may provide (or hire) a boat which is either free or subsidized. A holiday island may be served by an airport or a ferry which, like the car-park, is administered with both eyes on its primary purpose, which is to bring tourists to the hotels. A shop or restaurant, in deciding what goods to stock or what sort of menu to offer, would take into account the assortment that best suits the segment of the market it aims at, even if some items move slowly and are not profitable if viewed in isolation.

The car-park and ferry are examples of infrastructure, and infrastructure by definition must be deemed to have external effects which do not find full recognition in its own profit-and-loss account. If this is to be seen as involving irrational 'cross-subsidization', then few are free of guilt. Why, it may be asked, are all airports in the United States in the public sector? Clearly, because, while seeking to be efficient, the airport management at Pittsburgh (say) has specific responsibilities to the businesses and citizens of Pittsburgh which do not necessarily coincide with the maximization of the airport's own profitability. Why is almost every urban transport network in the world (a) publicly owned and (b) subsidized? Presumably because it is realized that:

(1) The beneficiaries of public transport include many who do not use it, because of the effect on congestion, and on property values. A clear case of externality.
(2) Urban transport is a *network*, best managed as such and subsidized *as a whole*. The idea that one can disassemble the network and (where necessary) subsidize separate routes, while outlawing cross-subsidization, would be regarded as preposterous outside the odd world inhabited by British ministers and their ideological advisers.
(3) Efficiency in this and in similar instances cannot be separated from purpose. No firm with a transport department would separately assess its profitability and efficiency without taking into account the punctual delivery of its goods.

Thus if, say, a brewery is seeking to organize the delivery of its beer to a few hundred outlets, it may choose to own all or most delivery lorries or hire sub-contractors, but in either case it is responsible, it is in charge of the operation. It does not leave the whole process to the automatically functioning forces of free competition. The ideologists who advise the government on public transport do not see this, and not only advocate privatization but also deprive the local transport authority of responsibility for the system. The separate assessment of the separate routes ('no cross-subsidization') makes no sense outside their world. Can one imagine transport in Washington, Toronto, Paris or Munich being fragmented in this way?

When there is a network with any standardized fare structure (with prepayment, tokens, commuter tickets, or whatever it might be, valid for the network or by zone), how is 'cross-subsidization' to be avoided? And is it not wrong in principle to consider (say) route 40 or a single metro line other than in the context of the network within which it operates? A letter in the *Scotsman*[5] asks how one can cope, with the 'newly deregulated bus services' in Edinburgh, with 'the problems of the sort posed by the bus stance in Chambers Street, which bears sixty different numbers, many of them duplicated, belonging to five different operators, but with no information as to the places they serve'. No more system maps, or exhibited timetables. Ideologically-engineered chaos, unknown in other countries of any political complexion. In Glasgow deregulation was followed by a sharp rise in congestion, as all the competing buses tried to use the same main streets at the same time.

The so-called Adam Smith Institute has also proposed that trains be run on (publicly-owned) tracks by competing companies – not as an exception (such as a special Pullman luxury service, or a train operated for a holiday firm) but as a replacement for the existing network of services. Again, disintegration is the name of the game. Conceptually, the 8.30 train to Manchester is a separate company, separately evaluated. Responsibility for the network disappears. This is the ideologically-motivated externalization of internalities.

Indeed, the separation of efficiency from purpose goes far even in totally non-commercial contexts. Thus the *Observer*[6]: 'The office of Arts and Libraries won't discuss what museums and galleries are actually *for* when determining "performance indicators".'

Here again, myopic marginalism and fragmented thinking dominate. Is one to evaluate the Uffizi gallery, or a cultural festival, only in terms of its own revenue, ignoring not only the value of art as such but also the extra revenue accruing to hotels and shops of Florence or of Edinburgh ('cross-subsidization' again?). Presumably such economists would condemn as 'irrational' the payments made by American municipalities to attract Republican or Democratic conventions to their cities.

Let me stress the question of public utility or public service efficiency criteria. Efficiency cannot be detached from the question of function, of purpose; 'efficiency for what'. For reasons already explored, any monopolist can improve financial results by worsening quality (or charging higher prices, or both). This would lead to losses if there were competition. From this the 'libertarian' thinkers could conclude that the solution is competition. However this runs into the problem of the natural monopoly, or into the fact that in some circumstances competition is wasteful or would tend to destroy the advantages of system, of having a managed network. This seems everywhere to be recognized (outside British government circles) for urban transportation, though the case is weaker for inter-city buses: thus, while a publicly-owned monopoly runs transport in New York and Washington, there is competition on the route *between* New York and Washington, since the network element is less significant. It is *prima facie* wasteful to lay parallel competing networks of water pipes, gas pipes, telephone lines, electricity transmission lines, or to have competing postmen delivering letters from Birmingham to Edinburgh. But we must never forget that private or public monopolist corporations will only have two reasons for *not* worsening service: a sense of duty to the public, or minimum standards imposed by a supervisory body equipped with teeth.

Otherwise it will speedily be found that rural post offices are loss-making, that urban ones yield a higher profit when customers stand in long lines all day. British Telecom has duly noted that telephone directories do not 'pay', so it has ceased to provide them to post offices, so that (unlike the situation in other countries) the traveller who arrives in a strange city has literally nowhere where he can consult a telephone book. A charge is to be made for directory inquiries. And industrial customers of British Gas have much to complain about too.

A few years ago I wrote: 'Who would advocate the break-up of the electricity grid? Not even Sir Keith Joseph.' I reckoned without the impact of ideology. Mr Parkinson *does* wish to break it up. The incredible has become possible. It is said that the nation-wide estimates of future demand have been mistaken. But without a nation-wide generating authority, there could be no estimates at all. If there are several independent producers, how can the needed investment decisions be taken? Frank Hahn once wrote that 'under perfect competition investment is profoundly mysterious'.

To take a public-transport example: DC Transit (Washington) invests in a metro extension because it knows that there will not be competing buses running parallel to the new route (while feeder services will be provided). The decision is taken by the transport planning authority, responsible also for seeking to reduce congestion in the centre of the city. Were it otherwise, it would be irrational to make the investment. Suppose that ten separate electricity generating companies supplied current to the national grid. Whose task would it be to estimate the demand for electricity in ten years' time? Whose responsibility to invest in new capacity? The government's advisers seem unable to grasp that these points have substance.

They also accept (what I hope is) a caricature of James Buchanan's view of public service or of duty to the public. It is correct to warn that public servants have interests of their own, which may well diverge from the (often ill-defined) public interest. It is quite another to assert (as I heard Dr Giersch assert at a conference) that 'it has been shown that public servants have no concern for the common weal'. It is surely more realistic to note that many officials identify with the interests of the segment for which they are responsible, be it nursery schools, artillery, libraries, tax-collecting or nature conservancy, and not only because to do so might advance their careers. There is a deplorable lack of understanding of the importance of pride in a job well done, loyalty, commitment (a mistake no Japanese would make), and this is equally important to the private as well as to the public sector. A fire chief takes pride in speedily putting out a fire, a ship designer in the quality of the ship he designs, the head of Glasgow's (excellent) parks department in the quality of Glasgow parks, and this not (or not only) because the effect could be to earn a bonus or promotion. Nor is this 'altruism'.

Norman Lear[7] cited a number of *conservative* American thinkers to the effect that excesses of 'materialistic hedonism' have led 'the free enterprise system to subvert the very values that help to sustain it – such values as social conscience, pride in one's work, commitment to community, loyalty to company . . .'. Short-term profit is all that matters. 'A commercial system needs taming and correcting by a moral–cultural system independent of commerce' (this 'quote' is from Michael Novack).

Lastly, some remarks about economic theory. I agree with Harold Demsetz (in his 'Theory of the firm revisited', mimeo) that 'perfect competition is an ineffective model for studying the firm', because it is really 'perfect decentralization'. 'The absence of substantive managed coordination is the *sine qua non* of the perfect decentralization model.' He (and I) argue that to base the theory of the firm on transaction costs, as Coase and Williamson do, is 'much too narrow'. He went on: 'All coordination is managed through conscious direction: managed coordination exists not solely because transaction cost is positive . . ., but because coordination is generally productive.' Not only are tasks not infinitely divisible, but the choice of what transaction to undertake is a function of firm's strategy, of its chosen role in the market. Just as within any organization what seems rational to do depends in part on the area of responsibility of the decision-maker. Obvious? Not to those who believe that the whole is *only* the sum of its parts, that each transaction is or should be separately evaluated in terms of its separate profitability, and that organizational structures do not affect decisions as to resource allocation.

It is not my contention that orthodox neoclassical economics is directly responsible for the policy errors here analyzed. Rather it is that the normal textbook predisposes its readers to certain misunderstandings by not warning them about the limitations of the theories. Some leading practitioners do warn. Thus Hahn has written: 'The analysis of the invisible hand in motion is still well beyond us';[8] Radner that 'the theory of the internal economy of the firm is in its infancy'.[9] However the reader of mainstream textbooks will not have his or her attention drawn to the inherent ambiguity of the concept 'margin', to the multidimensional nature of most firms, to the elements of system, to the effects of institutions upon decision-making, the effect of monopoly power upon quality, or to the extent to which 'cross-subsidization' in some form occurs within many firms much of the time. So the textbooks, if not actually predisposing the reader to certain kinds of error, do not equip him or her to identify them when they occur in real life.

NOTES

1. Capitalism and the factory system', in Langlois (ed.), *Economics as a Process* (Cambridge: CUP) 1986, p. 203.
2. A. Nove, 'Internal economies', *Economic Journal*, vol. LXXIX, p. 847, 1969.
3. B. Loasby, *Choice, Complexity and Ignorance* (Cambridge: CUP, 1976) p. 30.
4. P. Earl, *The Economic Imagination* (Armonk, N.Y.: ME Sharpe, 1983), p. 61.
5. *Scotsman*, 29 July 1987.
6. *Observer*, 23 August 1987.
7. *Los Angeles Times*, 15 March 1987.
8. *Economic Journal*, no. 97, Supplement, p. 14.
9. *Economic Journal*, no. 96, Supplement, p. 3.

14 Marxism and 'Really Existing Socialism'*

CRITERIA

What is the connection between the Soviet system, as developed under Stalin and as modified since his death, and the socialism envisaged by Marx? That there are differences is, of course, both obvious and inevitable, and this for several reasons. Firstly, Marx nowhere systematically set out any 'blueprint' of a socialist future, and indeed considered such exercises to be futile and even reactionary. His refusal to give any detailed description of a future world was no doubt part of his sincere conviction that *his* ideas on socialism were quite distinct from those whom he called utopian socialists. Secondly, Marx has been dead for over a hundred years, and even his most fervent and uncritical admirers would agree that this great man could not foresee all that was to come, computers to nuclear weapons included. Quite evidently he would have modified his doctrines in the light of experience, including the experience of socialist planning. Thirdly, since he could not modify his doctrines after his death, we must, unless we are incurable dogmatist believers, perform this task

* Written in 1984 and published in 1986 by Harwood Academic Publishers, as a volume in the Marxian Economics section of *Pure and applied economics*, this essay would now have to take into account the increasingly frank public discussion of Marx and of socialism that one finds in the press of the Soviet Union, Hungary, Poland and China. A whole number of authors point openly to the utopian or erroneous views of Marx and Engels about socialism, especially with regard to markets ('commodity production'). Lenin is no longer regarded as sacrosanct, though direct criticism is still rare. The question can be and is directly asked: which of the doctrines inherited from the Founding Fathers are relevant today and which can be seen as mistaken? Also the applicability of the term 'class' to Soviet society, the nature of the bureaucracy, its relationship to the party *apparat*, can be freely discussed in a challenging way. Indeed, it is now possible to envisage the publication of such a paper as this in Moscow, which shows how *glasnost*' has stretched the boundaries of the permissible.

ourselves: which of Marx's ideas on socialism appear to be contradictory or unreal, given the experience of 'really existing socialism'? Only then might it be possible to develop a critique of such socialism in Marxist terms. To take a simple example, there is in Marx the belief that under socialism the division of labour will be transcended (*aufgehoben*). In the USSR the reverse has been the case, in respect both of the horizontal (specialization, professionalization) and the vertical (hierarchical) division of labour. How far, we may ask, was this development the inescapable consequence of industrial development under state auspices, and, if it was such a consequence, does this not provide a basis for a criticism of Marx rather than of Soviet practice?

This brings me to the heart of the whole question of appropriate criteria, in judging both Soviet reality and the validity of marxian doctrine. To take another example to which we will return, what does Soviet experience tell us about the validity of the doctrine of historical materialism? In the introduction to my *Economic History of the USSR*, I quoted Lenin: 'Politics cannot but have dominance over economics: to argue otherwise is to forget the ABC of Marxism.' A Soviet critic cited that passage, and accused me (not unfairly) of omitting a subsequent passage in which Lenin spoke of 'politics as concentrated economics'.[1] (Olsevich, 1983) Of course the two are closely linked, particularly where the state owns and manages the economy, but to interpret Russian history since 1917 in terms of any species of economic determinism (even 'in the last instance') really does require an illegitimate leap of imagination – at least in my opinion.

But let us look first at how 'socialism' or 'communism' was understood by Marx and Engels, and by Marxists of the post-Stalin period.

Marx himself made no clear distinction between 'socialism' and 'communism', and the notion that one was the lower stage of the other first made its appearance after the Russian revolution (it was *not* an invention of Stalin. Bukharin, Trotsky, Preobrazhensky used such phrases too). Of course, Marx appreciated that full socialism/communism would not appear overnight, that there would be a transition period, a lower stage – of which more in a moment. However, socialism and communism for him were virtually synonyms, to be used interchangeably.

Let me briefly (too briefly?) set out what Marx's vision contained. Probably the most thorough collection of its contents, with appropriate references, is to be found in Bertil Ollman's article, in *Critique*, no. 8. The key elements were:

(a) *Abundance*. Capitalism has at least potentially overcome the problem of creating a sufficiency of productive potential to meet all reasonable needs. Capitalist relations of production are acting as a brake on the development of productive forces. Remove that brake, and production and productivity would rapidly increase. It is on this basis that we will see the end of acquisitiveness, selfishness, the struggle of each against each. Attempts to create socialism amid relative poverty would reproduce 'the old rubbish'.

(b) *Overcoming 'commodity fetishism' and the market*. Private property in means of production, the separation of production units from each other, requires ex post validation of the value of commodities through the process of sale and exchange, through the market. The relationship between men takes the form of relationship between things. Under socialism, labour power will be applied directly by the 'associated producers' to the tasks of satisfying society's needs for goods and services. It will be possible to calculate the number of hours of human effort required, and to relate this to the social utility of what is produced, without a detour via exchange-value and the market. 'There can be nothing more erroneous and absurd than to postulate the control by united individuals of total production on the basis of exchange value, of money.'[2]

(c) *Elimination of the wages system and of money*. Since calculations of cost are to be in labour-time, and there will be no purchase-and-sale, money will wither away as a medium of exchange. Under fully-developed socialism/communism there will be realized the aim of 'from each according to their abilities, to each according to their needs'. In the transition period, however, when people's consciousness is not yet fully socialist (and abundance is not yet achieved), people will be 'paid' according to their work. It is not clear if work is to be measured in hours, or whether differential rewards are envisaged for work of different quality or intensity. In any case, pay will not be in money but in non-circulating tokens, presumably denominated in hours and minutes.

(d) *Elimination of the division of labour and of alienation*. Educated, all-purpose human beings will interchange jobs. There will be no need for hierarchy, or where it is needed the task of coordination/command can be taken in turn. The causes of alienation will be overcome. There will be no professional bureaucracy, officers, etc.

(e) *The withering away of the state.* The state being essentially an organ of class oppression will no longer have any purpose. Since there will be no class conflict, no special repressive machine will be needed, therefore laws, judges, police, become unnecessary.

(f) *Planning*, undertaken in the advance knowledge of needs and of available means, will be a simple matter. It is the market, the separation of producers from the product and from each other, that makes it all so complicated. There will be a huge saving arising out of the waste (*faux-frais*) in the circulatory sphere, which Marx treated as unproductive.

(g) *The proletariat*, in liberating itself, will end class oppression and bring into being a classless society.

As is clear from successive versions of his reply to Vera Zasulich, Marx took very seriously the notion of a primitive communist society that once existed, in which there was an organic fusion of the individual with society. (Whether there ever was such a society is a question I will not discuss.) His socialism/communism involves a restoration of this organic fusion, but of course on the basis of the highest modern technique and the full development of the productive forces. This explains, as Agnes Heller has rightly pointed out, why Marx devoted no attention to the rather vital questions of how decisions are to be taken (on the economy or on anything else) and how differences of view are to be reconciled: 'there will . . . be no group interest or conflict of interests'.[3]

Already at this stage the attentive reader will have noted this author's belief that Marxian socialism and 'really existing socialism' diverge largely, but certainly not exclusively, because of the utopian-romantic aspects of Marx's vision. Utopian visions have their important role to play, in inspiring action and sacrifice. But by definition they are unrealisable, and this renders those who fail to realise them immune from the criticism of not having achieved the impossible. But let us now look at the socialist ideas of Marxists after Marx, and before Soviet experience could have taught any lessons.

August Bebel had worked closely with Engels, and, though not himself an intellectual 'heavyweight', can be seen as representative of much social-democratic opinion in pre-1914 Germany, a time when the party was considered to be orthodox-marxist in its ideological stance. For some reason the most systematic exposition of his view on socialist planning is to be found in his *Woman under socialism* (*Die Frau im Sozialismus*).

The complexities of real planning in a modern industrial society were not understood by him. Such phrases as 'child's play', the belief that socialist man would take the needed decisions on the basis of readily-available information, anticipate similar statements by Russian revolutionary theorists, which will be cited in a moment. Clearly Bebel derived from Marx and Engels the belief that a classless, socially coherent society will be one without conflict over resource allocation. To cite Bebel again: 'The gratification of personal egoism and the promotion of the common weal go harmoniously hand in hand and coincide'.

Kautsky was another of the associates of Engels in his last years, and more of a theorist than Bebel, with whom he collaborated closely. It is not clear whether he ever read, or took seriously, Enrico Barone's pioneering work on 'The ministry of production in a collectivist state', which was published in 1908 and put highly pertinent questions about how calculations could be made in an imaginary socialist commonwealth. Kautsky also envisaged a socialism without markets, which led him to envisage a number of relatively autarkic socialist societies (since it would be necessary to keep *trade* to a minimum). True, he specifically disavowed utopias, and, in one of his works (*Die soziale Revolution*) envisaged the use of prices in the 'circuit of commodities'. Oskar Lange saw in this an important contribution to economic theories of socialism, but since Kautsky imagined that price ratios 'historically given' (i.e. derived from the capitalist past) would be used, it really does not seem that he saw any active allocative role for prices. Acknowledgments are due to T. Kowalik and P. Sutela for drawing attention to these aspects of Kautsky's thoughts. And in his article on the Erfurt programme Kautsky wrote that 'in a socialist society, which is after all just a single giant industrial enterprise, production and wages must be organized in a planned way, like in a modern large industrial enterprise'. The reference to 'wages' is interesting: it implies money, though Kautsky did not enlarge on this point. His notion of socialist economy as one gigantic enterprise does have some marxian roots, and, as we shall see, Lenin saw things this way too. But Kautsky was committed to parliamentary democracy, as the political way towards achieving socialism under conditions of universal suffrage, and on this issue he clashed very sharply with Lenin after the Bolshevik seizure of power.

Lenin's pre-1918 ideas on the economics and politics of socialism should be well known, and it may therefore be unnecessary to dwell on them for long. The following would seem to be the key elements in the present context. *Firstly*, there is his concept of the role of the revolutionary intelligentsia in bringing specifically socialist ideas to the working class which, left to itself, would not go beyond 'trade unionism', i.e. demands for economic betterment. Thus they would seek higher wages, not the abolition of capitalism and of the wages system as such. While Lenin was criticized by Rosa Luxemburg, who had a greater belief in the virtues of working-class spontaneity, it has been pointed out[4] that similar ideas had been expressed by both Kautsky and the menshevik theorist Axelrod. *Secondly*, there was Lenin's concept of the party. Here again it is noteworthy that Plekhanov at first took his side, and it may well be that the disciplined, conspiratorial elite concept was largely the result of the peculiar circumstances of Tsarist Russia. It will be necessary to trace the route by which this concept of the party became the rather different notion of the one-party state. Just as Lenin's well-known article on 'party literature', which when it was written (in 1905) referred to the duties of party members in a situation when there were other parties and other literatures, became a justification for imposing *partiinost'* on everybody. But this is to run ahead. His authoritarian concept of the party was linked with a very strong emphasis on the *dictatorial* aspect of the 'dictatorship of the proletariat'.

The *third* element of Lenin's ideas was the oddly libertarian politics which are to be found in *State and Revolution*, which contrast strangely with the authoritarian Lenin. He imagined that everyone will be able to run their own affairs 'without compulsion, without subordination, without that special *apparatus* for compulsion which is called the state'. In the *State and Revolution*, surprisingly, the Party is not even mentioned. Oddly enough, he cited, in that same work, Engels's remark to the effect that 'wanting to abolish authority in large-scale industry is tantamount to wanting to abolish industry itself'. Yet here, and in such works as 'Will the Bolsheviks retain state power?' and 'The coming catastrophe', he insisted that capitalism had 'so simplified' the organization and planning of production and distribution that any literate and numerate person can perform these functions in turn. 'To organize the whole economy on the lines of the postal service, all under the leadership of the armed workers, that is our immediate [sic] task' he wrote in *State and Revolution*, in 1917. Like Kautsky before him, he imagined socialist industry as a kind of huge single enterprise, managed somehow by society as a whole. His study of the German war economy convinced him that if the Kaiser's government could control the economy and the big cartels, so could a proletarian government. So a *fourth* characteristic of Lenin's view of socialism is (following Marx) a gross oversimplification of the task of planning, a lack of any grasp of economic problems, as distinct from those of engineering and accountancy. He was quick to learn, but there was much he had to learn.

Bukharin had attended lectures in economics in Vienna. But he too, both in the *ABC of Communism* which he wrote with Preobrazhensky, and in his *Economics of the Transition Period* (1920), seemed blissfully unaware of *economic* problems under a future socialism. 'The factories, workshops, mines and other productive institutions will all be subdivisions, as it were, of one vast people's workshop, which will embrace the entire national economy of production.' This means that

> everything must be precisely calculated. We must know in advance how much labour to assign to the various branches of industry; what products are required and how much of each it is necessary to produce; how and where machines must be provided . . . The communist system of production presupposes in addition that production is not for the market, but for use . . . The work of production will be effected by the giant cooperative as a whole. In consequence of this change, we will no longer have *commodities*, only *products*. These products are not exchanged for one another; they are neither bought nor sold . . .[5]

Money is to wither away. Such ideas as these were typical of the Bolshevik party outlook in the period of 1917–20, and found their reflection in the party programme adopted in 1919.

Of course what was actually going on during the period of so-called war communism was vastly different. The peasants were subject to requisitioning, a centralized authoritarian system allocated resources, representative bodies (soviets, trade unions) were placed firmly under party control or were simply dissolved. It seemed to many at the time and since that this was due to dire emergency. But some important features of 'war communism' were the result of ideological fervour and illusions, as several of the protagonists were later to admit. Thus hyper-inflation was greeted by some comrades, Preobrazhensky for instance, as a positive step in the desired elimination of money on the road to communism. And Trotsky defended militarization of labour not just as a necessary emergency expedient, but as an integral part of the whole transition period to communism, when the higher consciousness of the workers would make compulsion unnecessary, and Bukharin agreed with him.

By the time the civil war was won, thousands of party officials had become accustomed to the brutal exercise of power, to arrests of all and any political opponents, to requisitioning and terror. Many were dismayed by the adoption by the tenth party congress of policies which became known as NEP (indeed, the full implications of NEP did not become clear until some months after the congress). It was recognized that this represented, in Bukharin's words, 'the collapse of our illusions'. A compromise proved necessary with the hated petty-bourgeoisie. Lenin called it a 'retreat'. No one equated NEP and socialism. When, in 1925, the Stalin–Bukharin majority put forward the slogan of 'socialism in one country' it was presented as a realizable aim, not as an attained reality. Even Trotsky found it hard, until after his exile, to deny the possibility of 'building' socialism in Russia.

It was Zinoviev in particular who denounced the notion of 'socialism in one country' as doctrinal heresy. At least until after his exile, Trotsky was more ambiguous. True, they had hoped for world revolution. It had not happened. Russia stood alone. But it was 'the sixth of the world'. It had immense resources. Having made the revolution, how could the aim of building a socialist Russia be rejected? As Bukharin argued, then it would appear that the mensheviks had been right, the October revolution had been premature. The slogan appealed to the still-very-real enthusiasm of the activists, and touched a nationalist chord too: we in Russia are pioneers, we will show the world. Mayakovsky had imagined 'Ivan leading the slum-dwellers of London out of their basements'. The internationale might unite the human race, but Moscow will show the way. A heady mixture, skilfully used by Stalin against the opposition.

Naturally, Trotsky denounced Stalin's claim that by 1936, socialism had *already* been built, for such a claim rested on defining socialism as the (almost complete) elimination of capitalism and private enterprise. By 1936 virtually all industry, trade, construction and transport had been nationalized, agriculture was predominantly collectivized.

The 'Stalin constitution' was adopted. So this was socialism. Or was it?

THE NATURE OF STALINISM

Let us now take a look at the end of the thirties, when 'Stalinism' had fully established itself as a political, social and economic system, leaving till later the task of identifying the changes which have occurred since. What relationship did the Stalinist system have to Marxism in any form? What was, or could be, a Marxist explanation or justification for such a system? Its key features could briefly be identified as:

(a) Despotic rule by reference to a supreme despot ('the cult of personality', to use Khrushchevian terminology).
(b) A one-party state, but with the one party organized on centralized and strictly hierarchical lines.
(c) Terror used, along with strict censorship, to enforce compliance with orders and with the formal ideology. Even suspicion of potential dissent was treated as a grave offence.
(d) A highly centralized economy, run on hierarchical lines, with a minimal role for markets or other spontaneous processes, with top priority for investment in heavy industry, neglect of agriculture, consumer services, housing.
(e) An emphasis, contrasting with the earlier period of Bolshevik rule, on traditional virtues: patriotism, family, discipline at work and at school, conventional art forms, so-called 'socialist realism' in literature, and so on.
(f) Minimal rights for workers, no question of even partially free trade unions, imposition of harsh delivery obligations on the peasants, after their forcible collectivization.
(g) The Comintern reduced to a minor branch of the soviet foreign policy establishment, with large numbers of its officials shot in the terror-purges.
(h) The emergence of a privileged stratum (class?) of office-holders in the state and party, the so-called *nomenklatura*, subject, however, to a high risk of arrest and worse.

Let us begin by examining the 'Marxist' justification of the *one-party state*.

As already mentioned, there was nothing suggesting a one-party state in the works of pre-revolutionary Marxists. Indeed, the party is absent from Lenin's *State and Revolution*. But Lenin's views about his own party (not yet seen as the only one) caused deep suspicion in the mind of Trotsky. In a well-known criticism he made in 1904, he vigorously attacked what he called 'substitutionism', i.e. substituting a centralized and authoritarian party for the working class in whose name it claimed to speak. 'These methods [of Lenin] lead, as we shall see, to this: the party organization substitutes itself for the party, the central committee substitutes itself for the organization, and finally a dictator substitutes himself for the central committee'.[6]

Perhaps even better known is the view of Rosa Luxemburg. Opposing Lenin's conceptions and methods, she wrote in 1918:

> Freedom only for the supporters of the government – however numerous they may be – is no freedom at all. Freedom is always and exclusively freedom for the one who thinks differently . . . With the repression of political life in the land as a whole, life in the Soviets must also become crippled . . . Life dies out in every public institution, becomes a mere semblance of life, in which only the bureaucracy remains as an active element. Public life gradually falls asleep. The few dozen party leaders of inexhaustible energy and boundless experience direct and rule . . . and an elite of the working class, is invited from time to time to meetings where they applaud the speeches of the leaders and approve resolutions unanimously . . .[7]

Was the suppression of all other parties a necessity of civil war? In part, yes. But the large majority of the Mensheviks did their utmost to behave as a legal and loyal opposition, and Lenin's remarks on the subject are worth recalling. Referring to NEP, he said: 'If a menshevik says: "you are now retreating, I always was for retreat . . ., let us retreat together", then we reply: "for public expression of menshevism our revolutionary courts must shoot you, otherwise they are not our courts but God knows what."[8] Lenin was on record repeatedly at this period asserting the right and duty of the Bolsheviks to rule alone. The essential point was class analysis, and this of two kinds. The first was the (correct) view that, in a country overwhelmingly peasant, freedom to organize and to vote would inevitably mean that the peasant majority would threaten the Bolsheviks' hold on power and would mean the abandonment of what was seen as a long and hard road towards socialism. Democratic institutions, a genuinely elected legislature, were thus excluded, and this explains the attitude of the Bolsheviks to the Constituent Assembly and its large (peasant-elected) Socialist Revolutionary majority. The other is best expressed in the language used by Trotsky, the same Trotsky who had denounced Lenin's concept of the party:

'The special role of the communist party in conditions of proletarian revolution is quite clear. We speak of a class dictatorship. Within the class there are various strata, heretogenous attitudes, different levels of development. Yet the dictatorship of the proletariat requires unity of will . . .'. Rejecting the notion of coalition with other socialist parties, he characterizes them as 'representing various levels of backwardness and prejudices of the toiling masses'. He continued:

> We have often been accused that we have replaced the dictatorship of the Soviets by the dictatorship of the party. Yet we have every right to say that the dictatorship of the soviets became possible only through the dictatorship of the party . . . The communists express the basic interests of the working class . . . The dictatorship of the proletariat of its very nature implies the direct domination of the revolutionary vanguard . . ., which, where necessary, compels the laggard tail to catch up the head . . .[9]

Essential here is the axiom that *the* party represents by definition the interests of the proletariat and the views of its advanced guard. Equally by definition, the view of any other party claiming to represent workers must be that of the 'tail': laggards, backward, prejudiced elements, in due course labelled 'petty-bourgeois' or worse.

Arguing at the tenth party congress (1921) against the workers' opposition, Trotsky (1925) declared that 'they have placed the workers' right to elect representatives above the party. As if the party was not entitled to assert its dictatorship even if it temporarily clashed with the passing moods of workers' democracy . . . The dictatorship does not base itself at every given moment on the formal principles of workers' democracy.' At the eleventh congress he repeated the same arguments:

> The 'workers' opposition' puts forward dangerous slogans which fetishize the principles of democracy. Elections from within the working class, were put above the party, as if the party had no right

> to defend its dictatorship even when this dictatorship was temporarily at odds with [*stalkivalas'*] the passing feelings of workers' democracy . . . It is essential to have a sense of – so to speak – the revolutionary-historical primacy [*pervorodstvo*] of the party, which is obliged to hold on to its dictatorship, despite the temporary waverings of the masses . . . and even of the workers.

Rejecting the workers' opposition demands for power to factory committees, he even more revealingly stated: 'Formally speaking this is indeed the clearest line of workers' democracy. But we are against it. Why? For a basic reason: to preserve the party's dictatorship, and for subordinate reasons: management would be inefficient . . .'. In these respects at least he was fully at one with Lenin. At the thirteenth party congress Trotsky's plea for inner-party democracy was necessarily muted by his own openly expressed fears that too much of it would leave room for alien elements to enter, and this is indeed an evident danger: if only one party is allowed, then views which would find expression outside might penetrate into it. He had no answer to Kamenev's retort: 'If you say today, let us have democracy in the party, tomorrow they will say, let us have democracy in the trade unions, the day after tomorrow, non-party workers may well say give us democracy too . . ., and then the millions of peasants . . .'[10]

Trotsky (and at that time Bukharin too) went further than most in demanding the militarization of the trade unions, but for Lenin there was no question but that the party must control them. This was in 1921, when Bolshevik popularity among the working class had much diminished. One more quotation from Trotsky may be apt in the present connection:

> If it is true that compulsory labour is unproductive in all circumstances, as the Mensheviks assert, then all our construction-plans [*stroitel'stvo*] are doomed to failure . . . Without compulsory labour, without the right to give orders and demand their implementation, the trade unions would become a mere form without content, since the process of building a socialist society needs trade unions not for the struggle for better working conditions – that is the task of social and state organs as a whole – but to organize the working class for production, to educate, to discipline, to group, to attach [*prikreplyat'*] specific categories and individual workers to their posts; i.e. hand-in-hand with the government, to coerce [*vlastno vodit'*] the workers into the framework of a unified plan.[11]

While Trotsky's 'militarization' thesis was rejected, one can see in his formulation the essential elements of the Bolshevik attitude to free trade unions or indeed to any organizations, whether or not of the working class, that they do not control. In the Stalin period it was taken to be axiomatic that a party represents a class, and that, in a society without mutually hostile classes, there is room only for one party.

Stalin later provided a sort of justification for the intensification of coercion, asserting in a well-known passage that, on the way to its final withering away, the powers of the state have to be greatly increased, to deal with the resistance of the opposing classes. It is customary, in and out of the Soviet Union, to criticize Stalin for this formulation. Yet, again, an almost identical thought is to be found in Trotsky's works. In the process of criticizing Menshevik arguments about the relationship between socialism and freedom, Trotsky asserted: 'the road to socialism lies through the highest concentration of state-power [*gosudarstvennosti*]. Like a light-bulb which, before extinguishing itself, flashes brightly, so the state, prior to its disappearance, takes the form of the dictatorship of the proletariat, i.e. of the most pitiless state, which coercively [*povelitel'no*] controls the life of citizens in all its aspects'.[12] Over and over again, when he was 'the prophet armed', Trotsky used arguments to justify extreme totalitarianism, and indeed also terror.

So one can say with some confidence that the Stalinist doctrines on the state and the party, in respect of their dominance over society in general and the workers in particular, rested on the firm foundations laid in Lenin's time, and reasserted by Trotsky and other Bolsheviks of the most varied hues.

Stalin added several elements. Under him the *centralized planned economy* was created on the ruins of NEP. (The 'war communism' episode of ultra-centralization was, in practice, what was described by Kritsman as 'the most complete form of natural-anarchistic economy', anarchistic because there was no coherent central plan.[13] While, needless to say, plans under Stalin were frequently contradictory and seldom fulfilled, none the less there was created an administrative planning-and-management hierarchy, which could impose central priorities on the economy and on society. This was part of the basis for his claim that 'socialism' had triumphed in the USSR.

Stalin added the *terror*, and with it the systematic identification of any opposition, whether within or outside the party, with treason and interventionist plots. Not only could there be only one party, there could be no non-subversive opposition at all, even among its members. Hierarchy meant just that, and the principle of 'democratic centralism' became totally meaningless (it was *becoming* meaningless soon after the revolution). Solzhenitsyn has argued that the 'Gulag' was already fully formed under Lenin. In so far as this related to repressive actions against what were seen as enemies of the revolution, this was so. But there was a vast quantitative and qualitative difference between the Cheka terror and the Stalin terror. During the civil war everyone's minds were concentrated on a temporary desperate emergency. Concentration camps, such as the notorious Solovki, did indeed become a feature of the Soviet scene after the civil war ended, and many a Menshevik or SR found him or herself in *politizolatory* or exiled to Siberia. But this was action taken against political dissidents. Stalin's terror was distinguished by scale, by coverage and by motivation, and by brutality too. We still do not know exactly how many were arrested and detained in the 1930s, but certainly many millions. Among them were countless peasants ('kulaks', so-called, and others who opposed collectivization or stole from their 'own' farms when they were hungry), and very large strata of Red Army officers, party secretaries, national cadres, intellectuals, party activists, and indeed very ordinary folk swept up in the great sweep of the purge. The motive was not any more one of isolating dissidents, or punishing specific actions; it was preventive, prophylactic, anticipatory. It spread to include families, subordinates, colleagues of those arrested. Charges, when made, were mostly fantastical, 'proved' by forced confessions, but millions were sent to camps with no charge, simply by decision of an NKVD troika (the so-called *osoboye soveshchaniye*). All this was legitimated by reference to the theory that, as socialism is achieved, subversive resistance mounts and has to be pitilessly crushed.

To cite Vasili Grossman: 'With Stalin's help the revolutionary categories of dictatorship, terror, the struggle against bourgeois freedoms, inherited from Lenin, and seeming to Lenin to be temporary, were made into the basis, the foundations, the essence, and merged with traditional, national, millenial Russian unfreedom. With Stalin's help these categories become the content of [Soviet] statehood, while survivals of social-democracy were turned into empty form, into stage decorations.'[14]

Stalin's concept of the party is perhaps best seen in his references to generals, officers and sergeants of the party. Hierarchy and obedience, uniforms with badges of rank, became part of the system with his active support. Similarly, Stalin strove to eliminate the traditional concern for egalitarianism, eliminating also Lenin's 'party maximum', i.e. the rule that party members' incomes should be analogous to those of a skilled worker. In his speech against 'petty-bourgeois egalitarianism' in 1931, he set the scene for the widening of the income gap between skilled and unskilled, bosses and workers, and the 'Stakhanovist' campaigns then deliberately created a highly-paid group of record-breakers. Privileges of high officialdom were institutionalized, and increasingly (like Stalin himself) they separated themselves from ordinary people, living under guard in the Kremlin, special houses, dachas, etc.

Under Stalin the *nomenklatura* system was made fully operational. Its origins were in the first post-revolutionary years, when party members were assigned to key jobs throughout the republic. The secretariat, under Stalin since his appointment as general secretary in 1922, gradually made of this a system. Party dissidents were complaining about the appointments system in the early years of Soviet power, as many sources, and speeches at congresses, testify. This was an aspect of an essential feature of party control to this day, referred to in party resolutions as *podbor i rasstanovka kadrov* ('selection and placement of personnel'). This in practice meant selection replaced election in both party and soviet institutions. Provincial party secretaries, senior economic officials, editors, deputies to the 'Supreme' Soviet, commanders of military districts, directors of research institutes, people's commissars (later renamed ministers), whosoever is supposed to elect or appoint them, became nominees to the appropriate section of the central committee apparatus. *Nomenklatura* meant both the list of posts which were subject to this nomination system and the list of persons deemed to hold such posts, who became known as *nomenklaturnye rabotniki*. (Note: a very common translation error is to render the word *rabotniki* as 'workers', as in '*partiinye rabotniki*'. Not to be confused with *rabochiye*, which really does mean 'workers'. In Soviet official language 'rabotniki' almost always means 'officials'.) Inevitably this led to rank-consciousness, to a hierarchical structure to which appropriate levels of salary and non-monetary privileges were attached. With, it is true, especially under Stalin, a very considerable danger of sudden demotion, or worse.

The elimination of the 'party maximum', referred to above, plus the campaign against 'egalitarianism', meant that the privileges of high officialdom could not be publicly criticized, and the very existence of such privilege (and of special shops, dachas, seaside resorts) was made a state secret – along with any details of the *nomenklatura* system itself.

In an early work on the subject[15] (Nove, 1969, p. 71), I likened the *nomenklatura* system to the *tabel' o rangakh* of Peter the Great. We will return to the theme of Stalinism as part of the Russian historical scene. At this point it is enough to note the similarity, a uni-hierarchy based on service, to monarch, state, party. Peter the Great as well as Stalin made the possession of rank and privilege full of occupational hazards.

We shall be examining various interpretations of the Stalinism phenomenon in subsequent pages. Here we will concentrate on Soviet interpretations of this period, and also of the post-Stalin stage of Soviet development. Unfortunately, the task is complicated by the silence which has descended upon any serious discussion of the nature and origins of Stalinism. Khrushchev's 'destalinisation' campaign loosened many tongues, but his own explanation was sadly deficient: 'the cult of personality', defects of Stalin's character, grave breaches of 'socialist legality', causing many innocent victims among party members. But he insisted that Stalin's line had been correct until 1934, that is, that forcible collectivization, the excessive pace of industrialization, the centralized planning system, the political and social order created under the authority of the despot, were all correct. Needless to say, this was seen by many as highly unsatisfactory. Non-party victims of the terror were not referred to at all, and indeed nothing was done to 'rehabilitate' the principal victims of the show-trials of the 1936–8 period: Trotsky, Bukharin, Rykov, Zinoviev, Kamenev and Rakovsky remained either unpersons or enemies (though no longer with any mention of being agents of foreign powers). So, while under Stalin all oppositionists were branded as treasonable, under Khrushchev and his successors their ideas were at no point seriously discussed, any more than was the nature of the regime that had them killed.

Some analysts had recourse to Aesopian language and circumlocutions. Thus *Novyi Mir* published a review of a book on the fall of the Roman republic in which an intelligent reader could see an analysis of the rise of Stalin disguised as the rise of Augustus, with Trotsky cast in the role of Cicero ('killed in the 'forties, far from his native land, accused in the terminology of the time of being an enemy of the Roman people'). Another and longer article purported to discuss the rise of Mao, with virtually every word applicable to developments much nearer home. However, serious discussions inevitably were by word of mouth, or in *samizdat*, or in emigration.

It was there possible to raise *the* taboo question: how far was Stalinism the outcome of Leninism, or of Marxism–Leninism? Can its nature be discussed without decanonizing Lenin? *Samizdat* authors vary widely in these respects, ranging from Roy Medvedev's continuing attempts to stress the virtues of Lenin (and so the contrast between him and his bloodthirsty successor) to Solzhenitsyn's insistence that the evils of 'Gulag' were already in full flower under Lenin. A full survey of these and many other ideas on this subject could fill a book, and would take us far from the subject. However, it may be worth citing the arguments of Vasili Grossman, the novelist, which are seldom cited in this context. In his fragmentary novel *Vsyo Techyot*, published abroad, he also helps to explain the massacre of the first generation of Bolsheviks, the 'fanatics, destroyers of the old world', who genuinely believed and hated, who were 'the dynamite with which the party destroyed the old Russia, clearing the space for new construction, for the granite of the idea of the great state'. The first group that followed them, tough 'builders' with minds of their own, also suffered heavily in the purges.

> Terror and dictatorship swallowed its creators. The state, which seemed to be a means, became the end. Those who created this state thought it was a means of realizing their ideals. But it turned out that their yearnings and ideals were a means used by the great and terrible state. The state ceased to be a servant, became a grim autocrat. The state became master, became national in essence as well as in form, drove the socialist element into appearance, phraseology, a shell . . .

Under Stalin, they needed not 'servants, but civil servants'. New men came forward to take the place of the fanatics and the first builders. Promoted young, they still occupied the top places in the hierarchy until today, they were the 'Brezhnev' generation.

An odd characteristic of the Stalin period was an insistence on a uniquely wide gap between what was and what was claimed to be. To this Stalin himself made a direct contribution. Three examples can be cited. One was the 'Stalin constitution', the 'most democratic in the world', while a popular official song announced that 'I know no country where man breathes so freely', this at the height of the terror. Another is Stalin's announcement, in 1948, that there were no slums in Moscow, at a time when overcrowding reached its highest point. Still another instance is his declaration, in 1933, that the people's living standards are rising, and that 'whoever denies this is an enemy of Soviet power' (no wonder cost of living indices ceased to be published!). Sergei Utechin rightly observed that

> Stalin's political theory was for the most part fictitious . . . There is little doubt that Stalin intended people to be aware of the fictitious nature of the theory, for an attempt on the part of the population to treat it as truthful (e.g. to believe that they enjoyed freedom of speech) would undermine the whole of his system of rule. Therefore any action based on belief (genuine or pretended) in the truthfulness of the official theory was treated as a most serious political offence. A profession of belief was obligatory, an action implying belief was severely punished.

Perhaps today's official characterization of the Stalin era is implied by the definition of the more recent stage as that of 'mature' or 'developed' socialism, sometimes also called 'real socialism' (not to be confused with Rudolf Bahro's *real existierender Sozialismus*). It emerged around 1970, apparently with Suslov's backing. It implies that the earlier period was one of immature or underdeveloped socialism. According to an article by V. Dmitrenko (1974) on the 'origins of the conception of developed socialism', the transition to this stage was being completed 'on the borders of the 'fifties and 'sixties'. In his article, Dmitrenko refers to 'the contradictions between the new potentials, the needs of social development, and old methods of control'.[17] This view finds many possibilities and ways of expression. If such terminology were not reminiscent of heresy (it had been used by Preobrazhensky, and Bukharin too), the earlier period could have been called one of 'primitive socialist accumulation', characterized by the priority of accumulation, of vast investment projects, and also the preparation for and the waging of war. Economic historians and would-be reformers contrasted the 'extensive' growth of that period with the needs of a more resource-constrained, efficient 'intensive growth' that was now required. Economic calculation and consumer tastes had been largely ignored, but could no longer be. In various ways, reforming economists would argue that the centralized system inherited from Stalin had become a hindrance to the development of the forces of production. The implication was that, when originally born fifty years ago, the system did fulfil its role, had its own rationality in relation to the tasks faced by the Stalin regime.

Dmitrenko, however, faced a difficult problem, that of reconciling the concept with the older notion of a transition period. 'The experience of the USSR is ever more convincingly proving the need for a critical examination of the idea of a relatively short socialist phase and of the possibility after a transition period of the gradual establishment of consistently communist characteristics. The functioning real socialism showed the inadequacy of characterising it as a merely transitional society', which 'bore the birth-marks of capitalism, such as commodity-money relations, the class structure of society, the existence of two kinds of property, the organic inequality arising out of distribution in relation to work, etc.'[18] This, according to Dmitrenko, led to unsound proposals to liquidate market relations, turn kolkhozy into state-farms, abolish producers' cooperatives, and 'some of these proposals, unfortunately, were put into practice'. The author deplores what he calls 'the damaging consequences of overestimating the level of development of our society, of unrealistic approaches to the forms and tempos of the movement towards communism'. This doubtless refers to Khrushchev's attempt to write into the revised party programme some specific promises about the transition to communism, such as free housing, free canteen meals, free urban transportation. These ideas have now been consigned to oblivion *sine die*. 'Developed socialism' is here to stay for a long time, as a first stage, to be followed at some date by a higher stage of developed socialism, when 'there will be created the conditions for a direct transition to communism'.[19] This comes close to declaring 'socialism' to be a mode of production, distinct from a shadowy communism of the future. This cannot be done in so many words, as it would be contrary to Marx's fundamental categories.

What is the significance of this sort of terminology? What does it tell us of the regime's self-definition?

The Czech emigré Lubomir Sochor stresses the conservative functions of the ideology of 'real socialism'. 'The affirmative function consists in justifying the established system at a time when it has lost its internal dynamism, in maintaining it in a state of immobility to make any change impossible, however necessary or urgent it may appear'; and 'the negative (polemic) function . . . is so evident that there is no need to go into details. Its aim is on the one hand to repress, on the other hand to forestall. The ideology of "real socialism" is the foundation of anathemas and maledictions decreed on schismatic ideologists . . .'. It also

> makes communist parties in power in the Soviet bloc countries immune against reformist ideas, if not once and for all then for a very long time. I am not suggesting, of course, that this ideology is the major cause of political and social sclerosis. On the contrary, it is determined by the latter and is merely its reflection and expression. But the ideology of 'real socialism' is an important factor in maintaining the immobility of Soviet society. This ideology helps to make immobility a chronic social disease, it generalises it by adding intellectual immobility to the immobility of social relations and institutions.[20]

This is a particularly clear way of stressing the inherent conservatism of the doctrine. Sochor indeed gives philosophical underpinnings to this interpretation: 'the ideological formula on "real socialism" was based on the identification of "real" with "existing" and the "essence" with the "existence"'. Adapting Hegel's well-known phrase, 'the Soviet ideologies have pushed the identification of the "rational", the "real" and the "existing" to absurdity . . . Their identity is purely static, devoid of internal tension and consequently unproductive and sterile . . . It changes while always remaining the same'.[21]

The official terminology is indeed being used for legitimation and apologetics for whatever happens to be, but Sochor may be overlooking its more 'reformist' implications. There is a parallel here with another apparently apologetic 'law', Stalin's so-called basic law of socialism: the maximum satisfaction of the evergrowing needs of the people on the basis of the highest technique. When used in this way by Stalin, it does indeed seem to imply that whatever exists is, by definition, providing the maximum possible satisfaction, and so on and so forth. But even Stalin found this identification of real and rational too much to swallow, since he also said that socialism provides the possibility of achieving maximum satisfaction (and of rational planning), but of course it is not necessarily realized in practice. This at once opens up the possibility of discussion about optimal planning and overcoming existing inefficiencies, and so the formula proved not to be a bar to reform discussions, after Stalin died (while he lived, he and he alone could point to any but the most trivial gaps between what is and what ought to be).

Similarly, 'real', 'mature', 'developed' socialism can be said to require major institutional changes, because the existing institutions and planning system were created in a period now implicitly characterized as immature, underdeveloped socialism, in just the way adopted by Dmitrenko 1974.[22] The 'leaked' memorandum by T. Zaslavskaya argues that 'the system of production relations and the mechanism of economic management reflecting it lags behind the development of productive forces'. In other words, while the official formula can be and is being used to strengthen conservatism and immobility, it can be and sometimes is used in a 'reformist' way. For example, under 'mature socialism' the working class is more mature, better educated, so forms of subordination appropriate to an earlier period are no longer appropriate today, this being another of Zaslavskaya's arguments. In fact one could easily assemble a quite long list of articles and books which use the 'mature socialism' formula as a 'reformist' battering-ram. Indeed Gorbachev spoke of 'the need to create an economic mechanism which corresponds to the needs of developed socialism.[23] Probably it is 'real socialism' that should be regarded as the inherently conservative form of words. 'Mature' and 'developed' can serve either the conservative or the reformist cause, depending on who interprets these words, even if they were intended by their authors to legitimize immobility and the preservation of the social–political *status quo*.

THE 'LEFT' CRITIQUE

For many years now the Soviet experiment has been studied and criticized by Marxists of what might loosely be called a Trotskyist persuasion, i.e. by people who believe that the revolution was 'betrayed', that it departed from true socialist principles. The same sort of analysis was aimed also at other countries that claimed to be socialist. Some temporarily embraced Maoism as an alternative, but the subsequent evolution of China has led to what could be called a generalized demaoization. For example, Coward and Ellis wrote the following: 'In China another revolution in ideology is taking place, overthrowing ideas of delegation, management, the handing of power to "representatives" or "responsible individuals"; ideas which are the keystone of capitalist production relations and bourgeois democracy. They are being replaced with ideas of collective decision-making, of active thinking by all the people'.[24] It is highly probable that the authors now wish to forget what they wrote in the middle 1970s. But this issue of unreal or semi-utopian criteria must be borne in mind throughout the pages that follow. It is easy indeed to list the many ways in which Soviet social, political and economic arrangements fall short of, or contradict, the ideas expressed at various times by Marx and Lenin. But some of the ideas could be seen as inherently unrealizable in practice. To take one example, to which we will have to return at length, it is no conceivable use criticizing the existence of 'bureaucracy' (e.g. in economic management) if one is advocating 'marketless' state planning, since bureaucracy and hierarchy then become inescapable functional necessities. That is, unless the term 'bureaucracy' is simply used as a pejorative phrase indicating the bad habits of officialdom, and no less a person than Trotsky himself regarded such a view as both un-Marxist and superficial.[25] (Trotsky, 1975, pp. 91–2).

All analyses and explanations of the type about to be analyzed face one major problem: that of adapting the traditional Marxist class-based analysis to circumstances radically different to those envisaged by Marx. Property relations, the acquisition and disposal of surpluses through exploitation which arises out of *ownership*, are categories of thought which cannot readily be applied to Soviet reality without considerable modification. Clearly, the rulers of the Soviet Union, howsoever one chooses to define or identify them, do not individually own the means of production. It could be argued that the same dilemma faced Marxist analysts of the Tsarist imperial past; was it useful to see Peter the Great's Russia in terms of a ruling *class*, and if so of what class? Pokrovsky's efforts to fit the tsarist autocracy into conventional Marxist categories caused him to attach to Peter the Great the not-very-convincing label of representative of 'merchant capital'. Others disagreed. Trotsky himself, arguing against Pokrovsky, wrote an eloquent article significantly entitled 'On the historical peculiarities of Russia', which some who call themselves Trotskyists find it convenient to forget. Indeed Marx himself, in his last years, puzzled over the question of the applicability of his doctrines to Russia, as is clear from successive drafts of his reply to Vera Zasulich and correspondence with Mikhailovsky.[26] This is linked with another controversial question: the existence within the Marxist canon of the 'Asiatic mode of production', a point to which we will return. Russia was not only geographically half in Europe and half in Asia. Russian Marxists found Marx's views embarrassing, and most of this correspondence remained unpublished until well after the revolution. Yet paradoxically Marx's own consciousness that Russia might find a road to socialism different from that of developed capitalist countries could serve as an answer to those who (like the Mensheviks) had argued that Russia had to await mature capitalism before moving towards socialism.

Trotsky himself defended almost to the end of his life the notion that the USSR was a 'degenerated workers' state', or a workers' state with substantial bureaucratic deformation, though of course he denied Stalin's claim that socialism had already been built. In exile he vigorously criticized the notion of 'socialism in one country'. This criticism should be seen in context, including the context not only of the history of the 1920's but also Russian grammar. As Richard Day (1973) pointed out, Trotsky did not at first challenge the Stalin-Bukharin claim that socialism could be built in Russia.[27] One reason related to the implications of his own earlier theories of 'permanent revolution': it was, after all, he, even before Lenin, who had argued that after the seizure of power one would have to go forward beyond the bourgeois-democratic stage, even in a predominantly peasant country such as Russia. Another was the consciousness that, given that revolution in advanced countries had not broken out, denial to the possibility of building socialism would be seen as defeatist, an admission that the Mensheviks had been right about the 'premature' nature of the seizure of power in 1917 (this specific point was made by Bukharin in anti-Trotsky polemics). The 'grammatical' point is that the word 'build' is ambiguous, unless it is used in either its imperfective or perfective aspect: *stroit'* is the process of building, *postroit'* is the completed action. Trotsky would certainly deny the possibility of *postroit' sotsializm* in one country, but was surely favourable to 'building' it. Indeed in his pamphlet *Chto takoye SSSR . . .*, published in 1936, he quotes with approval the view that it is nonsense to assume that socialism will triumph simultaneously in many countries; there will be some 'isolated' socialist states for a time.

Highly relevant to the present issue was his view, and that of some of his supporters (notably Preobrazhensky) as to what constituted the stages of 'building' socialism. It was equated in their minds with the extension of the ownership of, and powers over, the means of production on the part of the 'proletarian' state, the reduction of the role of market forces. On this last point Preobrazhensky was more rigidly dogmatic than Trotsky. He insisted on seeing the basic struggle as one between 'primitive socialist accumulation' and 'the law of value', i.e. the market. Trotsky (1932), as a number of his works show us, saw more clearly the role the market must still play 'throughout the transitional epoch', and he did criticize Stalin for going too far too fast in and after 1930 in industrialization and collectivization. But, despite this, Trotsky was inclined to see state ownership of the means of production as an essential stage in the process of building socialism, and the fact that, by 1935, state and collective ownership had become predominant seemed to him an important victory along the road. The problem was that the state was not what it should have been, the means of production were controlled by a powerful bureaucracy acting in the name of the dictatorship of the proletariat. The bureaucrats did not *own* the means of production, they ruled in the name of the proletariat, so, even if the real proletariat had few rights, none the less in some essential way it was a workers' state, albeit a highly distorted one.

This was too much for some Trotskyists, and even Trotsky himself in the end found it increasingly difficult to call the terroristic despotism of the late 1930s any kind of workers' state. Judicial forms are one thing, reality another. When he referred to the 'bureaucracy . . . freeing itself from the market and from Soviet democracy', he at least showed some consciousness of the fact that market and democracy were not mutually inconsistent antitheses, that there were circumstances in which the greater power of the state machine over the economy actually reduced the influence of ordinary people (the workers too) over their lives and environment. There was no necessary coincidence between the expansion of state power and the building of socialism. One had at the very least to ask: what sort of state is it? Whatever illusions there may have been in Trotsky's mind in his first years of exile, surely no Marxists could seriously regard the Soviet state as a 'workers' state' in any meaningful sense.

State capitalism is the label which some other 'left' critics prefer. The term is not without its ambiguities, as when Lenin used it to designate a species of mixed economy in which real capitalists were still playing some economic role. In the present instance, the argument is that the state plays the role of capitalist. The state owns and controls the means of production, dominates society, appropriates and disposes of the surplus, allocates resources, with little or no control from below over its decisions. This could be regarded as a sort of ultimate development of monopoly-capitalism, with the state as monopolist, the state as exploiter.

One obvious problem with such a theory is to identify who are the 'proto-capitalists,' *who* do the exploiting, the deciding, the appropriating. The party leadership? High Officialdom? The bureaucracy? Those who control any means of production, everyone down to junior management? Another is to define what it is that they appropriate: the entire surplus, or that part of it which they use for their own privileged purposes? Or, to put it another way, are they exploiters because they have power of decision, or because of what they decide? Would a dominant group of ascetic monks who exercise a paternalistic dictatorship also 'qualify' as exploiters, even if they were genuinely ascetic?

But let us return to the notion of the 'collective capitalist', for it is clear that no individual, however high in the hierarchy, owns factories and farms. The collectivity of rulers *jointly control* the means of production and dispose of the surplus. They would then be seen as the equivalent of a ruling *class*. Let us put aside for the present the problem of identifying just who is senior enough to be considered a member of this collectivity. After all, similar imprecision inevitably attends the definition of 'capitalists' in the real Western societies. Perhaps, though, one could question the validity or usefulness of the word 'bureaucrat': apart from the authentic function of political leadership, what of (say) generals, organizers of vast projects such as the Baikal–Amur railway or north siberian gas, or for that matter the heads of the KGB? The word 'bureaucracy' is associated with routine-bound office staffs. These do indeed exist in large numbers in the USSR, as elsewhere, but are they, or their normal *modus operandi*, quite what we have in mind in identifying the Soviet ruling stratum? Words like 'elite' are not of much help either; some would stretch the vague term all the way to include a manager of a small rural store, on the grounds that he does command something, though his or her power is somewhat less than the manager of a branch of a retail chain store in Plymouth.

But let us turn to the usefulness of the term 'capitalist'. It is true that bureaucrats do carry out important functions which capitalists perform in capitalist countries. This has led some critics, for instance Charles Bettelheim, to insist that capitalism was not overthrown by the October revolution, that it exists still today (Bettelheim, 1982). This is linked with his definition of socialism, which includes control by the 'direct producers', the elimination of commodity production and the wages system, and so on, and his belief that the term capitalism covers virtually every conceivable alternative to socialism so defined.

Yet to see the Soviet system as a variant of capitalism is surely to obscure some rather important differences. The point is well put in the Feher-Heller-Markus volume.[28]

> in what sense can societies characterized by an absence of private property in the means of production, by the far-reaching reduction of market mechanism . . . by a dissolution of the institutional separation between economy and state and by a general tendency to abolish the distinction between the public-political sphere and that of civil society – in what sense can such societies be called capitalist at all?.

Of course certain similar tendencies exist elsewhere, but 'the difference between East and West is not one of degree'. They also argue, and very effectively, that the treatment of these societies as *capitalist* must make them appear as quite irrational and inefficient, violating the 'economic rationality' of any sort of capitalism. They have, they rightly insist, a rather different goal-function: not the search for higher profit, but what Feher *et al*. call 'the maximization of material means (as use-value) under the global disposition of the apparatus of power as a whole'.[29] Furthermore the specific economic problems of soviet-type economies are radically different to those typical of capitalism, both in terms of the dominant criteria and in respect of outcome (generation of shortages, overcommitment of resources, the role of imposed plan targets, lack of feedback via the price mechanism, and so on). As one possible approach to an analysis of a complex phenomenon, 'state capitalism' does help to clarify certain issues, but it confuses by implying a degree of similarity with really existing capitalism which is surely misleading.

The point was well put also by Castoriadis:[30] 'In seeking to define this economic formation, it becomes evident that it presents no analogies with the capitalist economy, since, despite the continued existence of exploitation and the monopolization of management of production by a social stratum, its economic laws are quite different.' Arguing that the Soviet system has abandoned specifically socialist goals, he claims that it is 'neither capitalist, nor socialist, nor on its way towards either of these forms', and that consequently 'the Soviet economy represents a new historical type, and it matters little what one calls it so long as its fundamental basis is understood'.

An alternative approach is that of a *transitional society*. This case can be presented in several variants, one of which resembles that of the 'degenerated workers' state' referred to above. The defenders of the 'transitional society' view would all agree that the Soviet system is some sort of amalgam or hybrid of elements of capitalism and socialism. There is public ownership of the means of production, but distribution rests on 'bourgeois right'. There is planning, though of a bureaucratic and undemocratic sort, commodity–money relations are reduced in scope, but they do play some role. A wages system still exists. Enterprises, provinces, ministries, compete for resources. The 'associated producers' do not meaningfully control either the work process or the product. Thus it is not socialism. Neither is it capitalism.

Then what is it, dynamically interpreted? Is it evolving *towards* socialism? Or reverting back to capitalism? Or in a state of arrested development, in a sort of cul-de-sac? If it is a cul-de-sac, is it a durable and viable one, possibly even a mode of production not foreseen in the marxist tradition? The 'transitionalists' have to reject the last of these possibilities, for their case rests on the belief that there is no lasting resting-place between capitalism and socialism. It has to be one or the other, or else one is either in movement in one or other direction or doomed to collapse in some unworkable hybrid state.

There are some useful insights to be gained by stressing the coexistence in the Soviet system of contradictory elements, and the attempt currently being made to reform the centralized planning structures highlights some of these contradictions. The limited power and ability of 'the centre' to control its subordinates, or even to ensure coordination at the centre, the growing need to use the methods of commodity-money relations (the market) and the strong resistance of the party-state apparatus to such a development, problems of labour discipline and of linking incentives to the desired final result, these and similar problems are acute today. The plan supposedly incorporates use-values, i.e. the disaggregated needs of society (both of the citizens and of the productive units), but when 'the only connection between consumption and production is realized through the administrative decision of a centralized and hierarchical bureaucracy'[31] the outcome differs from both the intention of the planners and the requirements of the users. It might therefore be argued that the basic contradictions of the system arise out of its transitional and hybrid nature, and so the task is to find ways of overcoming the resistance of the ruling bureaucracy who have usurped workers' power and then move towards real socialism.

There are, however, some snags about this whole position. One of these relates to the definition of socialism which the advocates of this interpretation tend to adopt. For Mandel, or Bettelheim, or Ticktin, it broadly accords with Marx's socialism/communism, with planning as the democratic task of all the associated producers, with no market (commodity-production), no exchange, no bureaucracy, no money, no wages . . . If this conception is in fact an irrelevant and meaningless Utopia, then obviously one cannot be in transition towards it. Without for a moment denying the many contradictions which the present system faces, the dynamic of possible changes cannot in fact be in the direction envisaged by the 'transitionalists'. Worse still, as they regard the market and socialism as inherently incompatible categories, they must view the market elements that exist as the 'capitalist' part of the hybrid. This is another version of the error already referred to above, of regarding to extension of state power over resources and people as somehow synonymous with the 'building of socialism' and victories in the class struggle. As if, for example, herding peasants into pseudo-collective farms represented an increase in the control of producers over their work or their product!

At present it means oppositions to 'market'-type reforms, in the name of non-existent and ill-definable 'democratic' planning, with the unintended effect of supporting the most conservative elements in the bureaucratic power-structure. These, of course, resist reforms which reduce, or threaten, their grip on the economy. Trotsky's above-cited reference in the same sentence to 'the market and Soviet democracy' is ignored or misunderstood. The 'transitionalist' view in all its versions rests on what might be called a utopian alternative. To illustrate, let me cite an example. Suppose a productive unit exists, and requires for its activities ten material inputs. In the real world there are precisely two ways in which these can be acquired. One is by purchase, from their producers or via trading intermediaries. The other is by administrative allocation, requiring an allocational bureaucracy with appropriate powers (which involve social powers too). The bulk of the 'transitionalists' counterpose to both these alternatives a mythical democratic planning process in which the ten inputs are somehow transmuted in the right quantities and at the right time by comradely discussion among the 'associated producers'. Faced with elementary questions about how this might work in practice, they seek refuge in one of two lines of defence: either they assume the achievement of 'abundance', so that there will be enough for everyone, and mutually exclusive choices (and virtually all economic problems) will be a thing of the past; or, more commonly, one is treated to a diatribe in which the ill-effects and distortions attendant upon the market and competition will be listed. These, needless to say, are far from imaginary, and present authentic problems, economic, political and social. But how are they to be avoided? One last instance will suffice. In arguing against the present author, Ben Frankel[32] points out quite legitimately that if there is both central planning and market-type decentralization, some decisions taken at the lower (say at the enterprise) level will conflict with central plans. Surely this could happen. But the only way of ensuring that they do not is to concentrate all decision-making at the centre, which is both undesirable and impossible.

Involved directly or indirectly in all these discussions is the issue of *class*. If a group of people, even if not individual owners, even if unable to pass on their rights and powers to their children – actually control the means of production, are they a class in the marxist sense of that word? Some argue so, contrasting the juridical position (ownership by the 'state' or 'the people') with the real power relations. Castoriadis, in his already cited work, argues that 'bureaucratic property is neither individual nor collective', that it is 'exploited jointly (*en commun*) by a class, collective within this class, in which there are still internal differentiations. In this sense it can be called "private collective property"'.[33] A similar case is put by Claude Lefort:[34] the political apparatus forged by the revolution, having eliminated the old dominant social strata, freed itself of all control on the part of the proletariat; this political apparatus then directly subordinates to itself the apparatus of production', and then is itself 'pitilessly subordinated' to the task of management of the economy. Whence the existence of 'a new hierarchy whose common denominator is that it directs, controls, organizes at all levels the production apparatus . . .'. He too speaks of a 'new class', collectively appropriating, and he interprets the Stalin terror as the way of disciplining this apparatus. Unlike the capitalists, whose power rests on the activities (and ownership) of individual capitalists, 'the bureaucrats form a class [because] only their functions and status differentiate them collectively from the exploited classes'. And, of course, Djilas had long ago written of the 'new class' which controls, distributes and redistributes.

There is, however, some danger of seeing the stratum or class as 'parasitic', a view also to be found in Trotsky, and which follows from his (surely superficial) analysis of the power of the 'bureaucracy' in terms of its regulation of distribution. While of course some 'bureaucrats' may be surplus to requirements, surely it is going too far to imagine that the economy and society can function with no political leadership, or that one can have plans without planners, economic ministries without offices, armies without staffs. This is part of the cost of using terms as 'bureaucrats' with a pejorative implication, a fault already referred to.

In her interesting book, Maria Hirszowicz (1980) also identifies a 'sovereign bureaucracy', but even high officialdom 'must observe the rules imposed from above and follow the instructions of their superiors. A hierarchy – or rather a network of hierarchies – within the party state implies for this very reason the concept of "more" or "less" power, rather than a simple division between rulers and ruled'.[35] This is not very different from David Lane's[36] 'competing elites in a bureaucratic structure', and he too would reject ruling class. But these two critiques are not from a 'left' perspective, if by this is meant an attitude with direct or indirect links with Trotskyism or Maoism. There will be more on the relevance of the concept 'class' in the final section. We should now turn to those who might be called neo-marxists, whose inspiration might be called revisionist, or who have in fact abandoned Marxism after having earlier professed it.

Finally, it is worth recalling that virtually every possible interpretation of the system had already emerged in discussions among exiled oppositionists at the end of the 1920s. We will have occasion later to cite Rakovsky, but here is Ciliga's 1936 account:

> Some of us thought there was still a dictatorship of the proletariat, though it had a bureaucratic slant; others that there was no proletarian dictatorship left, but there were relics of it . . . Still others that there was no dictatorship of the proletariat at all and that we were faced with a new social regime that was neither bourgeois nor proletarian. Opinions on the Soviet economy were equally divergent. Socialist economy, transitional economy, typical bureaucratic economy, capitalist state economy'. (1979, pp. 124–5).[37]

'EUROCOMMUNIST' AND OTHER NEO-MARXIST INTERPRETATIONS

Konrad and Szelenyi (1979), two intelligent and imaginative Hungarians, argue for the notion of a ruling class of intellectuals. Their case rests in part on the undoubted fact that the days of unlettered commissars are over, that higher education is the path to power, that members of the ruling strata (class) must at least claim either professional competence or the knowledge of Marxism–Leninism (and thus the ability to read the compass of history), and preferably both, so their legitimation as individual holders of power-positions rests on an intellectual (or pseudo-intellectual) basis. This is supported in their analysis by the notion that the intellectuals as a whole live on the surplus generated by the productive workers, and this underlines the existence of a gap between intellectuals (or workers by brain) and proletarians (workers by hand).

It is true that there is a specific relationship between intellectuals and the regime, especially in some East European countries, notably Hungary. It is also true that some intellectuals do enjoy both power and privilege. However, one must, in the first place, be careful about how to define an intellectual. There are two opposite dangers. One is to adopt the old Russian notion of the *intelligentsia*, with its connotation of dissidence and creative critical thought. Obviously, *such* intellectuals cannot, almost by definition, be too near the seats of power. The other is to define intellectuals simply by possession of educational qualifications, in which case not only Brezhnev but an ex-Notre-Dame professional footballer are 'intellectuals', and so (if he has a degree) is the Duke of Argyll.

Some privileged members of the upper *intelligentsia*, for example academicians, do indeed enjoy very considerable status and privilege, but should be seen more as very senior servants. Under Stalin, the 'wrong' views even on strictly scientific matters could lead to disastrous personal consequences (for instance, for Vavilov), and in more tolerant times Sakharov found himself in exile for interfering in politics.

Defining 'intellectual' more reasonably as a person whose career and promotion are decisively influenced by intellectual qualifications of some sort, it is hard to avoid the very different conclusion of Bienkowski (a Polish ex-minister of education): 'promotion in the ruling group . . . excludes all meritocratic criteria such as qualifications or talent. The ruling apparatus takes particular care that nobody that even once betrayed a critical attitude to any problem . . . should be promoted'.[38] A similar point is made in the emigré journal *Sintaksis*: intellectuals, again almost by definition, seek to assert their intellectual qualities in pursuing their careers, but promotion within the hierarchy does *not* proceed on the basis of ability, the key qualities being adaptability, conformism, loyalty to one's boss, so that, in the opinion of that author, intellectuals suffer much anguish and frustration.[39]

One can recall the ideas of Makhaisky (Machajski) at the beginning of the century: he saw Marxist social-democracy as the ideology of the intellectuals, using the workers and peasants to remove landlords and capitalists and to ensure the rule of the intellectuals. It could possibly be argued that the dominance of the revolutionary intelligentsia in the first years of the Bolshevik revolution lends support to Makhaisky's theories. But in the USSR the Marxist *intelligentsia* was dealt a shattering blow, most of them perishing in the Stalin terror. Their successors, for all their sometimes half-baked education in *rabfaki* and technical colleges, had other qualities.

Then one must not overlook the fact that the vast majority of the 'beneficiaries' of higher education receive little pay and negligible privileges. Teachers, medical personnel, office staffs, librarians, activities classified as *Kultura*, even graduate engineers and technologists, earn on average less than skilled workers, and have (relatively) lost ground in the last twenty years in all communist-ruled countries. Many of these underpaid professions have become feminized in consequence.

Finally, it seems odd to regard the intellectuals as a whole as if they were exploiting the 'direct producers' by living on the surplus they generate. It is surely a misapplication of the already very dubious distinction between the 'direct producers' (defined narrowly as workers by hand) and the apparently unproductive 'other ranks'; these latter would then include so heterogeneous a group as members of the politbureau, traffic police, technologists, industrial designers, philosophers, school janitors, nurses, economists, firemen, kindergarten teachers, party ideologists, novelists and shop assistants. Of course by no means all are intellectuals in any definition. The one thing they have in common is not being 'direct producers' in the narrow sense used, surely wrongly, by Konrad and Szelenyi. It simply does not make sense, in any economy, whether socialist or capitalist, to regard all such persons as exploiters of productive labour.

The question of 'who exploits whom' applies also, though in a different way, to the ideas of those of the Trotskyist persuasion who see an exploiting class in the USSR. We will have to return to this question yet again later.

Another school (or schools) interpret the Soviet system as having taken peculiar shape due to the backwardness of Russia, and this merges into the application to the Soviet Union of the notion of oriental despotism, or, in some versions, of feudalism.

Long before 1917 Plekhanov wrote: 'A premature socialist revolution could lead to a political monster similar to the ancient Chinese and Peruvian empires, i.e. to a renewal of tsarist despotism with a communist lining.' Many years later Wittfogel (1957) wrote his challenging *Oriental Despotism*, which stressed the role of irrigation in the ancient empires, and this made its direct application to the USSR less than obvious. In the USSR itself this was virtually a banned subject under Stalin. Even in 1984 the attempt by one Yu. Semyonov to discuss 'Marx and the Asiatic mode of production' attracted criticism, though of an academic kind: Semyonov is said to have 'sought to assert a hypothesis on the existence of a social order founded exclusively on the supremacy of state property, with a total co-incidence of the exploiting class with the state apparatus', which could be called 'politarian' (*politarnyi*). This sort of formulation evidently raises sensitive issues, and the Soviet critic prefers to fit the ancient despotism into the category of a 'slave society' with a large role for the state machine.[40]

We have already discussed 'Russian backwardness' and Russian political culture in connection with the phenomenon of Stalinism. Neo-Marxist (and non-Marxist) critics in eastern and central Europe find obvious attraction in the idea that Soviet socialism was a backward and primitive sort. Many Eurocommunists, for instance in Italy, think likewise. This links with the position of most Mensheviks: the Bolshevik revolution was premature, the needed pre-conditions were lacking. As already noted, even the official doctrine of 'mature' socialism implies an earlier stage of 'immature' socialism. However, unlike the official doctrine, the neo-Marxist critics do not accept the notion of a 'mature socialism' today. In their various ways, they assert or imply that the Russian legacy of social and economic underdevelopment, traditions of autocracy and serfdom, civil war and isolation in a hostile world, led to distortions both substantial and lasting. Having started, or been forced, onto the path of despotically imposed 'revolution from above', they moved further away from the original doctrines and aims, and now exhibit features which repel many socialists, especially those who have absorbed Western humanist and democratic traditions.

Such critics vary widely in their approach. Some continue to regard Lenin as a basically positive figure, Stalin as having destroyed Lenin's legacy as well as most of his comrades. But an increasing number now ask themselves whether Lenin's one-party state, his intolerance of all opposition, his identification of the dictatorship of the proletariat with that of the party, his ban on factions within the party, made a major contribution to the features of the Soviet system they most dislike. Of course they are prepared to recognize that the pathological distortions of the period of the Stalin terror are past history. But the regime was seen by them, and not without reason, as similar in essence to that of high Stalinism, minus mass terror and a demi-god despot, of course.

The Asiatic mode, or other societies where domination is quite evidently not based on an *owning* ruling class, have been used as a parallel by many brought up in the Marxist tradition. Bukharin[41] made an early reference to the empire of the Incas, in which a non-property-owning priesthood dominated society, and Plekhanov has already been quoted. More recently the oriental despotism notion played a big role in Bahro's analysis of *real existierender Sozialismus*, and also in Alvin W. Gouldner's last works.[42] There are problems in using this perhaps too imaginative parallel. The purely personal–despotic element relates above all to Stalin, and applies with much less force to his successors. Marx's 'Asiatic mode' was static, based upon a predominantly rural society, and this fits badly into explanations of an industrializing and modernizing despotism, be it of the Peter the Great or a Bolshevik variety – though Gouldner argues that the inertia and lack of dynamism of today's USSR can be interpreted by reference (*inter alia*) to the 'Asiatic mode', in which pressure from above is the only way to overcome the system's tendency towards inertia.

So, while some feature of the Soviet system do recall elements related to what loosely can be called oriental despotism, possibly a better approach treats them as pre-capitalist, a return to a species of neo-feudalism. Markus,[43] in the volume cited above, speaks of 'relations of dependence' (*Herrschaft und Knechtschaftverhältnisse*, i.e. of domination and subjection). It is no coincidence that a bold Soviet theorist, Danilova (1958) asserted that the economic factor played a decisive role under capitalism, but that in both *pre-* and *post-*capitalist society the key factor was that of domination–subjection.[44]

Again, there are some elements in the system that may merit the designation semi-feudal. Markus[45] refers to 'striking remnants of some traditional social organization', including 'the use of forced labour . . . elements of semi-bondage to land . . ., the role of nonmonetarised covert privileges in the upper strata of the social hierarchy', as well as 'degrading personal dependencies'. Bienkowski (1981) among others, also speaks of a 'process of feudalization', Voslensky (1980) of 'feudal fiefs'. The use of such a term is questionable, in that in classical feudalism the lords exercised personal power (with fortified castles and even private armies), in contrast with a Soviet high official (or even a tsarist *dvoryanin*), whose power derives solely from position, from rank.

The image of feudal or oriental-despotic relations has its uses, highlights certain specific features of Soviet-type systems. It is not for nothing that Bukharin referred to Stalin's policy as the 'military-feudal exploitation of the peasantry'. The more one stresses the specifically Russian features of Bolshevism, the more likely are such images to appeal, the more so as the Russian revolution was in part a revolt against (capitalist) modernization, a rejection of the 'European' and indirectly the reassertion of older and cruder ways of ruling and industrializing. However, the Soviet system cannot, in my view, usefully be seen as inherently feudal or 'Asiatic', even if some features of the system have undoubtedly some resemblances to older modes and traditions. If Szelenyi, Castoriadis, Markus, are right, and this is a new hitherto unknown social formation, its peculiarities would be obscured by too much use of labels which relate to very different societies and historical periods. The extension of this system (with varying degrees of success, admittedly) to countries with quite different traditions is used by Markus and his colleagues as a further refutation of the 'oriental–despotic' type of interpretation, but this is not too strong an argument: such countries as East Germany, Czechoslovakia and Poland would scarcely have adopted this species of system without external coercion, whereas in the USSR it grew for reasons internal to that country, organically.

Many critics, who may differ in other respects, see the close connection between political and econonic power, the vital link between centralized planning and the centralized party-state machine, between privilege and the function of managing and allocating, the essentially hierarchical nature of economic (market less) administration and the hierarchical organization of power and of society. Thus Selucky (1979), Dora Shturman (1981) and also Feher, Heller and Markus (1983) stress the effect of the lack of economic and institutional feedback, the weakness of the citizen as a consumer and as a claimant on resources. The title *Dictatorship over Needs* speaks for itself. The powers-that-be do not, of course, simply ignore the needs of society, indeed they adopt a paternalistic posture. The point is that it is for them to decide, they know which are the needs that should be satisfied. Control, the combating of spontaneity in any sphere, become aims in themselves, and much will be said in the next section about the resultant contradictions with an increasingly necessary stress on economic rationality.

Finally, there is among some non-Marxists (some neo-Marxists, too) a debate about the meaning and appositeness of the word 'totalitarian' in relation to the Soviet system. Its use may be justified by the following consideration. There are three basic species of power: political (and police), economic, and ideological-religious. In Western societies they are in separate hands, even if there are some links between them, and this provides considerable freedom of manoeuvre for any adroit citizen, as does the disunity (in a democracy) of various segments of political-and-police power, e.g. a multi-party system, some degree of separation between legislative, executive and judicial authorities, federalism, and so on. In the Soviet system in principle all these powers are in the same set of hands. This, plus the degree of control over the press and other media, and the tendency to repress any unofficial association or pressure group, justifies the use of the label 'totalitarian'. The Soviet ideologists' own indignant opposition to the very notion of 'pluralism' points in the same direction. Confusion has (in my view) arisen because of a misunderstanding over the possible meaning of the word 'totalitarian'. If it is taken to mean real total control, a pure hierarchy in which subordinates have no influence over decision-making and always obey orders, with no pressure groups existing at all, then of course the Soviet system is not totalitarian. Sectional interests do find means of expression within the nominally monolithic party-dominated structure, orders are frequently drafted by their recipients, not all orders can be or are obeyed. Because plans are frequently contradictory, ambiguous, unfulfillable or unfulfilled, some scholars deny that the Soviet Union's economy is planned. This would be a correct judgment if one defines 'planning' to require a set of coherent, clear, fulfillable, balanced plan-orders.

So 'totalitarian' is a useful label. Others have devised alternatives: 'Partocracy' (Avtorkhanov), 'etatism' (Brus), 'bureaucratic Leviathan' (Hirszowicz), 'unihierarchy' (Rigby), 'organic Labour State' (Harding 1984). As Shakespeare has said somewhere, 'What's in a name?' A more important question is: what is the nature of the Soviet regime today? I would strongly agree with Feher *et al.* (1983)

when they wrote: 'A confrontation with the reality of these societies demonstrates deep conceptual ambiguities and inadequacies in the theoretical heritage of classical Marxism . . ., and that these systems represent a social formation the possibility (and the danger) of which was not only unforeseen by Marxist theory, but in a sense could not have been predicted by it.'

Very well, *what* social formation?

CONCLUSION: AN ATTEMPT AT AN INTERPRETATION

Having devoted many of the preceding pages to expounding and criticising the ideas of others, it now becomes necessary for the author to expose himself to others' criticism by attempting his own interpretation. This is not a strictly 'Marxist' one, since I do not believe in '-isms' in general or Marx*ism* in particular; Marx's favourite quotation, '*de omnibus dubitandum*', can and should be applied freely to Marx himself.

The USSR does seem to be a genuinely new kind of social formation, or mode of production, unforeseen by Marx. Attempts to use conventional labels derived from (or applied to) something very different are bound to give a misleading impression, they have to be modified to fit the new sort of social and economic structure. In my own first attempts to grapple with these problems I was attracted to the notion of the universal service state, and so to Peter the Great. Suppose, I reasoned, there existed a society in which everyone held civil and military ranks: this rank-based and rank-conscious society would not be one to which the Marxist term 'class' could be applied, since position and not ownership were the determining and defining factors. In Western society too we have senior officials and generals, but this can be held to be no more than a modification of (and to be understood in relation to) the basic distinction between those who own and those who do not. But suppose no one owned the means of production, and society was strictly hierarchical. The definitional problem would be where to draw the line, a necessarily rather arbitrary procedure. All officers, and their civilian equivalents? Senior officers only?

Of course no country can exist in which *only* rank determines position and influence: for example a widely-read author or great musician or pop star need hold no rank, and a successful black marketeer can make more money than a quite senior party secretary (unless he too becomes corrupt). In no country do orders simply travel downwards, without those 'below' having some influence on their contents. It is also true that within any hierarchy everyone below the topmost level has to obey his (or more rarely her) superiors. Nor do even the 'other ranks' of society merely passively obey; they may at times disobey or obstruct. None the less, though reality will always be more untidy than any model, the universal service state, or unihierarchy, is a useful way of looking at the essence of the system.

One hierarchy? Some might disagree. There are many, and they may be competing. This is partly true. There are hierarchies in the Soviet republics and regions, in management, in academe, in the central party machine, in retail distribution, the army, and so forth. Most people rise within their particular sphere or area. However this would also be true in (for example) the British army. Thus a colonel in the Royal Corps of Signals will not be appointed to command an armoured division, nor does an infantry major expect to be transferred to command an artillery regiment. None the less, the army as a whole is a highly rank-conscious hierarchy, within which there are specialized sub-hierarchies.

What binds them all together is the appointment system. In the British army it is (or was, when I was a soldier) the Adjutant-general's department. In the Soviet communist party it is the party apparatus, who operate the *nomenklatura* system, under which the head of the trade unions could be transferred to the job of deputy foreign-minister and thence to the deputy-chairmanship of the presidium of the Supreme Soviet, to take the actual case of V. Kuznetsov. As the example shows, there is some cross-posting between hierarchies, though one gathers that at lower levels one tends to rise within one's own particular locality or sphere (but this is also the normal pattern in the British army, up to the rank of major).

As all appointments to all posts considered to be significant (in political, social, cultural or economic spheres) are on the *nomenklatura* of the central committee, this seems a good definition to adopt, because it is a *self*-definition of the ruling stratum or class. As pointed out earlier, I was struck in one of my first articles on the subject by the parallel with the tsarist *dvoryanstvo* (service-gentry) estate. Voslensky's book (*Nomenklatura*, 1980), specifically identifies this group with 'the-dominant class', 'the directing class', 'the exploiting class'. It could be said, in answer to possible objections, that membership of the *nomenklatura* is not the *cause* but the *effect* of being in the ruling group. One is not a party secretary or general because one is in the *nomenklatura*, one is on the *nomenklatura* because holding these high positions so defines you within the system.

Privileges depend on rank and are lost when rank is lost, which may be one reason why there is such a pronounced tendency towards a geriatric leadership in the USSR – despite fairly generous 'personal pensions'. Rank is not, as such, hereditary. However, especially since Stalin's death, sons (much more rarely daughters) of senior officials benefit from sufficient educational privilege and other kinds of 'pull' to achieve fairly senior positions in some sphere, for example in prestigious research institutes. To make the parallel with the tsarist system again, *dvoryanstvo* status was (with some exceptions) inherited, but could also be acquired by promotion in the civil and military service, while some hereditary *dvoryane* held minor jobs (or small areas of land), and some – notably Lenin himself – even turned into professional revolutionaries. It may well be that, if we had family histories of the *nomenklatura*, there would be evidence of similar downward mobility, but quite possibly less of it. But we lack the necessary evidence, and in any case even the *nomenklatura* lists (what appointments figure in it, how many are involved at various levels, and so on) are state secrets.

Inevitably, as society has become more stable and economic growth has slowed, social mobility has become less, and so a gradual tendency exists for the consolidation of a 'class of rulers', who will tend to intermarry and to make promotion from below more difficult to achieve. But surely they will never be stupid enough to close the door to advancement. Indeed, were it otherwise we would be justified in referring to a *caste*. The old Russian word *sosloviye* (estate, a ruler's estate) may be suitable because it is unfamiliar, and yet reminds us (perhaps too much?) of parallels with the past. Still another approach emerged in the debate between oppositionists in Russia itself, before they were liquidated. Rakovsky (1928) could see that most of the men around Stalin were *former* workers, that they turned into full-time *agenty vlasti* (agents of authority), and in doing so ceased to be workers. This is obviously true, and represents a belated realization of the inherent meaninglessness of the 'dictatorship of the proletariat'. He might have gone further, and noted the fact that, in most societies, persons promoted from below value their privileges and pay little attention to the welfare of those who have now become their inferiors; to this the typical behaviour-pattern of sergeant-majors in any army bears eloquent witness. It helps to explain the *style* of the new men who rose with Stalin. In the course of discussion some anonymous oppositionists wrote (XYZ, 1929–30): 'Before our very eyes there has been and is being formed a large *class of rulers* (*klass pravyashchikh*).' They then discussed whether they exercise state power as a species of private property. But the point in the present context is the words 'class of rulers', as contrasted with the traditional Marxist 'ruling class'. This is more than a slight verbal rearrangement: if it is a class, it is so because it rules, whereas the Marxist would or should argue that capitalists rule (directly or indirectly) because of their class position as owners. Another example of the importance sometimes attaching to verbal reformulation is Bernard Chavance's (1981) distinction between *capitalisme d'état* and *capitalisme étatique*; in the first version the *state* is the 'capitalist', in the second the role of capitalists is played by 'concrete persons' under the formal ownership of the state. I do not myself share the view that Soviet society is usefully designated as capitalist, and only cite this argument to illustrate the importance that can attach to verbal variations.

Clearly, anyone even remotely influenced by the Marxist view of history or society is bound to seek the sources of the power of the rulers (be they a class, stratum or estate) in their relationship to the means of production. The connection here leaps to the eye. They do collectively decide what to produce, how incomes are to be distributed, what the surplus should be used for, how much should be invested and in what. Many if not most of the rulers are economic controllers or managers, the economy is under the supreme command of the apex of the political hierarchy, the politbureau being in a real sense the board of directors of the biggest firm in the world, USSR Inc. As already argued above, it is no answer to retort that the power of the rulers is limited, that they are influenced, and sometimes disobeyed, by those below them. All power everywhere is subject to constraints of some kind, outside of bad textbooks on politics.

But which way round does power go? Can one meaningfully speak of political power being derived from the economic? Surely not. The two are intimately linked, they reinforce each other, but the dominance of the political is hardly to be doubted. The 'class' interest is not profits, most certainly not economic rationality as such. Indeed, one of the biggest problems facing Soviet society today arises out of the resistance of the 'class of rulers' to the sort of reforms which are required for a more rational operation of the economy; a contradiction exists between the interests of the system's rulers in maintaining intact their domination over the everyday operation of the economy and these rulers' interest in achieving the economic objectives of their own policies, which do require increased efficiency.

In 1921, Chayanov[47] with remarkable prescience, wrote the following:

> The system of communism put all participants in economic life into a system of standardized rewards [*voznagrazhdeniye*] and thereby deprived work of any stimulus. Of course, work was done, but effort was lacking, as it had no basis. The lack of stimulus affected not only the executants but also the organizers of production, since they, like officials [*chinovniki*] everywhere, were interested in the perfection of the act of decision itself, in the precision and polish of the work of the economic apparatus, and not at all in the results of its work. For them the impression created was more important than material results.

He imagined a peasant Utopia (in 1984!) in which such problems had been overcome. Markus[48] made the point that 'the goal-function of the "planned" economic activities of the state' is 'the maximisation of the material means (as use values) under the global disposition of the apparatus of power as a unified whole'. He added: 'What is effectively accumulated outside the domain over which it can directly dispense does not count (for the power apparatus) as part of the "national" wealth, but constitutes a threat . . . because it can confer a degree of economic independence upon those who own it formally or practically.' This is not unlike the observation of Ken Jowitt (1983, p. 275)[49] 'The Soviet elite may be expected to disdain as well as fear a social order based upon the skills and ethos of businessmen and (competitive) politicians and to avoid the benefits and terms of private/market ownership: they are too threatening.'

But, to repeat, it is *also* true that, in their capacity as managers of USSR Inc., the rulers require that the economic system should function; one needs to be both 'red *and* expert'. In a conflict between power and efficiency one cannot give sole attention to power, if only because too much inefficiency causes loss of power, internally and externally.

What is the role, in this system, of Marxist ideology? This would be the subject of a book-length discussion. Some assert that ideology is dead, that it is either a formal catechism recited on appropriate occasions, or a card-index of quotations to justify a policy decided on practical grounds. It has important functions of legitimation, it is linked with important festivals and myths, is a new kind of 'opium for the people'. Any parts of the sayings of the founding fathers which happen to be inconvenient are forgotten or reinterpreted. It has been said, surely with good reason, that no member of the politbureau has the slightest interest in what Marx actually said on any subject.

Some (usually anti-Soviet) commentators claim that the regime is guided by ideology, *real* ideology. This, in their eyes, includes such characteristics of the system as the one-party state, censorship, ban on free trade unions, collectivized agriculture, militarism, capital punishment, privilege, hierarchy. Whatever the merits or otherwise of such a characterization of essential features of the system as it is today, this sort of approach *deduces* the ideology from what exists, and then asserts that ideology determines it – a not-very-useful tautology.

Yet ideology does influence policy and attitudes. There is, among the leadership, concern that policies should aim at improvements in living standards and welfare services, in line with a basically paternalist image. 'Workers' are not just given pride of place in official speeches. Security of employment is a valued right, and workers have indeed, as we have noted, overtaken most 'intellectuals' in the earnings league. Private trade is seen as immoral, as 'speculation', not only because it is outside the power of the apparatus, and this negative attitude is widespread also among ordinary people (this is an additional obstacle to 'market'-type reforms today). Since in no country is any decision ever taken on *purely* ideological grounds, there is no way of measuring its impact, in either domestic or foreign policy. It can be seen either in terms of a 'coloured-spectacles' image, or as blinkers, either colouring the way reality is perceived or excluding from sight some solutions to practical problems which might otherwise be perceived.

Does Soviet experience conflict with the basic tenets of the doctrine of historical materialism? Surely it does, on even the loosest definition of that term. To say, with Lenin, that 'politics is concentrated economics' is not to escape from having to recognise the dominance of politics, the use of political (and police) power to change fundamentally the relations of production, to transform the economy and the working lives of millions of citizens. Economics, needless to say, is always present as a modifying and constraining factor, interacting with the political. But the latter has been dominant even 'in the last analysis'. This should in no way downgrade the importance of economic factors in the process of political decision-making. They do have a life of their own, as do also scientific-technical factors. One can no more legislate economic laws than order water to run uphill. But one can still arrest unofficial traders as speculators (and build dams to prevent water from finding its own level).

So far, the international aspect of 'really existing socialism' has been ignored. Some Trotskyists ascribe much or even most of the distortions they see in Soviet development to the consequences of the 'socialism-in-one-country' doctrine. If by this is meant the consequences of the espousal of the doctrine, this does not make too much sense, since the USSR's isolation was not a conscious aim of policy; it was a fact it was necessary to live with. If, however, the point is that the isolation of an underdeveloped Russia in a hostile world had a profound influence on events, policies and institutions, this was indeed the case. It is also true that, in Stalin's time and since, the great-power interests of the Soviet Union were given priority, or were explicitly identified with the interests of the world communist movement. The questions that many ask, from left-wing or right-wing positions, are: How far is the USSR different from other great powers, how far does her professed ideology influence foreign policy, is it true that 'world domination' is the goal of this policy, and, if so, what impels the Soviet leadership to adopt such aims?

A case can be made for a totally non-ideological interpretation. Let us, for example, look at the discussions between Molotov, Hitler and von Ribbentrop in 1940, fully documented in the German archives. The crudest considerations of great-power spheres-of-influence seemed to prevail. The occupation of the three Baltic states at this same period may have been accompanied by ideologically-orthodox declarations, but the objective as such would have been very well understood by any Tsarist minister. When war with Finland broke out in 1939, Stalin set up a 'workers and peasants government' at Terijoki, under Kuusinen, and then, when its phoneyness was all too apparent, expunged its very existence from the record. (I fail to find any reference to it in Soviet histories of the period, or in Kuusinen's biography.) Dominance over Poland and the Balkans was an aim of Tsarist policies. Methods have changed, it is true. Catherine II could get one of her lovers 'elected' to the Polish throne, a solution unavailable to the present generation of Russian leaders.

Voslensky, in his book on *Nomenklatura* (1980), develops the thesis that territorial expansion is, for Soviet officialdom, an aim which parallels capitalists' attempts to maximize profits. This seems to me far-fetched. So, in its own way, is Richard Pipes's double-edged thesis: that the Soviet system is expansionist and aggressive because of its essence, *and* that it was equally so in the case of the Tsarist empire, even though presumably it had a quite different essence.

The expansion of communism as such is surely not desired unless it is of the 'moscovite' variety, as can be seen from the conflict with China (and, earlier, with Yugoslavia). The Soviets' evident desire for recognition as a super-power, with the right to nuclear parity and to have a say in the world's problems, requires no Marxist–Leninist doctrine to explain it. The United States prefers *pax americana*, and uses whatever weapons (military, ideological, economic) are to hand in defence of its position. The USSR's claim to parity, with the 'capitalist' powers remaining dominant in much of the world, is consistent with an expansionist push, modified both by fears of unleashing a nuclear holocaust and by the limits set by the aim of maintaining Moscow's control; thus a good reason for not incorporating all of Germany in the Soviet empire (even if this were in other respects practicable) is the likelihood that in a Russo-German partnership it would not be long before the Germans were in charge.

To identify and weigh the relative importance of 'normal' great-power objectives, of 'Soviet' or Russian nationalism, and of residual ideological conviction, is probably impossible. It may well be that members of the politbureau are themselves unaware in what proportions they are motivated by these various considerations. Marx, as is almost universally admitted even by orthodox Marxists, significantly underestimated the importance of nationalism ('the workers have no fatherland'). We now know that no stratum of society is exempt from nationalist or racist feelings, and, precisely because the present leadership cadres have risen from among ordinary people, it would be astonishing if their views (also about women, modern art and much else) did not reflect the attitudes and prejudices of their *milieu*. No observer of the Soviet scene today can fail to note the importance of Russian nationalism as a 'cement' for the regime. But of course too much stress on the *Russian* aspect is fraught with danger in a multi-national state, and so its extreme manifestations are repressed, a cult of *Soviet* patriotism advocated, but with Russians still presented as *primus inter pares*, an elder brother. It remains a matter of controversy among Western specialists how strong the non-Russian nationalisms are, how far they are likely to threaten the unity of the system. My own (doubtless fallible) judgment is that there is a tendency to exaggerate the centrifugal elements, that the republican hierarchies provide avenues of promotion for ambitious people of the main nationalities (the Jews being something of a special case). See Mary McAuley (1984) who criticizes the contrary views of H. Carrère d'Encausse and others. This is not to deny the existence of Ukrainian or Georgian nationalism, and of virtually open resentments in Estonia and Lithuania. But (as was the case also under the Tsars) this is unlikely to threaten political stability unless the regime is seriously weakened for other reasons. Much more serious is the resentment of Soviet domination in several East European countries, Poland especially, and it helps little that acceptance of Soviet policies is labelled as 'proletarian internationalism'. But it is not part of the present paper to indulge in prophecy.

How do the bulk of the population view the Soviet regime? Opinions vary, from Solzhenitsyn's picture of the people groaning under the tyranny of a tiny ruling group, to Alexander Zinoviev's view that the regime is accepted and more or less corresponds to popular desires. With regret one must conclude that – though he takes his argument too far – Zinoviev is nearer the truth. People do grumble, have many grievances no doubt, but hope to find remedies within the system, see no possibility to challenge it, and, more important, would probably oppose most proposals to reform it. Thus they do not like the shortage of meat, but would deeply resent the price increase which alone can get supply and demand into some sort of balance. There is no reason to suppose that the masses actually want socialism in a definition which would appeal to the radical *intelligentsia*. To cite Mihajlo Markovic:[50]

> But Marx did not solve the problem: how will the whole proletariat form its common will, make the step from a 'class in itself' to a 'class for itself', win power and run society 'organized as a ruling class'? How will this alienated and degraded class build up a consciousness about essentially new possibilities, a consciousness that requires enormous general culture . . . And if a vanguard of the class does the job, how to avoid the alienation of the vanguard, manipulation of the class by it?.

This brings us finally back to appropriate and inappropriate criteria. The Soviet system cannot usefully be judged or criticized in terms of an inherently unrealisable utopia. Having overthrown Tsars, landlords, capitalists, and later having destroyed the intellectual fanatics who flourished in the revolutionary years, an industrializing despotism imposed order, and in the name of a revolutionary ideology a 'class of rulers' has become firmly established. It survived the death of the despot, shed the extremes of terror and personality cult and made life reasonably secure for all who do not wish to profess dissent. It is, after all, thirty years since anyone was executed for an overtly political reason in the USSR, a remarkable contrast to the preceding thirty years.

Yet the regime's search for stability is in danger of achieving immobility and decay, not least because the centralized system of economic-and-political management is increasingly in conflict with the development of the productive forces. It matters greatly, both ideologically and politically, to believe that 'socialism' in its Soviet version can, in the foreseeable future, catch up and overtake the developed West. Khrushchev believed that it could. Experience has shown that this was not so, and this despite serious economic difficulties within Western capitalism. Analysts such as Bienkowski and Gouldner speak of 'petrification', 'stagnation', 'inertia'. The present leadership are aware of the challenge posed by the necessity of fundamental change. Their residual Marxist beliefs must lead them to be deeply concerned when quite visibly the relations of production act as a brake on the forces of production. We will soon discover whether they (or their immediate successors) can rise to the challenge, and what kind of new social forms (or conflicts) will be the consequence of the attempt. But at the same time the 'residual Marxism' in their minds, as well as the self-interest and habits of most members of the ruling stratum, incline them to oppose the market-type solution, which, by whatever name is given it, seems to them both alien and threatening.

Brus (1975, 1980), among others, has discussed with skill the relationship between democratization, market and efficiency. The experience of Hungary, and now also of China, suggests that while in some sectors at least (notably agriculture) the last two are closely connected, the first – democratization – is much less so. The market, by giving more choice to consumers and producers alike, and thereby diminishing the everyday impact of 'dictatorship over needs', does provide for an increase in economic freedom. It could even be said that this is a necessary condition, both for the introduction of any meaningful sort of workers' participation or self-management, and for the extension of democracy into the political–social sphere. Necessary maybe, but, in my view (and also Brus's) emphatically not sufficient. Not only Hungary and China, but also Chile and several other right-wing repressive dictatorships, demonstrate this all too fully. Still, what other path forward is there in Eastern Europe? The ultra-left can only counterpose a set of slogans about democratic planning without a market, which are recognized now even by most Marxists as being meaningless in practice.

This article has concentrated almost exclusively on the Soviet Union, as a sort of prototype of 'really existing socialism'. However, the term itself was coined by Rudolf Bahro in his book under that title, and he was writing in East Germany, using the term in a quasi-satirical, critical spirit. It is therefore appropriate to ask what light the experience of other countries sheds on the subject of the present inquiry.

While their experience is important and relevant to any full analysis of the impact in practice of Marxist ideas in the world, including the possibilities of alternative ways of managing the economy, their virtual omission is not a serious a defect as might appear. Firstly, because in many instances (especially in Eastern Europe) the Soviet-type system was imposed by outside forces, so that many problems arose out of the conflict between the political culture (and economic interests) of the country concerned and the Soviet model which they adopted, or were forced to adopt. Secondly, the less developed 'socialist' countries (Cuba, Vietnam, Mongolia and to some extent even China) are mainly of interest as models of economic development and modernization; it is in the USSR that the 'mature' version can be studied. China may be, indeed is now, taking a new road. However, in their first years China's rulers followed the Soviet example fairly closely, and the dramatic departures from the Soviet pattern – the Great Leap Forward, the communes, and then the cultural revolution – are now interpreted in China itself as disastrous. (There are some historical parallels with earlier stages of Soviet development, however, which will not be pursued here.) Time will tell whether the wave of market-type reforms, and the virtual decollectivization of agriculture, will eventually bring China to some new model of socialism, or whether this will prove a sort of delayed Chinese NEP, justified by the general poverty and low level of development.

There is much to be learned, and studied, in the experience of Hungary's '1956' and of the Hungarian 'new economic model', in the advantages, obstacles and stresses which accompany the attempt to introduce the market mechanism, to change Soviet-style centralized directive planning. The same holds for Yugoslavia's 'self-management' experience, though in the most recent years the Yugoslav economy (and the Hungarian too, though to a lesser extent) has encountered serious difficulties. Czechoslovakia's search for a new model ('socialism with a human face' plus economic reform) was suppressed in 1968 by direct military intervention. One cannot seriously consider Ceausescu's Romania other than as a crude despotism, politically reminiscent of Stalinism, and in economic trouble, contrasting with the less oppressive and economically more successful Bulgaria. Poland is a special case. Until the rise of Solidarity the Polish regime could be seen as a particularly notable example of an unrepresentative clique ruling over a basically disaffected people, committing major blunders of economic policy (e.g. the totally unsound boom of 1971–5) and unable to cope with its political consequences. Then in 1979–81 'Solidarity' demonstrated to the world the hollowness of the claim that the system was in any conceivable way representative of the workers, of their aims or aspirations, though the claim that this is so (however hollow in fact) is an ideological imperative of the first order. The party was utterly demoralized; many members joined 'Solidarity'. So total was the party's paralysis that the suppression of 'Solidarity' and the restoration of 'order', took the form of martial law, with the special role for professional army officers, a quite unprecedented turn of events. The special position of the Church is another feature peculiarly Polish. Furthermore, General Jaruzelski's government has now embarked upon an economic reform which, in its principles, is remarkably similar to that adopted in Hungary.

All these developments cannot but have some eventual influence on events in the Soviet Union itself, since there too one is witnessing what could be called a 'crisis of system', a degree of economic malfunctioning which the new generation of leaders is being called upon to remedy. Failure to act may have serious consequences both within the Soviet Union and on its relations with (and influence upon) the world outside. Indeed, Gorbachev made this very point, in describing the need for economic reform: 'the historic fate of our country, the position of socialism in the contemporary world, depends in large measure on how we tackle this task'.[51] And any remedy will inevitably involve action far removed from what Marx (and the Marxist tradition) had considered to be part of the transition to communism.

NOTES

1. Olsevich, p. 21.
2. Marx, pp. 138–9.
3. Heller, p. 130.
4. Notably by Harding, 1977.
5. Bukharin and Preobrazhensky, pp. 114, 116.
6. Luxemburg, 1978, p. 199.
7. Luxemburg, 1966, p. 134.
8. Lenin, p. 89.
9. Trotsky, 1925, p. 89.
10. Kamenev, pp. 142–3.
11. Trotsky, 1925, p. 136.
12. Ibid. p. 161.
13. Heller, p. 26.
14. Grossman, p. 189.
15. Nove, p. 71.
16. Utechin, p. 242.
17. Ibid. p. 8.
18. Dmitrenko, p. 6.
19. Ibid. p. 18.
20. Sochor, pp. 10, 12, 13.
21. Ibid., p. 10.
22. See quotation, Dmitrenko, p. 26.
23. *Pravda*, 11 December 1984.
24. Quoted from a critical review, in *Radical Philosophy*, winter 1979, p. 8.
25. Trotsky, 1975, pp. 91–2.
26. For a valuable discussion of this point, with supporting evidence, see Shanin.
27. In my view, Day overstressed the relative importance of foreign trade in Trotsky's argument, but on this views can differ.
28. Feher, Heller and Markus, pp. 23–5.
29. Ibid. p. 65.
30. Castoriadis, p. 66.
31. Feher, Heller and Markus, p. 14.
32. See *Radical Philosophy*, spring 1985.
33. Castoriadis, p. 85.
34. Lefort, pp. 147, 150.
35. Hirszowicz, p. 93.
36. Lane, p. 159.
37. Ciliga, pp. 124–5.
38. Bienkowski, p. 207.
39. Klenov, pp. 57–77.
40. Nikiforov, p. 132.
41. Bukharin, 1921, p. 69.
42. Gouldner, p. 334.
43. See Feher, Heller and Markus.
44. Danilova, p. 48.
45. Feher, Heller and Markus, pp. 38–9.
46. Ibid., p. 8.

47. Chayanov, p. 59.
48. Markus, p. 245.
49. Jowitt, p. 275.
50. Markovic, p. 312.
51. *Pravda*, 24 April 1985.

REFERENCES

Avtorkhanov, A. (1973) *Proiskhozheniye partokratii* (Frankfurt/Main: Posen).

Bettelheim, C. (1982) *La Lutte des Classes en URSS*, vol. 3, (Paris: Maspero/Seuil).

Bienkowski, A. (1981) *Theory and Reality* (London, Allison & Busby).

Brus, W. (1975) *Socialist Ownership and Political Systems* (London: Routledge & Kegan Paul).

Brus, W. (1980) 'Political System and Economic Efficiency', *Journal of Comparative Economics*, vol. 4, no. 1, pp. 40–55.

Bukharin, N. and Preobrazhensky, E. (1969) *The ABC of Communism* (Harmondsworth: Penguin).

Bukharin, N. (1921) *Teoriya istoricheskogo materializma, populyarny uchebnik marksistskoy sotsiologii* (Moscow).

Bukharin, N. (1920) *Ekonomik perekhodnogo perioda, obshchya teoriya transformatsionnogo protsessa* (Moscow).

Castoriadis, C. (1973) *La société bureaucratique* (Paris: Union Générale d'Editions).

Chavance, B. (1981) 'La nature du système soviétique', *Les temps modernes* (June).

Chayanov ('Kremnev'), A. V. (1981) *Puteshestiviye moego brata Aleksiya v strane krastyanskoi utopii*, reprinted in New York (The 'Utopia' was dated 1984!)

Ciliga, C. (1979) *The Russian Enigma* (London: Ink Links) (written in 1936).

Danilova, L. V. (1958), in *Problemy istorii dokapitalisticheskikh obshchestv*, vol. 1 (Moscow).

Day, R. B. (1973), *Leon Trotsky and the Politics of Economic Isolation* (Cambridge: Cambridge University Press).

Dmitrenko, V. (1974) 'Stanovlennie kontsepsii razvitogo sotsializma v SSSR', *Voprosy istorii*, no. 8.

Feher, F., Å. Heller, and G. Markus (1983) *Dictatorship Over Needs* (Oxford: Basil Blackwell).

Gouldner, A. W. (1980) *The Two Marxisms* (London: MacMillan).

Grossman, V. (1970) *Vsyo techyot* (Frankfurt: Possev verlag).

Harding, N. (ed.) (1984) *The State in Socialist Society* (London: Macmillan).

Harding, N. (1977) *Lenin's Political Thoughts*, vol. 1 (London: Macmillan).

Heller, A. (1976) *The Theory of Need in Marx* (London: Allison & Busby).

Hirszowicz, M. (1980) *The Bureaucratic Leviathan* (London: Martin Robinson).

Jowitt, K. (1983) 'Soviet Neotraditionalism: The Political Corruption of a

Leninist Regime', *Soviet Studies*, vol. 35, no. 3.
Klenov, A. (pseud?) (1984) 'Filosofiya neuverennosti', *Sintaksis*, no. 12.
Kamenev, L., cited in Feher *et al.*
Konrad, G. and I. Szelenyi (1979) *The Intellectuals on the Road to Class Power* (Brighton: Harvester Press).
Kritsman, L. (1924) *Vestnik Kommunisticheskoi akademii*, no 19.
Lane, D. (1982) *The End of Social Inequality*? (London: George Allen & Unwin).
Lefort, C. (1971) *Eléments d'une critique de la bureaucratie* (Genève/Paris: Droz).
Lenin, V. (1964) *Sochineniya*, vol. 45 5th edn (Moscow).
R., cited from B. Knei-Paz (1978) *The Social and Political Thought of Leon Trotsky* (Oxford: Clarendon Press).
Luxemburg, R., cited from J. P. Nettl (1966) *Rosa Luxemburg*, abridged edn (Oxford: Oxford University Press).
Markus, C. (1980) 'Planning the Crisis', *Praxis International*, no. 3.
Marx, K. (1973) *Grundrisse: Foundations of the Critique of Political Economy* (Harmondsworth: Penguin).
Markovic, M. (1977) in R. C. Tucker, *Stalinism* (New York: W.W. Norton).
McAuley, M., 'The state in socialist society', in N. Harding (1984).
Nikiforov, V. (1984) 'Teoria obshchestvennoi-ekonomicheskoi formatsii', *Voprosy istorii*, no. 8.
Nove, A. (1969) 'History, Hierarchy and Nationalities', *Soviet Studies*, vol. 21, no. 1.
Olsevich, Y. (ed.) (1983) *Ekonomicheskoye razvitiye SSSR: kritika burzhuaznykh kontseptsii* (Moscow).
Rakovsky, R. (1928) *Byulletin oppozitsii*, no. 6, and in C. Howe (ed.) (1976) *Essential Works of Socialism* (New Haven: Yale University Press).
Shanin, T. (1983) *Late Marx and the Russian Road* (London, Routledge & Kegan Paul).
Sochor, L. (1984) 'Contribution of an Analysis of the Conservation Features of the Ideology of 'Real Socialism', in *Research Project on Crises in Soviet-type Systems*, study no. 4.
Selucky, R. (1979) *Marxism, Socialism and Freedom* (London: MacMillan).
Shturman, D. (1981) *Nash novyi mir* (Jerusalem: Lexicon).
Trotsky, L. D. (1975) *The Challenge of the Left Opposition, 1923–1925* (New York: Pathfinder Press).
Trotsky, L. D. (1925) *Sochineniya*, vol. 12 (Moscow).
Trotsky, L. D. (1932) (1933), cited from *Byulletin oppozitsii*, nos 31 and 34.
Utechin, S. V. (1963) *Russian Political Thought* (New York: Praeger).
Wittfogel, K. (1957) *Oriental Despotism* (New Haven: Yale University Press).
Voslensky, M. (1980) *La Nomenclatura* (Paris: Pierre Belfond).
XYZ (anonymous) (1929–30), cited in *Byulletin oppozitsii*, nos 15/16 and 17/18.

15 Planning and Markets*

TWO 'EXTREMISMS'

We should, in my view, distance ourselves both from pure *laissez-faire* or crude Friedmanism which so influences Mrs Thatcher ('the market can solve all our problems') *and* from the untenable assumptions of traditional Marxism ('the market can and must be replaced by conscious planning by the associated producers for the needs of society').

It is important to devise a more effective strategy for combating the *economic extremism of the New Right*. It should be possible to mobilize the bulk of the economics profession against the theories produced by New Right think-tanks, as these theories are criticized by the large majority of our colleagues, yet much of the fashionable extremism goes almost by default, for want of coherent opposition. In my view, a counter-attack should concentrate on the following:

1 Macro foundations

(a) An attack on naive monetarism (while recognizing, of course, that 'money matters').
(b) A refutation of the equally naive but fashionable notion, fostered by the 'rational expectations' hypothesis, that government is helpless, that it cannot create real jobs, and so on. (No one has yet explained why jobs in the public sector, or those created by orders from the public sector, are any more or less real than any other jobs!)
(c) The economy is not necessarily self-righting, markets do not automatically clear, and this is not just because of removable 'market imperfections', for example in the labour market (though we do suffer from various inflexibilities).
(d) The government's almost incredible inability to distinguish be-

* This chapter was written for presentation at a conference, and has not previously been published.

tween current expenditure and investment expenditure, its blind adherence to PSBR targets and its prejudice against anything in the public sector should be shown up for the nonsense that it is – while not denying the need to keep a watch on spending (the converse to 'cash limits' is not 'no limits' or blank cheques).

(e) Apparent indifference to low investment in manufacturing capacity and in infrastructure, and a complacent attitude to large-scale capital outflow which modernizes our competitors.

2 Micro errors; (or misplaced marginalism, or inappropriate incrementalism)

(a) Ignoring externalities. Even in Reagan's America, airports, docks and urban transportation are in the public sector and will remain so, because even there it is understood that they benefit business and the population, in ways not reflected in their own profit-and-loss accounts.
(b) Ignoring natural monopolies and systems (networks). This is shown by the attempt to introduce competition into telecommunications and the absurdities of the government's policy on buses.
(c) Downgrading the public service aspect of public services. Efficiency becomes detached from purpose, from duty, from the question: 'efficiency for what'. It then becomes 'logical' to close rural post offices and telephone boxes.
(d) Attempts to introduce 'market' or 'commercial' criteria into health and education. The appallingly high cost of medical services in the United States should serve as a warning: the 'perfectly informed' customer (that is, the patient) is an evident myth.

3 Labour policy

(a) Deliberate and systematic efforts to underpay employees in the public sector generally, with poor morale and deterioration in quality the inevitable consequence. This is accompanied by hypocritical denial that the government *has* an incomes policy.
(b) An odd belief in a low wage economy as *the* solution to Britain's unemployment problem (though there are indeed strong arguments against excessive wage rises in relation to productivity).
(c) A preference for confrontation with trade unions (sometimes

admittedly unavoidable); disregarding of such qualities as loyalty, commitment, pride in work well done, a and sense of job security (important in such successful countries as Japan); in other words, naive marginalism applied to the labour market.

Many of these problems must face socialists too, so we will be returning to them. Indeed, there is a small school of economists (such as T. Liska in Hungary) preaching a sort of *laissez-faire* socialism, based quite explicitly on neo-classical economics.

A basic error of Thatcherism (even more of the New Right ideologists) is to ignore Schumpeter's dictum: 'no social system can work which is based exclusively upon a network of free contracts . . . and in which everyone is supposed to be guided by nothing except his short-run utilitarian interest'. If we have the morality of profit-maximizing doctors, why not profit-maximizing judges and policemen?

The extremism of the 'left' can be seen in two different aspects. One relates to current policy prescriptions, such as resistance to any incomes policy, or to 'wage restraint', belief in the desirability of price and import controls, commitment (sometimes now half-hearted) to extensive nationalization, 'soak-the-rich' tax policies which in fact would hit the middle (and upper-working) classes and do speedy political damage. (Chile in 1970–3 should be an awful warning.)

Underlying these attitudes is either a failure to appreciate the logic of a market economy, or a rejection of the market in favour of 'planning', with very little consciousness of what 'command' planning entails.

Although Trotsky expressed the view that 'the transitional epoch between capitalism and socialism, taken as a whole, will mean not the reduction of commodity turnover but, on the contrary, its great expansion',[1] this is far from the view of most who regard themselves as Trotskyists. While the need temporarily to use the markets and money is accepted, this is regarded as a sort of 'transitional' evil, and progress towards socialism is equated with the reduction of the area where 'the anarchy of the market' operates. Socialism being defined as the substitution of deliberate and conscious planning by the 'associated producers' for the market, evidently it seems to follow that planning and the market are incompatible in principle, even if they must temporarily and uneasily coexist. Preobrazhensky, in the 1920s, saw a kind of war to the death between the principle of socialist accumulation and 'the law of value', with one or other triumphant in the end. Indeed one can cite Marx in support; for instance: 'nothing is more erroneous and absurd than to postulate the control of united individuals of total production on the basis of exchange value, of money'.[2] This approach overlooks:

(a) *Scale*. The substitution of conscious planning of output and inputs, in a large country with hundreds of thousands of enterprises (engaged in industry, agriculture, construction, transport, distribution and so on) is a colossally complex task.
(b) *Social–political consequences*. To carry out this task requires a hierarchically organized bureaucratic structure, which must tend to dominate society.
(c) *Efficiency consequences*. Unavoidable bureaucratic fragmentation results in inconsistencies and imbalances. Aggregation, rendered necessary by scale, leads to failures to relate micro-assortment to demand (of industry or of citizens).
(d) *Problems of economic calculation*. How does one compare costs and results? How to evaluate alternatives (and who is to do it)? How to measure 'socially useful effect'? In what form, if at all, would the 'law of value' apply, and, if it did not, what is to take its place?
(e) *Labour incentives* imply inequality. The alternative to some sort of labour market is direction of labour (as was explicitly recognized by Kautsky, Bukharin and Trotsky). Yet socialism for the 'fundamentalists' implies the 'elimination of the wages system'. It was a reviewer in *Radical Philosophy* who wrote: 'A regime devoted to equality in its literal sense would have to be authoritarian, ready to crush inequalities whenever they reasserted themselves, as they inevitably and constantly would'.[3]
(f) *Human attitudes* are assumed to alter in implausible ways, unless one imagines real abundance (that is, the end of opportunity-cost). People identify the general good with the needs they know. Illegitimate leap is made from small community (Robinson Crusoe, peasant family, a commune) into a society of a hundred million and more.
(g) *Competition and choice* are inherently linked. One cannot envisage one without the other. Yet competition is seen as alien to socialism (that it *can* take ugly forms is not in dispute). The converse of competition is not cooperation, it is monopoly.

The left-fundamentalists are driven by their ideas to judge 'really existing socialism' by unreal criteria, and to attack reformers who wish to introduce or strengthen market elements in Soviet-type economies, alleging that they are anti-worker. One such recently informed me that they Czech reformers of 1968, and the Hungarians too, aimed to 'reduce workers' wages'. When I asked why, I was told that Dubcek and Sik desired to increase work norms, that is, to increase labour productivity. When I asked how real wages could have risen without a rise in labour productivity, I was told that this is indeed a contradiction, and an insoluble one until the 'direct producers' are in charge of the economy; in other words, until Utopia comes. *A fortiori*, if Kinnock were ever prime minister, measures designed to increase productivity would be vigorously combated by such fundamentalists (at least in Czechoslovakia there were no capitalists to reap the benefit!).

But the really key weakness of the dogmatic left is their lack of any clearly articulated alternative. Typically they attack the many genuine weak spots which must exist in any market economy: danger of unemployment, uncertainty leading to investment errors, excessive income differentiation, cyclical fluctuations, the stimulation of the acquisitive spirit, and so on. All these objections have point. But what is the alternative? How is a collectivity (whether under an appointed or an elected management) to obtain its material inputs, and to know what to make and to whom to supply it, other than via some species of market – or via instructions and administered allocation? *Tertium non datur*. At this point one has silence, or slogans empty of content.

WHAT SORT OF MIXED ECONOMY?

It follows from the above arguments that it is impossible to envisage a socialism both tolerable and efficient without a market mechanism, *and* that it is not possible to rely on *laissez-faire* either for macro balance or, in all spheres, for micro efficiency, even leaving aside (as one in the end must not) what are sometimes called non-economic considerations. (However, I recall Michael Kalecki once saying: 'The most stupid thing to do is not to calculate. The second most stupid thing to do is to follow blindly the results of your calculation.')

Let us begin with *the microeconomic sphere* and some elementary categorization:

(a) *The 'market' sphere*. This ought to cover a large part of production of goods and services. A precondition: the absence of major external effects (other than those that can be legislated against, such as atmospheric pollution, or marketed, as via sub-contracting). Another precondition: competition, actual or potential, thereby avoiding the danger of domination of producer over the user. This presupposes the absence of substantial economies of scale, which might justify the existence of one producer (for example, the electricity grid). Management (whether or not responsible to the workforce) would freely purchase inputs and make its own plans for output in free negotiation with customers, directly or via trading intermediaries. The profit motive would play a major role here, though its income-effects would require to be moderated by progressive taxation. For the market to operate one requires a price system either free to respond to supply and demand or, if controlled (or taxed, or subsidised), controlled with the aim of eliciting the required response – other than by issuing direct orders. Investment decisions of a minor sort, required for modernization or adaptation of existing enterprises, should be decentralized, but the principal source of capital would be either retained profits or the state banking system, with the latter keeping a check on possible unsound decisions, wasteful duplication and so on.

(b) *Externality-prone sectors*, particularly infrastructure, require a different approach. So do *public services*. Docks, airports, roads, public transport generally, water supply, posts, telephones, garbage collection – all require to be operated efficiently and economically. But here the profit-and-loss account is often misleading, or even perverse. Thus trains and buses are more 'profitable' if uncomfortably crowded. One is likely to encounter *subsidies* in those cases in which external economies are important, for example, avoidance of congestion on the effect of efficient docks on the hinterland. The public-service aspect relates to a key efficiency criterion: that of carrying out the desired *purpose*: thus garbage collection requires to be done not because it is, as such, profitable, and good financial results are no guide to efficiency unless the garbage is actually collected from all houses that require this service. Similarly all *must* be supplied with clean water, letters and telephone calls must reach small communities, and so on. An important distinction: in the 'market' sphere, as here defined, no question of any imposed duty arises, nor (usually) of subsidizing losses, since it is usually the case that what is profitable is what is needed, what is needed is profitable.

(c) *Monopolies, systems, networks*. There are large-scale industries and services which are either natural monopolies (electricity generation and distribution, telephones and urban transport networks for instance) or there are such large technological or informational economies of scale that centralized control and decision-making is the most rational way of handling production decisions. The list can change as a result of technological innovations, but could include most of the energy sector, heavy chemicals and steel. These tend to be sectors which are operated even under capitalism by large corporations, which are in varying degrees centralized. If the manager of an ICI plant at Billingham is subject to instruction on many matters from ICI headquarters, the same reasons could well apply to a similar chemicals plant in an imaginary socialist society. One reason why today one has 'Markets and hierarchies' (to cite the title of O. Williamson's book)* is that it is more economical and more convenient to administer some relationships rather than proceed through the market. (There is also the important and neglected intermediate category, the sub-contractor.) This is one reason why firms are large. In the case of public transport, the systemic or network element is so important that almost everywhere (except in the minds of Mrs Thatcher's fanatical advisers) it is considered evident that an integrated urban transit system is required (with a simple fares structure necessarily involving so-called cross-subsidization, and with public service a dominant success criterion). In these instances, competition can have a harmful, disruptive effect.

Clearly public authorities (central or local) must be involved in planning, evaluating, price-fixing and where necessary also subsidizing activities and sectors within categories (b) and (c) above. They should and must be efficient, but efficiency criteria cannot solely depend on financial results.

(d) *Social services* fall into a separate category, as to some extent does housing. It should be unnecessary to argue that the welfare state, with free education, medical services, old-age pensions, etc. etc., must play an important role in a socialist common-

* O. E. Williams, *Markets and Hierarchies*. (N.Y., The Free Press, 1985)

wealth of any kind. The boundary-line between what is free to the citizen and what must be paid for would be a matter of democratic decision, involving the national plan and its priorities.

Now on to the *macro economy*. Planners would have plenty to do:

(a) *Money matters*. While rejecting myopic monetarism, the state must keep a careful watch on inflationary pressures and avoid excess demand. This is not rendered simpler by the assumption of democratic freedoms, which must include the right to organize sectional pressure groups.
(b) *Employment and unemployment* are bound to present challenging problems. By manoeuvring with taxes and subsidies, and through public works and (labour-intensive) social services, it should be possible to keep unemployment at tolerable levels, but it is futile to imagine that this can happen automatically. Counter-cyclical measures may well be needed.
(c) *Income policies* would have to represent a compromise between the pressures of the labour market and the avoidance of what would be regarded as excessive income differentiation. Agreed norms for wage and salary rises, linked with the real resources available, might well encounter trade union sectional demands, but Austrian and Swedish experience suggests that this is not insoluble problem (provided ultra-left dogmatists are not listened to).
(d) *Major investments* must clearly be the central planners' responsibility, taking into account regional and employment problems as well as the expected demand for goods and services, including foreign trade in the calculations. The setting up of new enterprises is another vital function. Hungarian experience suggests that some sort of capital market may be needed, mobilizing retained profits (of those enterprises which do not need to invest in themselves) as well as private savings, these being sources additional to credits from the state banking system.
(e) *Setting the 'rules of the game'* for the micro economy, including environmental protection, regional development, the responsibility of management to the labour force and (where necessary) also to the customers, action to be taken in the event of failure, the rules within which foreign trade is carried on, and so on. For the monopolized (or very large-scale) sectors, which cannot be

> 'supervised' by competition, more direct forms of control over prices and performance would be needed, as argued above. Uncontrolled markets *can* cause major social and economic distortions, as the dogmatists rightly point out (except that their alternative is in fact no alternative).

In my *Economics of Feasible Socialism* I argue at length in favour of a multiplicity of different producers/providers of goods and services, including both cooperative and limited private-enterprise sectors. In general, the existence of unused profitable opportunities for non-noxious activity should be a legitimate reason to allow people to provide them, and to employ others, in the capacity of a working manager. There was also a discussion of the desirability and limits of self-management in the socially-owned sector. All this can be questioned from several angles. One, encountered in Hungary, was that to set a limit to numbers employed in private enterprises would cause distortions, and may reflect a subconscious belief that private enterprise would be superior unless subject to legal limitation! (I asked: 'So you believe that private enterprise should be either banned or limitless?' To which the reluctant reply was: 'Yes'.) But the question of what sort of enterprises should exist, and what should be the relationship of management to labour within them, will not be further discussed here.

Of course, the coexistence of plan and market can give rise to some predictable strains and stresses. Ben Frankel argued that, if managements were free to respond to market stimuli, their actions could well contradict the central plan. Of course he is right: they might. But how can such a risk be avoided, without snuffing out all possibilities of local initiative?

Finally, it may be asked: what have all these ideas on 'feasible socialism' to do with the present-day dilemmas faced by the Labour party, and indeed by socialists of any sort? What relevance has all this for devising 'a coherent socialist strategy for Britain in the 'eighties', to quote from this conference's programme? Alas, the answer could well be 'nothing', or very little. There is no electoral mileage in proposing to nationalize major sectors of industry. Electoral opportunity will come primarily out of the ideological extremism of Thatcherism and its consequences, and not from popular support for a programme to transform society. (Personally I would not favour such a programme, and am strongly against the 'hard left'.) A critic has argued that the model of 'feasible socialism' sketched out in my book has greater relevance to possible reform in Eastern Europe, or China. This is true, if by 'relevance' is meant the practical politics of today.

While I am aware of the validity of such criticism, I none the less hope that this essay, which explores the borderlands between theory and possible future practice, might shed light in areas where light is needed.

NOTES

1. *Certo tokoye SSSR* . . . (mimeo, Russian, 1936).
2. *Grundrisse* (Penguin edn, 1973) pp. 138–9.
3. Richard Norman in *Radical Philosophy*, spring 1985, p. 38.
4. In *Radical Philosophy*, spring 1985.

16 'Feasible Socialism' Revisited*

My book did have some effect. It has been translated into Italian, French, Spanish, Swedish, and now into Chinese. So it achieved its object of stimulating discussion about what socialists should regard as feasible, as well as on the relevance (or irrelevance) of what Marx and his followers thought about socialism in general, socialist planning in particular. The book was being written during 1980–1. Reviews, some of them highly critical, have appeared. Much has changed in the world. Yugoslavia and Romania, each in different ways, are in acute crisis. Poland under Jaruzelski has still to emerge from its own crisis. The Hungarian economy has also run into trouble. Meanwhile Gorbachev has placed the USSR on the road to 'radical reform', with an explicit link between economic and political–cultural change. China too is in the throes of large-scale reforms, which were in their early stages in 1981. Meanwhile in the West the forces of the anti-socialist right have gained strength and, particularly in Mrs Thatcher's Britain, are actively engaged in unmixing the mixed economy and privatizing everything they can, including social welfare. In many countries of the third world, too, one sees a reaction against socialist ideas and institutions.

For all these reasons, the book would have been somewhat different if it had been written in 1989. How different? Why different? First of all, *why was it written*?

---

* This way my contribution to a conference (March 1988) in Györ (Hungary), on the theme of the reform of socialist planning. My *Economics of feasible socialism* (George Allen & Unwin, 1983) had been read by many of the participants, and so this was an attempt at 'updating' it. Since then I have heard that it is also to be translated and published in Hungary. Indeed with the onward march of *glasnost'* it could conceivably be published in the Soviet Union too. In fact some of the Soviet reformers may consider that it did not go far enough! More should be said, for example, on the need for some sort of capital market, and on the implications of liberalizing foreign trade. I would now (1990) have to take into account the fundamental changes occurring in Eastern Europe.

As a student of Soviet-type economies, I was very conscious of the inefficiencies that seemed inherent in centralized planning. These clearly were indeed 'inherent', in the sense that they could not be ascribed to stupidity, bad will or a love of inefficiency for its own sake. I wrote many years ago an article on 'planners' preferences',[1] where I criticized those who thought that the product mix reflected the preference of the planners as against that of the consumers: surely in most instances the product mix was not consciously intended by the centre, it was a malfunction, and this in turn was due to the *impossibility* of determining at the centre either the detailed assortment of output or the most economical means of producing it. In 1958, that is, thirty years ago, I wrote an article on economic reform, published in *Social Research*, which argued that market-type reforms were necessary. Of course, this was premature, and I only mention this early and probably naive article to show that these questions worried me rather long ago.

The second motive arose out of contemplating the critique of the Soviet system from the left, by those who considered themselves to be true Marxists. It seemed to me that, while many of their criticisms hit the target, the implied alternatives, the criteria of judgment, were quite unreal. This unreality, it seemed to me, was deeply embedded in the Marxist tradition and stemmed from Marx himself. Their opposition to the market was combined with opposition to the inevitably bureaucratic centralized alternative. Marx, it appeared to me, was a utopian in his (admittedly fragmentary) remarks about socialism/communism. The two motives then combined: by what kind of realistic criteria could we criticize the Soviet system?

There followed another question: what other model or models of a socialist economy could there be? Would it be relevant to possible socialist programmes in West European countries? It was not enough to criticize, there had to be some sort of 'feasible socialist' alternative. I made clear that this was not so much a commitment, a statement of personal belief, but an intellectual exercise. If people preferred capitalism, or some other '-ism', that was their right. However, already then I felt the shadow of the offensive of the New Right; they all too often used the inefficiencies of Soviet-type planning as a stick with which to beat 'socialism' in general, and so a defence was needed against attackers from that quarter.

Let us look at *some criticisms* of these ideas which have appeared in the last few years. Several were from the left: Mandel in *New Left Review*, and also Louis Gill from Canada, among others. They broadly followed the line that could easily be foretold (*was* foretold in the imaginary review which I included in the book). The market's inadequacies were listed – and they undoubtedly exist. Then Mandel imagined a form of market-less supply of inputs which left me puzzled: how is it possible that he could not see the gaps in his own argument? He envisaged a footwear factory (his example) sending representatives for a comradely discussion to the producers of leather. Presumably the citizens who desire shoes have a comradely discussion in the retail store, which sends a request to the footwear factory. It is all so simple, and reminded me of my days in the British army. Soldiers are entitled to boots. Boots of various sizes are 'indented for' by the quarter-master. These requests (*zayavki* they are called in Russian) are aggregated, and the quartermaster-general of the Army ensures that boots are indeed provided. The soldier and the regiment do not pay for them. Since soldiers have only two feet, and their numbers are known, forecasts of requirements can be made with reasonable accuracy. Admittedly in the real world someone pays the factory for the boots, but, true enough, at the regimental level there is no market.

It is hardly necessary to list here the deficiencies of such an approach. Simplicity is achieved by eliminating choice (there is only one model of army boot). As well as consumer choice there is producer choice, and in my reply to Mandel I concentrated on the situation of a producing enterprise (whether and how far it is 'self-managed' is in the present context irrelevant). To produce any good or service requires several material inputs. Any change in decision as to what to produce calls for a change in these inputs, which vary in specification and quality. It is unrealistic to imagine that they are abundantly available in state storehouses, as they too require to be produced, and in turn require inputs. Production is a complex process through time, involving interrelated processes. In every system some of the necessary coordination is achieved through hierarchic subordination: that is, *within* firms or corporations. Markets or hierarchies – *tertium non datur*. Similarly the enterprise, having negotiated with its customers, can obtain the needed inputs either by *purchase* or by *administered allocation*. Also involved is the issue of complexity. It is in no way un-Marxist to speak of quantity turning into quality! When one gets away from a shoe factory seeking a supply of leather, and reaches the real world in which hundreds of thousands of production and service units require maybe millions of inputs, each of which has alternative uses, Mandel's approach is totally wide of the mark. But he is indeed in the tradition exemplified by Engels's well-known remark in his *Anti-Dühring*: 'everything will be quite simple without so-called value'.

'Value', 'commodity relations', arise out of the separation of production units from each other. But this separation is a prerequisite for meaningful enterprise autonomy, which in turn is the prerequisite for any sort of meaningful self-management or participation.

If Mandel valiantly defends the dogmatic position, this cannot be said of Bettelheim. He has largely abandoned his earlier arguments. In recent seminars in Paris I heard him admit that such criticisms as mine were well founded, that the elimination of markets does lead to the domination of what a Soviet critic has recently called 'the class of bureaucratic allocators' (*klass burokraticheskikh raspredelitelei*).[2] In discussion, he agreed that the alternative to the allocation of labour through incentives (wage-differentials, or a species of labour-market) can only be labour allocation by direction, hardly a step in the direction of workers' freedom. And yet, in his comments on my own model of 'feasible socialism', he asserted that it could not be socialism, since it involved both commodity production and the wages system ('marchandises et salariat'). This, if I understood him aright, leaves him in a theoretical vacuum. On the one hand, the elimination of the market leads to some form of highly undesirable state capitalism (he even makes out, in his latest work, that the October revolution itself was 'capitalist'). On the other, the very presence of commodity relations makes any system non-socialist. So, then, has he proved that socialism is impossible, on his own definition?

Another category of criticism has come (informally) from some Hungarian colleagues, and relates to the present difficulties of the Hungarian economy. Do these show that the desired mix between plan and market, with a sizeable cooperative and private sector, is not viable? As one of them put it, 'We have all the institutions which are in your model, so why are we in such a mess?' There are various replies which could be made. One, also made by a number of Hungarian critics, is that the 'new economic mechanism' in its present shape provides neither any effective macroeconomic policy nor a really functioning microeconomic market. There is little real competition (and where it does exist, as in retail trade, there are reasonable levels of efficiency). Price controls, subsidies, levies, import restrictions and pressure to export distort or paralyse the market. It is arguable how far this is due to social–political pressures and contradictions of the kind analysed by Kornai, and how far it is a by-product of the balance of payments constraint. In the USSR there used to be a debate on 'socialism in one country'. One could argue that 'reform in one small country' cannot be effective. A parallel: when Mitterrand was first elected, he tried an expansionist policy, which failed because France was alone in pursuing it (it might have worked had the whole of the EEC adopted it). Similarly, the adoption of a new economic mechanism by the whole of Comecon could have given a better chance to even an imperfect new mechanism.

Another critique from Hungarian colleagues was: why the limitation on private enterprise? (In my 'feasible' model, a limit was set on numbers employed, or on the value of capital assets, the choice being influenced by whether or not unemployment is a problem.) I replied that my 'limit was not so much a desideratum as simply definitional: if large sectors are dominated by privately-owned capital, then it would not be socialism'. Two counter-attacks were launched on this position. One: why not redefine socialism, to include (for example) Sweden, where a welfare-state with a large state sector coexists with large-scale private enterprise? The second: does not the very existence of imposed limits imply that private enterprise would grow rapidly unless this is artificially prevented? And does this not mean the silent assumption that the private sector is inherently superior? This ties up with an interesting paper presented at a recent conference in Florida, on the theme: why does cooperative enterprise not flourish in capitalist countries? Is there in fact an advantage in private ownership of the means of production?

This brings me to the neo-liberal critique, for example by Brian Crozier and Arthur Selden, and also Israel Kirzner. Most of the arguments are familiar, and indeed I set them out in the imagined right-wing review in my book. However Kirzner (in a paper presented at that Florida conference and not yet published) performed the valuable task of tying up the present controversies with the old debates between Mises and Lange. He argued that Mises was compelled to rethink his own position. Lange's case was a strong one within the restrictive assumptions of neoclassical general-equilibrium theory, so Mises, in making his case against him, cast many of these assumptions aside, and so arrived at the position still held by the so-called 'Austrian' school, of which Kirzner himself and Lachmann are distinguished members. This school stresses *dis*equilibrium, the functions of entrepreneurs and risk-takers in a dynamic and ever-changing world. A very different world to the textbook equilibrium neoclassical one in which, to cite Brian Loasby, 'the sub-systems of resource allocation known as firms have no function to perform', and nor has management, in a world of perfect knowledge and no interdependencies.[3] Similar arguments have been advanced by the West German economist Helmut Arndt, in his *Irrwege des politischen Ökonomie*.

One must recognize some validity in such criticisms. State-owned, self-managed, cooperative enterprises are vulnerable to the accusation that they would be risk-averse, and/or that there would be no one to bear the cost and blame for failure if the firm were unsuccessful. There can be no perfect system, there are advantages and disadvantages in every human institution. So there is no harm in admitting that the Kirzner type of criticism hits the target. Of course small-scale private enterprise would fill the risk-bearing gap to some extent, but suppose the optimal size (and the risk) is significantly above the limit, or a small entrepreneur is very successful and could expand rapidly unless prevented?

But let us now pass to the impact of *recent developments*, *changes*, *reforms* and *crises*, which, were I writing my book today, I would have to take into account.

China would need much more space. The apparently swift success of decollectivization of agriculture, the (partial) opening to foreign capital and the legalization of private trade and petty manufacture have been accompanied by only limited autonomy for state industrial enterprises. Difficulties have arisen, too, as is hardly surprising. Income inequalities have grown ever larger in agriculture, especially in the absence of an explicit land rent. A shift away from grain-crops has made increased imports necessary. Inflationary pressures have increased. There have been reports of increased corruption of the party and state apparatus – but similar things happened in the USSR also, and there at least they had no connection with reform. My last visit to China was in 1983. There is much to study to fill gaps in knowledge, before the needed new pages could be written. I have learnt that *Feasible Socialism* is about to appear in Peking in a Chinese translation. This is a surprise, as I thought that the critical chapter devoted to Marx would rule it out.

The USSR under Gorbachev is engaged in what is repeatedly described as a 'radical reform', and clearly this would call for many pages of analysis. Much that is described in my chapter on 'the lessons to be drawn from Soviet experience' is no longer controversial. Indeed Soviet critiques of their own system[4] and their amendments of official growth rates and price indices[5] paint a notably *less* favourable picture than even the CIA. Gorbachev speaks of 'a pre-crisis situation'. One can and should welcome the much greater frankness, openness and willingness to discuss and analyze fundamental issues, both of the past and the present.

However, the truly remarkable cultural changes, the much enlarged area of freedom of speech and of the press, contrast with the exceedingly slow progress of the economic reform. Declarations and decrees have had little effect. Enterprise autonomy and 'full *khozraschyot*' have remained on paper, with *goszakaz* becoming *gosprikaz*'; in other words, state orders (commercial) are in fact state orders (hierarchical–administrative), covering virtually all productive capacity. 'Trade in means of production' remains an intention not (yet) realized in practice. Price reform is not to occur until 1991, though other elements of the reform can scarcely begin to operate until the basis of price-determination is altered. Chronic shortages continue, as does the long-notorious scattering of investment resources over too many projects. In agriculture some highly desirable developments (such as the small group and family contract, leasing of land to families and mini-cooperatives) are contradicted by the energy with which local authorities repress (legal) private growing of early vegetables[6] reflecting widely-held prejudice against private enrichment. Complaints continue about arbitrary interference with farm management by the party and by the 'agro-industrial complex' (*Agroprom*) bureaucracy. A story widely told in Moscow goes like this:

> *KGB man* (to CIA man, in, say, Geneva): 'Tell me, honestly, you can be frank with me, did you have anything to do with the Chernobyl disaster?'
> *CIA man*: 'I swear to you, no. But *Agroprom*, that was us!'

So, were I writing my book today, I would have much more to say both about the ability of the new leadership realistically to assess the situation and initiate an ambitious programme of reform, *and* the powerful social and political forces which are delaying or blocking change. These forces are assisted by the undoubtedly very serious practical problems which stand in the way of the desired reform: the continued *defitsit*, the lack of trained personnel accustomed to work in new ways, the absence of some necessary institutions (thus a market requires information flows and trading intermediaries which are still rudimentary). Then the reform model itself has gaps: there is no clarity about a role for a capital market, there is still argument about the principles of price-determination, there is vagueness about the appropriate levels of decision-making. I would certainly quote a remarkably intelligent (and probably little-noticed) article in *Izvestiya sibirskogo otdeleniya Akademii nauk SSSR, Seriya ekonomika* . . ., by P. Aven and V. Shironin. They go even further than I do in stressing that the so-called 'command economy' is really a 'bargaining economy', and accuse those who devise reforms of not seeing how the real economy works. Thus: 'the real "economy of bargaining" remains practically unstudied, no one has examined the procedures by which agreements are reached and the "weight" of various resources in the "bargain"'. Yet 'how can one forecast the effect of the lessening of administrative pressures and of the introduction of economic stimuli and levers' without such knowledge?.[7] They also draw attention to the role in capitalist countries of 'large firms and corporations' (p. 39).

It is too easily assumed that under the reform the key decision-making level should be the enterprise. Yet in some sectors this is not the case in the West, if by 'enterprise' is meant one factory. A firm like Du Pont or Imperial Chemical Industries contains dozens of 'enterprises'. The same is true of Exxon or Shell. I made this point in my book.[8] After my recent visit to Moscow I feel that the point needs strengthening. Also needed is more emphasis both on what the market can do and on its limitations. Among some reformers I encountered what seemed to me to be 'Muscovite friedmanists', guilty of typical Chicago over-simplification. Infrastructure, like public urban transport, generates external economies, and their profit-and-loss account is an insufficient guide to efficiency, without also taking into account both the external effects and the *purpose* of their existence: just as the transport department of a Western corporation cannot be evaluated merely in terms of its own finances, ignoring the punctuality and reliability of the delivery of the goods it carries. All airports in America are publicly owned, usually by local authorities, because profit maximization of the airport's own operation is not necessarily consistent with attracting traffic for the benefit of the business community and citizens of that locality. Some reforming economists in the East need reminding that, in standard neoclassical theory, 'highly complex sub-systems . . ., containing within themselves many layers of great complexity, are regularly treated as simple elements, while components of a complex system are analyzed as isolated units'.[9]

Of course some Soviet economists – Maiminas, for instance – are aware of the complexities of decision-making structures. They could also remember the pioneering work on organization theory by Alexander Bogdanov.

Much is being written about the extent of corruption in high places, especially in some republics, and about the opposition of 'bureaucrats', of sectoral and regional interests, and, last but not least, of (especially) the intermediate levels of the party machine. There is genuine nervousness, too, concerning the possible consequences of loss of control, the confusions which inevitably occur when long-established arrangements are radically altered. Workers too are concerned about the effects of reforms on job security and the stability of their earnings. It is much too soon to express any firm view about the success or failure of a reform process which is still in its early stages, and I will not pursue this question further here.

If my book were written today, more would have to be said about the economic problems not only of Hungary but also of Poland and Yugoslavia, all of which remain acute or have become more so. Even the relatively successful Bulgarian agriculture has gone wrong in recent years (it is not clear to me just why), whereas the least 'reformist' of the Comecon countries, the GDR and Czechoslovakia, seem to have done better. Are there any lessons here? If so, which? More research is needed. No lessons can be learnt from Romania, other than on the need to avoid dynastic despotisms.

Finally, back to the West, and in particular to Great Britain and Mrs Thatcher's ideologists. It is necessary to stress that she has no majority in the popular vote: her parliamentary majority is a consequence of a unique electoral system. But it is true that Labour is in confusion, the would-be social-democratic–liberal centre losing ground. Many 'Thatcherite' principles have considerable support. Yet some of her recent actions are extraordinary, judged by the standards of other conservative governments. Let me give examples.

'Privatization' of natural monopolies is not on the agenda of the conservative governments of France, West Germany, the Netherlands or Switzerland. Who but extremist anti-socialist ideologues would privatize water, urban public transport, electricity, telephones and airports, would seriously consider privatizing the post office, would *order* local authorities and public-health bodies to put most of their services out to private tender? Who else would also *fragment* networks? Examples of the latter are the break-up of the unified electricity-generating system, and the disintegration of urban transport: different firms run buses in competition with each other, with no one responsible for the network. The privatization of health and education, based upon the profit motive, is on the agenda too.

I cannot explain why 'Thatcherism' is in some respects unique to Britain. (Even in America, *all* urban public transport and airports are in the public sector.) The underlying theories or ideology would be explored, were I writing my book today. Very briefly, the essential features of the 'economics' of those who advise Mrs Thatcher go beyond mere belief in the virtues of the free market, virtues that do exist and, indeed, which most of us share. Nor can one object to her views concerning the need for an 'enterprise culture', which is lacking in Britain both among management and trade unions. The key elements that distinguish her advisers' ideas are:

1. The whole is seen as *only* the sum of its parts. To quote Peter Earl (*The Economic Imagination*, a good book): 'The neoclassical theorist sees aggregated concepts as if they are simply the sum of their component elements.' The purposes of system, the logic of networks, are missing; hence the tendency to fragment, which extends far beyond economics, causing disruption also to the government of London and Greater Manchester, school districts and so on. (But pro-business ideology prevents them from even thinking about breaking up large private corporations!)
2. 'Methodological individualism' also asserts itself in a simple picture of utility-maximizing individuals and profit-maximizing firms. According to the ideologically convenient formulations of James Buchanan, public servants pursue their own personal utility, there being no such thing as a definable public interest. No one can deny that some public servants ('bureaucrats') do pursue self-interest, but clearly in the public as well as the private sector people also try to do their job well and derive satisfaction from this. The postal service used to take pride in punctual delivery of letters (less so now, because of the stress on 'commercial criteria'). Naively narrow psychology sees nothing between personal utility maximization and 'altruism'. In Buchanan this is combined with the typical 'Chicago' belief that the pursuit of individual profit in the market is always conducive to the general good. In which case, it follows that the maximum possible reduction in the public sector is

a good in itself. It is clearly important for socialists, in East or West, to distance themselves from this view of human motivation. In my own book I argued, at length, that it is unrealistic to expect human beings to identify with 'the *general* interest', but Buchanan-type doctrines go far beyond this. In my view, the heads of the Glasgow parks department, of Budapest transport, of the British Museum, do try to do their job well, tending to identify the general interest with obtaining more resources for parks, transport and museums. In Buchanan's, they pursue their own personal 'utility', unless they are 'altruists'. Of course pride in a job well done also adds to personal utility, but so would bureaucratic indifference if the individual happens to be bureaucratically indifferent. The theory is a tautology. We all do what we prefer. Thus I prefer to be writing this paper because I am writing it. If I had preferred to spend the time on a yacht with a beautiful blonde, I would be on a yacht with a beautiful blonde. The ultimate achievement of this sort of logic is the assertion that involuntary unemployment is impossible: you must be 'preferring leisure'. Lucas *does* say this.

3. Externalities are ignored or downgraded. This follows from the belief that whatever is profitable is (almost) always good, whatever is loss-making ought to be abandoned. Hence the aim to eliminate subsidies to public transport, the neglect of infrastructure generally, cuts in housing, the subordination of anything to do with quality of life to commercial considerations. Research grants, as well as university finance, are repeatedly cut.
4. 'Planning' is rejected, not being seen as needed. Thus there is (almost) no energy policy. It is believed that competitive markets will take care of investment, despite the arguments of those economists (still a minority) who point out that the competitive model does not generate the needed information, especially about, for example, the investment intentions of others.[10] (The 'high growth' of the British economy in recent years is accompanied by modest levels of productive investment, and the very large increase in imports could lead to a balance of payments crisis quite soon.) Space forbids further exploration of this and similar themes.

What is depressing is the lack of a coherent reply from Labour, from the moderate centre, and indeed from the mainstream economics profession (the far-out think-tanks that have Mrs Thatcher's ear are not typical). The Labour party is much handicapped by having to battle with its own left wing, whose 'socialist' slogans are unpopular with most voters and lack an economic base, while the trade unions are slow in taking a positive attitude to productivity. The public image remains unconvincing.

But then perhaps the prospects for democratic socialism in Western Europe depend decisively on something going badly wrong with the existing system. Does the stock exchange crash that reverberated round the world in October 1987 signify the start of another Great Depression? That would change all our points of reference.

NOTES

1. *Economic Journal*, June 1966.
2. See Nuikin A., *Novyi mir*, no. 1, 1988, p. 198.
3. Loasby B., *Choice, Complexity and Ignorance*, Cambridge, 1976, p. 63.
4. For example, N. Shmelev, *Novyi mir*, no. 6, 1987.
5. See, for example, Khanin and Selyunin in *Novyi mir*, no. 3, and Bogomolov in *Literaturnaya gazeta*, 16 September 1987.
6. 'Axes and even bulldozers' have been used to destroy glasshouses, according to *Voprosy ekonomiki*, no. 7, 1987.
7. See no. 13, 1987, p. 35.
8. See Nove, 1983, pp. 201–2.
9. Loasby, p. 30.
10. See Richardson, G. B., *Information and Investment*, Oxford, 1960.

17 Soviet Reforms and Western Neoclassical Economics*

> It is known that Marx and Engels held that socialism and commodity production [that is, production for the market] were not only contradictory but also incompatible. Lenin adopted the same position. Even today no one would have the 'theoretical cheek' to claim that Lenin was the founder of the theory of commodity production under socialism. Was the theory of Marx, Engels, Lenin, about socialism then incorrect, or was their theory on commodity production incorrect?

This was said by Professor A. Sergeyev at a conference devoted to a draft of a new textbook on political economy.[1] The director of the Institute of Economics, L. Abalkin, declared at the same conference that

> for historical reasons we are facing the necessity to reassess anew many of our conceptions of socialism, . . . to take into account phenomena which could not have been foretold in the 19th century, when Marx and Engels worked, and which Lenin could not observe or investigate in the first years of Soviet power.[2]

The new editor of *Voprosy ekonomiki*, V. Popov, stated: 'We lack a decisive break-through towards the elaboration of a contemporary theoretical model of socialism . . .'.[3]

What could they learn if they were all to attend a course in

---

* This paper was written for a conference on planning and markets in Eastern Europe, which was held in Vienna in December 1988 under the auspices of the Institut für Wissenshaften von Menschen. There is certainly more that could be said about the potential relevance of some Western theorizing, for example principal-and-agent, organization theory, models of disequilibrium, and 'monetarism' too (the USSR has suffered from lack of attention to excessive growth of money supply). However, the critique of 'mainstream' teaching appears to me to have been basically correct.

neoclassical economics? Having read the standard textbooks, what could they apply to their reality? Needless to say the phrase 'neoclassical economics' or 'the neoclassical paradigm' covers a wide range of different writers, and all would freely admit that their theories do not and cannot pretend to 'realism' in the assumptions, with respect to any real, functioning economy. All theories involve abstractions. This is as true of Marx as of Milton Friedman. Thus the assumption in *Das Kapital* about the rate of profit is an equilibrium assumption; in real life, as Marx well knew, rates of profit vary widely. In his definition of productive labour under capitalism he abstracted from the existence of the self-employed, and so on. As will be seen, part of my critique of the relevance (to *any* economy) of the neoclassical paradigm lies not in what the theory or its interpreters say but in what is left unsaid, or not emphasised. For example, no one denies that what appears to be profitable to do depends in some degree on the area of responsibility of the decision-maker – but no one says so either.

Let us begin with the question of *shortage*, the *defitsit* which worries Soviet economists and managers in equal measure. The same issue of *Voprosy ekonomiki* carries a full and fair account of Janos Kornai's interpretation of its causes. But Kornai, whether he be right or wrong, is not a neoclassical economist, and is the author, among other things, of a book entitled *Anti-equilibrium*. The neoclassicals generally assume that 'markets clear', or would do so if there were not some imperfections, such as price controls, trade unions and the like. If some labour or materials remain unused, then this cannot be 'Pareto-optimal' as more could be produced without diminishing anyone's income. In general equilibrium everything is fully utilized, and this is the *optimum optimorum*.

Yet this view is, I submit, false. False because it is inconsistent with the assumption of competition. For competition actually to be occurring there *has* to be spare capacity, at the very least among the less successful. Competition must mean losers as well as gainers, and this is already inconsistent with the 'Pareto' principle which speaks of gainers with no losers. (I once said to a neoclassical: 'Surely you cannot envisage a situation in which any innovation or indeed any major act would cause no loss to anyone!' He replied: 'In that case the situation is already Pareto-optimal') Equally important, a situation in which aggregate supply equals demand with full employment of material and human resources will guarantee the existence of shortages at the micro level, and all experience shows that fear of shortages generates a mode of behaviour (hoarding, overapplication for resources, concealment of capacity) which makes shortages more acute. The basic reason is simple, and applies to all systems: precise knowledge of the future does not exist; the unexpected always happens; there are millions of variants of goods and services when fully disaggregated. Since these are not and cannot be perfect substitutes for one another, spare capacity must exist if demand is to be satisfied, to cope with the unexpected. It cannot be achieved by price manipulation (or fluctuation) alone, because of innumerable instances of complementarities in production. Long ago Kornai correctly observed that, for user demand to be satisfied, it must be difficult to sell; one needs a buyers' market. He had in mind, among other things, the psychological effect on the would-be seller: he may not bother to adapt the product to new requirements if there is a sellers' market.

It follows that – except in a static world confined exclusively to textbooks – markets not only do not clear, they *should* not clear. A smoothly functioning system requires excess production capacity; competition presupposes its existence. Unless, that is, one assumes perfect micro foresight – a situation never encountered anywhere at any time.

The neoclassical paradigm lays overwhelming stress on the concept of equilibrium. There are some good theoretical and pedagogic reasons for this. It is, as Frank Hahn likes to say, a 'beautiful' theoretical construction. No alternative can match its beauty and its completeness. Economics has become highly mathematicized, and important elements of reality tend to be excluded because they are not amenable to mathematical techniques. Everyone, including the authors of equilibrium models, are well aware that the real world is full of disequilibrium. There are indeed disequilibrium models, but they are, so to speak, equilibrium–disequilibrium models. To quote Henry Wu (Hong Kong University) 'disequilibrium [becomes] a merely reconciliating experience employed to reconstitute the disequilibrating concepts within the equilibrium framework'.[4] Similarly, uncertainty is recognized, but, as Shackle and others have been pointing out, the models incline many users to imagine insurable, actuarial uncertainty, to which one can apply theories of probability, and in the end it becomes (almost) certain uncertainty, as in the case of 'rational expectations'. It is clear, of course, that people (East and West) adjust their behaviour to expectations and try to be rational, but this is no excuse (to quote Keynes) for 'reducing uncertainty to the same calculable status as that of certainty itself'. Furthermore, to cite Brian Loasby,[5] 'equilibrium models cannot explain, since they specify no causal process'. Phyllis Deane[6] points out that 'it was the notion of taking uncertainty into account that proved most difficult to absorb into the neoclassical paradigm. For a world of uncertainty is a world of perpetual disequilibrium.' Three quotations from Frank Hahn, an intelligent *defender* of 'neoclassicism':

(a) 'We have no good reason to suppose that there are forces which lead the economy to equilibrium. By that I mean we have no good theory. If indeed there is order we do not understand how it is brought about.'
(b) 'It is a fair question whether it can ever be useful to have an equilibrium notion which does not describe the termination of actual processes.'
(c) 'If price changes are themselves the outcome of the rational assessment of their consequences for the agent making the change, then we can no longer take the neo-classical axiom for granted.'[7]

The so-called 'new classical economics' is far worse. One of its principal creators, Sargent, wrote: 'It's very hard to do disequilibrium work . . ., the reason being that the possibility of disequilibrium complicates agents' decision problems. One reason in favour of equilibrium models is that it solves a lot of technical problems.'[8] So much the worse, therefore, for the real world. Solow noted that 'new classical economists wonder why rational people do not always see that a 10% increase in the money supply is equivalent to a 10% increase in every price overnight and that all real things remain in pre-existent equilibrium'.[9] Instantaneous adjustment is assumed, and for Lucas all things are by definition in equilibrium. Thus he denies the very possibility of involuntary unemployment: since everyone does what he or she prefers, they must prefer leisure! (Opponents of this school refer mockingly to the fact that 15 million Americans happened to have 'preferred leisure' in 1933!). I will not pursue these ideas further, but it is wrong not to note (and deplore, with amazement) the very considerable spread of 'new classical economics', explicable only by its elegant mathematics, at least in my view, and its helpfulness to extreme *laissez-faire* ideologists (they claim that the doctrines prove that government intervention can achieve nothing). It is a species of *reductio ad absurdum* of formal neoclassicism, 'an admirably consistent and logical outcome of the neo-classical assumptions of rational maximizing behaviour', to cite Prychitko.[10]

I pass to two attacks directed from 'ideologically' very different quarters. One comes from the unjustly neglected Oxford economist G. B. Richardson, the other from the 'Austrian school'. Both are highly relevant to East European reform models.

The essence of Richardson's critique also concentrates on uncertainty, with special reference to *investment decisions*. He shows that, paradoxically, uncertainty and imperfect knowledge are not regrettable imperfections, as implied by neoclassical theory. To cite an admirer of Richardson, Brian Loasby:

> The conventional view, of course, is that in perfect competition the price and output of every unit within the economy is precisely determined, whereas under oligopoly they are indeterminate. Richardson demonstrates that, in the absence of the (Walrasian) auctioneer, formal perfect competition provides no basis for expectation, whereas oligopoly does at least define the apparently relevant set of competitors and may well promote the exchange of information which gives firms the confidence to make commitments. It is perfect competition that is indeterminate. The imperfections are what makes the system work.[11]

Richardson argues that:

> under perfect competition it would be impossible for any firm to know how much of any good to produce . . . Presumably firms are supposed to equate future marginal costs with future prices. But how is a producer to predict future prices, depending as they do on the demands of the consumers and on the supply plans of all his competitors? This the textbooks do not tell us . . . If the future price of a good were known to be greater than the current cost of making it, then a profit opportunity may be said to exist; but if there are an unlimited number of firms able to respond to the opportunity, no individual firm will know what to do. A profit opportunity equally available to everyone is in fact available to none at all.[12]

Neoclassical textbooks do not, as a rule, handle investment satisfactorily. They appreciate, of course, that investment raises the question of time, of *future* prices, interest, exchange-rates. But most neoclassical models are of their nature static. To cite Hahn again, investment 'is profoundly mysterious under perfect competition'.[13] Investment involves risk, an estimate of what the future might bring. It involves estimating the future actions of actual or potential competitors, the plans of the providers of complementary inputs. In the real world, as Kornai pointed out long ago, no one takes a major decision on the basis of price information alone, yet many models (including the Lange model of 1938) assume that they do. The theoretical gap is visible also in the Soviet reform model, with its emphasis on 'self-financing' and on decentralized investments. These are, in themselves, desirable, since the system has suffered from overcentralization. However one does not see in the reform proposals an adequate stress on the availability of information on the basis of which investments should be made. In Richardson's universe, which is the real world, investment takes place because of so-called imperfections: imperfect knowledge (one firm knows something the others do not), collusion, market domination, government-sponsored coordination (Japan's MITI undertakes this) or long-term links with large customers. The greater the anticipated competition, the less the incentive to invest. (The British governments's economic advisers seem quite unable to understand this.)

Now to the Austrians, typified by Lachmann. He too believes that the real market 'maintains itself through a divergence rather than a convergence of expectations, and this cannot be defended as a strictly equilibrating process'.[14] He too follows Shackle in stressing 'true uncertainty', which he counterposes to 'late classical formalism', formalism under which 'the economist's focus on functional relationships between the prices and quantities of things' eliminates 'human intentionality' and 'learning by doing'. It is assumed that 'the probabilities of certain outcomes are given and known', and this is needed for formal mathematical modelling. *Different* expectations, disequilibrium, actual or anticipated, are the bases for entrepreneurship, which itself can disequilibrate. 'Austrians', such as Hayek, have been pointing out that the standard neoclassical treatment of competitive price '*assumes* the situation to exist which a true explanation ought to account for as the effect of the competitive process'. Israel Kirzner, a New York 'Austrian', stresses 'the extraordinary assumptions concerning availability of information' which underlie standard theory. This 'simply assumes that firms know the nature of "given" preferences and supply perfectly appropriate products. I wanted a theory that could be practically applied and did not assume out of the way all the interesting informational issues in order to reach determinate solutions in a highly formalized manner'.[15] But back to the 'Austrians' and to Kirzner. He pointed out that L. von Mises, in trying to show that Lange's socialist model was inadequate, 'emphasized with unsurpassed clarity how important it is to see the market as an entrepreneurial process rather than a state of equilibrium affairs'.[16] Again, 'markets work, in the Austrian view, because they are characterised by a continual process of entrepreneurial discovery', and profits are a consequence of actions under disequilibrium. Indeed, in the formal general-equilibrium theory profits tend to zero, since there is no function for an entrepreneur and so no reward for entrepreneurship. The German economist Helmut Arndt made a similar point: 'The manager or entrepreneur, and also the purchaser, are in fact almost totally deprived of function . . . What they "do" could just as well be left to a robot!'[17] W. Baumol wrote: 'The entrepreneur has virtually disappeared from the theoretical literature.'

Richardson and the 'Austrians' are surely more relevant to Soviet reforms than is the neoclassical paradigm (even if the Austrians may idealize the 'entrepreneur' in an age of corporate bureaucracies). One need not accept their conclusions, but one must take their arguments seriously. In the USSR too the investment decision and the managerial function relate to the world of disequilibrium and uncertainty. Socialist entrepreneurship involves risk in a dynamic world, with imperfect (but not non-existent) information. One thinks too of Schumpeter, who linked large-scale research and innovation with large firms, which possessed or hoped to possess market domination, for in its absence the risk involved would be too great. (Yet an excessively protected monopoly may not wish to innovate, so the conclusion is controversial.)

This brings me to the theory of the firm. The general-equilibrium perfect-competition model has problems with the firm and, to cite Shubik, sees no difference between a giant like General Electric and the corner ice-cream store. The question of the internal organization of firms was left unexplored: a firm is a 'black box'. ('Outsiders' such as H. Simon and H. Leibenstein tried to enter the box.) Efforts to fit the firm into the neo-classical world have been made by Coase, and more recently by O. E. Williamson. In the latter's *Markets and Hierarchies*, he explored the reason why some activities are undertaken under hierarchical orders and not through the market. He centred his analysis on the concept of 'transaction cost'. Indeed markets are not costless, nor is the obtaining of information. If a given transaction costs less if under the authority of the firm (and 'cost' includes the cost of ensuring that contracts are observed), then the answer is 'hierarchy'. Soviet reformers should indeed devote more attention to the role and logic of hierarchy in capitalist market economies. However in doing so they should bear in mind the incompleteness of Williamson's interesting and valuable analysis.

In my view, the problem arose from over-concentration on 'the transaction' as the basic unit of the analysis. It is true that, in deciding whether to perform a *given* task oneself or to use a sub-contractor in the market, the considerations advanced by Williamson do apply. But this leaves out of account the factors guiding the decision-maker to undertake that transaction. It is tacitly assumed that all transactions are profitable *as such*, that the firms's overall strategy and role do not contribute to the decision.

This is connected with another 'lack' in conventional neoclassical theory, which in fact inspires the title of Axel Leijonhufvud's Information and Coordination. Let me quote him:

> In Walrasian general equilibrium theory, all transactors are regarded as price takers. As noted by Arrow, 'there is no one left over whose job it is to take a decision on price'. The job is in fact entrusted to a *deus ex machina*: Walras' auctioneer is assumed to inform all traders of the prices at which all markets are going to clear. This always trustworthy information is supplied at zero cost. There are no situations conceivable at which 'demand and supplies do not mesh', since firms face 'perfectly elastic demand and supply schedules without ever having their trading plans disappointed'.[18]

He too points out that 'the model leaves no room for the production manager, product designer, distribution expert, etc.' In the neoclassical model there is no need for conscious coordination. There is also a problem with time. Hahn agrees that the Arrow–Debreu neoclassical model is 'careless in its treatment of time', collapsing the future into the present, or else assuming that inter-temporal market signals exist, so that future equilibrium prices are somehow known. In another of his articles, Leijonhufvud points out that the use of production-function analysis predisposes the analysts to seeing the actual process of production as an instantaneous combination of production factors. Yet in fact production takes place in a series of interrelated *sequences*, through time. The separate marginal or incremental assessment of the contribution of each of the sequences is thereby complicated and sometimes rendered impossible. Furthermore firms have strategies, choose a role in the market, and the profitability or otherwise of a specific transaction is judged *within* a wider whole. In identical situations firm A may act when firm B does not, because of where the given transaction fits into the more general pattern. This aspect, which arises prior to a decision whether to do it oneself ('hierarchy') or hiring a sub-contractor ('market') is missing from Williamson's analysis, and from the neoclassical textbooks generally.

In my own critique of conventional theory I referred to 'myopic' or 'one-dimensional' marginalism. This analytical deficiency can be illustrated with numerous examples. Neoclassical theory silently assumes that every transaction is directly market-related and earns a profit as such. Yet a large number of marginal decisions, whether on current production or on investment, can only make sense if seen as part of the larger whole. Thus, given the prior decision to invest in the oil industry in northern Siberia or Alaska, a large number of choices must be made on the routing and diameter of pipelines, location and equipment of pumping stations and a great deal else. These are margins *within* a hierarchy of margins.

Consider another and very different example. A shop, like Fauchon in Paris, Fortnum and Mason in London or Eliseyev in old Moscow, bases its profitability on its reputation for a very large assortment of foods. In Glasgow 'myopic-marginalist' accountants destroyed a similar shop by removing from its shelves those products that did not 'pay', thereby destroying that shop's raison d'être; eventually the shop closed. Common sense says that in all businesses the part must be related to the whole: that is why there *is* a whole, yet conventional neoclassical theory fragments. Textbooks are full of references to margins, yet the nature of marginal decisions is not discussed or defined. Yet the 'marginal' pumping-station or pâté de foie gras in the two above examples must be judged in relation to their effect on the oil project and the food store respectively. In the real world, decisions are marginal, but within a *hierarchy of margins*, to which there is a corresponding *hierarchy of decision-makers*, whose task is to relate the part to the whole. In neoclassical models the issue of optimal organizational and decision-making structures seldom arises, yet it is a vital, decisive aspect of the Soviet reform process. An American economist, Harold Demsetz, pointed out that the so-called perfect competition model has 'little to say about competition or the inner organization of firms', since 'what is modelled is not competition, it is extreme decentralization'; real competition and real firms 'require at least a modicum of authority in the allocation of resources . . . . The framework necessary for understanding most competitive activities, the very possibility of which depends on superior knowledge and real time lags and which is motivated by a desire for best orders, is lacking in the perfect decentralization model.' He also stresses that 'the real roles of management . . . to desire or discover markets, products, production techniques and actively to manage the actions of employees, have no place' in such a model. It cannot handle 'managed coordination'. He rightly criticizes the 'transaction costs' approach as 'much too narrow', as it ignores the positive importance of coordination. 'Prices, and the markets in which they are revealed, simply provide information about the value others place on resources, they do not themselves "allocate" or "coordinate" the uses made of these resources' (quoted from 'The theory of the firm revisited', UCLA discussion paper, 1987).

Hahn touched on a related point when he wrote: 'There are theoretical difficulties for accounting for the existence of firms unless we allow there to be increasing returns of some sort.' Yet most neoclassical models find increasing returns a problem, since they are inconsistent with equilibrium, which requires firms to be on a diminishing returns curve. (Otherwise they would already have expanded . . . But this again is a static concept; in real time *some* firms are expanding, others not.)

A similar critique of 'one-dimensionalism' was made by Brian Loasby: 'Even in economics, where the proliferation of multi-level interdependence is the essential basis on which the subject has been built, very drastic simplifications are the rule. Highly complex subtypes, such as firms or even whole sectors of the economy, containing within themselves many layers of great complexity, are regularly treated as simple elements, while components of a complex system are analysed as isolated units'.[19] Kornai made the same point more briefly in his *Anti-equilibrium* 'It is surprising that economics should have neglected for so long the problem of multi-level phenomena.'[20] Let us consider two illustrations of error caused by incorrect approach to multi-level problems, one from Great Britain and one from the Soviet Union.

The British government has decreed the privatization of all municipal bus services, allowing free competition and outlawing 'cross-subsidization', that is, the covering of losses on one service with profits from another. Apart from the confusion and congestion such a decision has caused, its inherent unsoundness rests on the implied belief that, conceptually, each bus service, perhaps even each bus, is a separate profit-making or *khozraschyot* unit, to be evaluated separately. The *system or network* aspect disappears, i.e. is disrupted. In no other civilized country is this example being followed: in every European, American and Canadian city known to me there is a publicly-operated *network*, with the subsidy (if any) paid to the network, which inevitably implies cross-subsidization between parts of the whole.

The Soviet example relates to service enterprises in agriculture. Decrees promulgated in 1982 and in 1985 set up an 'agro-industrial' hierarchy, *Agroprom*, to resolve the problem caused by the tendency of the service organizations such as those for repairs, drainage or 'chemicalization' to fulfil their own turnover plans in roubles rather than to serve the farms economically. It was decided that they should be rewarded in relation to their contribution to the 'final result', for example the harvest. There was a fallacy here, which the student of neoclassical economics would not be able to spot (but Leijonhufvud would!). Of course, in a tidy formal model a service organization *would* be paid in relation to its marginal productivity contribution. However this overlooks a very important aspect of reality. The reason why Soviet 'service' organizations could not be paid in relation to their contribution to the final result is that *no one knows what it is or was*. We can know that the harvest on a given land area was a thousand tons or bushels, but how to discover what proportion of this was the consequence of insecticides, or drainage work, or repairs? The key to the answer, as Soviet reformers do now realize, is to place decision-making and coordination in the hands of whosoever is in charge of *all* the sequential operations. Thus an American or British farmer makes estimates about the need to use insecticides or for tractor repairs and can also decide whether to do the job himself or hire a sub-contractor in the market, but in both instances *he is in command*, he decides, in relation to the entire sequence of tasks. The area of responsibility of the decision-maker, as well as his success criteria, *matter*. As Demsetz pointed out, the task of coordination is itself productive.

This brings me to another vitally important aspect of real competitive economies, *goodwill*. Firms find it important to maintain or improve quality, to undertake actions which *in themselves* may not pay, because reputation pays, and to maintain reputation it is worth spending time and effort. Obvious? Then I suggest that sceptics should look at any ten economics textbooks and look for the word 'goodwill' in the index. It is almost invariably missing. (Samuelsen does mention that it is a saleable asset, but without examining its nature or stressing its importance.) Yet here is a vital missing ingredient in the Soviet system: under conditions of monopoly or a sellers' market, bad service or poor quality cannot be 'punished' by the customer's going elsewhere, so loss of goodwill does not matter; nor do the customer's requirements. Why is goodwill missing from most neoclassical textbooks? Because under so-called perfect competition and in equilibrium the firm can by definition sell all it produces at the equilibrium price, *and* because of the analytical simplification that quality is *given* (a different quality is a different product; incidentally, 'quality' is also almost invariably absent from the index to a neoclassical textbook). Under pure monopoly, of course, goodwill does not matter either. It matters under *real* competition. But goodwill raises another analytical complication: it links together different transactions by the same firm, they react upon one another, whereas theory prefers to separate them, linking them only with the market. (Analysts do sometimes discuss brand names and product differentiation, under the heading of 'imperfect competition', and do note that it does have some effect on quality. But this is another example of so-called 'imperfections' being in fact necessary, and so not imperfections.)

The neoclassical view of human behaviour, whether of capitalists, managers or workers, is quite remarkably narrow. Firms maximize profits, individuals maximize utility. This approach is frequently linked with so-called Methodological individualism: the whole is but the sum of its parts. (Mrs Thatcher has said that 'society' does not exist, only persons and families do.) If this implies that the separate pursuit of profitability by parts of a large firm are necessarily and always consistent with the interests of the firm as a whole, that is surely nonsensical: why, then, is the firm large; why does it maintain a head office and an expensive corporate bureaucracy? This too is highly relevant for Soviet reformers. In the West there are a multitude of firms of all sizes, and within large ones there are different degrees of financial and operational autonomy of the parts. I would refer back to what I wrote earlier about hierarchy of margins and also the coordination of sequential or interrelated operations. It is by no means a matter of technological economies of scale; Du Pont operates nearly a hundred factories and plants, so the economy must be informational and/or arises out of the interconnections between the parts. Some Soviet reformers have frequently sought to devise a model within which the interests of the parts are always consistent with the interests of the whole. We must realize that this can never be completely achieved in any system. There are bound to be contradictions, conflicts of interest, to be resolved by higher authority, whether this be within the corporation or within the state. These dilemmas are in no way illuminated by the neoclassical paradigm, which, as we have noted, assumes 'perfect decentralization'. But back to human motivation. H. Simon has properly reminded us of its complexities: capitalists or managers do not 'maximize profits' in any meaningful way; it is an axiom which can neither be proved nor refuted, any more than it can be shown that individuals maximize utility, except in the purely tautological sense that whatever the firm or the individual does *is* maximizing behaviour. Suppose a capitalist takes a holiday in Honolulu, or I address a conference here in Vienna; are we 'maximizing profits' when we could be in our office? Do I prefer talking to this conference to taking a holiday?

Out of these over-simplifications have emerged so-called theories of 'public choice', which serve (in the West) the ideological purpose of denigrating public services and justifying privatization. It is undoubtedly useful to be reminded of the fact – well known also in the USSR – that some politicians, public officials and bureaucrats feather their own nests and pursue power and privilege. But it is quite another matter to assert that this is the rule throughout the public sector, that the officials in charge of kindergartens, public parks, hospitals or artillery do not identify with and desire improvements in the areas of their respective responsibilities. The problem, much discussed in the USSR, of 'departmentalism' (*vedomstvennost*) arises out of such identifications and is neither purely personal selfishness nor altruism. Thus (to take another example) the librarian of Moscow or Glasgow University desires to acquire more books, periodicals and shelving space because he is morally committed to his (or her) work, and not because he is 'maximizing his personal utility'. Unless, of course, we adopt the tautology that everyone prefers whatever he prefers, in which case we will be unable to distinguish between the devoted and honest librarian and one who secretly sells old books on the black market! Both would be 'maximizing'. There are two serious dimensions to this over-simple approach. Firstly, it is used to justify privatization, because it is held that in pursuing profit the capitalist will be compelled to be efficient (which is true subject to two conditions: that there is competition, and that profitability is the appropriate guide to efficiency, and, as we shall see, neither is necessarily the case). Secondly, it abstracts from pride in work done, loyalty and commitment, which affect performance of management and labour alike. The maximizing robot may 'fit' mathematical models, but is a poor substitute for real 'economic men', who pursue a whole number of sometimes inconsistent objectives, in the USSR, Austria, Britain – everywhere.

Neoclassical theory does recognize the existence of 'public goods', where the market cannot function effectively, though there are disagreements as to where to place the 'boundary' between public and private, for example in health, education and garbage collection. Water, electricity, gas and posts, are seen by many to be 'natural monopolies', where competition is either impossible or wasteful (competing water-pipes down the same street?). In most countries such considerations would apply also to urban public transport. Important too are *externalities*, positive or negative. This applies particularly to infrastructure, a point duly noted already by Adam Smith, who advocated public expenditure on roads, canals and ports, and, of course, there are external *dis*economies, such as congestion and environmental pollution. In such instances the profit rate is a misleading guide; state intervention or a subsidy may be appropriate. In Britain there have been debates for many years concerning efficiency criteria for public or private monopolies. They, and the controversies surrounding privatization, are directly relevant to the present Soviet discussions on what they call 'full *khozraschyot*', profit-and-loss accounting, wherever considerations of monopoly, externalities and public service are important. I read years ago of a Soviet town where each bus driver en route to suburban destinations was instructed to turn his passengers off the bus if their number fell below a minimum figure, as the rest of his journey was unprofitable! If there were competition, this would be 'bad for business' through loss of goodwill; where competition is absent then there must be an obligation, a duty to the public, which may require to be enforced. This is, by the way, another example of the fact that, in the real world, firms (even profit-oriented private firms!) find it necessary to undertake some loss-making activities to maintain goodwill, under competitive conditions.

Neoclassical price theory in 'perfect competition' models suffers from the assumption that all firms are 'price-takers', that prices are given. It is of course recognized that real firms frequently 'administer' prices, the range of choice being limited by what they believe their competitors will do. This acts as a restraint in both directions: price cuts may involve a price war, in which they and the competitors could both lose; ruthless use of opportunities for price increases afforded by a degree of monopoly could attract competing firms. Very useful here is Baumol's notion of 'contingent competition': a firm may be dominant in the market, the cost of entry (the investments needed) may be high, but if it raises its prices and profit rates too much it may well attract a competitor. (This is one reason why 'profit maximization' is so vague and indefinable a term. Loasby wrote that it 'has no unequivocal meaning outside of economists' models'). This too is a point worth pondering in the context of Soviet reforms. In some sectors there are real economies of scale, a dominant producer, who could raise prices excessively; one solution is price control, another is to provide the means for a competing enterprise to be created, and thereby influence price behaviour. The new law on cooperatives can do this, provided the cost of entry, the minimum scale of efficient operation, is fairly small.

In discussing Richardson's challenge to orthodoxy, we have already raised by implication the 'cobweb' problem. This is most evident in agriculture, but is of wider application, whenever time is involved. Suppose prices of (say) onions or pork go up. Producers expand output. The price then goes down. Producers reduce output. The resultant shortage causes the price to go up. Fluctuations can be severe, and no tendency to equilibrium can be discerned. It is not only political considerations ('the farmers' vote') that cause agricultural prices to be controlled in virtually all the countries of the world. A similar phenomenon can be envisaged as occurring in industrial investment: prices rise, many invest in new productive capacity, there is then over-production, prices and output fall, and so on. It is the risk of such an outcome that could discourage investment, or alternatively lead to over-investment. Such a danger would exist even if prices were wholly free and there were a smoothly-functioning capital market. My reading of Soviet writings on self-financed investments suggest that this has not been taken sufficiently into consideration, though the problem of the absence of a capital market has been discussed. In this whole area there is little in neoclassical economics that could help. The cobweb does not 'belong' in the paradigm, in which 'the future is collapsed into the present'.

There is taking place in the USSR today a discussion about currency convertibility, so the question of exchange rates has become a topical issue. Exchange rate instability is a matter of evident concern to businessmen and planners alike: costs and profits depend greatly on exchange-rates, uncertainty discourages enterprise. The pound–dollar exchange rate has fluctuated wildly in recent years, from $2.60 to $1.05 and back to $1.80. Some argue strongly for intervention to limit these fluctuations, others (for instance, Milton Friedman and Alan Walters) believe in strict non-intervention. As and when the rouble becomes a convertible currency, these issues will be of concern in Moscow also. The neoclassical paradigm predisposes the 'believers' to the Friedman–Walters view, in that the market tends to be idealized by them. However some economists who would consider themselves to be in the neoclassical tradition disagree with them.

Finally, what *is* there that Soviet reformers should learn, positively or negatively, from neoclassical textbooks? Certainly there are some generally accepted propositions which are valid and important, but nearly all (or even all) of them were already to be found in Marshall almost a hundred years ago, and indeed in the work of early Russian economists too (I have been reading Shletser and Shtorkh, respectively the first professor of economics in Moscow University and the first economist–academician, who lived in the reign of Alexander I). Prices controlled below the supply-and-demand balancing level ensure shortages and black markets. Budgetary deficits financed by money creation contributed to inflation in 1806 and also in 1986.[21] Credit too freely granted at artificially low rates of interest, or which turn out to be non-repayable grants, have some predictable consequences. People in Russia, as elsewhere, try to improve their material position, subject to constraints, which must be taken into account in wages policies. Arthur Koestler (in his *Janus*) warned against two opposite excesses: seeing the parts *only* in the context of the whole, or seeing the whole as *only* the sum of its parts. In the USSR the individual was surely for too long subordinated to the collective, to 'society', to 'needs' defined by the party leadership. A corrective is desirable, and here the neoclassical stress on the individual is helpful. However this is accompanied by neglect of intermediate categories. The firm is accommodated within its paradigm with some difficulty, an industry not at all; social needs tend to be downgraded. Neglect of institutions causes neglect of the study of what Hahn called 'the invisible hand in action', the way the market actually works, as well as what goes on *within* firms. The general equilibrium framework of analysis seems to me quite irrelevant, and its mathematical refinements equally so, if one is concerned with modifying the functioning of the real Soviet (or any other) economy in a practical way. We must be concerned with *processes*, not with equilibrium.

One final observation. In 1958 I was at the London School of Economics, listening to a lecture by Danzig introducing linear programming. I was sitting near to Lord Robbins who, as is known, believed that a socialist economy could not function because of the large number of simultaneous equations that had to be solved. He told me that Danzig's lecture worried him. The USSR, unlike the West, had a political authority which could define and determine an objective function, which could then be realized through a computerized programme, and socialism then could be efficient, a prospect which alarmed him. It is of interest to see why and where he was wrong, for we know that Soviet mathematical economists have for many years sought to devise SOFE (System of Optimally Functioning Economy), and one reason why it does not exist is precisely that it has not proved possible to define an objective function. One is further reminded of the last work by Norbert Wiener, the inventor of cybernetics: *God and Golem, Inc.*, translated into Russian as *Chelovek i robot* and published in *Novyi mir* many years ago. He warned against the use of cybernetics in the social sciences and presented an example of how difficult it is to define for operational purposes the wishes of just one person (let alone society as a whole). In a story by W. W. Jacobs, a British sergeant returns from India with a magic monkey's paw, which will grant three wishes. Someone steals it and wishes for 200 pounds sterling. Soon a man arrives and tells the 'wisher' that his son has been killed in an accident, and that he will receive £200 in compensation. The second wish was to undo the result of the first wish. Moral: even so simple an objective as £200 is in fact conditional upon a long and almost infinite list of circumstances in which one would prefer not to have it, and all must be incorporated in the computer's programme, or else disaster could befall.

And yet we still have models with clear, simple and unambiguous 'preference functions'. Their authors live in an unreal world. Wassili Leontief rightly condemned the tendency to 'preoccupation with imaginary, hypothetical rather than observable reality', and complained that the pure theorists 'drive out' of the profession those who study the actual economy; they produce mathematical models 'without any data'. (Leontief himself is a fine mathematician.) There is a moral here that transcends geographical and ideological boundaries.

So what kind of economics *do* we all need? That is a subject for another paper and another conference.

NOTES

1. *Voprosy ekonomiki*, no. 7, 1988, p. 40.
2. Ibid., p. 59.
3. Ibid., p. 5.
4. Henry Wu, *What's Wrong with Formalization in Economics*, p. 91.
5. Brian Loasby, *Choice, Complexity and Ignorance*, p. 26.
6. Phyllis Deane, *Evolution of Economic Ideas*, p. 223.
7. *Equilibrium in Macro–economics*, pp. 10–11, 48, 85.
8. A. Klamer (ed), *Conversations With Economists*, 1984, p. 68.
9. Ibid. p. 139.
10. *Critical Review*, no. 1, 1987.
11. Loasby, p. 187.
12. G. B. Richardson, *Information and Investment*, pp. 156–7.
13. *Oxford Economic Papers*, July 1986, p. 360.
14. David Prychitko, *Critical Review*, no. 1, 1987, p. 65.
15. Peter Earl, *Economic Imagination*, p. 8.
16. Israel Kirzner, 'Some crucial implications of the socialist calculation debate', 1987, unpublished.
17. Helmut Arndt, *Irrwege des politischen Õkonomie*, pp. 217–18.
18. Axel Leijonhufvud, *Information and Coordination*, p. 6.
19. Loasby, p. 30.
20. Kornai, *Anti-equilibrium*, p. 84.
21. An article in *Kommunist*, no. 11, 1988 estimates the deficit in that year at 15–17 per cent of the total revenue.

Part IV
Contemporary USSR

18 Has Soviet Growth Ceased?

My interest in index numbers began in the context of discussions on Soviet growth. Until 1950, this had been expressed in terms of so-called '1926/7 prices', and official claims appeared to be both startling and exaggerated. Already by 1950 national income was alleged to be 17 times above 1913 levels, and industrial output was said to have soared since 1928 at rates which seemed (and were) incredible, though no one doubted that growth had been impressive.[1] Critical literature on the subject in the West, beginning with Colin Clark's pioneering *Critique of Russian Statistics*[2] and Naum Jasny's little volumes[3] and a series of Western recomputations, e.g. by Bergson, Nutter, Seton and Hodgman,[4] sought to arrive at more reliable and less exaggerated figures, using physical output data and/or price indices derived from such data. It is not the task of the present paper to analyze, let alone criticize, these computations. The point is that they drew attention to several distinct sources of possible distortion of the index numbers. The first was the use for too long of *obsolete* price-weights, at a time of rapid structural change. It is in connection with indices of Soviet machinery prices that we learnt of the 'Gerschenkron effect',[5] that is, the fact that the use of early-year weights in an industrializing country will tend to yield a much higher rate of growth than would the weights of a later year. This was amply confirmed by the results of Bergson's computations. Thus the same physical output data yielded a growth rate of 11.9 per cent in 1928

---

* This paper was presented to the Manchester Statistical Society in November 1983, and is reprinted with their permission (they own the copyright). It is worth noting that virtually all Soviet economists, and Gorbachev too, now speak of the early 1980s as a period of 'stagnation' (*zastoi*), and all now accept that the official index of volume and of price distorted reality, by being too high and too low respectively. Gorbachev expressed the view that such growth as there was could be attributed to increased sales of vodka and to the consequences of improved terms of trade (that is, the high price at which oil could be exported). Also under discussion is the effect of shortage and lack of choice on international comparisons of purchasing power.

prices, but only 5.5 per cent (or 4.9 per cent) in 1937 prices, because the *relative* prices of machinery and equipment and of other rapidly-growing items had fallen.

If this were all, we would merely have to note another consequence of the not unfamiliar index number problem and then pass on to other business. But this is far from being the end of that particular story. For apart from using 'obsolete' price weights, Soviet statisticians were accused, particularly by Jasny, of using improperly high 'so-called 1926/7 prices' for new products. Under conditions of inflation, such as were certainly present in the USSR in the first half of the 1930s, costs and prices tended to rise. Numerous new products, or modifications of old ones, had to be 'inserted' in the volume index. Not only the index but also the plans of enterprises were expressed in '1926/7' roubles. Management was evidently interested in giving the new products the highest possible '1926/7' value. Counter-pressures seemed unlikely to be effective since the enterprises' hierarchical superiors also wished to fulfil plans in '1926/7' roubles. Jasny made a heroic effort to calculate an index in 'real' 1926/7 prices. But of course this was and is an impossible task. For how can we know, or ever discover, what *would* have been the price in 1926 of a product which first entered production in, say, 1936?

Further questions then arise, and Seton was particularly active in asking them. Assuming that our recomputations are based on physical output data, these are of their nature both incomplete and aggregated. A thousand tons of crude oil, or kilowatt-hours of electricity, are what they are, and remain so. But what of machine-tools, ball-bearings, cloth, cars and even sausages? They are produced in a multitude of types, qualities, designs, all of which change. Can we be confident that, in using physical output data, we are making the appropriate comparisons through time? (I abstract here from the question of whether the physical output data are themselves inflated, which raises different issues).[6]

'1926/7 prices' may be said to be obsolete today in another sense: they have not been used since 1950, although the official growth data up to that year are still based upon them. Soviet price and volume indices are now computed in prices of recent years, and with the slow-down in structural change there is not much room for the Gerschenkron effect to operate. The choice of base-year is no longer decisive. The key problem relates to the way in which price indices are, and can be, computed, and how they reflect changes in product mix and the introduction of new products.

A strong *prima facie* case can be made for the proposition that Soviet official price indices understate actual rises in prices, both of producers' goods and consumers' goods, and the case rests on analyses published in the USSR. Given that officially claimed growth both of production and consumption are based on these prices indices, it would follow that both are likely to be significantly exaggerated. Since these growth rates are very modest by past standards (2 per cent–3 per cent per annum), it raises the question of whether growth has ceased altogether. It raises other questions too. What of other countries' statistics? Do they suffer from the same defects? Is it proper for us to criticize Soviet official claims while silently allowing our readers to imagine that those of other countries can be taken at face value? No one who has read Morgenstern's admirable book[7] – and anyone who has not should repair the omission forthwith – will be under any illusions: global price and volume indices are everywhere little better than approximations. However, I will argue that whereas any errors in *our* 'approximations' are likely to be random and could lead either to overstatement or understatement of the 'real' state of affairs, the Soviet system tends to bias the statistics in the direction of understating price increases. The basic reasons, which will now be analyzed, relate to the coexistence of three factors: a sellers' market, price control and the interest of the producers in fulfilling plans. At least the first two factors are present in many countries today; not only those with Soviet-type economies, but also many developing countries suffer from shortages (sellers' markets) and price control, and there is direct inducement to use the former to evade the latter, a procedure which has certain statistical consequences. Also of great importance in the present context is what has come to be known as 'Goodhart's Law': if something is controlled or becomes a target, it ceases to be a good measure. Several vivid examples will be cited to illustrate this.

First let me cite the 'Soviet' evidence. Referring particularly to the official index for machinery and for construction, which (as we shall see) shows 'a continuous fall in prices', Krasovsky wrote: 'We regard [this] as of dubious reliability. It seems that the price indices were based on a comparatively narrow and unrepresentative sample, untypical of the whole volume of capital investments. In reality the overwhelming majority of new investment and new capacity . . . is characterized by a substantial and sometimes excessive increase in costs.' He then gave examples, showing large increases in costs (prices) of investment.[8] In the same journal, Faltsman sought to calculate what he called the 'capacity equivalent' (*moshchnostriyi ekvivalent*) of investment. He argued that investment costs per unit of new productive capacity are rising faster than the rate at which investments are financed, so that in real terms (those measured in terms of the capacity they create) investments are falling; he gave numerous examples.[9] Yet the official index shows a rise in investment volume. The same point is made more forcefully by Val'tukh: 'In the tenth five-year-plan period (1976–80) there occurred an absolute decline in productive capital investments in real terms . . . In monetary terms the volume of capital investments, including productive investments, appears to have risen in the tenth quinquennium. However costs rose still faster. The real volume of investments is determined not by its financing but by its results'.[10] Of course it must be recognized that investment costs can rise for reasons unconnected with price rises of the various components of the investment process (machinery, building materials, etc.). For example, there are labour costs, environmental protection, and the need to invest in high-cost areas such as North Siberia. However, the above sources do assert that machines and building work are rising in price, and there is both direct and circumstantial evidence to that effect from many other sources too. Thus a large number of Soviet analysts have pointed out that agricultural machinery has become more expensive. Fal'tsman, in another article, tried to calculate the overall increase in machinery prices, basing himself on a sample which covered 20 per cent of total output. Per unit of installed capacity, prices of Soviet-produced machinery rose by 15 per cent in the period 1976–80 (prices of imported machinery rose much faster).[11] Yet the official price index for 'machinery and metal-working', far from increasing, shows a continuous fall. Figures have been published up to 1979 as follows:

Machinery and metal-working: wholesale prices (1949=100)

	A	*B*
1960	—	44
1965	43	41
1970	40	39
1975	35	33
1979	32	30

A includes turnover tax. *B* excludes turnover tax.
Source: *Nar.khoz.*, 1979, p. 165.

The figures seem all the more dubious since, at this period, there have been substantial increases in the prices of energy and metals, while money wages doubled. After the publication of the figure for 1979, the Soviet authorities decided to omit the wholesale price indices from published statistics. These appear in neither of the two annual volumes published subsequently. (This may have causes not directly related to the subject of the present paper; some US analysts have been using the official index for machinery and metal-working in the process of calculating the rise in output of military hardware, a procedure which seems illegitimate to me.) Anyhow the evidence does suggest that the official price index is misleading. From which it follows that the volume index significantly inflates both the output of machinery and the volume of investment.

It may be asked: why do the customers purchase expensive machinery? Thus, if farms are offered machinery at prices so high, the use of which would increase costs and reduce profits, surely they would refuse to buy them? For reasons to be explained, this is not so under Soviet conditions, where machines are allocated administratively and the farms 'are in the position of supplicants, receiving what the (agricultural machinery) industry decides to produce and not what is required . . .[12] In several Soviet analyses of the causes of the rapid increase in agricultural costs, the main reason given is the sharp rise in price of industrial inputs.[13] Many of these inputs are the products of the machinery and engineering industry, and this is yet another pointer to the misleading nature of the price index. Similarly, the economist O. Novikov ascribes a 'significant part' of the fall in the rate of return on capital investments to 'economically unfounded increases in prices of machine-tools and technological sets'.[14] An indirect, but useful, indication of how the deliberate action of the producers can distort the index may be found in an article by P. Bykov. He pointed out that, whenever a new machine enters production, the planning organs impose targets for subsequent years for a reduction in material utilization, labour utilization and costs. Management therefore deliberately incorporates in the machine, when it first appears, unnecessary extra weight of metal, labour inputs and inflated costs, in order to be rewarded for fulfilling economy plans in the following years. The waste includes the hiring of staff whose sole purpose is to redesign the machine, by introducing economy measures which could have been incorporated in the original design. The author interviewed factory directors who agreed that this was wasteful and irrational, but, they argued, unless these excess expenditures were made, 'the first downward revision of the price would cause losses for enterprise, the targets for the reduction of material and labour utilization would not be reached, and as a result the factory would face serious economic difficulties'. The point, as Bykov does not fail to note, is that the planners do not know what the design of that particular machine *should* be, and are also unaware of the real possibilities of economizing labour and materials, and the effect of their pressure is to stimulate waste.[15] But in the present context we should observe the effect on the price index of machinery of the above procedures. Thus the new machine, when it first appears at its high price, is not 'comparable' with old ones and so does not figure in the index, but the subsequent reduction in this high price does.The production and sale of expensive machines is facilitated by the prevailing shortage, by the system of material allocation, and by the interests as well as the weaknesses of the user – a vital point to which we shall return.

Before doing so, what of consumers' goods? It so happens that in a paper entitled 'The purchasing power of the Soviet rouble', which appeared in the *Bulletin* of the Oxford University Institute of Statistics in 1958. I utilized a large number of price observations of my own, gathered in 1956 in many parts of the USSR. If the official index is to be believed, these observations would still be largely valid today: the consumer price index shows an increase over the period 1956–80 of just 5 per cent.[16] Substantial rises in some items – such as coffee, restaurant meals, carpets, jewellery – were supposed to be balanced by cuts in textiles, watches, radios, etc. Since average money wages have risen substantially, from 73 roubles per month in 1956 to 169 roubles in 1980[17] it might seem to follow that living standards have risen very rapidly.

Any Soviet citizen would react sceptically if told that the cost of living had remained unchanged for the past quarter of a century. It is also clear that many manufactured consumer goods are not now obtainable at anything like the prices I had observed in 1956. Popular scepticism is not evidence, particularly where the cost of living is concerned. However, there are other indications. Thus the Soviet economist Lokshin has drawn attention to the fact that prices per unit of many manufactured consumers' goods have shown sizeable increases: for instance, while the official price index for footwear showed no change between 1970 and 1980, average prices of footwear rose by 33.6 per cent. In the same period, men's suits priced under 70 roubles fell from 22 per cent to 6 per cent of total sales, those costing over 100 roubles rose from 25 per cent to 41 per cent of the total, and so on.[18]

Another Soviet economist, Sverdlik, cites other examples. Thus 'between 1965 and 1975 the average price of socks and stockings rose from 0.66 to 1.29 roubles'. He is forthright in his criticism of the official index:

> It must be stressed that the published index . . . of retail prices reflects only the changes in the listed prices [*preiskuranty*] of specific products. Yet there is taking place in practice a concealed rise in prices and services significantly exceeding the improvement in quality, increasing the output of dearer goods at the expense of cheaper ones which are in demand. As a result there is a rise in price per unit which is not reflected in the existing method of calculating retail prices.[19]

Attempts have been made to correct the official index. Thus the late R. Greenslade sought to devise a more reliable index for producers' goods, and Schroeder and Severin have sought to calculate independently the real (concealed) price increase for consumers' goods. There is another computation by Schroeder and Denton, prepared by the CIA, using the same methodology, that is, one based on physical quantities with Soviet prices used as weights.[20] For reasons to be discussed in a moment, it is difficult to compute the 'correct' index for reasons both conceptual and informational. Both Lokshin and Sverdlik point out that an increase in price per unit could be due to an improvement in quality welcomed by the consumer, *and* could be due also to the producers deliberately shifting to dearer variants and foisting them on the helpless customer. To cite Sverdlik again: 'If cheap and dearer models are on sale . . ., then the increase in the price per unit reflects an increase in demand for better quality goods. But if industry and trade reduce the production and sale of goods that are cheap, i.e. for them unprofitable [*nevygodnykh*], but which are in demand, then the rise in price per unit has an adverse effect on welfare and results in a fall in real incomes.[21] Under conditions of a sellers' market, the fact of purchase does not necessarily reveal any preference. As Kornai has well argued, under conditions of chronic shortage one makes do with substitutes. He also noted that prices under such conditions can be divided into controllable and less (or non-) controllable, depending on the definition and homogeneity of the product in question.[22] Soviet experience illustrates the validity of his argument: thus in the ten years 1970–80 the unit prices of such items as sugar, butter and milk were indeed unchanged and conformed precisely to the official index, whereas Lokshin's above-cited article showed that in every instance quoted by him, the unit price of manufactures rose. (All this must have a probably unintended effect on price relativities over time, as prices of products are changed at very infrequent intervals.)

Let us now see by what 'mechanism' an upward price drift can occur, and then ask whether similar distortions cannot be encountered in Western 'capitalist' countries also.

Soviet enterprises have clear material inducements to raise the prices of their products. Value of turnover is frequently a plan target, and if this can be increased by changing the product mix and/or introducing new products at higher prices, the motive to do so is clearly present. So management would be directly interested in charging more for its products, and in opting for dearer variants when possible.

It may be objected: do not Western 'capitalist' managements behave similarly? Of course, they too prefer to charge higher prices. However, in my view, their situation is different in three important respects. The first is the existence of competition, the absence of a sellers' market (i.e. of physical shortage); the second is the absence of price control; and the third is that the firm is concerned with profits, not gross value of turnover, and if lower-priced variants yielded higher profits they would be chosen.

So far as producers' goods are concerned, there is a further difference affecting customer behaviour. Let us for a moment examine the position of a Soviet manager as a customer. His sales resistance is subverted not only by the sellers' market situation. The manager actually benefits from higher prices of inputs, so long as these find their reflection in the officially-fixed price for his output, as this will tend to increase the value of total turnover. Here is the latest of the many Soviet sources which provide evidence of this. 'The users have no economic influence on the enterprises which make new machinery, and, as a rule, agree to pay any price, even when it is excessive. The explanation is that, when higher prices are paid for inputs, the financial plans of the users are corrected. The rise in price of inputs has the effect in most cases of increasing the measured result of their (the users') activities, that is, the value of output.[23] In the case of construction enterprises, their plan was expressed (until 1981 at least) in roubles *spent*, and numerous instances have been cited in the press in which they tried to reject cheaper inputs. In any case there may be no choice; while enterprises try to influence the supply plan by their own requests, in the end their inputs are allocated administratively, they are tied to a specific supplier, who is therefore in a *de facto* monopoly position. True, he is enjoined to supply what the customer actually requires. However, as Kornai's book and large numbers of Soviet sources amply demonstrate, supplier goodwill is more important than insisting on one's legal rights in respect of price and specification. Indeed a recent Soviet publication has noted not only the 'domination of the supplier over the user', but also the fact that only one in ten breaches of delivery obligation is the subject of any penalties (*sanktsii*), and that these cover only an insignificant fraction of the loss even when they are applied.[24] One has *de facto* competition between customers, rather than between suppliers; planned allocation under conditions of chronic shortage may or may not actually materialize. For all these reasons, sales resistance is weak and indeed there may be active collusion between supplier and customer in raising prices, for reasons already given. The customer buys expensive cost-increasing machines under circumstances in which the Western capitalist entrepreneur would refuse to do so.

The presence of price control is important because of its effects both on behaviour and on statistics. Soviet officials are, of course, well aware that there could be unauthorized price increases, and there is a conscious effort to combat these. However, this brings 'Goodhart's Law' into operation. If it is forbidden to increase prices of (say) clothing, lathes or canteen meals, then any increases which do occur must take 'evasive' forms: supplying fewer of the cheaper varieties, introducing new items of supposedly better quality at higher prices, reducing quality at the same price, and so on. All concerned would then claim, indeed have the duty of claiming, that no price increase had occurred. The fact of control affects the measure of what is controlled. There is no point of evading price control unless it exists, and so this motive is usually absent in the West. It must be added that a lively informal barter trade exists between managers in respect of industrial materials and machinery. Corruption is said also to have some effect on material allocation. This, however, would only affect price and growth indices if it becomes more prevalent over time, or bribes become relatively larger. Without wishing to deny the importance of the informal or black sector, we will leave it aside in the present analysis.

The situation for consumers' goods differs from that of producers' goods in that the citizen is not formally rationed, does not have goods allocated to him or her and is interested in lower prices. Here the sellers' market is a decisive factor. This also gives rise to phenomena of corruption and black markets, which still further complicate the task of computing a reliable price index, as does time spent queuing.

Let us return to the problem of evaluating or computing a price index. One must distinguish two different potential sources of distortion. One is a shift in the product mix among already existing variants. The other is the appearance of new products, with or without the disappearance of older ones.

In the USSR white bread costs roughly twice as much as black (rye) bread. For some reason or other, white bread is considered superior (the nineteenth-century Russian poet Kol'tsov wrote: 'Even white bread tastes bitter among strangers'). With rising money incomes demand shifts towards white bread. Prices of bread have remained unchanged for over twenty years, but the *average* price of bread rises. However, if both kinds are available, clearly it is correct that prices have *not* risen. As in analogous circumstances in the West, one is in the presence only of an adjustment of output to changing consumer demand, and any increase in expenditure can in this instance be explained, and indeed be held to reflect, higher consumer satisfaction. However, to return to the points made by Lokshin and by Sverdlik: suppose that there are several widely different prices for men's suits (or footwear, or vodka, or socks), and *despite* the existence of unsatisfied demand for the cheaper varieties, they cease to be produced, or are produced in reduced and insufficient quantities; the resulting increase in average price per unit is now forced, and, even though it may be that no price of any specific article has risen, a realistically computed price index would have to take into account the rise in average prices. The existence of such a tendency in the USSR has been frequently referred to in the Soviet press. If the equivalent tendency exists in the West, it should be exceptional. Given a degree of competition and of choice, it is reasonable to assume that actual purchases of dearer models do reveal preference. If more canard à l'orange is eaten in Glasgow restaurants, and less of the cheaper fish and chips, we conclude that this is what the customers prefer to eat. (Not so if only duck is on the menu, as was actually the case in a Polish provincial town in 1976 when I was there!). But we will return to the issue of choice in a moment.

New products present a rather different problem, that of comparing the non-comparable. In every country some products or models made in 1970 were not made in 1980, some made in 1980 were not made in 1970. A price index must none the less, at least implicitly, answer the unanswerable question: what *was* the value of output in 1980 in 1970 prices (or vice versa) of goods not made in one or other of these years? There is specialist literature on this subject, but it is important for us to distinguish between *theoretical* solutions and their practical application, or indeed applicability. Grilliches and others have written of 'hedonic indices' which quantify changes in product characteristics, and there are some valuable articles by Nicholson on the subject with which we are concerned and also on the related question of the welfare implications of rationing.[25] The distinction is made, rightly, between new products which appear alongside the old, and those that totally replace them. As in the case cited earlier, if people buy the new by preference, this, in a market economy, is an important indication which is relevant also for price indices: thus it validates the claim that the new and perhaps dearer product is of higher quality in the users' eyes. An interesting controversy involved Nicholson and Gilbert. The latter claimed that, if a new product was no dearer than the old, then this was evidence that there was no change in the quality. No, argued Nicholson (in my view correctly), a better product at the same price is the equivalent of a cheaper product. We cannot compute a price index which includes new products without knowledge of their quality characteristics.[26]

But what are these characteristics? One can derive a long list from the works of the above authors: comfort, speed, size, durability, reliability, after-sales service, elegance, convenience, efficiency in use and many other 'technical characteristics'. These, *and* consumers' preferences (even 'indifference curves') require to be known, and turned into statistically measurable quantities. In a few instances 'hedonic' indices could be computed, though one is left wondering what relative weights should be assigned to different quality characteristics (and why, and by whom). It seems to me reasonable to assume that this cannot be done systematically by any actually existing central statistical office; hence my reference to (necessarily) inspired approximations. Hence also the typically vivid remark of Wiles, who roundly asserts that 'all price indices compare like with like, so unlike must be reduced to like to fit at all', and therefore that 'all existing output and cost of living indices are wrong'.[27] One would also like to know more about Western countries' computations of the volume of investment. Here too, as in the USSR, unlike has to be compared with unlike, a process complicated by inflationary price rises (and the tendency, in both East and West, for actual investment costs to exceed the initial estimates). Houses and factories built, machines installed and replaced, all change characteristics. Economists use statistical data, and make comparisons through time and between countries, and far too seldom inquire as to how the data is collected and computed. In this area too, one sees the potential statistical effect of 'Goodhart's Law'. Thus one way of measuring the output of the building industry is via its inputs, its consumption of building materials. We can measure the output of goods transported in ton-miles or ton-kilometres. But we can do these things only if they are not plan targets, that is, if they do not influence the building and transport industries in their conscious choices. In a 'capitalist' country the enterprises concerned would not care one way or the other, they are concerned only with profit. But we have seen that the Soviet building industry's plan was expressed in money spent (more and dearer inputs were preferred) and transport *plans* are in ton-kilometres, which affect management's preference for heavy loads which travel long distances, thereby subverting the intended meaning of the measurement, as well as unintentionally stimulating waste, since rewards and penalties attach to plan fulfilment or non-fulfilment.

So, while we should recognize that we must not compare Soviet imperfections with unattainable Western statistical perfection, the fact remains that the institutional and incentive arrangements in Soviet-type economies will tend towards understatement of price rises (and, proportionately, an overstatement of growth rates), while Western measures are imperfect in a random way. Unless, that is, Western governments have some direct interest in price indices, in which case the same strictures would apply. Thus one could imagine a situation in which, when wages and pensions are indexed, a government might tamper with the cost of living index. Indeed, in Great Britain during the Second World War the government deliberately froze or even reduced certain prices of rationed goods which were over-represented in the 'basket' used to compute the cost of living index.

Let us now assume that we have enough evidence to assert that the Soviet price index is understated, the growth index overstated. By how much? It may be contended that we cannot say by how much, because we have a double obstacle to overcome: lack of the required data on quality, and lack of information on consumer preferences, which cannot be 'revealed' under conditions of shortage. Indeed all monetary sums and aggregates assume that prices and quantities are the result of free exchanges under equilibrium conditions, with market prices serving, in Nicholson's words, as the best approximation to 'relative marginal utilities and relative marginal productivities'. Imperfect though the real Western world is by these criteria, they seem inapplicable altogether to the 'East'.

A precise answer is indeed impossible. However, a useful indication may be found in a fascinating paper by the Czech émigré economist, P. Havlik, in the *Forschungsberichte* of the Vienna Institute of Comparative Economic Studies. His paper compares living standards in Austria and Czechoslovakia. He proceeds by calculating purchasing-power parities. The outcome puts the Austrian wage-earner far above his Czech counterpart: the latter's purchasing power in 1980 was of the order of 49 per cent–52 per cent of the Austrian's, depending on the weights used and the inclusion or exclusion of dependants and the 'social wage'. The exact figures need not concern us in the present context. What matters is the clue which his calculations indirectly provide as to the degree of exaggeration in the Czech aggregate indices.

Czechoslovakia and Austria were at approximately the same level in the 1930s, with the former perhaps slightly ahead. Austria suffered more war damage, and was surely behind the level of Czechoslovakia in 1946. Calculations cited by Havlik and made by Czech statisticians in the 1960s put the 'real wages' of the two countries at an approximate equality in 1960. The official statistics, such as those published by the UN agencies, show both national income and consumption in the two countries growing at similar rates, or the Czech figures to be marginally higher. For example, UN statistics show the following for national income (material product in the case of Czechoslovakia):

	(1975 = 100)		
	1960	*1970*	*1978*
Austria	52	83	112
Czechoslovakia	50	77	113

Since there was no appreciable change in the percentage of accumulation, the above figures ought to reflect consumption too. So, it may be argued, how is it possible to move as fast, or faster, than your rival and yet fall so far behind? The official claim must be seriously misleading.

Havlik compares the purchasing-power parities (Czech crowns: Austrian schillings) in 1964 with those of 1980. An Austrian schilling equalled 0.70 Czech crowns in 1964, 0.52 Czech crowns in 1980, in terms of the calculated purchasing power, averaging Czech and Austrian weights. So Austrian prices did increase faster than Czech prices. The Austrian cost of living index was 227 (1964 = 100). The implied Czech index was 169. But the official price index was only 124.7, on a 1964 base. That is to say, the implied price rise was 3.3 per cent per annum, and not 1.4 per cent, as is officially claimed. Such a difference is what might plausibly be expected. It is of the same order as the calculations made by Schroeder and others using admittedly imperfect Soviet unit-price data.

It may be objected that Czechoslovakia is not the Soviet Union, that it should not be assumed that Austrian indices are perfect, that the purchasing-power parity calculations are not entirely accurate. To this one can reply, firstly, that the Czech economic system is similar to the Soviet and should give rise to similar tendencies in the price-and-volume index field; secondly, that there is no reason to suspect the Austrian price indices of bias in any particular direction (that no such indices are or can be perfect we would all accept); thirdly, yes, the weights and the prices of representative commodities used by Havlik could well involve some margin of error, as Havlik himself would surely be the first to admit. But he shows all his workings, and no systematic bias is apparent. Furthermore the 1964 and 1980 calculations use a similar methodology, and the comparison between the official and the implied price index is a sort of unintended by-product of his purchasing power parities. Thus, while there can be no pretence that this is a *precise* measure of the understatement of price increases (and the symmetrical overstatement of growth) in either Czechoslovakia or the USSR, it provides, in my view, confirmatory evidence as to orders of magnitude.

A different and challenging approach to the question of how to measure the exaggeration of official indices in the USSR is contained in a remarkable article by G. Khanin.[28] Unfortunately he did not (evidently could not) spell out his conclusions, but his methodology is interesting and deserves closer study than it can get here. Khanin begins by establishing the fact that there *is* serious distortion, and that it is unevenly spread about the economy. It is least in the energy and materials sectors, greatest in multi-product industries. 'Yet the planning organs usually regard the statistical data as either equally reliable or equally unreliable for all sectors.' This can have deplorable effects on the planning process. Thus, he writes, suppose that reports of past performance show a 20 per cent increase in production of materials and a 60 per cent increase in output of (multi-product) manufactures. The former was not exaggerated, the latter was, by such familiar means as 'inflating [*vzduvaniye*] of prices, increase in double-counting, increase in material intensity, etc.'. Suppose this relationship is projected into the future by the planners. Then there is a built-in certainty that the honest, undistorted fulfilment of the plan would be rendered impossible by the shortage of materials, and therefore enterprises and ministries would be compelled to continue the distortions they practised in the past. 'The relative ease by which improved performance can be achieved by fictional increase in output' is attributed to the fact that the enterprises' superiors (the economic ministries) are judged by the same indicators of performance, and thus have no incentive to combat these practices. Some economists hoped that the (Soviet) central statistical office would 'calculate the hidden increase in wholesale prices', but this is more difficult in a planned economy than it would be in a market economy. 'The fact that in the last 10–15 years there was a hidden price rise in a number of sectors . . ., which distorted synthetic economic indicators, does not require proof.' The question is how to calculate its extent.

To do this Khanin has recourse to six kinds of calculation, which he applies to industrial output:

1. Physical volume weighted by labour inputs.
2. Changes in costs of production of comparable products, and in labour productivity.
3. Change in volume of material inputs utilized.
4. Utilization of electric energy and its relationship to changes in industrial output in the United States.
5. Plan-fulfilment in physical quantities.
6. Changes in foreign trade (external, world-market) prices of Soviet manufactures that are exported.

Each calculation has its imperfections, for reasons that he lists, but together they can in various ways act as cross-checks on the others, and the results do not greatly vary. He roundly asserts that 'price rises constitute the basic cause of the overstatement of the growth of machinery production', and then argues that his recomputation shows that 'in the last 2–3 quinquennia' machinery output did not rise

2–2½ times as fast as metal consumption but only 1.2 times (metals include ferrous and non-ferrous metals). Similarly, while according to official claims there had been a relationship 'unprecedented in any developed country' between the growth of industry's electricity consumption and industrial output, industrial output in fact did *not* rise faster than electricity consumption; it rose somewhat slower. His recomputations also show that national income (in its Soviet definition) rose only slightly faster than the rise in the volume of goods transported by rail and road.

Obviously, Khanin was not allowed to spell out his detailed conclusions. Let us see what we can reconstruct, using his indications.

Firstly, we see that these are *major* distortions. As he points out, they cause serious imbalances because the indices are used by planners. Increases in costs and prices are underestimated, volume increases over-estimated, labour productivity gains overstated, and this contributes to imbalances between supply and demand (personal incomes rise faster than real production). Investment statistics are also distorted, the real volume being significantly overstated.

Secondly, let us look at his machinery figures. The official index for 'machinery and metal-working' is 256 in 1980 (1970 = 100). Khanin states that this represented 2–2½ times the growth of metal consumption in this sector, which implies that it rose by 62 to 78 per cent. His calculations indicate that the 'real' increase was only 1.2 times that of the metal; therefore the correct index should be not 256 but somewhere between 174 and 194. It is interesting to note that a US recalculation by Ray Converse (in *USSR: Measures of Economic Growth and Development 1950–1980*, Joint Economic Committee of the US Congress, 1982) comes up with an index for machinery of 190 for 1980 (1970 = 100), or very close to the upper end of Khanin's range.

Now let us look at total industrial production. In 1980 the industrial output index stood at 178 (1970 = 100). The use of electricity in industry no longer appears as such in Soviet official data, but a table in the 1979 handbook shows electricity consumption by industry in that year to be 751 milliard Kwh, against 488 milliards in 1970. Extrapolating to 1980, this would show a rise of 57 per cent. If industrial output rose 'somewhat slower' than this, if the effects of concealed price rises and increased double-counting were eliminated,[29] then the 'real' figure could be roughly 150, a long way below the official 178. Finally, national income. The volume of goods transported by rail and road rose in 1980 to a level 42.6 per cent above that of 1970 (*Nar.khoz.SSSR.*, 1980, p. 293, gives the data in tons). The official index of national income (material product) was 162 (1970 = 100). Khanin's recomputation suggests that it was only 'slightly faster' than that of rail and road transport; that is, it was nearer to 145 than 162.

Yes, this is all exceedingly rough. It does seem to me useful all the same, as suggesting orders of magnitude. These are not very different from those implied by Havlik's calculations, cited above. Thus the gross value of Soviet industrial output at current prices increased from 374.3 to 616.3 milliard roubles in the period 1970–1980, that is, by 64.7 per cent. Therefore the official indices imply a fall of 7.4 per cent in prices in ten years. If one takes Khanin's recalculated volume index to be around 150 then prices in fact rose in the ten years by almost 12 per cent. This is a 'swing' of very close to 20 per cent in ten years.

One surmises that figures for consumption would be similar. It is worth citing the CIA's results, which use the Schroeder methodology referred to above – physical output data weighted by Soviet expenditures. For the period 1971–80, the annual average rate of growth calculated by the 'Schroeder' method comes to 2.5 per cent, against the official Soviet 3.9 per cent. Since the official retail price index remained virtually unaltered, the difference between the two figures would represent their estimate of concealed price increases, that is, 1.4 per cent per annum,[30] or 17.5 per cent in ten years. One must bear in mind that there is little distortion in the index for food, unlike manufactures. Of course, even a 2.5 per cent rate of growth is far from negligible. One must add that this has declined in the most recent years; similar methodologies, used by several contributors to the East European volume of studies prepared for the Joint Economic Committee of the US Congress, point to similar distortions for the countries concerned.

It would seem that the distortion is greater in the wholesale price index than in the retail price index. This would be partly because of the higher weight of the relatively undistorted foodstuffs in the latter, and partly (so it may be surmised) because consumers do at least try to buy cheap, whereas Soviet managers as buyers are often in collusion with their suppliers to raise prices.

Anyhow, the evidence does suggest an overstatement of volume increases sufficient to support the view that Soviet growth has fallen to a level little above zero.

There is one other question which is raised by the coexistence of shortage (sellers' market) and price control: the welfare implications of consumption measured at these prices under conditions of limited choice and 'forced' substitution. All our evaluations are based on the supposition that the consumer chooses freely between alternatives and that goods are available at the going price.

Of course, choice is in no way infinite. There are (say) 60 cheeses to choose from in Bordeaux, twenty in Glasgow, and the contrary may be true for whisky. In many American cities it is hard to find edible bread or more than one kind of bacon. Once again, we must not compare Soviet reality with an idealized perfect market. Nor do our prices measure up to the demanding standards of our textbooks. None the less, there is an important qualitative difference between 'capitalist' countries and Soviet-type economies in this respect.

Let us look at the 'welfare measurement' problem, using the following, perhaps too imaginative, parallel. Let us assume that we have a country with a normal market economy and rational prices, but within it there is a segment of society set apart, deprived of choice: conscript soldiers of an old European army, say (or prisoners, or slaves). It will certainly be possible to utilize the prevailing prices to measure the *costs* of maintaining these persons. But it would be a totally inappropriate measure of the consumer satisfaction or welfare of the conscript soldiers. Their food, their clothes are chosen for them. They may, for all we know, detest them, though it is also possible that some enjoy their food and wear their uniform with pride; we do not know unless we ask them, for they cannot choose alternatives. Contrast the volunteer professional soldier in the same army, eating the same food and wearing the same uniform (he will usually receive much more pay than the conscript, of course). He has, if a genuine and informed volunteer, opted for a package which includes the uniform and army food. This has a parallel in a package holiday, or table d'hôte, in which the food is chosen by the 'producers' of the service, so that the satisfaction of the holiday-maker in respect of each meal may vary considerably, but the holiday or restaurant was chosen freely. This is no different from the situation of a man whose wife chooses what he eats, but he may at least be presumed to have chosen the wife. Or, to take a different example, relating to work satisfaction: few indeed are the university teachers who enjoy reading a hundred examination scripts, but this is part of a basically higher satisfying package which we are lucky to be able to enjoy and we have freely chosen. However, the conscript (or prisoner, or slave) has had the whole package thrust upon him.

Thus we can conceive of a society in which prices fulfil all the functions assigned to them by theory, and yet a portion of that society is excluded from choice, in effect excluded from the market. In such a case, as argued earlier, their welfare, their consumer satisfaction, cannot be measured in market prices, though the *cost* of providing the goods can be.

Of course, the ordinary Soviet citizen is not a slave, prisoner or conscript. We have to deal with situations of *limited* choice, of queues, of shortages. Perhaps a better parallel is wartime in Great Britain, when there was rationing, price control and frequent shortages. As mentioned earlier, Nicholson discussed in a theoretically stimulating and ingenious way how to incorporate rationing into price and welfare indices, but the individual demand schedules and indifference curves which would be required were not and are not available. It is also worth recalling that, in wartime Great Britain, the poorest segment of the population actually improved their diet as a result of rationing at low controlled prices. It is also significant that, in conditions of wartime shortage, the acquisition of some scarce item brought to its acquirer a quite disproportionate sense of satisfaction: I recall my joy at being able to take four oranges home; four oranges freely bought in a free market cannot now give such pleasure! In my view no index of 'real' incomes in Great Britain based on wage and price indices covering the years (say) 1938–44–54 can have much meaning. It is bound significantly to overstate 'welfare' in 1944; the words 'purchasing power' were misleading at a time when one had such limited power to purchase! But since we have no statistical measure of frustration, we have in practice no means of 'correction' for this.

Similar problems arose – to take other examples – in Poland in 1974–83, and in the USSR itself in 1928–38. In both instances a period of relative market equilibrium at official prices was succeeded by serious physical shortages (amounting in parts of the USSR to famine in 1932–3). 'Real wages' seemed to be rising at the controlled official prices, but consumption in physical terms fell. Prices were then raised by 100 per cent and more (in Poland in 1982, in the USSR in 1934–5). Conditions gradually improved; yet the relationship between wages and prices would show a quite misleading deterioration. Real wages in the USSR in 1983 may be similarly subject to distorting influences. A sharp rise in many prices occurred early in the year. Suppose – as is possible – its effect on the retail price index will be to raise it by (say) 5 per cent, while money wages rise by 2.5

per cent, but that output of consumers' goods and services is unchanged, or rises by 1 per cent. 'Real incomes' would seem to fall, but this would not be so, though there will have been some redistribution. Similar problems arise in measuring the change in real incomes in many countries affected in recent years by price control and shortages: Ghana, Algeria, Chile, Libya, Iran . . . These are not trivial matters, nor are they confined to the USSR.

It is sometimes possible to take into account prices in a legal free market, for which official statistics are published. Thus in the USSR in 1980 food prices in the free market were twice as high as in state shops on average, and the difference has been increasing. However, where transactions are 'black', or take the form of unofficial barter deals, there is inevitably little reliable information either on quantity or prices. The fact that goods may not be available affects the desire to acquire and hold money, and also has an adverse effect on wage incentives, but – unless shortages become truly catastrophic – the need to acquire money remains. Indeed savings bank deposits have risen sharply in the USSR, not only because of frustrated purchases; large sums in cash must be paid if and when scarce consumer durables (such as a car, or a cooperative apartment) become available, and also cash may be needed for 'second economy' deals. Side by side with these transactions are a multitude of barter deals and mutual favours, payments in kind (bottles of vodka for plumbers have become proverbial, and their charges are said to be denominated in bottles) and so forth. Of course, we in the West also have a 'black economy', excluded from the official statistics. Two differences between the two kinds of black economy may be surmised. One is that in the West lower prices are frequently charged ('Pay me in cash and I will only charge you X'). The other is that in the West the motive is usually one of avoiding tax and social insurance payments, while in the USSR what is being avoided is price control and also the official planning and allocation circuit. It is probable that a greater proportion of the informal economy in the USSR is engaged in redistribution, and less on additional production of goods and services, than is the case in the West. However, this is an area where we must be conscious of our ignorance.

Still another dimension has significant statistical effects: this is called in Russian *prinuditenyi assortiment*, compulsory product mix, or sale of one item (scarce) on condition that one also buys another (abundant, but not in demand). There is massive anecdotal evidence about this phenomenon. Thus a customer (in one case reported in

Krokodil) could only buy chairs if he also bought a specified number of elderly herring. More recently *Pravda* (16 February 1983) reported that an attractive tie could only be bought along with otherwise unsaleable shirts and eau-de-cologne; volumes of Pushkin and Mayakovsky poems on the condition that the customer also bought *The Administration of Forests in the Belorussian Republic* and a handbook on the maintenance of tractors. Another article cites (critically) the view that 'in an epoch [*sic*] of general shortage the customer will take anything' (*Pravda*, 8 February 1983). So along with 'take it or leave it' one also has 'if you take this you must also take that'. In intra-Comecon trade, a similar practice has been widely commented upon: goods entering into trade are divided into 'hard' and 'soft', depending on their degree of shortage and importance for the respective economies; and bilateral barter takes the degrees of 'hardness' into account, and so one has both the exchange of goods of equal hardness and the making of sales of 'hard' goods conditional upon the partner also purchasing some 'soft' ones. This vastly complicates any attempt to evaluate terms of trade and comparative advantage. It also raises another perplexing question, which is familiar wherever there are non-convertible currencies: what is, or should be, the exchange rate as between convertible and non-convertible currencies? Suppose that country A (say Romania) can earn a million dollars or a million roubles; with the dollars one can buy anything, including roubles; with the roubles one can buy only what the Soviets can be persuaded to sell. The official exchange rate is meaningless; the black market rate is also inappropriate, reflecting a narrow range of usually illegal transactions. This question was discussed by Hungarian economists in connection with their economic reform; they settled in the end on an exchange rate between roubles and dollars related to the price levels in East and West, without taking non-convertibility as such into account, but there were and are some counter-arguments.[31] The point at issue is the one we stressed earlier: choice, or lack of it, and for the consumer what could be called 'the cost of consumption' (waiting in line, searching, the rudeness of shop assistants, and so on), and their effects on the evaluation of consumption, production, welfare and currency.

The matters discussed here are related to a different controversy, which concerns the existence and degree of *macro* disequilibrium, or excess *total* demand, in Soviet-type economies. Of course, by definition every observable shortage is 'micro'; that is, it relates to some specific product or products. Econometric 'macro' models applied to

Soviet-type economies have led to some surprising conclusions: that in most cases there *was* no excess demand, though, of course there were partial or sectoral disequilibria.[32] However, the practical (and even theoretical) significance of such conclusions may be questioned. Thus, even if the deficiency of window-glass were precisely balanced by an excess of roofing material, and shortage of butter by unsold copies of the collected works of Brezhnev, the phenomena of shortage, bottlenecks, sellers' markets and the restriction of choice would still be both real and important. (That in the end the money is spent on *something*, or saved, is not in the least surprising!). The theoretical point could be formulated as follows. Suppose that aggregate demand equals aggregate supply at the official prices, but that the product mix does not accord with demand. It would appear that the 'value' of unsold products is equal to the sums the consumers have failed to spend on the goods they desired to acquire; so we have a 'macro' balance. But the whole point is that the *user valuation* of the unsold products is lower than the prices which the planners have assigned to them. Let us imagine that it would be necessary to halve their price in order to sell them; a macro disequilibrium would then become visible. But in any case a very large number of Soviet sources attest to the fact that money incomes in recent years have risen faster than the supply of goods and services at the officially fixed prices. Of course, if one were to assume a different product mix and/or a radical change in pricing, the picture would be quite different. One can undertake econometric exercises on such assumptions, though their use and purpose seems (to put it mildly) more than somewhat problematical. One such study, by Podkaminer, came to the totally astonishing conclusion that meat prices in Poland in the period of acute meat shortage (e.g. 1980) were *too low*, and this by a breathtakingly irrelevant analysis, which included the pattern of consumption in Ireland, and drew no conclusion from the fact that meat prices in Poland had been unchanged for twenty years while average wages trebled.[33]

CONCLUSION

This paper may seem an unsatisfactory collection of allegedly insoluble problems, but I believe that it is useful to stress the importance of such problems. These arise in the main from two very different factors: the need to compare the non-comparable (which is a universal phenomenon when the range and nature of products alter), and the effects on such comparisons of shortage, sellers' markets, price control, 'compulsory assortment' and the like. Involved in this is the problem of the economic meaning of prices, and of aggregates expressed in value terms, when these prices do not reflect either the relative scarcities of inputs or the use-value (or relative scarcity) of outputs, and when the goods in question are frequently unobtainable or rationed, or represent substitutes for those actually sought by the user. It is a regrettable fact that these phenomena do not lend themselves to precise quantification, the more so because of their importance in many parts of the real world. It is not only in the Soviet Union that the published price and volume indices can cause the analyst to reach seriously misleading conclusions.

NOTES

Grateful thanks to Dr Philip Hanson for drawing attention to sources and for critical remarks on the first draft.

1. For a summary of these claims, see A. Nove, *An Economic History of the USSR* (Pelican, revised edn, 1982), and also A. Nove: '1926/7 and all that', *Soviet Studies*, October 1957.
2. Colin Clark, *Critique of Russian Statistics* (London: 1939).
3. N. Jasny, *The Soviet Economy During the Plan Era* (Stanford, The Ford Institute, 1951), *Soviet Prices of Producers' Goods* (Stanford, 1952), *The Soviet Price System* (Stanford, 1951).
4. A. Bergson, *The Soviet National Income and Product*, in 1937 (New York: Columbia University Press, 1953). W. Nutter: 'The Growth of Industrial Production in the Soviet Union', NBER (Princeton: Princeton University Press, 1962). F. Seton: 'The Tempo of Soviet Industrial Expansion', *Manchester Statistical Society*, January 1957. D. Hodgman, *Soviet Industrial Production, 1928–51* (Cambridge, Mass.: Norvard University Press, 1954).
5. A. Gerschenkron, *A Dollar Index of Soviet Machinery Output, 1927–8 to 1937* (Rand Corporation, 1951).
6. On this question see the controversy started by S. Rosefielde in *Slavic Review* (December 1980) and the counter-arguments of R. W. Davies (ibid.) and A. Nove (ibid., December 1981).
7. O. Morgenstern, *On the Accuracy of Economic Observations* (Princeton: Princeton University Press, 1963).
8. V. Krasovsky, 'Ekonomicheskiye problemy fondo-otdachi' (Economic problems of rate-of-return on capital) *Voprosy ekonomiki*, no. 1 (1980) p. 109.
9. V. Faltsman, 'Moshchnostriyi ekvivalent osnovnykh fondov' (Capacity

equivalent of basic capital) *Voprosy ekonomiki*, no. 8 (1980) pp. 120–3.
10. K. Val'tukh, 'Investitsionnyi kompleks i intensifikatsiya proizvodstva' (The investment complex and intensification of production) *EKO* (Novosibirsk) no. 3 (1982).
11. V. Fal'tsman, in *EKO* (Novosibirsk) no. 7 (1983) p. 18.
12. V. Tikhonov, in *Voprosy ekonomiki*, no. 11 (1982) p. 49.
13. See for instance A. Arkhipov: 'Prodovol'stvennaya programma i razvitie ekonomiki kolkhozov' (The food programme and the development of the collective-farm economy) *Voprosy ekonomiki*, no. 1 (1983) p. 86.
14. 'Stimulirovaniye rosta effektivnosti kapitalnykh vlozhenii' (The stimulation of investment effectiveness) *Voprosy ekonomiki*, no. 1 (1983) p. 56.
15. *Pravda*, 30 March 1983.
16. *Narodnoe khozyaistvo SSSR* (Soviet statistical annual) (1965) p. 653; (1981) p. 439.
17. *Narodnoe khozyaistvo SSSR* (1981) p. 364.
18. R. Lokshin, 'Stoimost i struktura roznichnogo tovarooborota' (Value and structure of retail trade turnover) *Voprosy ekonomiki*, no. 10 (1981).
19. Sh. S. Sverdlik, *Obschestvennyi produkt i denezhnyi oborot* (Social product and monetary circulation) Novosibirsk (1981) pp. 166–7.
20. R. Greenslade, 'Soviet industrial production statistics', in Treml and Hardt (eds), *Soviet Economic Statistics* (Durham, NC: Duke University Press, 1972) and G. Schroeder and B. Severin, in *Soviet Economy in a New Perspective* (Joint Economic Committee of the US Congress, Washington DC, 1976); also G. Schroeder and E. Denton, in *USSR: Measures of Growth and Development, 1950–1980* (Joint Economic Committee of the US Congress, Washington DC, December 1982).
21. Sverdlik, *Obschtestvennyi produkt*.
22. J. Kornai, *The Economics of Shortage* (Amsterdam, Oxford, North Holland, 1980).
23. V. Tarasov, *Voprosy ekonomiki*, no. 2 (1983) p. 38.
24. P. Bunich (ed.), *Sistema upravleniya ekonomiki razvitogo sotsializma* (System of management of the economy of developed Socialism) (Moscow, 1982) p. 105.
25. For instance, see J. L. Nicholson, 'The Measurement of Quality Changes', *Economic Journal*, September 1967 and his 'Rationing and Index Numbers', *Review of Economic Studies*, Volume x (1943) pp. 65 ff.
26. For Gilbert's view, see *Economic Development and Cultural Change* (April 1961).
27. P. Wiles: *Political Economy of Communism* (Oxford: Basil Blackwell, 1962).
28. *Izvestiya Akademii nauk, Seriya ekonomicheskaya*, no. 6 (1981).
29. The Soviet gross industrial output is the total sum of the output of all industrial enterprises, without any deduction for the value of inputs. Of course, this only makes a difference to an index of growth if there is a change in the degree of vertical integration. Clearly the author is suggesting here that sub-division of tasks between different enterprises is resorted to as a means of inflating the gross output total.

30. *USSR: Measures of Economic Growth and Development, 1950–80* (Joint Economic Committee, US Congress, 1982).
31. See A. Dezsenyi-Gueullette, 'Taux de change, prix extérieurs et efficacité du commerce extérieur hongrois . . .', *Revue d'études comparatives est-ouest* (December 1979) pp. 277–321.
32. For example, see R. Portes in *Economica* (May 1979).
33. *Review of Economics and Statistics* (August 1982).

19 Labour Incentives in Soviet *Kolkhozy**

This paper has a cause: the appearance in the *Journal of Comparative Economics* (June 1980, vol. 4, no. 2) of an article by D. Israelsen, in which it was argued, *inter alia*, that labour incentives are *more* effective in a *kolkhoz* than in a capitalist enterprise; the latter pays its employees the equivalent of their marginal product, whereas in a *kolkhoz* the pay of members equals the hours they work divided into the net product, and extra effort would earn somewhere between average and marginal product, which, on conventional assumptions, must be more than the marginal product. Since any *kolkhoz* member can increase his share by working more, this would particularly benefit him/her in a *large kolkhoz*. The specific conclusion is then drawn that those who argue that *kolkhoz* labour incentives are in principle ineffective, and 'that the large size of collectives exacerbates the problem' are in error. Somewhat similar conclusions were reached by John P. Bonin.[1] Were this so, both Soviet and Chinese reformers would be in error too.

There can scarcely be any observer of the Soviet *kolkhoz*, in and out of the Soviet Union, who doubts that labour incentives are notoriously poor. It seemed to me that there were some clear fallacies in Israelsen's argument. But the editors of the *Journal of Comparative Economics* were unconvinced by my rebuttal, and indeed refused to publish it. (They did not like the rest of my MS either!) On reflection, my rebuttal did take too many things for granted. This encourages me to try to formulate the argument step by step, more carefully.

One point is surely worth making at the very start. If we are discussing the eliciting of *extra* labour effort in realistically envisage-

* This was a paper for the (seventh) conference on Soviet and East European agriculture, held at Grignon, (France) in July 1984. Since it was written there has been even greater frankness about the ineffectiveness of incentives in Soviet agriculture, together with new decrees on small (genuine) cooperatives and family farming (contracts, leasing), designed to create a real sense of responsibility for work well done, a feeling that the land in a real sense 'belongs' to the peasants (*chuvstvo khozyaina*). Unfortunately, results to date have been disappointing.

able situations, the assumption of diminishing marginal productivity can be a misleading simplification. One has to ask: what is the reason for which the work is wanted? This is a particularly important point in agriculture: thus in winter there may be little work to do, whereas it is vital to secure extra effort at harvest time. Industrial firms too may require additional labour, or extra hours from their existing labour force, to meet specific requirements, such as agreed delivery dates, or to ensure that the product reaches a port in time for loading, or a variety of similar reasons. In these conditions, a capitalist firm or farm would pay overtime rates or bonuses to elicit the extra effort, a situation not envisaged in a simple world of smooth curves and diminishing marginal productivity, in which overtime pay would make no sense at all. (In fact, increasing returns are by no means rare in real life, despite their inconvenience for neoclassical model builders, as Kaldor, among others, have been pointing out).[2]

It is essential to distinguish between two different questions: the *offer* of work to the labour force, and that labour force's *willingness* to work. Also essential is the correct specification of the incentives of management. Let us accept the simple assumption that the capitalist is interested only in profit. What, then, is the *kolkhoz* management interested in? This question is of key importance. Suppose it were democratically elected, as it would be if it were a genuine cooperative. Suppose further that it was free to decide what to produce, and how much to sell. Management would then be charged by the members with maximizing net revenue per member. This would bring us close to the 'Illyrian' model, or to some variant of 'Yugoslav' self-management, a world explored by many economists including Ward, Domar, Meade and Vanek. It is generally agreed that this sort of cooperative would tend to employ fewer people than would a capitalist firm. So we may find some who were willing to work denied the opportunity to do so for as many hours as they wished, because it would not 'pay' the cooperative to use additional labour if the effect would be to reduce the average 'dividend' per member, even when this is significantly above the marginal product; management would seek, on behalf of the members, to limit the number of hours worked. On the face of it, then, in this situation the member would have better incentives for work when work is offered, than his equivalent in a capitalist firm, for the reasons advanced by Israelsen, though allowance would have to be made for seasonal and other peak requirements for labour. The point about requirements is important. It is neither sensible nor remotely realistic to assume that work is necessarily available for anyone who wishes to work at any time, any more than its converse: that peasants will necessarily be ready to work whenever they are required. Tasks are finite and are not regularly spread through the year; they have to be undertaken in sequence. To abstract from this means that one is abstracting from agriculture when writing about agriculture.

However, even in this imaginary picture there is one very important difference with the worker in a capitalist enterprise. The latter is a *wage*-earner, who knows in advance the wage-rate (or overtime rates for any extra work) and so, whatever the marginal product might be (of which the worker has no idea and cares less), he knows what he will receive for his additional efforts. The *kolkhoz* member cannot know this in advance. Even if the peasant fully trusts the management, even if the latter is free to decide what to do, even if agricultural prices are fixed at acceptable levels, the peasant can know in advance neither the size of the net revenue nor the total number of hours worked by his fellow-members, and therefore the dividend per hour is a question mark. There may be a guaranteed minimum payment, as there is in *kolkhozy* today but, if the cooperative is to be solvent (as many *kolkhozy* today are not), this minimum must be significantly below the average. This would also affect the distribution of time and effort between collective work and private activities, since the *kolkhoz* member has a private plot, of which more in a moment. So the relative effectiveness of incentives must be affected by uncertainty as to what the income might be, even on these favourable institutional assumptions. But those assumptions are, of course, quite unreal.

Kolkhoz management is *not* genuinely elected by or responsible to the peasants. Nor is it free to decide what to produce or what to sell. It has its own success criteria, which are not linked with peasant incomes at all, but with plan fulfilment. This totally changes the interest and attitude of management to the use of labour. Suppose that output or sales are below plan. Then it will seek to utilize additional labour which produces *some* increase in output, even if the marginal product is small, even when its utilization will diminish the 'dividend' per hour and per peasant. Therefore management would be willing to 'employ' labour in circumstances in which no capitalist (or self-managed firm) would do so. *For it* the marginal *cost* of the extra labour is zero or close to zero; the total size of the net product divided by the hours worked is what determines the total 'dividend'. More hours worked simply reduce the pay per hour. The peasants know this, and also that plan orders from above may and frequently do require an increase in output of some product which it is plainly unprofitable to produce, and this further affects their morale and commitment to collective work. They are also painfully aware that procurement quotas may be arbitrarily varied, that machines may break down, that there may be power cuts, that deliveries of fertilizer and pesticides may or may not arrive, that some tractors will be out of action at harvest time for lack of spare parts. They also know that the outcome depends on the quantity (and quality) of the labour of fellow-peasants, which may or may not be forthcoming. All this, and the weather too.

In Israelsen's model there was no guaranteed minimum, which makes his conclusions totally untenable. The introduction of a guaranteed minimum does reduce the disincentives to work. In the actual Soviet experience of recent years, the combination of high costs, lavish use of labour, the priority of plan-fulfilment and the guaranteed minimum have led to serious losses and a very rapid increase in state credits granted to farms, many of which have had to be written off.[3]

In the present instance we cannot assume perfect foresight. The peasant members cannot know in advance what they would receive for their work. To assume that they do would be an example of illegitimate use of an otherwise legitimate simplifying assumption. If an essential difference between a wage-earner and a member of a *kolkhoz* is precisely that the wage is known in advance and the 'dividend' is not, one cannot usefully eliminate this essential difference by assuming that it does not exist!

Furthermore there is another piece of knowledge which each peasant cannot have, especially in the large *kolkhoz* which Israelsen is discussing. Suppose for a moment that each member has the 'rational expectation' that his or her labour will be well remunerated (he or she will have no notion of either the average or the marginal product of labour, before or even after the event). The same knowledge must be assumed to be in the possession of all the other peasants. In a large *kolkhoz* (say with 500 members, scattered over several villages) he cannot possibly know how many others will offer additional labour with the same expectation. Yet, on the posited assumption, their hourly remuneration is determined by the total hours worked divided into the total net product. The expectation of additional earnings is in some degree dependent on the others' abstaining from increasing the total number of hours worked, if this would reduce the pay per hour. One cannot meaningfully introduce perfect knowledge into this model. It is almost as if it was known that a particular horse would win the race at odds of ten to one: the odds would then not be ten to one.

It may be useful to cite two examples of the lavish use of labour by *kolkhoz* management. One of these dates back to the early 1950s, the other to 1983, thereby demonstrating that these habits are of old standing and persist. The first was used in an article I wrote together with Roy D. Laird. It appeared in *Soviet Studies* in April 1953. We noted then that a Soviet source singled out for praise the following phenomenally labour-intensive way of using a threshing machine: two shifts of 70 (seventy) persons each, working almost round the clock. Commenting on this and on similar examples of the lavish use of labour, Roy Laird and I remarked that, since 'the total distributed to kolkhozniki is in any event limited to what is left over after all other commitments are met . . ., if labour days are wasted the only result is to reduce the payment per labour-day'.[4] So, as can be seen, we drew the conclusion at the time that marginal cost of labour must appear (to the management) to be zero, given the method of payment then in force. Many have been the changes since that date; prices, peasant incomes and investments, are now much higher. But certain habits do persist. Thus *Pravda*[5] reported on the excessive use of urban 'mobilized' labour on *kolkhozy* in harvesting cotton in Turkmenistan. They kept this labour on, even when the extra amount of cotton that could be harvested was quite small, and in no way justified the extra expenditure involved; furthermore delays in ploughing adversely affected the next year's harvest. The article gives this as one reason (the others related to machinery, seed and lack of effective defoliants) to explain the fall in net *kolkhoz* revenue by 25 per cent in five years. Why, then, was there such waste of labour? The article explains: because of 'struggle to fulfil the plan'. These examples support the view, for which plenty of other evidence exists, that the *kolkhoz* management does not give priority to achieving a high level of remuneration per hour, as compared with reporting plan fulfilment or over-fulfilment to higher authority.

But it is time to introduce the private plot. Peasants can divide their time between collective work and private production and marketing. Let us look at the many variables which could determine this division.

(a) The minimum time which *must* be devoted to collective work, either because of a regulation to that effect, or in order to avoid informal sanctions which could be imposed by a hostile chairman.

(b) The expected rate of pay for collective work, and thus the amount likely to be foregone by choosing not to do it.
(c) Free market prices.
(d) Distance to the market, means available for the journey (bus? train? hitch-hiking?), cost of journey, number of fleas (if any) in a hostel (if any) in town, and so on.
(e) Opportunity to shop in town, contrasted with the availability of goods in the village store.
(f) The labour actually required on the (small) plot, the number of private animals, and so on. (One cannot milk a cow one does not possess. The seasonal nature of agricultural labour must also be borne in mind. One cannot plant private or collective onions in February, or gather fruit in March. Peak labour requirements for the harvesting and marketing of private produce tend frequently to coincide with peak labour requirements for the *kolkhoz*).
(g) The opportunities available to sell private produce (for example to cooperative trade) without having to take it to urban markets.
(h) The family's needs for food, and its availability from sources other than the private plot,

In (say) 1953 the average rate of pay for collective work was miniscule. Private plots supplied almost all of the family's food (other than bread- grains) and most of the cash as well. There is clearly no need to explain further why incentives for collective work were ineffective at that time. It is quite a different situation today. We now have to explain the inadequacies of incentives when average pay is much higher. It is only right to add that acute problems in respect of labour incentives are encountered in *sovkhozy* (state-farms), which do pay a regular wage, which sets up the presumption that the element of uncertainty ('what will my pay per hour in fact be?') cannot be the sole explanation. Other negative factors may be more important.

This must bring us to another of Israelsen's arguments: the one which concerns the size of the *kolkhoz* (*sovkhozy* tend to be, on average, even larger). It is by no means only a question of not knowing how many hours will be worked by fellow-peasants or what pay per hour will be. It is also very important to know how well the work will be done. Agriculture (and not only agriculture, but particularly agriculture) requires that a number of tasks be performed in sequence. When these tasks are divided among different persons or groups, it becomes particularly difficult for management or rank-and-file peasants to relate the final outcome to the quality with which each task is performed. Good ploughing can be wasted if sowing is poorly done or weeding is neglected, or if the harvesting begins late because the combine-harvesters are out of order. Tractor-drivers given a ploughing plan in hectares may increase their 'output' by refraining from ploughing deep enough, but the disappointing harvest could well also be the result of poor work somewhere else along the chain of sequences. Add the well-known difficulty of supervising work in scattered fields, and we see several different forms of diseconomies of scale. Incentives become detached from the desired end-result, and sometimes (as in the case of tractor ploughing) have the perverse effect of rewarding poor-quality work.

These defects are common to state and collective farms, and critical articles in the Soviet press tend to cite examples 'impartially' from each. Thus, for instance:

> Sometimes the harvest is many times lower but the pay is higher. Why? Because it is not based on final output . . . If one has carried out additional tasks, recorded a larger number of hectares, then one gets more pay. With such a system of rewards, why should a 'mechanizer' bother with the size of the harvest? . . . In the old days, did the peasant ever try to calculate separately how much he would earn for ploughing, then sowing, then harvesting? It is the final outcome he had in mind.

The author, a *kolkhoz* brigadier, concludes that the contract brigade or the *zveno* is the answer.[6] Later the same year, the director of an efficient State farm complains that, though yields are much lower and costs higher on neighbouring farms, they earn more than the workers on his farm because earnings depend on plan-fulfilment and plans depend on past performance. As Stefan Hedlund says in an unpublished paper, 'the system fails to motivate the peasants to work well, to relate quality as well as quantity of work to the final result'.

This is why, in *kolkhozy* and *sovkhozy*, it has long been proposed that there be autonomous work-teams (*beznaryadnye zvenya* or *brigady*, now often referred to under the designation of *kollektivnyi podryad*.) The principle is simple: a small group of anything from four to thirty peasants contracts to carry out all the sequences and tasks in respect of some crop or livestock, over one or several years; in some instances the group is given a 'crop rotation' for several years; they keep the same land, but change the crop.[7] The farm undertakes to supply the needed equipment and other material inputs, and to pay this small team previously agreed sums which are directly related to the harvest, the milk yield or whatever the product may be. There is a long and frustrating history to this solution of the labour-incentive problem. It was already being discussed and experimented with in the second half of the 1960s. At the international congress of agricultural economists held in Minsk in 1970, Roy Laird asked the then minister of agriculture, Matskevich, if he favoured the *beznaryadnye zvenya*, and got the short answer: no. The sad fate of one of the experimenters, Khudenko, has been documented several times: he died in prison. As he undoubtedly ignored a number of rules and regulations, his fate was perhaps not due directly or solely to his experiments with the *beznaryadnye zveno*. None the less, the issue disappeared for several years from the public press, to re-emerge at the end of the 1970s. *Pravda* and other official publications began to publish articles in praise of those who organized such *zvenya*.[8] But until May 1982 there was no official party pronouncement, for or against. In the May 1982 decree, in Breznev's last year, there is a positive mention of the *kollektivnyi podryad*, but a more definite and strongly positive note was struck by Gorbachev in *Pravda* of 20 March 1983. Before analyzing these policies, let me make one last reference to Israelsen's article. Were he right, then, as already pointed out, not only is Gorbachev wrong to back the small work-unit, but the Chinese are also mistaken in introducing the 'household responsibility' system, which has the same objective: to relate effort more directly to result, and relate incentives to both. Gorbachev's article insists that the group is to elect its own leader, and to determine its own work assignments. Clearly its members would see directly what cannot be observed in the larger unit: who does what, when and how. There would be no need for supervisory personnel (one Soviet source gave this as one reason for the opposition to the proposal among petty officials!).[9] Members can jointly regulate their labour inputs in relation to the task in hand with some confidence that success will be rewarded. True, they have to contend with weather hazards (the standard contract does provide for a minimum reward in the event of natural disasters). As will be pointed out in a moment, severe practical problems will remain, but at least in this model it does seem rather self-evident that, *pace* Israelsen, peasants will have better incentives than in a large *kolkhoz*. Surely it is unnecessary to seek formal proof for the proposition that any incentive scheme involving payment by results loses its effectiveness if these results depend on the work of a large number of scattered individuals? Economists in general do have an unfortunate tendency to treat labour as a species of homogenous robot, and to neglect quality as well as work-motivation. It is true that such unquantifiable considerations as pride in work well done, conscientiousness and a sense of responsibility, do not lend themselves to mathematical treatment, cannot be fed into a computer. The question of work morale and commitment is a key one in Soviet agriculture. One cannot but echo the heartfelt words of Fyodor Abramov: 'The old pride in a well-ploughed field, a well-sown crop, well-looked-after livestock, is vanishing. Love for land, for work, even self-respect, are disappearing. Is this not a cause of absenteeism, lateness, drunkenness?'[10] It became urgently important to find a remedy.

So let us return to the autonomous work-group (whether the term *zveno* or *brigada* is used is immaterial: these days some *brigady* are small). Why was its introduction so long delayed? Will it now be introduced throughout Soviet agriculture? With what effects?

Among the obstacles to overcome was a long-established belief in the existence of organizational and technical economies of scale in agriculture. The Marxist roots of this belief have been well analyzed by Michael Ellman.[11] These ideas have doubtless been reinforced by considerations of a more practical kind: planners prefer a smaller to a larger number of units to whom to send their orders, and the notion of autonomy (no imposed work-assignments, which is what the word *beznaryadnyi* means) runs counter to a habit of mind which stresses hierarchical subordination. Uncontrolled spontaneity, *samotyok*, is a word of pejorative connotation. It should be recalled that *kolkhozy* were greatly enlarged in the years following 1950, through successive waves of imposed amalgamation. Petty supervision requires petty supervisors, whom such a reform threatens with unemployment.

Then there is the long-ingrained distrust of peasants and concern for the rebirth of private-property instincts. This too is linked with practical considerations: if an area of land is assigned to a work-group for too short a period, it may have no interest in its longer-term fertility; if for a long period (many years) then they may come to regard it as 'their own'. The more so as there are now 'family *zvenos*' (*semeinye zvenya*) and 'their numbers are growing'.[12] But we must also be aware of problems of a totally non-ideological kind. It so happens that I discussed them with a Soviet official at the Minsk conference in 1970. The official (unlike Matskevich) was favourably inclined to the idea, but pointed to serious frictions and conflicts which could result among the peasants themselves. Not all tasks are divisible into small groups of the *zveno* type, many tasks undertaken by a *zveno* could be seasonal, with little to occupy the members the rest of the time. Members may well be chosen who have skills (to operate tractors, for instance) and they could earn much more than the less skilled general-purpose workers. Nor is it an easy matter to negotiate a contract with each that would be regarded as fair by others. There would most likely be very wide disparities in earnings, some predictable, others not, which could give rise to protests and discontent.

The same point struck me in China during my visit in 1983. The 'household responsibility system' is also based on contract; the household has delivery obligations, at fixed prices. Much depends, therefore, on the prices and the obligations. As one Chinese official said to me: 'No one will get rich growing rice'. When I then asked him what was raised in his district by those who do get rich, he replied: 'ducks'. It was admitted that it could well be what the household is ordered or allowed to do, rather than the skill and energy they show in doing it, which will have a decisive bearing on their income.

To estimate the possible results of the autonomous group system in the Soviet Union it is important to examine carefully the type of contract which is to be made.[13] Gorbachev and others have rightly stressed that one must show care and imagination in drafting such contracts (there must be 'economically soundly based tasks') and that the mutual obligations must be strictly observed if the new system is to function smoothly. There have been instances reported of such *zvenya* falling apart when the conditions necessary for their functioning are not observed (see, for example, *Pravda*, 9 January 1983). Here it is necessary to stress one vitally important difference between the USSR and China. Chinese agriculture is still using traditional techniques, with relatively little mechanization and few industrial inputs (apart from mineral fertilizer). Soviet agriculture, however, is now capital-intensive, with production depending on a wide range of supplies from industry. The autonomous groups are to be issued with the needed machinery and equipment, and will require regular and reliable supplies of fuel and other inputs. No doubt the regular supply of these will figure in the contractual obligations of the *kolkhozy* and *sovkhozy*. But, with the best will in the world, will they be able to carry them out, bearing in mind the notoriously poor record of the agricultural machinery industry and of *Sel'khoztekhnika* in supplying the farm's requirements?

Attempts to introduce forms of *brigadnyi podryad* in the building industry have foundered on this very same rock: how can workers be expected to accept payment by results if these results are repeatedly affected by non-arrival of the needed materials, or the non-repair of equipment?

So a precondition of success is a drastic overhaul of the system of material supply, of the links between industry and agriculture. Will this be achieved by the 'agro-industrial complex' approach? We will have to wait and see. Decrees have been adopted before now which changed little. After all, the shortage of spare parts has figured in satire, song and story for at least 40 years, and has so far proved incurable. Similarly, decrees on *malaya mekhanizatsiya* have been frustrated by the priority given to plan-fulfilment in aggregate terms, which turns industry's efforts towards the large-scale machines. So cautious scepticism is not out of place.

There is, furthermore, another obstacle of a more psychological kind, and which was mentioned also in China. A reform of this sort requires officials (*sovkhoz* directors, *kolkhoz* chairmen and others) to negotiate and observe contractual obligations with their own subordinates, those to whom hitherto they had the power to give orders. A big change in approach is needed, complicated by the fact that these officials will themselves be under pressure from above to fulfil production and delivery plans. Gorbachev in his speech stated that the autonomous groups must be 'given the fullest autonomy (*samostoyatel'nost'*) for the carrying out of their assignments (*zadaniya*)'. Let us assume that he is sincere. But a number of times party and state officials have been urged, or even ordered, to cease petty interference with, and tutelage over, farm management, yet it has continued. Thus, despite the decision published in May 1982 on this subject, a *kolkhoz* chairmen (Y. Ipatenko) bitterly complained about the flood of peremptory orders: 'when to spread manure, when to connect up the spraying machines, even how to combat mice'.[14] Nor is this surprising, bearing in mind that decrees of various sorts, such as that criticizing the work of the Saratov *obkom* of the party,[15] urge and instruct party officials to ensure that various agricultural problems are resolved, and hold them responsible if they are not. Another decree[16] orders officials to take priority measures with regard to sugar-beet and so on. This cannot but impel them to interfere with farm management and with the new 'agro-industrial complex' organs which, in their turn, are all too likely to issue orders to farm management.[17] (Complaints on this score have already appeared – see *Pravda*, 17 December 1983.) For all these reasons, the smooth functioning of the *kollektivnyi podryad* system is hard to envisage. At the very least there must be acute growing pains in the first years. Particularly vulnerable will be that part of the reform relating to the obligation to ensure the regular supply of industrial inputs of all kinds. However the reform is surely along the right lines, and it is even possible that the efforts to implement it will lead to closer links between the needs of agriculture and the providers of industrial inputs, and thereby force industry at long last to 'turn its face to the village customer' (*litsom k derevnye*, to recall a slogan-phrase of the 1920s) and, who knows, the much-needed practice of producing for the customers' needs might 'infect' all of Soviet industry. Far-fetched? Yes, but not impossible.

Let us therefore withhold judgment and observe events.

NOTES

1. *Journal of Comparative Economics*, March 1977, vol. 1, no. 1.
2. See, for example, N. Kaldor in *Review of Economic Studies*, 1966, vol. 33.
3. See I. Suslov, in *Voprosy ekonomiki*, 1982, no. 12.
4. *Soviet Studies*, April 1953, p. 442.
5. *Pravda*, 7 July 1983.
6. *Pravda*, 9 January 1983.
7. See, for example, *Ekonomischeskaya gazeta*, July 1983, no. 31, p. 15.
8. See, for instance, *Pravda*, 25 November 1979; 14 July 1980; 25 and 26 March 1981, and 25 May 1981.
9. See Rebrin, *Nvoyi mir*, 1969, no. 4.
10. *Pravda*, 17 November 1979.
11. See Ellman's contribution to *Socialist Models of Development*, Pergamon Press, 1982.
12. A. Vyugin in *Pravda*, 9 January 1983.
13. Various kinds of contracts have been publicized, for instance in *Ekonomischeskaya gazeta*, 1983, nos. 15, 27, 31, 36.
14. *Pravda*, 3 January 1983.
15. *Pravda*, 7 July 1983.
16. *Pravda*, 20 August 1983.
17. Complaints on this score have already appeared – see *Pravda* 17 December 1983.

20 Soviet Agriculture*

There is general agreement, in and out of the Soviet Union, that agricultural performance has been deficient. Allowance must, of course, be made for unfavourable climatic conditions. However, it remains true that harvest yields are modest, while labour productivity has increased too slowly, very large investments have not been effectively utilized, machinery is of poor quality and costs have risen very rapidly, as have the subsidies which cover the difference between prices paid to the producers and the prices in state retail stores. There have been serious problems in motivating the labour force on state and collective farms, and one consequence is the need to mobilize millions from outside the villages to help bring in the harvest. Imports of grain and meat have reached very high levels. Altogether, agriculture has become a serious burden on the rest of the economy, while there are numerous complaints of shortages of such foods as meat and dairy produce, though part of this is due to the low, subsidized, retail prices, unchanged for 25 years. Allowing for weather variations, output has risen, but too slowly and at very high cost.

I doubt if any Soviet economist would dispute that there are serious difficulties to overcome. The object of the present paper is, firstly, to analyse the principal causes of these difficulties and, secondly, to consider the remedies which have been adopted or are under discussion, and evaluate their effectiveness.

Firstly, there is *labour*. The problem comes in several parts. One is the out-migration of the younger and more skilled, partly because the

---

* This was written in June 1987 and published in *Détente*. Since then there have been more radical changes, especially the legalization of family farming (on long-term leases and on contract), the creation of small genuine rural cooperatives of many kinds, the scrapping of most of the agro-industrial complex bureaucracy, the reassertion of the autonomy of farm management. However *kolkhozy* and *sovkhozy* remain dominant, leasing is still making very slow progress, and its unpopularity among many citizens may be illustrated by a *Krokodil* cartoon which appeared in March 1989. Villagers are shown singing and dancing, and a passer-by asks: 'Why are they so happy?' The reply: 'The leaseholder's pig has died.'

city lights beckon (in Russia as elsewhere), and partly because of the still wide gap in living standards and amenities. In some areas this has led to serious labour shortages. Secondly, labour on large state and collective farms has little desire to work and little sense of responsibility for the land. This has been the subject of heartfelt published comment by, for example, the late Fjodor Abramov, cited above page 298. Or here is another comment: 'In the old days they did not work because they knew they would get nothing. Now they do not work because they know they will be paid anyway'.[1] Thirdly, there is the question of the availability of goods to buy with any extra money earned. And finally, there is the question of how to relate incentives to good-quality work: thus there was the well-known instance of the tractor-driver fulfilling a ploughing plan expressed in hectares by ploughing too shallow.

The solution put forward a quarter of a century ago was the so-called *beznaryadnoye zveno*, autonomous 'link' or small work-group, now more usually referred to as *kollektivnyi podryad*, or group-contract. The principle is that fields or a livestock sector be the responsibility of a small number of peasants, who sign a contract with their farm and are paid by results. They are left to run themselves, that is, they have no imposed work-assignments (*naryady*, hence *beznaryadnoye*). The farm undertakes to supply the needed inputs (such as seeds, machinery and fertilizer) on terms written into the contract. Specific fields would be the responsibility of the group for at least a complete crop rotation, to give them an incentive for soil improvement.

Experiments on these lines began in the 1960s. One enterprising director of a state farm in Kazakhstan, Khudenko, achieved excellent results and nationwide publicity. But politics and ideology intervened. The sad story recently received attention in *Literaturnaya gazeta*,[2] in an article by Belkin and Perevedentsev, who had witnessed the original experiment and drawn attention to its remarkable effectiveness. Khudenko was arrested, and the whole scheme was dropped for many years. Belkin and Perevedentsev comment: 'if the Khudenko model had been adopted in good time . . ., the Soviet Union might no longer be an importer of agricultural produce, but an exporter'. Since the problem would not go away, the idea was revived in the late 1970s. However it was not until March 1983 that, at a conference held in Belgorod, Gorbachev (then the party secretary responsible for agriculture) gave the politbureau's formal blessing to this solution of the problem of motivation. It has received strong support in numerous party resolutions since.

How has it worked? It is important to appreciate that it is not at all a simple matter to negotiate hundreds of thousands of contracts, covering a wide variety of work, some of it seasonal. There is also the problem that the farms are frequently unable to obtain the material inputs they require (for reasons to be explained in a moment), and also find themselves compelled to pass downwards orders which they receive from party and state officials, which involves breach of contract and operational interference. The evidence so far is best summarized in the speech of Nikonov, the central committee secretary in charge of agriculture: after noting the impressive number of contract groups, he stressed that results have been modest. There

> must be punctual and full observance of contractual obligations made with brigades and *zvenya*. This means that . . . material-technical supplies must be delivered in good time, for without guaranteed supplies of inputs the contractual scheme cannot function [*podryada ne byvayet*]. And whatever is earned by the mechanizers and livestock workers must be paid to the last kopeck. Because of breach of these principles, people lose faith in the possibility of effective collective labour and its just reward. For these reasons during each work season a sizeable proportion of *zvenya* and brigades fall apart.[3]

Much is being said in favour of *family* contract (*semeinyi podryad*) and greater flexibility generally. The principle is a good one. Its implementation is still at an early stage, and we may be seeing 'growing pains'. There must be very considerable local variations. More data and more research are needed. Peasant sense of belonging, of participation, may well increase if the promised real election of management actually occurs (*kolkhoz* chairmen, nominally elected, have in the past been nominated by party officials).

Now let us consider *material supplies*. Here agriculture has been a victim of the deficiencies of industrial planning and of the administered allocation system. Complaints abound concerning quality of farm machinery, lack of spare parts and gaps in mechanization (which contribute to labour bottlenecks at peak periods and so to the mobilization of millions of townspeople). Far too often the purchase-requests (*zayavki*) are unsuccessful, and indeed many instances can be cited when equipment which has not been ordered is foisted on the farms, or the fertilizer is of the wrong type: '. . . orders placed with industry have nothing in common with what the farms require' (*Pravda*, 1 December 1986). Gorbachev himself has been very critical of the performance of the agricultural machinery industry, and a recent article in *Novyi mir*[4] speaks of the supply to farms of 'obvious rubbish' (*otkrovennuyu lipu*).

The proposed solution is 'trade in means of production' scrapping the clumsy and bureaucratic allocation system, and allowing farms to buy what they wish, as has long been the case in Hungary. Experiments on these lines are now in progress in some areas.[5] However, for this to function on an all-union scale, it would be necessary to alter radically the planning process in the relevant industries: to give them freedom and incentives to produce for the customer and not for plan-fulfilment statistics. This too is proposed, but not (or not yet) adopted. There is also the vital question of monopoly; a peasant is quoted (in Chernichenko's article) as advocating the replacement of *monopoliya* by *mnogopoliya* (multipoly? polypoly?) with user choice of supplier. The setting up of the 'agro-industrial complex' (hereinafter *Agroprom*) has not solved the problem; nor has the appointment of the former head of the agricultural supply agency (*Selkhoztekhnika*), Ezhevsky, as minister of agricultural machinery. There is also the complex question of prices, for inputs and for farm output, which will not be further pursued here.

This brings one to planning and the *Agroprom*. First let me define the disease, before examining the efficacy of the cure. There were in fact two diseases. One was the frequent interference with farm management by party and state officials. Citations from the Soviet press could fill a sizeable book. 'Why regulate our daily activities, what field to sow on Friday and which on Saturday?', wrote one farm chairman.[6] Or: 'now everything is planned from above: by crops, hectares, head of livestock, the value of work to be done, repairs, servicing. Why?'.[7] And so on and so forth. The observant reader will have noticed the date of the second quotation, and there are others still more recent, and this despite many a decree on respecting the autonomy of farm management. Officials also have frequently varied the supposedly fixed and unchangeable delivery quotas for produce.

The second disease became particularly acute during the 1970's. It arose because, in the process of investing heavily in the modernization of agriculture, the central authorities decided to set up or strengthen a number of specialized service organizations, which functioned separately from the farms. Thus *Selkhoztekhnika* not only became a supply agency but also took charge of repairs and some of the transport. Fertilizer, insecticides and herbicides became the preserve of *Selkhozkhimiya*, drainage and irrigation of sub-units of the ministry of water resources, and so on. Farm management lost control of operations, and the 'service' organizations were interested in fulfilling their own plans. One example can be cited: land improvement (*melioratsiya*) was undertaken by 'meliorators' who were interested in increasing the gross value of work, so chose 'capital-intensive activities' . . . the use of expensive materials, the choice of the worst land that is most costly to improve . . . ignoring the interests of *kolkhozy* and *sovkhozy* . . . '.[8] *Selkhoztekhnika* was interested in dear repairs.

The cure to this disease came in two instalments. As part of the food programme adopted under Brezhnev in May 1982, a new *Agroprom* hierarchy was set up, to try to coordinate the farms and the various service agencies, and also rural construction, procurements, transport and food processing. In each district they were all to be under the *raion* agro-industrial association, known by the initials RAPO. In its first incarnation *Agroprom* did not solve the problem, in that the various organizations survived and still aimed to fulfil their plans rather than do what most needed doing in the cheapest possible way. The quotation from Bobylev, above, is dated over three years after this problem was supposed to have been solved.

So in November 1985 they had another try. This time they abolished most of the separate organizations: no more *Selkhoztekhnika*, *Selkhozkhimiya* and so on. They were all incorporated bodily in *Agroprom*, and the RAPO in the localities was to be fully in charge of them all, even while it was supposed to respect the autonomy of farm management. The agricultural machinery ministry survived, but was to work closely with *Agroprom*.

The result? So far, patchy. There was evident danger in a 'bureaucratic' solution, and a better alternative was to put authority clearly in the hands of farm management, leaving them free to hire the service agencies as sub-contractors if they wish, or (for example) acquire their own insecticide if this seemed more effective. Again, this is the situation in Hungary. What in fact happened could (alas) be forecast: the 'dead' service agencies came alive under other names, within *Agroprom*. Thus. *Selkhoztekhnika* became *Agrosnab*, and several reports speak of its local agencies foisting unwanted machinery on farms, over-charging for badly-executed repairs, refusing to supply spare parts for *kolkhoz* workshops, and so on, in seeking to fulfil its plans.[9]

The reformers had intended that all the service agencies be rewarded in proportion to their contribution to the 'final result'– the harvest, the milk yield or whatever it might be. Unfortunately, this proved impossible, for one extremely simple reason: no one can know what it is. Suppose that one is responsible for repairs to tractors, or for applying herbicides; suppose further that the actual harvest turned out to be 18.3 centners per hectare; how does one even begin to identify the contribution to this output of repairs and herbicides? So, given the habit of relating pay to the achievement of some sort of plan target, inevitably there emerged plans for repairs and for 'chemicalization' which the providers of these services would endeavour to fulfil. If, instead, farm managers were in charge of the entire cycle of operations, they could use their best judgment about what needed to be done and at what cost it was worth while to do it. There is a link here with the point already made in connection with 'trade in means of production': farms should be able to choose the most effective assortment of material and service inputs, and whether to hire or to do their own thing. It is my sincere conviction that the *Agroprom* solution is, in its present form, wrong in principle. And, predictably, the RAPO interferes in farm operations, despite protests from many farm managers and indeed from Gorbachev himself.

Gorbachev has also sharply criticized the surviving habits of local party committees (*raikomy*) to issue operational orders. There is here a strong sense of *déjà vu*. How often has this been said! Similarly, delivery quotas were supposed to be fixed and unalterable under Khrushchev and Brezhnev too, or so they said. Yet, according to *Novyi mir*[10] today 'in many places is like 1952, 1962, 1972 and 1982 . . . first the plan, then the plan-task, then the first supplementary plan, then the second . . .' And this despite Gorbachev's stress, at the 27th party congress, on the principle of *prodnalog*. One can only echo the opinion of an anonymous official of *Agroprom* in Moscow: 'People in the localities are vastly indignant; what has been promised them is quite different. I lie down at home after work and think: what is going on? With one hand we write good decrees, promising the village scope for decision, fresh air, stimuli, while with the other hand we tear them to shreds'[11] Why? And what or who are 'we'?

One aspect of imposed plans has not yet been mentioned. This relates to investment projects. Huge sums have been spent on modern livestock complexes, in a well-meant attempt to overcome short-

Table 20.1 Cost of production, roubles per ton

	1970		*1985*	
	Sovkhozy	*Kolkhozy*	*Sovkhozy*	*Kolkhozy*
Beef	1277	1166	2922	2527
Pork	1111	1194	1975	2313
Milk	189	177	380	340

SOURCE: *Nar.khoz.* of the respective years.

ages of livestock products. A similar operation has been reasonably successful in the case of poultry and eggs, but the livestock farms have been an economic disaster of the first magnitude, because of high cost, lack of reliable fodder supplies, frequent power cuts, lack of paved approach roads, and so on. Costs of production have risen fast, much faster than other costs and prices (see Table 20.1)

Protests from farm managers have been in vain. Thus 'on the orders of the *obkom* and *oblispolkom*, farms were compelled to build expensive giant complexes . . . cow palaces . . . I begged them not to build at least the last unit, but they would not listen to me. Yet we have no workshop, no cover for grain storage'.[12] Chernichenko[13] is equally critical, referring to 'monstrous increases of the cost of production of milk' and a sharp reduction in the life-expectancy of cows. This is one reason for the too-modest rate of return on investments.

Agriculture has long suffered from inadequate *infrastructure*, in particular the lack of hard-surface roads. This has been fully recognized and very large sums have been devoted in recent years to road-building, and also to building grain elevators and other storage space, providing more packaging materials, improving links with the trade network, and so on. All these are desirable objectives. Delays in implementation are due to lack of resources of the building industry in rural areas, but progress is being made. Much attention is now being paid to rural housing and amenities, but it takes years to catch up with the consequences of past neglect.

Finally, there are the *private plots*, which still provide about a quarter of all agricultural output. Official policy is favourable to their growth, and the extension of 'family contract' for example, to fatten pigs for the farm) will tend to blur the dividing-line between collective and private (even the pigs will not know which they are!). However old habits die hard: it is still very difficult for individuals to obtain simple tools and implements and, in particular fodder for private livestock (fodder is still often in short supply). The campaign in 1986 against 'unearned incomes' was interpreted by some officials as a signal to prevent peasants from reaching urban markets with their produce. This 'distortion' (*peregib*) has been corrected, but many sources speak of the slow growth of marketing facilities, which are supposed to extend also to collective and state farms, while consumer-cooperatives are supposed to be much more active in buying produce from farms and peasants and marketing it in their shops in cities. This may now develop faster, after a slow start, if the local authorities do not obstruct it.

So, to summarize, what can one say about recent developments? In one of her interviews, Tatiana Zaslavskaya said that the reform process should begin with agriculture, as it had done in other countries.[14] She evidently had Hungary and China in mind. If so, the slow and contradictory progress of reform in agriculture is a warning of difficulties to be encountered. Little has yet changed. 1986 was a better harvest year, but the main reason was the weather. There remain many obstacles to overcome. Gorbachev and his colleagues know all this well, of course. He had a legal education, and it is perhaps no accident that he has been emphasizing the need to observe legal norms and contractual obligations, to end the bad habits of arbitrariness. Indeed the entire economic reform and its success depends in large measure on the replacement of orders from above by '*economic*' relations based on contract. This in turn links up with the *perestroika* of the behaviour of party cadres, whose arbitrary interference with economic enterprises (and with judges) was inconsistent with the necessary legal order. Here there is much to be done, and many uncertainties. Thus if *obkom* and *raikom* secretaries are judged, promoted or demoted on the basis of economic performance in their areas, if they are held responsible for whatever may go wrong, how can they not interfere? But it is by no means only a question of the behaviour of party officials. As we have seen, the small-group contract is under threat when *kolkhozy* and *sovkhozy* fail to observe their side of the contract, and they in turn are often victims of breach of contract: for example, though entitled to a large payment from the procurement agency for grain deliveries in excess of quota, a *sovkhoz* was refused payment in money, being offered fodder concentrates that it did not need instead, and could obtain no redress.[15] Another case involved demand for payment for combine-harvesters which had not been ordered. When payment was refused, the supply agency refused to sell urgently-needed coal to the farm, and appeals to the procuracy and to the RAPO had no effect.[16] It is appropriate to quote V. Skvortsova, writing in *Selskaya zhizn*[17] (22 January 1987). After mentioning several more instances of breach of contract, she asks: 'whose fault?' She replies as follows to her own question:

> For many years conflicts of departmental interest, exacerbated by shortages of resources, created a situation in which it was not contract which determined the rights and duties of the partners, but either an order 'from above' or some special relationship between the respective managements. Times have changed, but the habit of looking on contractual agreements as a non-obligatory empty formality has survived.

There is no easy cure. People's attitudes cannot change overnight, no matter how a new decree is worded. It must take time.

We are still in an early stage of the reform process, and it would be wrong to draw any definite conclusions, except perhaps one: that the process is bound to be difficult, and that – to cite another Soviet author – some local officials will do their utmost to 'turn the hurricane of radical reform into a storm in a teacup'. There is bound to be a conflict between old and new; big changes are never painless. It will be fascinating to see what happens, with the *podryad*, with material–technical supply, with *Agroprom*, with the rural party machine. The promise of 'radical reform' has yet to be fulfilled, but we must anticipate further endeavours to impose the needed *perestroika* in the years ahead.

NOTES

1. S. Vikulov in *Pravda*, 4 February 1987.
2. 1 April 1987.
3. *Selskaya zhizn*, 25 January 1987.
4. Y. Chernichenko in *Nvoyi mir*, 1986, no. 12.
5. Among them Lithuania, Moldavia and Stavropol, according to *Ekonomika selskogo khozyaistva*, 1987, no. 1.
6. *Pravda*, 26 March 1981.
7. *Pravda*, 22 January 1986.
8. See Bobylev in *Voprosy ekonomiki*, 1985, no. 9, p. 94.

9. For one of several published examples, See L. Mazlin, *Ekonomischeskaya gazeta*, 1987, no. 8.
10. A. Shvelyany in *Nvoyi mir*, 1986, no. 12.
11. Ibid.
12. *Pravda*, 18 May 1966.
13. Chernichenko in *Nvoyi mir*, 1986, no. 12.
14. *Izvestiya*, 1 June 1986.
15. S. Obolensky, *Selskaya zhizn*, 12 February 1987.
16. A. Ulyanov, *Ekonomischeskaya gazeta*, 1987, no. 5.

21 The Contribution of Imported Technology to Soviet Growth*

'Econometricians, like artists, fall in love with their models' (alleged modern proverb).

This may look like an essay in destructive criticism. It is not intended as such. It will, however, express its author's belief that we have here a question which cannot in fact be answered, other than in the most general terms. There are such questions in other branches of knowledge. Thus Sir Peter Medawar, eminent geneticist, commenting on attempts to measure the relative contribution of 'nature and nurture' to differences in intellectual capacity, asserts that 'in my opinion it is *not* possible to do so' (his emphasis),[1] for the two interact in ways which makes it virtually impossible to separate them. Economic growth and its causes are issues on which thousands of pages have been written. One is uneasily aware, when using Cobb-Douglas functions, that investment embodies new technology, that the residual is what one cares to make it, and might as well be called the *x*-factor ('*x*-efficiency', including all and any improvements in productivity due to higher-quality management methods, improved labour incentives, better education and training, successful geological exploration, and so on, as well as technical progress). Growth retardation too can have multiple interacting causes: in the Soviet case the burden of the arms race, the need to seek higher-cost materials and fuels in remote places, more serious planning deficiences, weaker labour incentives and even increased vodka consumption could figure on a list which, if Gorbachev is to be believed, also includes serious lags in design and production of modern and efficient capital equipment.

Amid all these multiple chains of causation and effect, how can one isolate the specific contribution of technology in general, let alone *imported* technology? That its contribution is positive, at least in *ex*

---

* This paper has not previously been published in English.

ante intent, is not to be doubted. Soviet planners will usually give preference to their own domestic production or, failing that, to Comecon suppliers, before turning to Western sources. It is as if there was a differential import duty. The motive for buying from the West can, of course, vary, with different analytical and policy implications. Thus:

(a) It *may* be due to the fact that certain types of Western technology are so advanced that they (or their allies) cannot replicate them; in other words, the cause is technological backwardness. However, there could be other reasons, such as the following.
(b) They have the know-how, and could produce the machines, but it is cheaper and quicker to rely on the international division of labour and buy them from, for example, Japan or West Germany.
(c) They have the know-how and do produce the machines, but in insufficient quantity.
(d) A particular component within a technological chain or package is unavailable and the gap is plugged with imports.
(e) They have all the technological know-how but the 'bottleneck' is lay-out and production organization. (This was, for instance, the motive for getting the Italians to equip and start up the 'Togliatti' car plant to make Soviet Fiats.)

When we speak of the contribution made by the imports of *high* technology, we should be aware that this is only a fraction of what is imported, the size of the fraction depending in large part on what is considered to be 'high'. This in turn should lead one into the very promising path, trodden very interestingly in work by such men as Philip Hanson, Ron Amann and Julian Cooper, of disaggregating, studying the contribution of imported Western technology to specific industries, such as chemicals, motor vehicles and so on.

Here too the quantification of the 'contribution' is no easy matter, with much depending on the object of the exercise. If it is linked with measuring the possible effectiveness of embargos, of economic warfare generally, then the key point is less the high level of the technology than the short-term bottleneck effect, and this can be enhanced by surprise. This effect is only loosely connected with technology as such. Thus the sudden denial of urgently-needed large-diameter pipe can cause severe delay to Soviet plans and cost them dearly. Similarly, the refusal to supply a key component on which the planners are relying can seriously delay the completion or functioning of some major project. Fears that the Reagan administration might act along such lines is one reason why Soviet planners seek to reduce what could be for them a dangerous degree of dependency. But such considerations do not usually enter into the process of measuring the contribution of imported technology to growth. Analagously, a strike in one component factory can bring a large part of the car industry to a halt, causing (let us say) loss of production worth $100 million in a matter of weeks. But we do not measure the contribution of this component factory to the value of the car industry by the loss that would ensue from its sudden and unexpected demise. In the longer term there are usually alternatives, though presumably more costly ones.

Strictly speaking, in measuring the impact of any particular purchase of Western technology, we might envisage the Soviet planners making the following *ex ante* calculation: 'If we purchase this equipment for $$x$, this promises to be more effective than a similar machine we might obtain from Czechoslovakia for a sum in transferable roubles (or by way of barter for n tons of iron ore); we could probably develop the machine ourselves at the cost of $x + y$ (internal) roubles plus two years delay (but the delay may not matter if the rest of the project is behind schedule, as it usually is).' If they decide to go ahead with the import from the West, the measurement of the gain will involve comparing it with the cost of the alternatives, but this is to some extent hypothetical. Thus they could not know what it would actually have cost in terms of R & D to produce the machine themselves, even assuming the needed know-how was available or could be obtained. This is not for a moment to deny the high probability of there being a gain in reality, as well as in the *ex ante* calculation. But how do we *measure* this gain? What *would* have been the cost of the alternatives? An inevitable limitation of specific case studies is that they do not and can not 'catch' spread effects: technology transferred for one purpose, and the know-how that accompanies it, can and does have an influence on productivity in other sectors and projects. One must also recall that imported machines may be used directly to make better Soviet machines; thereby having wide-ranging diffusion effects; so would foreign equipment in Soviet research establishments. The 'macro' studies would encompass all of this, if a reliable methodology could be devised to enable us to measure the immeasurable.

All this is not for a moment intended to criticize case-studies. On the contrary, they are highly desirable, and can (and do) give much more solid results than macro studies can. The Birmingham project can only be applauded.[2]

There is another possible source of confusion, which could arise from an attempt to correlate the performance, in terms of growth, of those sectors which contain large elements of Western technology with those that do not. For example, the chemical industry grew faster that (say) the steel or textile industries. This, however, may simply reflect the larger share of the chemical industry in plans for growth, and its relative priority could also account for an above-average quality of the complementary domestically-produced inputs and for the greater speed of completions. (There was a charming little article in *Pravda* about *dolgostroi* ('longbuild') citing the Tower of Babel as proof that uncompleted construction existed without the Soviet system being responsible for it!)

The *reductio ad absurdum* of crude correlation would be to note that Soviet growth was much more rapid in the period 1951–60, when little Western technology was imported, that in 1971–80, when much more of it was. No one has yet based on these facts the conclusion that imports of Western technology are a cause of slowdown in growth! Possibly Faltsman might argue that shortfalls in Soviet machinery production necessitated the import of more Western machinery which was dearer and misused, and then this *would* be such a cause. But Faltsman may be exaggerating (see below).

Let us imagine a Soviet research institute seeking to determine the contribution of imported technology to the growth of any major Western economy. The mind boggles. It is reported that the United States has become a net importer of high technology, but how can this be related in any way to the growth path of the US economy? What is the contribution of imported technology to West German growth? Or of imports in general? The Soviet institute in question would be justified in dropping such a project.

Where a multiplicity of causes exercise an influence, in unknown proportions, on a given outcome, there must be an element of arbitrariness in assigning weights to each. For example, those British monetarist neo-liberals who have the ear of the government ascribe the US business recovery to tax cuts, wage-restraint and their effect on stimulating entrepreneurship; while the Keynesians and other opponents of the British government's deflationary strategy naturally emphasize the stimulating effect of the huge budget deficit. Econometric models prepared by and for the British Treasury build into their assumptions the success of the chosen policy, and these also 'predict' the failure of any action by government to stimulate the economy by investments in the public sector. The conclusion is built into the premises. The group at Cambridge University which opposes the government and advocates import controls builds into *its* model the success of *its* strategy, and the specifications and assumptions within the model exclude or minimize the adverse effects of the proposed policies.[3]

Or, to take an example nearer to our subject, Gorbachev has singled out slow diffusion of technical progress, along with excessively slow withdrawal of obsolete machinery and failure to produce modern equipment of the requisite quality in the USSR, as important causes of growth slowdown, and has urged vigorous action to put all this right. What proportion of the slowdown was in fact due to this particular cause? How much gain would be registered if these matters *were* put right, with other things held constant? Could they be put right if other things *were* held constant?

In a book on *East–West technology transfer* (Paris, 1984), written by S. Gomulka and myself for OECD, we tried to analyze in detail some econometric calculations which sought to measure the contribution of such transfers. The detailed arguments are set out there, as are the references to the works in question. Green and Levine, in two calculations, concluded that one rouble's worth of imported machinery was as productive as 14 roubles of non-Western capital, accounting for as much as a quarter of all Soviet industrial growth in the period 1961–74. A recalculation using SOVMOD III concluded that one rouble of Soviet machinery imports in 1973–8 increased Soviet industrial production during that period by 8 roubles.

To arrive at these or any other results, one has to make some assumptions, notably on substitutability (of Soviet or Comecon equipment for whatever was imported from the West), on comparisons of and changes in quality of domestic and imported machines, and so on. Obviously, the more essential, i.e. non-substitutable, the import is, the greater is the loss from not having it, but in the absence of hard data, this has to be rather arbitrarily specified. In separate articles published in the *Journal of Comparative Economics*[4] Martin Weitzman and Yasushi Toda vary some of the Green–Levine assumptions in a not implausible manner, and both reach very different conclusions: that the results *could* show that 'the marginal productivities are indistinguishable between domestic and imported capital'. Rosefielde, by building into his assumptions the view that in the period 1950–73 the Soviets had been to some degree 'closing the relative technological gap', concludes that Soviet technical progress 'must largely be attributed to domestic Soviet science and engineering'. While many of the assumptions made by all the above-cited scholars can be (and have been) queried, I would strongly agree with Weitzman, who, in commenting on Rosefielde's study, wrote: 'The evidence so far is that we cannot determine any influence of technology transfer on Soviet economic growth using existing data. It's too bad, but nothing consistent seems to emerge from the numbers'.[5]

It is, of course, quite wrong to conclude that what cannot accurately be measured does not exist. I certainly do not wish to deny that technology transfer has positive effects on Soviet growth and productivity. This is also the conclusion of Gomulka's study of the direct and indirect effects of 'international technological diffusion' on countries 'behind the technological frontier', but he emphasizes (rightly, in my view) that machinery imports from the West may well be much less important for the USSR than other kinds of technological and scientific diffusion. These take many forms. 'Unembodied' technology transfer, obviously, does not show up in trade accounts. Purchase of know-how, the systematic scanning of Western technological literature, the activities (legal and not-so-legal) of specialists attached to embassy staffs and participation at international scientific conferences are some examples. Some significant part of the Soviets' own R & D doubtless benefits from the import of technology or of ideas, but there is no way of estimating the importance of this. Again, such considerations apply to any country: even the most advanced import both technology and ideas, patents, and so on from others, with spread effects which must vary greatly from case to case.

Both Gomulka and Rosefielde, in their different ways, note that the relative growth-effect of new technology (by whatsoever means, including via domestic R & D) declines 'if and when the technological gap diminishes, i.e. there is a sort of diminishing marginal return'. Gomulka in addition stresses the obstacles to diffusion of technology embodied in the centralized planning system, and on this there will be more to say in a moment.

Several other points are worth making first. One is to re-emphasize the 'bottleneck' argument: the Soviet economy is one where resources tend to be fully utilized, where reserves are insufficient to cope with the unexpected. In such an economy the positive effects of an import (or the negative effects of denying it) may be disproportionately large. In each individual instance this can be seen as short-term, but the continuous availability of any needed import is of longer-term effect, perhaps greater than elsewhere. This applies to any 'bottleneck-enlarging' import, not only to technology. This is also relevant to estimating the real cost, in terms of resources foregone, of imports of technology. By this I mean not just the value of the exports required to pay for them, but what George D. Holliday has called 'the resource-demanding aspect of technology transfer'. He writes: 'Thus both the Volga (Tolyatti) and Kama plants require not only direct high-quality Soviet inputs, but also generate substantial indirect demands, e.g. for special kinds of metals, plastics, high-octane gasoline, new highways, service facilities and other infrastructure, in competition with other Soviet requirements.'[6] (In other words, bottlenecks are created elsewhere.)

A second point is also related to the cost to the USSR of importing technology. V. Faltsman has noted, firstly, that prices of imported technology have risen very substantially and, secondly, that (at these prices) it is often *less* cost-effective than Soviet technology.[7] It is worth citing Faltsman's own words (which, it must be remembered, relate to imported machinery and equipment from all sources): 'As an analysis of [investment] projects has shown, investments in imported technology subsequently provides 2–4 times less output than analagous machinery and equipment domestically produced. Because of the absence of the required materials or breach of other needed conditions, often only part of the potential of foreign technology is realised.'[8] Arguing in another article for a reduction in imports, the same author writes: 'The rising trend in imports, when its prices were rising, was one of the most important factors in raising capital cost [*kapitaloyomkost'*] of new capacity. On the basis of project analysis it was found that the capital cost of new capacity with mainly imported equipment was on average three times higher than capacity with domestically produced equipment.'[9] All this supports other evidence to the effect that, for reasons that may have nothing to do with the inherent qualities of the technology, its actual use to the economy is far below what was both possible and desired. The reference by Faltsman to high and rising prices must also be a factor in low cost effectiveness.

Faltsman's argument, which so strikingly contrasts with that of Green–Levine, can be reinforced by that of Trzeciakowski and Tabaczynski: 'The impact of the transfer of technology . . . can be diminished, or even become ineffective, if the receiving partner does not dispose of skilled labour, intellectual capacity and adequate infrastructure . . . The same negative effect can appear if the receiving partner does not dispose of adequate and sufficient contracting capacity' (by 'contracting' the authors presumably mean building, assembly and installation).[10] The authors clearly have in mind the disastrous effect of the over-rapid expansion of Polish imports of technology in the 1971–5 period, but their warnings are of wide application: without the needed complementary domestic inputs, foreign technology may contribute little, or even less than nothing, to growth. Nor, as Holliday reminded us, should be overlook the opportunity-cost (alternative uses foregone) involved in the use of complementary Soviet material and human inputs into projects involving imported technology.

This brings me to a third point. The *share* of imported technology in the total value of installed capital equipment is larger than it looks at first sight. Thus Hanson, right on so many things, was surely wrong to cite a 'peak' figure as low as 5–6 per cent. In terms of *domestic* roubles the share must be higher. It constitutes one reason (relative grain prices are another) why Soviet imports in domestic roubles are so very much higher than the total in *valuta* roubles (in domestic roubles there is a substantial trade deficit, that is, an import surplus). However an interesting point of interpretation arises. Suppose a machine is bought for a million dollars, and that this represents 750 000 roubles at the official rate of exchange. Suppose further that this machine is sold to its Soviet user for 2 million internal roubles. Might not the difference – or some substantial part of the difference – be treated as a species of import duty? Such sums find their way to the state budget, helping to explain the very large increase in 'other revenues'. What is the real opportunity-cost of these imports? Is it represented by the value (in what prices?) of the exports that pay for them, or by the cost to the USSR of the alternative (if there be one) to importing this machine and, if so, do we mean the short-run (including the bottleneck-enlarging effect) or the long-run cost?

It may be worth citing in this connection V. Faltsman's estimate: according to him, in 'the last five-year-plan period' the share of imports in the 'installed total of tools of labour' rose to a third of the total.[11] Since about two-thirds of Soviet machinery imports come from Comecon countries, this suggests that a figure of 10 per cent would be close to the 'real' share of Western equipment in Soviet capital equipment being installed in or around 1980 (of course, in some sectors the degree of expenditure is much higher).

We should consider further the quality and availability of the Soviets' own technology and that of their Comecon allies. To some extent all estimates of the impact of Western technology must depend on the quality of available alternatives, now and in the future. The Soviet fear of excessive dependence has led to a cutback in imports of machinery and equipment in the early eighties, and to pressure on Comecon partners and on Soviet machine-builders to supply better quality. Such pressures are unlikely to have much effect without reform of the clumsy system of centralized planning and material allocation. Complaints about the consequences have filled the press for years, and have recently been reinforced by strong words from Gorbachev.

Let me cite a few of literally hundreds of sources. 'A large proportion of the work-force operates obsolete machines, which reduces the application of new technology and so leads to a substantial loss of productivity of both labour and machines, excessive use of metal and deterioration of product quality. Also the obsolete nature of the equipment causes over-expenditure on major repairs'; 'At present in ferrous metallurgy more than half of rolling mills are obsolete, non-mechanized units; labour productivity is much lower there. The modern rolling mills provide only 45% of rolled metal'.[12]

'In our national economy the influence of the user on the producer is virtually insignificant . . ., acts with great delay, and because of shortage of some products it practically disappears, and the rule comes into effect: take it or leave it; if you do not, others will'.[13]

'[Soviet] Machinery manufacturers are in fact not responsible for the effectiveness in use of their machines. The transaction once completed, the manufacturer disappears and the user has to correct defects himself, very often by primitive methods.'

'As a result of the existing organization of the production and repair of machinery, there are engaged in this about 20 million persons, and a larger number of machine tools and forging and pressing machines than in the United States, Japan and West Germany combined. The law of "self-supply", providing "one's own", is stronger than any criteria of effectiveness . . . How can one improve the quality of machinery on such a basis! The practice continues of scattering the production of many basic and auxiliary machines and components among many ministries and enterprises, showing lack of product specialization. 22 factories in the Ministry of Heavy Machine-building produce 17% of materials handling equipment, the rest being scattered among 400 factories within 35 different ministries . . . We have at present no machine-building enterprises or associations where user-enterprises or research institutes can place orders for non-standardized items of equipment or technology'.[14]

Finally, there is the critique of Aganbegyan. He begins with the elementary point that innovation is not a good in itself, that it must be economically effective. 'However, this is far from being generally the case.' He cites the example of robots, 'expensive and unreliable', which cost 40–50 000 roubles and save very little labour, so that in the end total costs do not fall but actually rise. These robots are made largely by hand (*polukustarno*) in many factories and ministries for their own use, 'because it is the fashion'. He deplores the very expensive (*fondoyomkoi*) form of R & D, 'which in many respects in ruinous for society', and 'which must cease immediately'. To achieve the desired results, 'it is necessary to smash [*slomat'*] departmental, organizational, planning, financial, psychological and other barriers between science and production . . .'.[15]

Numerous other articles refer to the lack of interest in innovation, notably in the machinery and engineering industry itself, with many others pointing out that, with the present system of success indicators, the innovator is more likely to be penalized than rewarded. There is excessively slow retirement of obsolete equipment, excessive duration of decision-making and of construction (so that a new machine might be obsolete by the time it is installed), price inflexibility, the absence of competition and therefore also of customer choice, and the familiar deficiencies of the material supply procedures, which often make it impossible even for a well-motivated producer to obtain inputs of the requisite specification. Gorbachev's speeches[16] show that he knew all these things very well, and he is surely intelligent enough to know that neither exhortation nor appeals to discipline can be sufficient remedies.

So, as so often in recent years, we have to return to the question of reform. Will there be any basic change in the system? Would reform have the desired results, or might it cause confusion? Is Gorbachev committed to fundamental change, and can he carry the central committee with him if he is? How much improvement can be generated within the centralized model? These are not the sort of questions which this paper is intended to answer. They are put all the same because they affect the ability of the Soviets' own R & D and machinery industry to provide and install their own 'native' technology, reducing without too much harm their dependence on imports, and they could also increase the effectiveness with which imported technology is used, for, as Hanson put it, 'the domestic diffusion of technologies imported from the West is a particularly slow and problematic process in these eastern economies'.[17]

So to one last question. Is the import of Western technology (or, for that matter, grain) a *substitute* for reform or a *stimulus* to reform? I doubt if anyone seriously believes that the politbureau ever consciously faced this as a dilemma, that anyone actually said: 'Comrades, we do not like the reform which will bring about efficiency, so let us import grain and technology instead.' A more sustainable view would be that the undesired and probably unanticipated effects of non-reform have contributed to the need to import – while the big improvement in Soviet terms of trade after 1973 made such imports possible without incurring major debts. It could be argued that pressure for reform would have been greater had these imports not been available. However the opposite case is strong: large-scale imports of Western technology frequently turn out to have disappointing results and do not 'fit' the system, causing strains which could be seen as reform-inducing rather than the reverse. As also for grain, the evident concern of the Soviet leadership at having to import so much from the capitalist world is surely also a stimulus to finding urgent solutions, rather than a substitute for the search for such solutions.

To conclude: unless the Soviet planners have been very foolish, which is very unlikely, it is clear (*pace* Faltsman) that imports of Western technology have benefited the Soviet economy overall, with the benefit very unequally spread between sectors. However to quantify this benefit on a macro scale appears to me to be an inherently impossible task, given the number of variables simultaneously influencing outcomes. Similarly, no one (not even Gosplan) can know the longer-term cost in terms of growth of reducing dependence on Western technology, since this requires one to estimate the extra cost and degree of success of R & D which was not or would not be undertaken in the event of reliance on Western sources. We must also recall that we are in a period in which major reforms are likely to be introduced in the USSR and in some at least of its Comecon allies, with unforeseeable consequences.

We seem to be dealing with something significant, but which we cannot quantify, to any more precise extent than asserting that the effect is positive, that there is a plus sign. This is often the case. What precisely was the contribution of Roosevelt's New Deal to the recovery after 1933 of the US economy, or of rearmament to the recovery at the same period of the German economy, or of Mrs Thatcher's policies to the rise in unemployment in Britain, or of the US deficit to the fall in unemployment in the United States, or of higher pay for collective work in increasing yields on *kolkhozy* from the low level of the 1950's? At the individual level too we act from multiple motives, which even the individual him or herself frequently cannot disentangle, let alone quantify. This is emphatically not to be read as an argument against trying to quantify whenever possible. Of course we should! But, if we cannot, it is as well to recognize the fact, and recognize also that unquantifiable factors must not be ignored.

To take a totally different example, Japan's remarkable economic performance has been contributed to by (*inter alia*) the discipline, commitment and loyalty of the firms' employees, and also by the ingenious use Japan has made of imported scientific and technological advances. Which of these, along with other factors, has contributed how much to Japan's growth? Or indeed if we confine attention only to Japan's R & D sector, what is the relative contribution of the imported and the domestic? Or, within any country, how does one separate the effect of R from that of D?

Let us keep production functions and Cobb-Douglas in their place, and not present them with tasks which are beyond their competence.

NOTES

1. *Plato's Republic* (Oxford: OUP, 1984), p. 171.
2. This refers to work by Annan, Cooper and Hanson.
3. An effective critical review by Paul Hare appeared in the *Scottish Journal of Political Economy* in 1982.
4. June 1979.
5. Quoted from a Report for the Strategic Studies Center, June 1978.
6. *Issues in East–West Commercial Relations*, Joint Economic Committee, US Congress (12 January 1979) p. 47.
7. *Voprosy ekonomiki*, no. 6 (1984) and EKO, no. 7 (1983).
8. V. Faltsman and A. Kornev, EKO, no. 7 (1983) p. 16.
9. *Voprosy ekonomiki*, no. 6 (1984) p. 42.
10. *Industrial Policies and Technology Transfers between East and West* (ed. C. T. Saunders) (Vienna: Springer Verlag, 1977) p. 133.
11. V. Faltsman, EKO, no. 7 (1983) p. 16. According to V. Seltsovski, *Planovoye Khozyaistvo*, no. 7 (1984) p. 123, the share of imports rose from 15 per cent in 1970 to 35 per cent 'now'.

12. G. Kurbatova, EKO, no. 3, 1982.
13. V. Trapeznikov in *Pravda*, 7 May 1982.
14. S. Kheinman, EKO, no. 5, 1980.
15. *Pravda*, 13 July 1985. Similar criticisms of robots have appeared in *Voprosy ekonomiki*, no. 7, 1985.
16. See reports in *Pravda*, 12 and 24 April 1985.
17. *Journal of Comparative Economics*, no. 6, 1982

22 The Defence Burden: Some General Observations*

THE OBJECT OF THE EXERCISE

Being to some extent responsible for initiating this discussion, it seems only right that I should begin by explaining the reason.

In the postwar years, this author detected a strong tendency to exaggerate the scale of Soviet military might and so also of its cost. In the early 1950s we were told of 175 Soviet divisions, a formidable force, showing such vast superiority in conventional force that only the nuclear deterrent kept them from sweeping on to the Atlantic. While there is indeed some evidence (for example, from Czech, Hungarian and Polish sources)[1] that Stalin in his last years thought that war was likely, hardly anyone today would maintain that the 175 divisions actually existed, in the sense of actually being mobilized (a great many must have been skeleton formations, and skeletons do not fight wars). Then came the story of the missile gap, which, as Kennedy must have quickly discovered, did not exist, or rather existed in reverse: US superiority in nuclear weapons could have been of the order of 15: 1 in 1960, and the Cuban missile crisis of 1962 occurred precisely because Khrushchev wanted to narrow it by installing medium-range missiles within range of the United States. It is an interesting question for historians how far the exaggerated estimates of Soviet strength were due to human error, how far they were

* This was my contribution to a conference on this subject held under the auspices of the Stockholm International Peace Research Institute (SIPRI) in Stockholm in 1987 and published in Carl G. Jacobsen (ed.), *The Soviet defence enigma*. (Oxford: OUP, 1987). The Soviets have repeatedly admitted that the real figures for defence expenditures have been concealed, and promised to publish these shortly, justifying the delay by the distortion engendered by pricing. Gorbachev said this too, in his Guildhall speech in London in April 1989, and has now given a figure; 77 billion roubles plus military space. Some consider that the real figure is higher. There has also been a lively and open controversy in Soviet periodicals concerning the level of hidden inflation.

deliberate (to help get money from the US Congress), and how far they were the consequence of the Soviet Union's own efforts to conceal weakness, to present itself as stronger than it really was. There was also the tendency – which still exists – to present the Soviets as hell-bent on aggression, aiming at superiority, and so on. All this developed in my mind an attitude of cautious scepticism about some published Western estimates.

On the Soviet side there was, and still is, almost complete silence. If their publications cite any figures on Soviet hardware, they usually come from US sources. This author is not competent to assess the quantity and quality of modern weaponry, having, in his army days, fired nothing more up-to-date than a Lee-Enfield rifle. But the burden to the economy, the scale of military expenditures, those are matters of evident interest to an economist. The only figure available was, and is, the Defence vote in the budget. This was supposed to cover 'the cost of weapons, ammunition, technical equipment, fuel, food and other equipment supplied to the Soviet armed forces', plus military schools, hospitals, sanatoria, sports, pay of those employed, 'the financing of capital construction', and so on, to cite one of several textbooks on the Soviet budget.[2] While vague at the edges (this seemed to exclude R & D and did not mention pensions), this definition would seem logically to cover the bulk of what is usually called military expenditures. But the budget total remained very low, it even fell slightly from 1970 to 1983, and it was in total and blatant contradiction with the Soviets' own claim that they were in the process of achieving parity with the United States. So, while Western propaganda may have overstated Soviet military strength and capabilities, Soviet sources were unusable, virtually non-existent: clearly, a large part of Soviet defence expenditure was not on the reported *smeta* (estimate) of the Ministry of Defence. Where, then, was it? What did the published *smeta* actually mean? Did its meaning and coverage change, and if so, when, due to what logic or sleight-of-hand? I agree with Peter Wiles that we must look for an accounting logic of some sort. To cite one of my own books, submarines are not likely to be disguised as expenditures on aid for lonely mothers.[3] They must be somewhere where they could be said to 'belong'.

SOME WESTERN RECOMPUTATIONS

Faced with increasingly incredible Soviet official figures. Western intelligence agencies made their own calculations, involving the conversion of their estimates of Soviet hardware and other expenditures into dollars and into roubles. This led to much controversy: what was the appropriate rouble–dollar ratio for defence goods? Is the high priority of the defence sector a reason for supposing it to be much more efficient and low-cost than civilian industry, or could the high priority be a reason for tolerating extravagance? The US Central Intelligence Agency (CIA), one recalls, had the embarrassing task of doubling their rouble estimate of Soviet military expenditure overnight, in 1976, not because they had discovered weaponry they had previously missed, but because they decided that they had grossly underestimated its cost. Then there was a further question, to which I will return: if we do compute a series in roubles, what price index is it appropriate to use? Finally, what can or should be the relationship between monetary magnitudes and the physical evidence of actual weapon development? In other words, suppose the growth indicated by these two measures is different, which is more likely to be wrong? For example, Steven Rosefielde arrives at a much higher growth figure in roubles than does the CIA.[4] This could mean: (a) Rosefielde's results overstate volume because of rising costs and prices; (b) these results are mistaken, because they are inconsistent with intelligence estimates of the weapons buildup; or (c) the intelligence estimates of weapons build-up are mistaken, either because the Soviets successfully conceal it or because the higher expenditure implies higher quality, accuracy, and so on. I would like to make clear that I do not agree with Rosefielde's methodology and reject his conclusions. But he is not alone in challenging the CIA's computations, and this cannot be ignored.

SIPRI also published estimates, but they were midway between the CIA's revised version and the official Soviet figures, and I was unaware of their methodology.

Other approaches existed, including Bill Lee's attempt to calculate the value of military hardware by identifying a residual in machine-building and metal-working (MBMW), subtracting all known civilian uses from the published total value of MBMW. This yielded a plausible total for 1970, and indeed was in line with the CIA's revised figure, and the method appealed to me at the time.[5] However, subsequently the figures ceased (in my view) to make sense; it is possible that Soviet statisticians made sure that they could no longer be used in this way. In any case, evidence is lacking on the use of MBMW within the MBMW sector itself, which renders calculation by residual subject to serious error.

Finally, there were two other approaches. One was to try to identify the military component in the input–output tables published for the years 1967 and 1972. The other was to analyse the Soviet national-income accounts. In both instances one had to look for residuals, items whose end-use was military but which did not appear as such. Peter Wiles's paper has much to say about the input–output tables, and he also refers to the work of Gillula and others, so I leave this aside, except to say that this is certainly a very useful approach which can also cross-check other calculations. As for national income, together with the late Alfred Zauberman I wrote an article, entitled 'A Soviet disclosure of rouble national income'.[6] We there reasoned that, since presumably there was no separate 'Annihilation fund' (S. G. Strumilin's phrase for the defence sector),[7] defence expenditures must be divided as follows:

(a) Material consumption of the Defence Ministry is part of 'Material consumption in institutions and enterprises of the non-productive sphere'.
(b) Consumption by military personnel is, of course, 'Personal consumption'.
(c) Accumulation (i.e., increase in numbers of weapons) appears as 'Investment in State reserves'.
(d) Some military construction (e.g., new barracks) is 'Investment in the national economy'.

We suggested that there was room in the figures we had computed for 'State reserves' for the increase in numbers of weapons. In my textbook on the Soviet economy, I had also surmised that some military hardware could be financed out of the budgetary heading 'Allocations to the National Economy', which also contains a sizeable item for 'State reserves'.[8] But it was clear that the national-income accounts and budgetary expenditures were two different ball games, since accumulation is a net figure (net of depreciation and/or retirements) and so is different from (smaller than) gross expenditures on capital investment or acquisition of weapons in any particular year.

Then, in 1970, the Soviet statistical annual began, and continued for several years, publishing a utilization-of-national-income table which included explicitly an item for 'defence' (*oborona*). I duly noted that it was identical with the budget defence vote, but considered that this showed that it was meaningless.[9] Peter Wiles took a different view, since it suggested to him that the defence vote is equal to what it seems legitimate to enter in the national accounts, that is, current consumption plus *net* additions to weapons (i.e., net of retirements, amortization). We will return to this question when discussing what the budget defence vote could or could not mean. Peter Wiles then tried to combine this interpretation of the budget vote with the defence elements hidden in the input–output tables. But in more recent years the *oborona* figure disappeared, along with the breakdown of national income utilized.

The Soviet national income tables divide the total into two main heads: 'consumption', and 'Accumulation *and other expenditures*' (my emphasis), which formulation gives rise to the attempt to compute the 'accumulation residual', possibly equal to non-consumption military expenditures (for example, see Duchêne's paper).

By the mid-1970s it became abundantly clear to every serious observer that Soviet defence expenditures were very substantially in excess of the defence vote. But the higher rouble estimates began to be too big to 'fit' anywhere in the national accounts or in the state budget. For example, Rosefielde's figure for weapons acquisition for 1980,[10] 54 billion roubles, is roughly double the CIA's estimate, and Steinberg's figures for defence expenditures in total are also well above CIA estimates, and he points out himself that such figures cannot be accommodated within the published Soviet totals. This raised two sorts of question. One, already mentioned, is whether these high figures, and the high growth rate calculated by Rosefielde, Lee and Steinberg, are consistent with the physical data on increases in military hardware which all the protagonists seem to accept. The other is whether the fact that the rouble figures seem too high to 'fit' into the accounts means that these figures are too high, or the accounts (and the budget) omit some significant part of military expenditure.

This last view is vigorously defended by Steinberg. Yes, he says, part of expenditures are not in the national income statistics, or in the budget, just as those engaged in producing weapons are not in the statistics of the labour force. This creates, in his view, demographic and expenditure inconsistencies which can be identified, and used to reconstruct the 'real' figures. Otherwise his methodology is open to the objection that, without an agreed total (e.g., of national income), the sky becomes the limit, since there is no total to subtract from, so to speak.

Steinberg's computations cannot be compared with the CIA's, or with those who claim that the CIA has too low an estimate, because, firstly, the CIA series (for some reason) are in what it describes as 1970 prices, not current prices (but note partial update in a joint CIA/DIA (Defence Intelligence Agency) presentation in March 1986). Secondly, the authors of the higher estimates (or the CIA for that matter) have not tried to fit them into the Soviets' own national accounts (the CIA recomputes GNP, that is, if, uses Western statistical categories). The comparison with Gérard Duchêne's computations is a particularly interesting one to make, because Duchêne's considerably lower figures are capable of being fitted into various national-income residuals without having to assume that Soviet official statistics understate the national income (net material product), industrial production and budgetary expenditures (as Steinberg does). Steinberg's views are a challenge to everybody, and it is quite a formidable task to prove that he is wrong, if indeed he is wrong. (It is interesting to note that the notion that those engaged in the defence industries were omitted from the labour statistics also came to Abram Bergson, and may be found in a contribution written 40 years ago.[11] He was analysing the gap, also noted by Steinberg, between the total population reported as employed and their total disposable incomes, which is greater than the number employed multiplied by their average wage.)

All of this leaves multiple question marks, to the clarification of which the rest of this note will be devoted. But it is worth saying again, with regret, that any effort to prove that Western propagandists exaggerate 'the Soviet military build-up' has been hampered by the Soviet publication of increasingly incredible budgetary defence votes. One appreciates their embarrassment, however. Imagine the following conversation in the Kremlin:

> *Comrade A:* 'Look, why not publish what we really spend? That will help to put a stop to some of the wilder over-statements of our enemies. We can blame Brezhnev, after all.'
> *Comrade B:* 'Sorry, *tovarishch*, impossible. It involves admitting that the real figure is four times what we said it is. They will say we lied all these years.'
> *Comrade A:* 'Oh well, I suppose you are right. Pity, though.'

THE BUDGETARY DEFENCE VOTE

So let us pass on to the meaning of the budget defence vote. Wiles, as we have seen supposes that, for some years at least, it was equal to the value of the item *oborona* (defence) in the national accounts, and that this item included the increment in weapons, that is, the gross volume less depreciation (write-offs). But he too is unable to fit the level of expenditures of recent years into the defence vote defined in this way, he supposes that additional concealment was occurring. Another interpretation is that the defence vote covers all current operational expenditures, such as pay, subsistence, administration, material utilization (e.g., fuel, heating, the use of practice ammunition, etc.), but that weapon production and stocks are separately financed, as in investment (and, of course, R&D).

Given the virtually unanimous view that the major part of defence expenditure is not in the budget defence vote, then where is it? Everyone agrees that most if not all military R&D is financed out of the 'Science' vote (i.e., out of 'Social-cultural expenditure'), and the paramilitary police troops out of the 'Ministry of the Interior' vote. Where can the rest be more or less legitimately hidden? It is well hidden; so we do not know. One obvious 'candidate' is 'Allocations to the National Economy', the budget's largest item, and within it the allocation to 'Heavy Industry' – or, in another categorization, in the allocation to 'State Material Reserves'. The accounting logic would be: not to sell weapons to the Ministry of Defence (unless it needs them in, say, Afghanistan), but to put them in special State stores. Also in the most recent years there has been a sharp rise in the overall budget residual, though this may have other explanations. But these are just hypotheses, which cannot be proved. It has also been argued that these residuals, when their other contents are allowed for, are too small. Thus the National Economy residual by use-category includes agricultural subsidies and foreign-trade expenditures, among others.

So – extra budgetary financing? If so, from where? One idea is Peter Wiles's: a transfer to 'Defence' of a part of the civilian amortization account. Obvious objection: it is fully committed (indeed, real depreciation may well be higher), and such a transfer would simply create another gap which would have to be filled with other revenues. I am unconvinced. An alternative argument is advanced by Igor Birman,[12] and in effect also by Dmitri Steinberg:[13] a large (even very large) concealed budgetary deficit, which contributes to inflationary pressure. Birman claimed that the State Bank issued extra money to the government, which appeared nowhere in the published accounts. Steinberg seemed to envisage the granting of credits, which are never repaid, which cover a large part of expenditures on weapons. Interestingly, the existence of fictional budget *revenues* has been pointed out by several Soviet economists,[14,15] but their point is a different one: that many sums paid into the budget by normal *khozraschyot* enterprises consist of turnover tax and profits in respect of goods not sold, so that the State Bank has to issue extra credits to cover the resultant gap in enterprise funds.

Presumably it is possible that direct grants are made to defence-industry enterprises (which Steinberg believes to be 'on the budget' in the same sense as, say, schools or hospitals; that is, they make no profits and their expenses are covered by public funds). These *could* masquerade as long-term credits. But this seems a not-very-probable masquerade, which finds no precedent in what we know of Soviet accounting. The very large budget deficit which such procedures imply is *very* unsound finance. (True, Reagan tolerates a vastly bigger deficit! But it is not concealed.) So, speaking for myself, I am agnostic on this question. If extra sources of finance do exist, why not some of the proceeds of arms exports? But again, there is no proof.

Some estimates of Soviet military expenditures, notably the CIA's, put in a very high figure for R&D, and seem to be using a definition of R&D that is a good deal wider than that which the Soviets put into their budget statements. Otherwise one would reach the ridiculous conclusion that close to 95 per cent of all Soviet R&D expenditures are military. This definitional problem bedevils all such international comparisons. (Indeed, I recall being asked to fill in a form specifying how many hours a week I spent on 'research'. I had no idea of the answer! In writing this paper, am I engaged in 'research'?) There is also the point that much military-type research in the United States is undertaken by private firms and does not appear in US figures of military expenditure. But, as was pointed out by Mary Acland-Hood, some of the estimates used by the CIA for Soviet military R&D are, to put it mildly, lacking in any solid basis and may well be substantially overstated.

HOW MUCH?

To return to rouble estimates of Soviet military expenditures. There is considerable difference of opinion as to the actual figures. But

Table 22.1 World military expenditures (billions of US dollars at 1980 prices and exchange rates)

	1977	*1980*	*1985*
USA	137.1	144.0	204.9
Other NATO	103.3	112.3	122.8
Total NATO	*240.4*	*256.3*	*327.7*
USSR	[126.1]	[131.8]	[146.2]
Other WTO	11.9	12.5	13.9
Total WTO	*138.0*	*144.3*	*160.1*

NOTES: Square brackets in original indicate estimate by the analysts.
NATO = North Atlantic Treaty Organization
WTO = Warsaw Treaty Organization

SOURCE: SIPRI, *World Armaments and Disarmament: SIPRI Yearbook 1986* (Oxford: Oxford University Press, 1986) p. 231.

apart from this, one can have very differing views as to how they can be compared with US expenditure data in dollars, and also on the price trends which rouble figures reflect.

The first of these points was dealt with by Franklyn Holzman,[16] and there is no need for me to enlarge on it, other than to stress that his points are serious and cannot be ignored. It may also be apposite to cite SIPRI's own calculations, published in the *1986 Yearbook* (see Table 22.1).

These are the sort of figures that led Admiral LaRoque's publication, *Defense Monitor*,[17] to assert, contrary to what is seen as Pentagon propaganda, that NATO substantially outspent the Warsaw Pact. And indeed even if *Soviet* expenditures in real terms were equal to, or somewhat exceeded, the US figures, 'Other NATO' is vastly bigger, in total, than 'Other Warsaw Pact'. As Jacobsen pointed out in the same SIPRI volume,[18] the CIA's own revisions, made in 1983, also effectively show Soviet military expenditures below US levels, and indeed, after allowance for R&D, show no growth since 1976, a conclusion which was bitterly attacked by Rosefielde.[19]

The growth (or non-growth) in question, to have meaning, should be in constant prices. So straight away the problem of price indices raises its head, not this time in the form discussed by Holzman (which relates to the different results obtained by using dollar or rouble weights), but as a different question: can one use the official Soviet index for MBMW as a surrogate for a price index for military

Table 22.2 Wholesale prices excluding turnover tax, 1965 = 100

	1975	*1981*	*1985*
All industry	106	103	114
Electricity	131	125	155
Fuels	172	173	290
Ferrous metals	150	155	190
Machinery & metalworking	80	74	72

SOURCE: *Vestnik Statistiki*, no. 9 (1982) p. 78, and no. 9 (1986) p. 79.

hardware, and is that index in fact usable for civilian MBMW because of its understatement of real price rises (or 'hidden inflation')? Thus suppose, using current roubles, one calculates that Soviet military expenditure rose from (say) 60 to 90 billion roubles over the previous seven years. If one takes the view expressed by Rosefielde, and (in an early draft of his paper) by Steinberg, and adopts the official Soviet index for MBMW, this would mean an increase in *volume* of well over 50 per cent. If, however, using the lower of the two estimates of S. Zhuravlev,[20] one accepts a cost-increase (*udorozhaniye*) for civilian investment goods of 5 per cent per annum, the increase would be just over 6 per cent, that is less than 1 per cent per annum. It makes quite a difference!

So it is important to show why the use of the official Soviet price index for machinery, or for investment in general, cannot be accepted.

MACHINERY PRICES AND INVESTMENT VOLUME

Investment statistics in value terms are very tricky to handle. Some purport to be in constant prices, some are in current prices, some relate to estimate prices (*smetnye tseny*) which are known to be exceeded, and it is not clear how and when this excess is financed. There are official price indices for machinery and for construction, but . . . Let us first turn to machinery. The wholesale price index disappeared from *Narkhoz* in 1979, but it can be carried through 1985 with the help of Table 22.2. Bearing in mind that average industrial wages rose by over 85 per cent, the index for machinery looks distinctly improbable. A whole long list of Soviet sources publicly regard it as incredible. Thus: 'It seems that these price indices were based on a comparatively narrow and unrepresentative sample, untypical of the whole volume of capital investments.'[21] Krasovsky, writing six years later, deplores the effect on construction costs of the deliberate choice of dear materials, and dear machinery, to fulfil plans expressed in *stroitelnyi val* (gross value of output).[22] He clearly states that series in so-called comparable prices are misleading. Furthermore he tells us that 'the fixing in 1984 of new estimate-prices and norms for construction led to a rise in the cost of investment by about 50 [fifty!] milliard roubles'. How indeed can all this be reconciled with the official index for construction costs, which show very little change, and indeed are lower, supposedly, in 1984 than in 1971!?[23]

Similar points, plus some quantitative estimates, were made by V. Faltsman:

> Rises in costs in 1976–80 exceeded for the first time the rise in the value of capital investments. The consequence was an absolute decline in completions [*vvoda moshchnostei*] compared with the previous quinquennium. In the period 1971–82 there was a significant rise in costs per unit of productivity of machinery. A rough measure of this rise can be deduced from the fact that total value of sales [*tovarnaya produktsiya*] of the machinery sectors rose by 8%, while the total energy capacity [*energoyomkost'*] of all the produced equipment rose by only 3% per annum . . . The annual average increase in prices per unit of productivity of the machinery was about 5% (earlier calculations had put it at 3%).[24]

The same author noted that it had recently been claimed that the volume of metal used to produce one million roubles' worth of machinery fell by 5 per cent per annum. This 'created the illusion of economy of metal', yet Soviet machines remained as heavy as before. 'We must take into account *udorozhaniye* (rising costs), and when this is done then the economy of metal in real terms was less than 1%.'[25]

The same points, stressing the exaggeration of figures for investment volume, were made by K. Val'tukh. He too drew the conclusion that 'in 1976–80 there occurred an absolute decline in productive investments in real terms'.[26] He tried to calculate the real rate of increase in machinery output in recent years and puts it at only 1 per cent per annum, far below the official index.[27]

Other sources abound. Thus A. Deryabin:[28] 'Analysis shows that the present method of determining wholesale prices actually incites the makers of new products to overstate their economic effectiveness', so that prices rise faster than their 'effect' (i.e., the productivity the new machines engender). Here is a quote from *Pravda*:[29] 'Enterprises are incited [*natseleny*] towards continuous price increases. Just alter some component, get the mark N (novelty) and the product becomes 20% dearer.' Then there is General Secretary Mikhail Gorbachev himself: 'On the excuse of modernization, prices of machinery and equipment, estimate-costs of construction, are increased . . . Unfortunately, state and economic organs prefer not to notice [*smotryat skvoz paltsy*], since they are often directly interested in the increase of the volume of output by "playing" prices.'[30] Nor does the customer resist. Thus, say L. Evstigneyeva and V. Perlamutrov:[31] There is 'the possibility and incentive to increase prices . . . since the users are in fact indifferent: higher prices for raw materials and equipment will find their due reflection in cost estimates, in the financial plan, and the required financing . . . will be forthcoming. The effort of the producer to increase prices does not meet any resistance from the user.' V. Medvedev[32] wrote of 'more or less concealed price increases'. Similar remarks were made by O. Novikov,[33] D. Palterovich[34] and G. Khanin.[35] Khanin is particularly interesting, since he does not confine himself to just saying that 'considerable rises in prices find no reflection in the price index', but also tries to recompute the 'true' volume. So far as machinery production is concerned, the effect of his recomputation is to reduce the official volume index of 256 to somewhere between 174 and 194 (for 1980, 1970 = 100). Interestingly, the CIA's recomputation is close to the upper limit of Khanin's, who had to indicate his results indirectly.

L. M. Gatovsky, referring to price supplements for new technology, wrote: 'The growth of these supplements exceeds even the exaggerated data on effectiveness . . . As a result there is a stimulus for the production of ineffective technology through increasing prices . . . The excessive rises of price contradicts the nature of intensification . . . Finally there is created a clear exaggeration of the volume of production'.[36]

In case there is still some doubt, I will end with S. Zhuravlev:[37] 'The rising cost of investment activity, taking quality improvements into account', he puts at between 5 and 7 per cent per annum. He also estimates that if 'negative tendencies, irrational resource utilization and losses' which distort the growth statistics were eliminated, a growth rate of 4 per cent in national income would be the equivalent of 5.4 to 5.8 per cent in previous years. One can turn this around and say that a growth rate of between 5.4 and 5.8 per cent claimed for previous years would really be the equivalent of 4 per cent if various distorting elements were eliminated.

In a remarkably vigorous critique of Soviet price and growth indices, written after this paper was completed, two Soviet specialists – G. Khanin and V. Selyunin – write the following: 'We know that machinery holds the record in inflating wholesale prices, which are used to compare growth rates. According to our calculations, in each of the four past quinquennia the rise in prices varied from 27% to 34%' [in each five-year period].[38]

A FEW COMMENTS

Firstly, the valuation of new products and of investment projects in constant prices is nowhere perfect. Secondly, all accept that some part of *udorozhaniye* (cost increases) of investments is due to more ecological expenditures and higher investment costs in remote areas, and also high-cost imports. Thirdly, some contribution was made by the large volume of uncompleted construction. Fourthly, some *udorozhaniye* was the result of the deliberate choice of dear investment variants (particularly notorious in agriculture), which is not the same as a rise in price. Fifthly, it is hard to compare different qualities of machinery. Sixthly, any index relating to Machinery & Metalworking includes many items which are not productive capital goods (such as cars, refrigerators, bicycles, perhaps also the arms industry).

However, the evidence really is overwhelming: it is *quite wrong* to apply what is clearly a distorted price index for civilian machinery to military production.

It is also worth asking the question: even if we had a good index for civilian machinery, would this be a guide to military hardware costs? Some have close civilian analogies (for example, means of transport), but some have not. There must also be an unknown but large sum spent on development, testing, false starts, such as is the case also in the West. And finally, when there is radical change to the products through time – as is certainly the case with modern weapons – what do we precisely mean by a price index? How much would it have cost to make an SS-20 in a year in which it was still only an idea in its inventor's head? Do any of us, do Soviet statisticians, know the answer to such questions? Do we, with respect to our own weapons?

On balance we ought surely to expect some *udorozhaniye*. So the CIA's estimates in 1970 prices could be consistent with some high rouble estimates in *current* prices, and still be consistent with the CIA's view that weapon acquisition in real terms increased very slowly.

CONCLUSIONS

There are still plenty of unsettled problems; some have to do with methodology, some with how to interpret Soviet statistics and gaps in these statistics; there is no agreement either on how many roubles they spend or just what this means in terms of volume over time, as well as real cost in terms of resources foregone (given the nature of Soviet prices and the prevalence of physical shortages, especially of materials and technologies of high quality). Yet the participants entertain the belief that this exposé of current knowledge and lack of knowledge may spark more informed debate, chart more useful avenues of future research and perhaps stimulate more *glasnost* from Soviet statisticians and CIA analysts alike – withholding data from the scrutiny of academic expertise may facilitate subterfuge (and prevent embarrassing challenge), but it does not facilitate rational choice.

NOTES

1. For example, see interviews with Polish 'Stalinists', in T. Toranska *Oni* (An Eks: Warsaw and London, 1985), interviews with E. Ochab (p. 37) and J. Berman (p. 312).
2. V. V. Lavrova and K. N. Plotnikova (eds), *Gosudarstvenny byudzhet SSSR* (State budget of the USSR) (Moscow: Izdat. dp, 1975).
3. See A. Nove, *The Soviet Economic System* (London: George Allen & Unwin, 1986) p. 247.
4. See S. Rosefielde, *False Science* (New Brunswick, NJ: Transaction Books, 1982).
5. W. Lee, *The Estimation of Soviet Defence Expenditure* (New York: Praeger, 1977).

6. A. Nove and A. Zauberman, 'A Soviet disclosure of ruble national income', *Soviet Studies* (Oct. 1959).
7. S. G. Strumilin in N. Fedorenko (ed.), *Planirovaniye i ekonomiko-matematicheskiye metody* (Planning and economic mathematical methods) (Moscow: Nauka, 1964) pp. 50–2.
8. Nove, *Soviet Economic System*, p. 246.
9. Ibid., p. 340.
10. Rosefielde, *False Science*.
11. A. Bergson, 'A problem in Soviet statistics', *Review of Economic Statistics* (Nov. 1947) p. 240.
12. See I. Birman, *Secret Incomes of the Soviet Budget* (The Hague: Nijhoff, 1981).
13. D. Steinberg, (paper 2.1 in this book).
14. V. Belkin and V. Ivanter, *Planovoya sbalansirovannost* (Planning equilibrium) (Moscow: Nauka, 1983).
15. I. Petrov, *EKO*, no. 1 (1986).
16. F. Holzman 'Are the Soviets really outspending us on defense?', *International Security* (Spring 1980) vol. 4, no. 4, pp. 86–104.
17. For example, in *Defensé Monitor*, vol. 12, no. 2 (1983).
18. C. G. Jacobsen, 'Soviet military expenditure and the Soviet defence burden', *World Armaments and Disarmament: SIPRI Yearbook 1986* (Oxford: Oxford University Press, 1986) p. 264.
19. The latest such attack by Rosefielde is in *Russia*, no. 12 (1986) pp. 49–59.
20. S. Zhuravlev, in *Ekonomicheskaya Gazeta*, no. 24 (1986) p. 4.
21. V. Krasovsky, in *Voprosy ekonomiki* (Economic questions) (Moscow) no. 1 (1980) p. 109.
22. V. Krasovsky, in *Voprosy ekonomiki*, no 4 (1986) pp. 41–5.
23. *Narkhoz 1984*, p. 395.
24. V. Faltsman, *Voprosy ekonomiki*, no 3 (1985) pp.49 and 53.
25. V. Faltsman, *Voprosy ekonomiki*, no 6 (1986) p. 95.
26. K. Val'tukh, *EKO*, no. 3 (1982).
27. K. Val'tukh, *EKO*, no. 2 (1986) p. 19.
28. A. Deryabin, *Ekonomicheskaya gazeta* (The Economic Newspaper) no. 19 (1986) p. 11.
29. *Pravda* (15 June 1986).
30. *Pravda* (17 June 1986).
31. L. Evstigneyeva and V. Perlamutrov, *Voprosy ekonomiki*, no. 12 (1985).
32. V. Medvedev, *Planovoe Khoziaistvo* (Economic Planning) no. 9 (1983).
33. O. Novikov, *Voprosy ekonomiki*, no. 1 (1983).
34. D. Palterovich, *Voprosy ekonomiki*, no. 1 (1986).
35. G. Khanin, *Vestnik akademii nauk, seriya ekonomicheskaya* (Herald of the Academy of Sciences, economic series) no. 6 (1981) and no. 3 (1984).
36. L. M. Gatovsky, *Voprosy ekonomiki*, no. 6 (1986) pp. 9 and 10.
37. Zhuravlev, *Ekonomicheskaya Gazeta*.
38. G. Khanin and V. Selyunin 'Lukavaya tsifra' (Cunning figures) *Novyi Mir*, no. 2 (1987) p. 184.

23 Is Within-system Reform Possible?*

Six years ago (in 1979) I wrote a piece, entitled 'The economic problems of Brezhnev's successors', which appeared in the *Washington Papers* (published by the CSIS of Georgetown University). This took the form of an imaginary report of an imaginary committee, which had been (in my imagination) set up to recommend reform. In all countries, the powers-that-be tend to appoint committees which will give them the advice they want to hear. So it would have been improbable, to say the least, for Brezhnev to have appointed 'my' committee, which represented what might for short be called the Novosibirsk view, and was presided over by Academician Aganbegyan, known to favour fundamental change. Despite Brezhnev's quite

* This was written for a conference held in Geneva in August 1985 and is reprinted by permission from *The Soviet Union and the challenge of the future*, vol. II (New York: The Paragon House, 1989), © PWPA. Since then there have been many decrees, laws, resolutions, speeches and articles, on radical economic reform in the Soviet Union. Many of the decisions represent important steps towards 'marketization', notably the law on cooperatives adopted in 1988, and the encouragement of family contract and family leasing in agriculture. The need for competition has been explicitly recognized. So has the need for a move to 'trade in means of production' (the elimination of administered allocation), the abandonment of imposed output targets and the strengthening of market-based contractual relations. Many statements have been made linking radical economic reform with a fundamental change in the political system. However, while political and cultural freedoms have expanded in a most impressive way, economic reform has made very little headway, owing in no small measure to the consequences of serious imbalances, shortages, budget deficits and inflationary pressures. These were superimposed upon the already very difficult problems of transition, and utilized by those forces in society opposed to these reforms. Unfortunately these include not only bureaucrats but also millions of rank-and-file citizens, concerned with job security and the maintenance of the (huge) food subsidies. Also "the fall of the Soviet empire", which seemed a remote prospect as recently as 1985, is a major issue today. Two questions arise: if the reform succeeds, could it be regarded as 'within-system', and can, or will, the undoubtedly radical intentions of the reformers be realized? Present indications give us no grounds for optimism.

explicit recognition that 'in the age of scientific–technical revolution, basic changes in our methods of economic management are essential', as he told the last party congress but one, the prevailing policy was one of cautious drift.

We now have the successor of the successor of Brezhnev's successor, a younger and evidently more intelligent (and less patient) man than either Brezhnev or Chernenko – we cannot really pass judgment on Andropov's views and actions, as he had too little time. Unofficial reports suggest that Gorbachev is well aware of the 'Novosibirsk' view, including the (leaked) Zaslavskaya paper, and at the very least is willing to listen to such ideas.

There was some overlap between my imaginary report and the Zaslavskaya paper, but this is no occasion for surprise. The key elements in any realistic analysis of what is wrong with the system are, so to speak, common property. Whatever its original rationale, it has outlived itself. The overwhelming scale and complexity of 'traditional' centralized planning renders its efficient operation impossible. True, the Western (and Southern) economies have their problems also, and mass unemployment is a source of major economic and human waste from which the Soviet system has not suffered. It is true also that some Western commentators exaggerate Soviet economic weaknesses (while simultaneously exaggerating Soviet military strength), which produces various kinds of wishful thinking about 'the fall of the Soviet empire', and policies designed to speed this collapse by speeding up the arms race.

Yet there are serious weaknesses, *systemic* weaknesses, which plainly are a source of grave concern to the leadership. It is not the task of this paper to analyze them, since, as its title indicates, I am to concentrate on the feasibility of reform. But a few words about the basic nature of what is to be reformed are none the less indispensable.

I have already emphasized scale and complexity. We are concerned in the main, in my view, with various aspects of *diseconomies of scale*. In any large organization, if headquarters knows precisely what needs doing and how, the simplest and most effective way of getting it done is to issue appropriate orders. It would be silly and pointless to proceed indirectly through manipulating the price mechanism. Marx's error was to suppose that in a socialist society the centre ('the associated producers') *would* have this information. Of course sometimes the centre does know, indeed sometimes only the centre *can* know. In these instances, the Soviet economic system is reasonably effective, provided that the sectors concerned are also given administrative priority, are not starved of resources. Armament production is an obvious instance, and so are oil, gas and electricity. Errors can happen in these sectors too, but there is no reason to assign them to the nature of the system. Thus electricity generation is centralized in West European countries too, for similar reasons: present and future demand is best seen at the centre, the power stations are an interconnected system, the product is clearly definable and homogeneous.

However there are hundreds of thousands of varieties of machinery, equipment, components, textiles, clothes and consumer durables; there are an almost infinite number of ways in which new designs and new techniques of production can be developed. To produce any manufactured good, or to provide a wide variety of services, requires numerous material inputs. There are hundreds of thousands of enterprises in industry, agriculture, construction, transport and distribution. Most make a variety of different goods, or different models of similar goods. Academician Fedorenko has remarked that, for next year's plan to be balanced, checked, corrected, disaggregated, and so on, *with* the help of computers, might require roughly 30 000 years.

Since next year's plan must be ready 29 999 years before that, it cannot be balanced, consistent, checked, corrected, disaggregated or stable. Hence the familiar list of problems: aggregated indicators in tons, roubles, pairs and so on cannot ensure that the product mix accords with needs; quality cannot be defined or rewarded; technical progress, though ardently desired, is frequently frustrated; the material allocation system repeatedly malfunctions, not because of bad will or stupidity, but because there are simply too many inputs to allocate to too many users; harassed directors over-apply for inputs, understate production possibilities, and hoard materials and labour; supply–demand imbalances frustrate management and ordinary citizens in almost equal measure, causing unofficial and/or corrupt practices to flourish and reducing the effectiveness of labour incentives. Unbalanced plans are necessarily and repeatedly amended in the course of their currency. Management repeatedly receives plan instructions which are internally contradictory. And so on.

The leadership knows all this and deplores it. It is wrong to stress, as some have done, the conflict between planners' preferences and consumer (user) preferences. Such a conflict can be seen at macro level (over, say, the share of consumption in the national income), and sometimes at the micro level too (for example, more Lenin, less Dostoevsky). But in general the centre can be assumed to wish that user micro needs be satisfied; there is nothing in the works of Marx, Lenin (or even Stalin) to the effect that women desiring brown size 5 shoes should not get them, or that a manager who needs thin steel sheet should get only thick steel sheet (because the supplier's plan is in tons). These are seen by *all* concerned not as a conflict of preference but as a *malfunction*, to be corrected.

A complication arises, however, to which we shall have to pay particular attention. The planners (or the party-state ruling apparatus as a whole) are in one sense a disunited set of competitors for scarce resources, which is why a chapter in my *Soviet Economic System* is headed 'centralized pluralism'. But, as the Hungarian emigré economist Markus remarked, they do have the goal-function of maximizing (or at the very least not decreasing) their control over resources.[1] In other words, citing this time myself, 'they prefer to be able to prefer'.[2] Can we therefore see these malfunctions as an inevitable, and thus necessary, *cost* of centralized control over material and human resources? In a very real sense the answer must be: 'Yes'. The question, then, becomes one of seeing when, and whether, the cost becomes intolerably high.

The word 'reform' needs careful qualification. In one sense, to cite the phrase correctly used by Gertrude Schroeder, the Soviet economy has been 'on a treadmill of reforms'. In a similar spirit, Zaslavskaya used the word 'labyrinth' to describe the sheer bewildering number of rules, plan indicators and amendments to these which face Soviet managers. Indeed there have been numerous reforms of (and within) the centralized system, culminating in the so-called 'large-scale experiment' now being extended. Some of these 'reforms' have been in contradictory directions: thus the 1979–81 measures had the net effect of increasing control over resource allocation and resource use (through tighter utilization norms), which resulted in a still greater proliferation of detailed plan-indicator orders. The 'experiment' is designed to reduce these (not for the first time), while giving much emphasis to the fulfilment of delivery contracts. However the basic principles remain untouched: plan-orders are the basis of production and of delivery obligations, and material allocation is still the rule, though the idea revives of extending 'trade in means of production', which figured in the abortive 'reform' of 1965.[3]

Just one example will illustrate what happens even to the best-intentioned plan-indicators. *Pravda* (30 March 1983) published a note entitled: 'Waste in the name of economy'. It turned out that designers of new machines sought to put into the design the greatest possible waste of metal, labour inputs and cost. Why? Because imposed on them in subsequent years would be obligatory plans for reducing metal use, labour inputs and cost. Therefore . . . One sees here in summary much of the disease. Aggregate plans in tons, roubles and so on stimulate management to waste. The central planning agencies do not and cannot know exactly how much metal, labour and so on should be used to produce each of many thousands of kinds and models of machines. So, rightly suspecting that managers might waste metal and labour and inflate costs, they introduce compulsory economy targets. These, however, have the effect just described.

Much has been heard in these last years about the need for stable plans and stable norms on which to calculate wage payments and incentive bonuses. On paper this seems sensible and logical. If plans once determined were stable for the whole year, or even for a quinquennium, then management could be confident of being rewarded for aiming higher (through so-called 'counterplans', *vstrechnye plany*) without fear of the so-called ratchet effect; that is, having their plans arbitrarily altered upwards if successful. Indeed plans have been altered too often in both directions, and this does make nonsense out of the attempts to encourage managerial initiative – which is in any case frustrated by the materials allocation system, tight financial controls and numberless other regulations. But the 'stable plan' is not only a fantasy, it is undesirable too. It is a fantasy because, given the huge scale of the task of the planners, it is quite inevitable that errors and omissions, unforeseen circumstances of some kind, would require a change in various plan indicators. Not to change the plan would actually enhance the already great systemic rigidities. (Ministries also change plans for less good reasons, but that is another story.) 'Stable plans' are undesirable in any kind of economy from which perfect foresight is absent (that is, in any kind of economy!). We all of us require to amend our behaviour in the light of unforeseen circumstances. So it is not surprising to read, in the report on the consultative meeting called by Gorbachev,[4] a criticism by the director of a clothing factory: 'for us, a fixed quinquennium, rigid long-term plans, combined with built-in growth percentages, obstruct the adaptation of output to changing user demand'. The 'stable plans' road is surely a blind alley.

Among the other measures introduced in 1979 is a shift from gross to 'normed value added' monetary indicators. For predictable reasons, this has proved unworkable and caused its own distortions; condemned in vigorous style in the specialist press,[5] it is unlikely to survive. But can any substitute be any better? The problem is the imposition of *any* aggregate plan target, howsoever expressed, on a multi-product enterprise or industry.

To repeat, the leadership is deeply concerned. Economy, efficiency, 'intensive growth', these are rendered necessary by the proliferation of needs – for investment, for consumption, for agriculture, for the military . . . The party's programme is being amended to reflect the theory of 'mature' (or 'developed', or 'real') socialism. But it must still be the objective and legitimation of the regime to catch up the West, and this they are plainly not doing, whether in computer technology (or, more important, its use) or in the quality of almost any manufactured product. Something must be done, and Gorbachev blamed delay in doing it on, *inter alia*, 'lack of insistence in the elaboration and implementation of major measures in the sphere of the economy'.[6]

What is the alternative, if any, to a Russian version of the Hungarian reform model, to a reform which frees most enterprises from having current output plans imposed on them from above, while leaving them free most of the time to purchase their inputs, without having them administratively allocated?

It is the virtue and value of the Zaslavskaya report that its author did discuss obstacles to necessary change (plainly change in the 'Hungarian' direction) in a systematic way. I assume that most participants have read one of several published versions of her report. What follows is based on her categories, but does not dwell on or repeat her arguments.

Let us begin with *ideology*. In her account she refers both to the (false) ideological picture of a Soviet society united and free of contradiction, and that part of the formal ideology which regards socialism as inherently incompatible with the market mechanism, and which therefore sees 'commodity–money relations' as a temporary necessity to be carefully circumscribed and made subordinate to the obligatory central plan. She is obviously right in stressing that major changes in the economic mechanism in the Soviet (as in any other) society would affect different groups in the population in different ways, engendering support from some and opposition from others. I will return to this theme in a moment. First let us look at ideology as such, and also at Soviet official 'political economy'.

What *is* 'ideology as such'? This is a not unimportant question. Some attempts have been made (the last one by Neil Harding),[7] to distinguish between the formal ideology and the operational set of beliefs. These are sometimes in contradiction. Thus the sayings of the Founding Fathers clearly and repeatedly assert the rights of the workers to organize and run the state (until it finally withers away). The operational version emphatically denied them that right, and on the contrary regarded any free and spontaneous organization of workers (or of anybody else) as impermissible. So which was the 'real' ideology in this rather important question? One cannot assert that what they do is determined by the 'real' ideology, having first deduced the 'real' ideology from what they do, except possibly with an ironic aside about the unity of theory and practice.

There may in fact be three 'faces' of ideology, not two. One is a formal set of doctrines, based on what the Founding Fathers said, fulfilling an important religious-legitimating function, with the monopoly of interpretation clearly located in the central committee. The second is indeed a sort of digest of operational principles (one-party state, censorship, repression of dissidents, and so on), together with sometimes cynical or hypocritical or purely practical justifications. The third is real beliefs, which can be sincerely held, and may be related to either of the first two, but not always (as with, for example, racism). Let us call these ideologies 1, 2 and 3.

Now let us return to 'political economy'. There is no doubt that Marx did believe that there would be no market under socialism. Whatever might be necessary in a transition period, the process of transition was envisaged as the gradual replacement of the market by planning, by society for society. The complexities of this process were neither anticipated nor understood. So ideology 1 is against a market-type reform. Ideology 2 is far more flexible, perfectly well able to suppress or reinterpret whatever bits of ideology 1 prove inconvenient to authority. It is in this sense that I interpret a conversation I once had in Moscow with a Soviet economist:

> AN: But would the price system that you propose be consistent with the Marxist labour theory of value?
> SE: Look, if we can persuade the leadership to adopt it and it works, I assure you it *will* be consistent with the Marxist labour theory of value.

The problem, however, is that there is a tie-up between ideology 2 and vested interest, of which more in a moment. Enemies of reform can and do refer to ideology 1. A good if rather low-level example may be seen in the article by Glushkov, the then head of the prices committee, in *Voprosy ekonomiki*, no. 1, 1984. He assails the very notion of *ravnovesnye tseny*, that is, supply-and-demand-balancing prices. Yet without a major reform of prices, which must be an integral part also of eliminating excess demand (for both producers' goods and consumers' goods), a serious reform can scarcely get off the ground. Another example is Koryagina, significantly on the staff of the party's school, who criticizes the notion of utility (*poleznost'*), counterposing and preferring *potrebnost'*, need.[8] The point is that utility, of its nature, can hardly be evaluated other than by the user. Need can be determined by planners. Not for nothing did the three emigre Hungarians, Feher, Heller and Markus, entitle their critique of the system *Dictatorship Over Needs*.

Reformers take one of several lines. One is to use the apparently conservative slogan of 'Mature (developed) socialism'. Not only Zaslavskaya did this; so did Gorbachev. After all, the system was created in its essentials 50 years ago, when presumably socialism was immature and underdeveloped. So reform is needed to bring the system of planning and management into line with the requirements of mature, developed socialism.

As for the labour theory of value, there are basically two ways of circumventing it: one is to reinterpret it, bringing in demand via the effect of use-value on the 'socially necessary' labour which produces the use-values, or (as did Novozhilov) by stressing feedback effects and legitimating opportunity-cost. Another is simply to disregard what Marx said about value under capitalism because he analyzed value under *capitalism*: socialism is a different ball-game.

If reforms of the Hungarian type were to be adopted, ideology 2 could accommodate them. But now we must bring in ideology 3; widespread in all strata of Soviet society. Among not only local party bosses but also many millions of ordinary citizens, there is a genuine and sincere suspicion of markets and traders ('speculators') and hostility to the price increases which are certainly necessary to bring supply and demand into balance. A market might also mean having to work harder and lessen the much-prized job security. Even if unemployment does not threaten, an end to labour hoarding would have to mean some redundancies and transfers. Ideology 3 can be seen and heard when local officials respond to popular demand (or prejudice) and impose ceilings on free-market prices, as has happened quite frequently (even though it is contrary to the official rules). The anti-market elements of ideology 3 are a serious obstacle to reform, affecting as they do both the conservative elements of party officialdom and ordinary folk.

Now let us pass to vested interest. Here we must avoid oversimplification. 'The party' is 18 million strong, and it contains both protagonists and enemies of reform. Zaslavskaya correctly points to the necessity of analyzing the effects of proposed changes on different strata of officialdom and management. Some would certainly lose. This would include many ministerial and local-party officials, heavily engaged in replacing the invisible hand with the visible hand – theirs. At the summit of power, however, the functions of the top men would be little affected: it is not they who allocate ball-bearings and issue detailed plan-orders in thousands of tons to specific enterprises. Management itself would require to take greater responsibility, to stand on its own feet, and this would frighten the less competent, those who are happy with the system which Hegedüs calls 'organized irresponsibility'. As for the party-state machine as a whole, those whom Markus described as aiming to maximize control over resources, the picture here is not quite as clear as some make out. Certainly the centralized planning system appears to give (and in important ways actually does give) the political organs the maximum degree of power. They are indeed anxious to maintain this, using for the purpose arguments drawn from ideologies 1, 2 and 3. Any automatically functioning system, any freedom for spontaneous forces to operate, anything smacking of *samotyok* (a pejorative term for any uncontrolled process) produces an instant negative response. One can go on at length on this theme: here is indeed a formidable obstacle. However . . .

However, it is not enough to prefer to be able to prefer. One must also be obeyed. The outcome must, to some degree, conform to the intentions of the rulers. The whole problem, as seen from the angle of such as Gorbachev, is that the existing system of management too often produces perverse results, results no one actually desires: not the planners, not the customers, not even the producers.

'Why is it that enterprises that produce obsolete goods of low technical standards, or consumer goods which are not in demand, can live normally and even flourish? Our economic mechanism allows such things to happen. How can we put this right, and with maximum speed?' This was Gorbachev at a consultative meeting with managers.[9] Summarizing numerous speeches at the meeting regarding increased powers and responsibility at enterprise level, the *Pravda* reporter wrote: 'Therefore what is needed is not partial improvements of the economic mechanism, but its complex all-round reconstruction.' The influential economist P. Bunich wrote, with regard to obstacles to technical progress:

> If they [any 'work collective', i.e. enterprise] try to introduce innovations at the stage of plan drafting, this would make the plan harder to fulfil . . . If the innovations are introduced in the course of plan fulfilment, then their effects will show up in the plan for the next period. Then this new obligatory plan will be tougher and more complex, since it is drafted on the base [of past performance], while wages and salaries remain unchanged.[10] (*Pravda*, 19 April 1985)

This same point was made several times at the round-table discussion reported by *Voprosy ekonomiki*. We all know that such quotations can be multiplied.

I cite them to illustrate the point that the leaders want not only power in the general sense, but also results. 'The historical fate of our country, the position of socialism in the contemporary world, largely depend on how we now act'.[11] Gorbachev well knows that technical progress is frustrated, output does not match the needs of industry, of agriculture (several speeches were devoted to *this* theme at the above-mentioned consultative meeting) or of the consumer. The party leadership urgently desires and requires greater efficiency, the sharp reduction of waste, production for use and not for plan-fulfilment statistics, and repeatedly says so. What price is it prepared to pay to achieve this?

In China, when I was there in 1979, there was also much talk of urgently needed reform, but several Western China-watchers were highly sceptical: the party would never allow such changes to occur. On my return in 1983 I saw that many far-reaching changes *had* in fact occurred, on orders from the party leadership itself. Yes, the reforms in industry have not yet been nearly as sweeping as in agriculture, and yes, China is not Russia. But this example shows that we cannot be certain that the powerful forces of conservatism will triumph. (They *probably* will, but not certainly.)

A major additional obstacle is constituted by the military. Even in a report not intended for publication, Zaslavskaya could not so much as mention the military–industrial complex. Yet in the short run this is a double problem for the reformers. Firstly, the arms industry is evidently a sector which benefits from central planning, and secondly, the military are beneficiaries of centrally imposed priorities, which are of particularly vital importance when the economy as a whole suffers from chronic shortages. So the bigger the claim on resources of an influential and high-priority sector which *is* centrally plannable, the stronger is likely to be the opposition to radical change in the 'Hungarian' direction. True, the military also have reason to be concerned with deficiencies in technical progress, but this may be seen by them as a factor only in the long term. The immediacies of the arms race must, on balance, strengthen the enemies of reform.

Some analysts see political danger for the regime in extending the role of the market mechanism. Indeed, some liberal reformers hope that such an extension will contribute to political liberalization. In my view, there is a connection, but it is a remote and very long-term one. The political dangers are surely exaggerated. Suppose that most enterprises base their current production plans on their customers' requirements, and obtain the needed inputs by straightforward purchase. While certain medium and low-grade planning officials will have to find other work, where is the threat to *political* stability? Why should such a situation not coexist with repression of dissidents, or a one-party state (though there would have to be some change in party officials' *modus operandi*)? One answer frequently given is that the right to interfere arbitrarily in resource allocation, at various levels, is of the essence of the system, as is also the subordination of judges to party functionaries, with all *its* consequences on the judicial system. So there is indeed much to be said on both sides. I do not doubt that the habits of mind and established practices of party officialdom represent a major obstacle to change. I do pose the question whether this is necessarily an insurmountable obstacle.

Let us now pass to the practical problems of *implementation*, which are formidable. It is possible to envisage a man like Gorbachev accepting most or even all of the analysis of the radical reformers, and still deciding that their proposals cannot be put into effect, both because of the opposition it would arouse among influential functionaries, *and* because in purely practical terms no 'Hungarian' reform could be implemented without intolerable risk of confusion or even, for a time, chaos.

It is sometimes said that Hungary is a small country, that what could be done there is impossible in the huge Soviet Union. But this is a double-edged argument. Hungary depends very heavily on foreign trade, and this provided an added motive for reform there; had Hungary been autarkic, it would have been much simpler that in the USSR to control resources centrally. I recall on my first visit (in 1964) asking whether a product was administratively allocated, and being told: 'Yes, but we have only one enterprise producing it'! The reform argument rests above all on *scale*, so that the size of the USSR is not an objection, on the contrary.

The USSR is not only large, it has also operated the centralized system for over 50 years. No one remembers any other. Functionaries and managers at all levels have learned to operate within it, to make it work through a huge network of informal links of many kinds. Reform would disrupt them, would face hundreds of thousands of executives of all sorts with the unknown. Furthermore it would do so when excess demand is prevalent, shortages chronic, financial discipline (the 'hard budget constraint' of Kornai) weak, and prices quite irrational from the standpoint of the logic of this sort of reform. Even without the fears engendered by the international situation, the whole operation would seem to be fraught with risk. The risk becomes the greater, given the likely desire of many functionaries to obstruct the process. The 'reform constituency' is not large, and change would have to be imposed from above. Furthermore, as Zaslavskaya pointed out, there exists as yet no carefully prepared reform model or blueprint, nor is it anyone's job to prepare one. Partial, piecemeal reform is apt to be self-defeating, for familiar reasons.

What alternative strategies might suggest themselves? Is there another road, not a 'Hungarian' one at all? In a typically percipient essay, Joseph Berliner envisaged four possibilities.[12] I will follow him by eliminating the 'Stalinist' or authoritarian line (unless war actually threatens). The second possibility is one of continuing to tinker and muddle through, and amounts to no real reform; this is possible, but would leave the USSR in a position of stagnation, falling further behind technologically, a prospect which cannot be acceptable to the new politbureau. Berliner then suggests that the authorities, fearful of the consequences of subjecting the state sector to the market mechanism (that is, the Hungarian model), might prefer to allow small-scale private enterprise alongside it. Of course Hungary allows some significant private and cooperative enterprise, and so, since 1979, does China. China has adopted a much more radical solution in agriculture ('the household responsibility system'), which bears some relationship to the *kolletivnyi podryad* or *beznaryadnoye zveno* to which Gorbachev has personal commitment, as evidenced by his speech in Belgorod in March 1983. In the USSR, too, the specific problems of agriculture, of which motivating the peasants to work is a key one, may bring about the adoption of major reform in that sector first.

My own belief is that private enterprise, in the form of allowing some to employ others for profit, will be too much for the Soviet leaders to swallow, challenging simultaneously ideologies 1, 2 and 3. But the revival of urban cooperatives, for small-scale manufacture and, especially, for a wide range of services, seems sensible, and may be acceptable politically. It is perhaps significant that a serious article on the origins of the concept of mature socialism, by Dmitrenko[13] (*Voprosy istorii*, no. 8, 1984) assigns blame for trying to force the pace towards communism, citing as one example the premature and unnecessary elimination of producer cooperatives. (They were finally abolished under Krushchev, in 1961.)

Other alternatives? An article by the director of the Institute of Economics, Kapustin[14] (*Voprosy ekonomiki*, no. 3, 1985) argues for what could be called product-based cartels. This would seem more logical than the all-union *obyedineniya*, which, being within existing ministries, cannot be responsible for all the output of their product in the very many cases in which it is made by enterprises under many different ministries. The inspiration of this idea could be East Germany. I myself heard Bogomolov, the director of the Institute for the Study of the Economy of World Socialist Systems, suggest (in a lecture in Vienna) the possibility of combining the East German and the Hungarian models.

This is not at all a silly idea, bearing in mind the point made earlier: that there are important sectors (energy, for instance) that should and could remain under centralized management and control, even while production of a wide variety of other goods and services is carried out by reference to customers' requirements, that is, via some species of market mechanism.

The evident difficulty of implementing an idea such as Kapustin's is that the elimination of ministerial boundary-lines is only one aspect of the problem. Refrigerators, bicycles, building materials, components of many kinds, materials handling equipment, and so on are made within enterprises which also manufacture large numbers of other things. To unscramble this omelette would be a fearsomely complex undertaking. This is apart from the fact that creating product monopolies (responsible, in Kapustin's conception, for satisfying all the needs for their particular commodity) runs directly counter to the logic of any market-type reform, which requires customer choice and therefore competition. It may be significant that uncomplimentary remarks about all-union *obyedineniya* figured in the *Pravda* report of 12 April 1985, covering the consultative meeting addressed by Gorbachev.

It could be pointed out that East German industrial performance is in fact superior to Hungary's, that the real lessons to be learnt relate more to the impressive performance of Hungarian agriculture, which has indeed been noticed and studied in the USSR. However it is probable that the real explanation is that (as one Pole said to me) 'no system has yet been invented under which Germans can be prevented from working'. (Even the Soviet system of trade and catering works better in Estonia than in Russia proper; traditional attitudes and the work ethic are important factors.) But, to repeat, there may be a point in applying the 'cartel' approach in some sectors.

So, finally, while the obstacles to major reforms are formidable, the arguments for tackling these obstacles have become more powerful. The leadership faces a perplexing dilemma. It is quite likely that Gorbachev is personally convinced that the internal and international security of the USSR depends on altering in a new and decisive way the established methods of ruling, planning and managing, because only thus will it be possible to carry out the party's own economic programme. While such new policies would require time to prepare, and so cannot be introduced or implemented immediately, even if the politbureau favours them, we *may* be in for some surprises in the course of the next two to three years.

NOTES

1. *Praxis International*, no. 3.
2. *Economic Journal*, December 1969.
3. The inadequacies of this 'large-scale experiment' are well set out by contributors to a round-table discussion in *Voprosy ekonomiki*, no. 4 (1985) pp. 102–23.
4. *Pravda*, 12 April 1985.
5. See, for example, *Planovoye Khozyaistvo*, no. 8, 1984.
6. *Pravda*, 24 April 1985.
7. *The State in Socialist Society* (London: , 1984).
8. *Voprosy ekonomiki*, no. 7 (1983).
9. *Pravda*, 12 April 1985.

10. *Pravda*, 19 April 1985.
11. See Gorbachev in *Pravda*, 24 April 1985.
12. In *The Soviet Union to the Years 2000*, edited by Bergson and Levine.
13. *Voprosy istorii*, no. 8, 1984.
14. Ibid., no. 3, 1985.

24 Soviet Economic Reform: Progress and Frustrations*

For the purpose of this paper I am assuming that the basic outline of the reform package is known. It has, for example, been set out by A. Aganbegyan in his *Economics of Perestroika*, to which I wrote the preface. It has been the subject of many speeches by Gorbachev. There have been a whole number of well-publicized decrees and declarations: on small-group and family contract and leasing in agriculture, on the state enterprise and full *khozraschet*, on cooperatives, on foreign trade, on reform of prices and of material–technical supply. We can all agree that, as and when these basically desirable and progressive measures are implemented, this will be a truly radical reform, and not yet another half-hearted attempt at 'further perfecting' a basically unchanged system.

However it is also clear that little has changed so far. Gorbachev said this in his speech to the nineteenth party conference in June 1988. So did Abalkin, the director of the Institute of Economics. He wrote the following in a recent article:

> If we speak of real economic successes . . ., then very little has been achieved. Is this really unexpected? In my view it is logical. Have we in fact brought into operation all the necessary levers, factors, powers? We have adopted a few laws, made decisions, approved various documents. But it is naive to hope that by decrees and regulations we can change real life. It is not several years but several months ago that we began to change real economic relations. Furthermore a coherent and effectively functioning system of administration [of the economy] does not yet exist.[1]

In an interview, Abalkin also spoke of 'the most serious' (*tyazheleishiy*) condition of the economy.[2] 'Why does the reform not function?'

---

* Conference paper, end- 1988.

is the headline under which the well-known economist P. Bunich referred to measures which are still half-hearted and inconsistent; state enterprises should have the sort of rights granted to cooperatives under the recent law.[3] Numerous articles speak of the preservation of the command system in a supposedly new guise. Some of this is explained by the delay in implementing a reform of prices, and by the fact that the five-year plan, drafted and adopted before the reforms began, is still supposed to be operational. Many articles refer to the many problems arising out of structural imbalances, shortages, inflationary pressures, fiscal and monetary disorder, transport bottlenecks and a grossly excessive number of investment projects leading to long delays in completions. All this cannot but complicate the introduction of reform measures. For example, how can one enforce strict financial discipline on enterprises, and relate wages to performance, when it can all be distorted by irrational prices, supply bottlenecks and state orders. Workers and management naturally feel that it is unreasonable that they should be penalized for reasons quite outside their control.

Then there are repeated complaints that Gosplan and the economic ministries interpret the party's reform decisions in their own way, while pretending to obey them. Bunich cites an example which relates to foreign trade: while many enterprises now have the right to engage in trade directly, their foreign-currency receipts are turned into roubles by conversion coefficients which are deliberately differentiated so as to relate these receipts to the internal prices of analogous goods; there are over three thousand such coefficients! This removes an important incentive to export. Similar manipulation affects norms of profit retention, which are differentiated by enterprise. Gorbachev has spoken of the continued dominance, despite all declarations to the contrary, of what he called 'His Majesty the *val*' (the gross output target). Repeated criticism of arbitrary interference by party functionaries and state bureaucrats has apparently had little effect, judging from many protests from managers of farms and factories. The problem is not so much, or not only, centralization, since for example Selyunin[4] expresses the view that 'the American economy is more centrally managed today than ours', because so much power resides in departmental (*otraslevye*) empires. A similar point was made by E. Gaidar[5] while B. Bogachev[6] claims that 'far from being centralized, the economy is torn apart by feudal departmental principalities [*udely*]'.

There are many obsolete rules and regulations that stand in the way of progress, but also obsolete human attitudes, at all levels. Thus in a discussion printed in *Voprosy ekonomiki*,[7] it was reported that some local officials actually destroyed private greenhouses and plastic sheeting used for growing early vegetables and tomatoes, using 'axes and even bulldozers'. A Soviet economist whom I asked about this replied sadly: 'Unfortunately there are millions of people in our country who prefer not to have any early vegetables rather than to see their neighbour make money by growing them.'

In assessing the various obstacles to reform, one must distinguish between *deliberate opposition and obstruction* by those who oppose reform, *the practical problems of implementation*, which are in themselves formidable, and *gaps and contradictions in the reform model*, if indeed it is correct to speak of a reform model in the singular, since there are still a number of obscurities and controversies to be resolved.

One reason for the slow progress of the reform is that many people do not understand or do not share the reformers' aims, or approve the measure which it requires. This has a number of aspects. One is a gut rejection of the increased inequalities which follow from payment by results, from freedom to set up cooperatives, to increase prices, to market early vegetables. It is not only bureaucrats who take this view: it is widely held among ordinary citizens. Or to take another example: price reform should include steps to bring official prices of basic foods, and also house rents, into line with economic reality: at present they are far below supply-and-demand balance, and far below costs as well, necessitating subsidies which have grown to fantastically high levels. Many have to have recourse to the free market, where food prices are up to three times higher than the official ones. Substantial rises in the official prices are long overdue. Yet when Gorbachev broached the subject, many were opposed, even though he promised compensatory wage rises. Many workers are worried about the effect of the efficiency drive, and of the stress on financial discipline, on their job security: it is not that unemployment is likely to be a problem, but redeployment of labour from overmanned to undermanned sectors and areas can be a painful process, too, for those who have to move. Gorbachev is seeking support 'from below' for his measures, but is not finding the going easy.

Perhaps even more important is the negative attitude of many functionaries of party and state, who see in the reforms a challenge to their power and privileges, and in many cases a threat to their jobs, since the reformers' object is to strengthen the market mechanism at the expense of administrative decision-making. Theirs is the visible hand that replaces the 'invisible hand' of Adam Smith. All the reformers, from Gorbachev down, speak of excessive numbers of ministerial and party officials, of too many supervisors, of bureaucratic deformations, of the need to cut staffs severely. The *glasnost'* (openness) which has been part of the reform movement has also, for the first time for close on 60 years, allowed a public discussion of the hidden privileges of officialdom. Officials' salaries (a secret too, until average figures were quoted to the nineteenth party conference) are in fact modest, but they have special shops where goods unavailable to ordinary citizens are sold to them at low prices, they have their own hospitals, country villas and transport. All such matters were strictly hidden from public view. It was *Pravda* itself, on 13 February 1986, which broke the taboo by printing a letter, under the heading *Ochishchenie* ('Cleansing'), drawing attention to these privileges, and suggesting that shortages and queues might be fewer if wives of officials had to stand in line with ordinary citizens. The publication upset some high officials, but a precedent was set, and the press frequently returns to the issue. Indeed *Literaturnaya Rossiya*[8] printed an article by F. Dymov in which the author, a rank-and-file member of the party, complained that in his twenty years of membership he has never seen any party accounts showing how much is spent on providing these privileges, or indeed on salaries or on anything else. Abel Aganbegyan, in an interview with the popular illustrated weekly *Ogonyok*, cited a 'high Soviet official' who visited Hungary and complained to him that in Hungary anyone can get anything in the shops: 'Is this socialism?' So for this official 'socialism' was equated with privileged access to goods and services which ordinary people cannot get! Evidently radical reform would not be popular with such persons, if only because the aim is to achieve balance between demand and supply.

They can utilize for their purpose what remains of 'ideology'. Of course it can be shown that ideological principles have been frequently reinterpreted to suit the political needs of the time, never more so than in Stalin's long reign, but some beliefs are genuinely held. Thus it has long been a principle of Marxian socialism that socialism and the market are incompatible, that gradually production for sale will be replaced by conscious planning and planned distribution. The present reforms, as also those already adopted in Hungary, Poland and China, point in the opposite direction, and so opponents of reform can draw strength from the uneasiness this causes.

They can (and do) appeal also to the egalitarian tradition in the ideology. This may seem contradictory, since the privileges of officials are not exactly what Marx or Lenin meant by equality. But they are out of the public eye, they go with rank and are lost when rank is lost; whereas market-based inequalities, such as those arising from the sale of early vegetables or out of the operations of successful cooperative or private enterprises, are visible and quite widely resented.

It would be over-simple to treat all 'bureaucrats' as opponents of reform. Tatiana Zaslavskaya, the eminent economist and sociologist, reminds us that much depends both on the effect of the proposed changes on the career prospects and functions of the given official, and indeed also on his (rarely her) confidence in his (or her) abilities to work in new ways. Similarly, she points out, younger and more skilled workers are likely to see advantages and opportunities in the proposed changes, whereas the older and less skilled may resent them. Some managers welcome new responsibilities, others fear them and prefer the old ways. The essential point is that, taken together, human attitudes present serious obstacles to reform implementation, and those of officials are of particular significance since it is they who must do the implementing.

We must now turn to a different, though related, point: the practical difficulties of implementation, which would make the transition to reform very difficult even if all concerned desired that it should succeed. Obviously, these difficulties provide ammunition for those who desire to obstruct the process of change.

The first point to make relates to what might be called the inevitability of gradualness, and the contradictions to which it gives rise. As was already pointed out, the reform, to be effective, requires a new set of prices and the abandonment of administered material allocation. However existing shortages, excess demand and imbalances, render impossible a swift introduction of these necessary measures. Material imbalances coexist with financial imbalances. As Gorbachev confirmed in his speech to the nineteenth party conference, the budget is in deficit, credit discipline is poor. One cannot rely on the price mechanism if the monetary system is in disorder. One reason for imbalance between supply and demand for consumers' goods has been the reduction in the supply of vodka, part of a (necessary) campaign for sobriety; it has proved impossible to cover the gap by a sufficient supply of other goods, while loss of revenue from vodka is part of the reason for the budget deficit. On top of this, the fall in oil prices has adversely affected the balance of payments and led to a reduction in imports of consumers' goods and in budget revenue from foreign trade. So there are powerful reasons for not implementing the whole reform package at once. However, gradualness creates contradictions, with two 'logics' uneasily combined. This is particularly awkward in an economy beset by shortages: then anything that does not figure in the central production or allocation plan is deemed to be low-priority, and therefore liable to suffer from non-delivery of some of the needed inputs. A large and growing literature discusses the reasons for the chronic shortages, which are often accompanied by excessive inventories and stocks of unsold or unsaleable goods, because of mismatches between the production plans and user requirements. Gorbachev himself has stated that the allocation system itself generates shortages, and that to wait before abolishing allocation for the end of shortages would mean waiting for ever. It is certainly hoped that the emphasis on financial discipline, the end of 'soft' credits, a balanced budget and payment of wages strictly in relation to performance will eliminate excess demand for both consumers' goods and producers' goods, and facilitate the introduction of new prices together with much greater freedom to vary or fix prices by negotiation. Meanwhile difficulties persist. One consequence of *glasnost'* is that they are frankly and openly discussed. Thus, to cite another example, under the reform enterprises are to have more resources to devote to investment. However, if machinery, equipment and building materials, are in short supply and 'rationed', they may well be frustrated in their intentions.

Another problem area is concerned with overcoming habits and relationships formed by decades of working within the old system. Thus management has not had to bother with finding customers, since they were designated by their superiors in the planning hierarchy. So they benefited from virtually guaranteed sales. Under the reform they would have to learn the arts of marketing, under competitive conditions, to which they are not accustomed and for which they were not trained. Furthermore the needed information-flows and marketing intermediaries are barely in existence. No wonder many managers seek out state orders, to stay within the procedures they know, and also in the hope of getting some priority in supplies of inputs. Another example: under the reform a much larger segment of investment will be decentralized, financed partly out of retained profits and partly out of bank credits. Yet most bank managers have had little or no experience in assessing the soundness or otherwise of investment projects, since in the past their functions were mainly to channel funds in accordance with planners' instructions and to check on enterprises' use or misuse of funds. Again, a period of training will be needed.

There is repeated criticism, too, of the existence of too many contradictory rules and regulations, while at the same time contracts prove to be unenforceable, or breach of contract results only in a fine, which is paid out of enterprise funds and hurts no one. There are far too many instances of hierarchical instructions overriding contractual obligations. All this is very well known to Gorbachev, who has a degree in law. Much is being written about the need for a legal order, affecting society as a whole as well as the economy (arbitrary interference with judges in ordinary criminal cases is notorious). Party functionaries have been repeatedly instructed not to interfere with justice, or in managerial decision-making.

Here, however, is another element of uncertainty; what precisely are to be the functions of the Communist party and its full-time officials, and of the economic ministries too? If they are held responsible for the carrying out of policies in (say) the chemical machinery industry or in supplying fodder concentrates, how can they not interfere? At the nineteenth party conference, in June 1988, Gorbachev produced some new proposals about the role of the Party, seeking to eliminate duplication of function between party and state officials, by turning many party functionaries into state officials, that is, combining the two roles; thus a city party secretary would be at the same time the chairman of that city's soviet, and presumably the central committee's department on the chemical industry would be merged with the ministry of chemical industry. Which still leaves unclear what are to be the relationships between that ministry and chemical industry enterprises, or how the party's role in making all key appointments (the *nomenklatura* system) can be reconciled with elections, of management or of soviets.

The example of the chemical industry highlights yet another obscure corner in the reform 'package'. A Soviet industrial 'enterprise' is, as a rule, one factory or workshop complex. A typical Western corporation (such as Du Pont or Imperial Chemical Industries in chemicals) contains literally dozens of 'enterprises' so defined. True, there are in the USSR a number of 'associations' (*obyedineniya*) in which several enterprises are combined, but it does seem that the Soviet reformers have not fully taken on board the question of the *level* at which managerial decision-making is best exercised. This can vary widely in different sectors, both in capitalist and in socialist economies.

There are other possible gaps in the reform package itself. Thus little attention has been paid to externalities, to situations in which micro-profitability may be a misleading guide to efficiency. The one exception is ecology: there is now a growing awareness of the importance of this question, and public opinion is playing its part (thus the press reported demonstrations of citizens in a Siberian industrial city demanding an end to air pollution). There are gaps also in the whole area of investment. Apart from the point, already made above, about ensuring the availability of the needed machinery and equipment, the decentralization of investment decisions raises the question of the need for a capital market, or some other ways of enabling those enterprises with financial reserves to invest in other enterprises, if the holders of the reserves see no need to expand their own productive capacity. (The sale of stocks and shares (*aktsii*) has been proposed.) There is also the question of information about future costs and needs, which, in any economy, cannot be conveyed by today's prices, howsoever reformed: to invest one must estimate what prices, costs and demand could become in the future, and one also needs information about the investment plans of one's potential competitors and/or suppliers of complementary inputs. The question of investment decisions raises also the question of risk: who bears it, who is rewarded in the event of success or penalized in the event of failure? There is formal provision for bankruptcy, but it is very seldom applied even in such 'reformed' economies as Hungary's, because of strong pressure to maintain full employment. If, as a result of a mistaken investment decision, the enterprise is unprofitable, should its own workers suffer wage cuts, when they can claim with justice that they did not take the original investment decision? Would this not still be the case even if the decision was taken by a manager whom they had elected?

The issue of risk-taking in state-owned enterprises is a difficult one to resolve. Mises used to claim that this was an incurable weakness of socialism, that entrepreneurship and private ownership of capital were indissolubly linked. It may be objected that 'ownership' in large Western corporations is diffused, that the managers actually in charge of operations are salaried employees, no different in this respect from Soviet managers. This is not the place to pursue the argument. It is noteworthy, however, that a number of Soviet-bloc economists have become aware of the importance of the question, and the recent decisions in the USSR to encourage the creation of *cooperative* enterprises is a part-answer: cooperative property is not state property; cooperatives are to take risks in responding speedily to market stimuli; they can be allowed to go bankrupt if things go wrong. But can they be allowed to make a lot of money if things go right? The Soviet press has published on the one hand complaints from the public about cooperative profiteering, and on the other complaints that cooperatives cannot be expected to show enterprise when heavy taxes are levied or an arbitrary ceiling is imposed on members' incomes, this in the name of the still-influential egalitarian ideology. One is reminded of the sub-title of Ed Hewett's book: 'Equality versus efficiency'.[9]

So, to recapitulate: the Soviet leadership is indeed trying to introduce radical reforms. Progress is slow for three basic reasons: *opposition*, much of it (but not all) due to defence of vested interest and privilege; the sheer *practical difficulties* of implementing the desired changes, which would exist even if there were no opposition at all; and *gaps and ambiguities* in the reform model itself. Very much involved is the long-recognized dilemma of plan versus market: in what form can the two be effectively combined? Where lies the boundary between them? Here we are still conscious of a process of trial and error. There is no agreement about just where to place this boundary. There is a discussion of this very issue in an article by two well-known reforming economists, G. Popov and N. Shmelev, devoted to analyzing how it is that the rigid centralized system, based on an indissoluble link between production and supply-of-input plans, none the less generates a chronic supply deficit. ('The answer is trivially simple . . . One cannot foresee everything', especially the remoter indirect requirements, for instance of wire for electric motors required for oil pumps which pump oil required for the petrochemical industry, which supplies dyestuffs that are needed for the cloth that – finally – is needed for the clothing industry.) The authors go on to discuss 'indicative planning' and 'market-automatism', and possible combinations of these, stressing the importance in this connection of rational and flexible prices, and of the dangers of monopolistic abuses if price controls were eliminated. They show themselves aware, too, of the dangers of the pure 'free-market' solution, especially in long-term decisions, affecting structural change, ecology and the quality of life. They stress that every system must have disadvantages as well as advantages. Their own preferred solution: planning and price control limited 'to a few hundred of the most important products, i.e. the quantity which under favourable circumstances we are able to count in physical units at the present level of knowledge and techniques for the gathering and processing of information. All the rest of output should not be planned at all, either directively or indicatively.'[10] But this is the authors' view, not an authoritative judgment or programme. They emphasize that by trying to plan everything one can end up by planning nothing. They quote the words of one of the best of the reformer-economists, N. Petrakov: 'In a state supposedly planned, we have for long developed chaotically [*stikhiino*, uncontrollably, spontaneously]. Plans rubber-stamp inertia tendencies, "determine" what just occurs on its own, from quinquennium to quinquennium.'[11] It cannot be too strongly emphasized that in recent years centralized controls have not just been inefficient, they have failed to control. Several authors have used the word 'anarchy' to describe a situation in which sectoral ministries have become too strong for the agencies called upon to coordinate them.

I have drawn up a long list of problems, difficulties, snags, inconsistencies, and also referred to opposition from various strata of society. Does this mean that failure is inevitable? I do not think so. As Gorbachev repeatedly tells us, 'there is no other way'. Stagnation would threaten the security of the regime, internally and externally. It used to be said that 'the party' would resist any serious reform, because the existing system maximized its power and privileges. Without wishing to deny that this is one factor in the opposition to change, it is none the less a fact that reforms have been adopted and are being pressed forward by the *party* leadership, since it has realized that economic failure has a profoundly negative effect also on its own power. So a serious attempt will be made, *is* being made, to introduce radical change in the economy and in society.

Two points with which to conclude. One is that the initial period of reform implementation, with a necessary learning process and trial and error, is hardly likely to be associated with rapid improvement in either productivity or living standards. There may even be temporary regress, unless the radical measures being introduced in agriculture (family leases and small genuine cooperatives) have a quick and positive effect on food supplies. It will also be difficult to restore fiscal and monetary order (an article in *Kommunist*, no. 11, 1988, has at last spoken openly of the hitherto concealed budget deficit, which is there estimated at 15–17 per cent, and at long last there are increasing signs that the real figure of military expenditure will be published).

My second point relates to the attitude the West should take. Some dedicated cold warriors believe that we should do our best to ensure the failure of Gorbachev's reform programme, because a more efficient USSR would represent a more dangerous enemy. The argument often then becomes zoological: a leopard cannot change his spots, the wolf cannot by negotiation be turned into a vegetarian, a more powerful bear is a greater menace (though, when it suits them, the same ideologists point out that a hungry bear is even more dangerous . . .). I entirely disagree, and all these references to the animal kingdom must be seen as variants on the theme that fundamental change in the USSR is in principle impossible. Yet fundamental change is being attempted, and quite clearly it is not confined to the economy. *Glasnost'*, a legal order, 'socialist pluralism', wider cultural and trade links with the West, arms reduction – all these should surely be welcomed as being conducive also to a reduction in international tension. Whether all these measures, including the economic reform itself, will actually succeed is still problematical. They should, however, be welcomed, not obstructed.

NOTES

1. *Moskovskie novosti*, 26 June 1988, p. 9.
2. *Argumenty i fakty*, no. 26 (1988).
3. Ibid., no. 25 (1988).
4. Selyunin, *Novyi mir*, no. 5, 1988.
5. Gaidar, *Kommunist*, no. 2, 1988.
6. *Voprosy ekonomiki*, no. 5, 1988.
7. Ibid., no. 6, 1987.
8. 17 June 1988.
9. Ed. Hewett, *Reforming the Soviet Economy* (Washington: Brookings Institution, 1988).
10. G. Popov and N. Shmelev, 'Anatomiya defitsita', *Znamya* (May 1988) p. 180.
11. Ibid., p. 181.

Index

Abalkin, A. 244, 355
Abramov, Fyodor 298, 303
abundance 173
accumulation 14
Acland-Hood, Mary 332
Adam Smith Institute 167
Aganbegyan, A. 321, 340, 355, 358
agriculture 302–11
  labour incentives in *kolkhozy* 290–1, 352
  Second World War 90–103
  service enterprises 254
  Tugan-Baranovsky 36–8
  see also peasantry
Agroprom (agro-industrial complex) 305, 306, 307, 310
Alexander I, Tsar 3, 18, 22, 259
Alexander II, Tsar 116
alienation, elimination of 173–4
Amann, Ron 313
Andropov, Yuri 341
Aniskov, V. T. 90, 101, 102
Arndt, Helmut 237, 250
Arrow, K. 251
Arutunyan, Yu. V. 90, 92–6 *passim* 99, 101, 102
AT&T 150
Austria 277–8
Austrian school of economists 249–50
autonomous work-teams 296–9, 303–4
Aven, P. 239
Avtorkhanov, A. 206
Axelrod, P. 176

Bahro, Rudolf 188, 204, 217
Baldwin, Stanley 84
banks 20, 21–2
Baran, P. 15
Barone, Enrico 133, 175
Bebel, August 174–5
Belkin, V. 303
Bell telephone network 150
Belov, V. 88
Berdyayev, N. 118
Bergson, A. 287, 330
Berliner, Joseph 351
Bernstein, E. 30
Bettelheim, Charles 195, 198, 235
Bienkowski, A. 201, 205, 216
Birman, Igor 331, 332
Bobrinsky, Count 116
Bogachev, V. 356
Bogdanov, Alexander 45, 240
Bogomolov, O. 352
Bolsheviks 43, 44, 46, 48, 55
  demand right to rule alone 180
  impact of revolution on modernization 117–18
  liquidation of first generation 187
Bonin, John P. 290
Borodin, Alexander 3
bottleneck effect 313, 317–18
Bovin, Alexander 124
Brest-Litovsk, Treaty of 46
Brezhnev, Leonid 297, 340–1
  agriculture 306, 307
  petrification under 121
Britain
  diplomatic relations severed 83
  economic theories in the 1980s 144–9 *passim*
  industrial crises 26–8
  Thatcherism 241–3
British Gas 160
British Telecom 150, 168
Brus, W. 206, 216, 217
Buchanan, James 169, 241, 242
budgetary defence vote 328–9, 331–2
Bukharin, N. I. 80, 172, 182, 186, 204, 225
  Lenin and 60, 64–6, 68
  NEP 84–7 *passim*
  planning 132

'socialism in one country' 178, 193
socialist production 177
Stalin's exploitation of peasantry 205
Trotsky and 71, 73, 75, 85
war communism 46, 47, 178
Bulgaria 218, 240
Bunich, P. 349, 356
Bykov, P. 269, 270

Cambridge school of economists 316
Carr, E. H. 80
Carrère d'Encausse, H. 215
Castoriadis, C. 196, 199, 205
Catherine II (the Great), Empress 19, 30, 115–16, 118
centralization
planning model 134–41
under Stalin 118–19, 179, 183, 188
Chavance, Bernard 210
Chayanov, A. V. 64, 87, 211
Cheka, the 43, 46, 184
Chelintsev, A. 87
Chernenko, Konstantin 341
Chernichenko, Y. 305, 308
'Chicago' school of economists 148, 150, 239, 241
China 217, 232, 300
economic difficulties 237
'household responsibility' system 138, 297, 299, 351
planning model 138
reforms 349
Chulkov, M. 19
CIA 327, 329, 330, 332, 333, 336, 338
Ciliga, C. 200
civil war 45–6, 47, 53
Clark, Colin 265
Clark, J. B. 33, 34
class, Marxism and 199–200
classless society 174
Coase, R. 169
Cohen, Stephen 71, 73
Comecon countries, technology imports from 319–20
Comintern 63, 179
command planning *see* planning
commodity fetishism 173
compulsory product mix 284–5
Congdon, Tim 145
consumer goods 270–5, 284–5
Converse, Ray 280
Cooper, Julian 313
cooperatives 36–8, 352
corruption 240
Crozier, Brian 236
Cuban missile crisis 111, 112, 325
Cushman, Robert E. 161
Czech legion 46
Czechoslovakia 218, 240, 277–8

Dallin, Alexander 91
Danielson, Nikolai 26
Danilov, V. 88
Danilova, L. V. 204
Day, Richard 73, 74, 75, 85, 193
Deane, Phyllis 247
defence burden 325–39
Defense Monitor 333
Demsetz, Harold 169, 252, 253, 254
Denikin, General 46
Denton, E. 271
'departmentalism' 256
deregulation 162–3
Deryabin, A. 335
despotism 118–19, 179
oriental 203–5
Deutscher, I. 72
Diderot, Denis 115
distribution 33–4
division of labour, elimination of 173–4
Djilas, Milovan 199
Dmitrenko, V. 188, 189, 191, 352
Dostoevsky, Fyodor 117, 343
Dubcek, Alexander 226
Duchêne, Gérard 329, 330
Dymov, F. 358
Dzerzhinsky, Felix 87

Earl, Peter 165, 241
econometrics 151–2
Ellman, Michael 298

Engels, Friedrich 31, 154, 171n, 174, 175, 235
  commodity production and socialism 244
  planning 27, 131, 132
equilibrium, neoclassical 246–8, 249–50, 253
Eurocommunism 200–4
Europeanization 114–17
Evstigneyeva, L. 336
exchange rates 259

factories 28–30
  see also industry
Faltsman, V. 267, 315, 318, 319, 335
feasible socialism 230, 232–43
Fedorenko, Academician 133, 342
firm, theory of the 250–2, 259
fragmentationism 164–70
Frankel, Ben 230
Free Economics Society 18
freedom 156–9
Friedman, M. 148, 153–63, 259
Friedman, R. 153

Gaidar, E. 356
Garvi, P. 85
Gatovsky, L. M. 336
George V, King 118
German Democratic Republic (GDR) 240, 352, 353
German invasion 90–1, 94–5, 102
Gerschenkron, Alexander 115
'Gerschenkron effect' 265, 266
Giersch, H. 169
Gill, Louis 233
glasnost' 121, 123, 358, 365
Gomulka, S. 316, 317
'Goodhart's Law' 146, 267, 273, 276
Gorbachev, Mikhail 88
  agriculture 122, 303–4, 305, 307, 309, 351–2
  autonomous work-groups 297
  defence costs 325n
  growth retardation 312, 316
  modernization 121–4
  'pre-crisis situation' 238
  prices 336
  reform 347, 348, 353, 355–61 *passim*, 364; delays 345; need for economic 191, 218; radical 232, 237
Gossen, H. 31
Gouldner, Alvin W. 204, 216
great-power objectives 213–15
Green, D. 316, 318
Greenslade, R. 271
Grilliches, Z. 275
Groman, V. 88
Grossman, Vasili 114, 184, 187
growth 265–89
  imported technology's contribution 312–24
'Gulags' 184, 187

Hahn, Frank 170, 251, 253, 259
  equilibrium 246, 247
  investment 168, 249
Hansen, Alvin 28
Hanson, Philip 313, 319
Harding, N. 206, 347
Havlik, P. 277, 278, 281
Hayek, F. 152, 249
Hedlund, Stefan 296
Hegedüs, A. 348
Heller, Agnes 174
Hewett, Ed 363
Hirszowicz, Maria 200, 206
Hitler, Adolf 213
Hodgman, D. 265
Holliday, George D. 318, 319
Holzman, Franklyn 333
Hungary 240, 358, 362
  intellectuals under communism 201
  New Economic Mechanism (NEM) 136–8, 217–18, 235, 345, 347, 351
  private business 138, 230
  success in agriculture 353

imperfect information 151–2
imported technology 312–24
incentives, labour 290–301, 352
income policies 229
incomes, peasant 98–100

individualism,
methodological 241–2
industry
output 278–80
under Khrushchev 105–13
see also factories
intellectuals 200–2
investment
agriculture 307–8
defence 334–7
mixed economy 229
neoclassical economics 248–9
rising costs 267–8, 276
Ipatenko, Y. 300
Israelsen, D. 290, 291, 293, 295, 297

Jacobs, W. W. 260
Jacobsen, Carl G. 333
Japan 131, 249, 323
Jaruzelski, General 218, 232
Jasny, Naum 265, 266
Jevons, S. 25, 28, 31
Joseph, Sir Keith 168
Journal of Comparative Economics 290, 316, 322
Jowitt, Ken 211

Kaganovich, L. M. 88
Kaldor, N. 291
Kalecki, Michael 226
Kamenev, L. 85, 88, 186
Kantorovich, L. 105, 112, 140, 141
Kautsky, Karl 131, 175–6, 177, 225
Kennedy, President J. F. 325
Keynes, J. M. 152, 246
Khanin, G. 278, 336, 337
hidden price rises and growth 279–81
Kheinman, S. 321
Khrushchev, Nikita 102, 186, 216, 307
cooperatives abolished 352
Cuban missile crisis 111, 112, 325
industry under 105–13
promises in transition to communism 189
Khudenko, I. 297, 303
Kinnock, Neil 226
Kirzner, Israel 236, 237, 249, 250
Klyamkin, I. 88
Knei-Paz, Baruch 79
Koestler, Arthur 164, 259
Kolchak, Admiral 46
kolkhozy 302, 309
labour incentives 290–301, 352
Kommunist 364
Kondratiev, N. D. 25, 34, 38, 87
Konrad, G. 200, 202
Kornai, Janos 140, 236, 245, 253, 273, 351
buyers' market 246
decision-making and price 140, 160, 249
sellers' market 271–2
Koryagina, T. 347
Kowalik, T. 175
Krasovsky, V. 267, 335
Kritsman, L. 43, 53, 183
Krokodil 285, 302n
Kronstadt revolt 47, 48, 58
Krzhizhanovski, M. 67
kulaks 58, 86
Bukharin 65–6
Lenin and 48, 63, 68
Kuusinen, Otto 213
Kuznetsov, V. 208

labour incentives 290–301, 352
Labour Party, British 242–3
labour policy, British New Right 223–4
Laird, Roy D. 294, 297
land reform 36–7
land rent 15
Lane, David 200
Lange, Oskar 161, 175, 236, 249, 250
planning model 139–40
Soviet planning as war economy 118–19, 132
Larin, Y. 46
LaRoque, Admiral 333
Leamer, Edward E. 152
Lear, Norman 169
Lee, W. 327, 329

Lefort, Claude 199
left-wing extremism 224–6
Leibenstein, H. 250
Leijonhufvud, Axel 164, 251
Lend-Lease 91
Lenin, V. I. 78, 88, 114, 171n, 209, 244
  capitalism 117
  Eurocommunist criticism 203–4
  NEP 53, 56–70, 72, 81, 178
  'party maximum' 185
  politics 172, 212
  trade unions 182
  Tugan-Baranovsky 38
  view of socialism 176–7; economics 66–7; one-party state 180; planning 131, 132
  war communism 43, 44–5, 47, 48, 56–7, 58; view of 50–6
Leontief, W. 152, 260
Lerner, Abba 139, 161
Levine, H. 316, 318
Lewin, Moshe 71
Liberman, E. 112
Liska, T. 224
List, F. 22
Literaturnaya gazeta 303
Literaturnaya Rossiya 358
livestock 101–2
living standards 277–8
Loasby, Brian 165, 237, 247, 248, 253, 258
Lobanov, P. 96
Lokshin, R. 270, 271, 272, 274
Lucas, R. 242, 247
Luxembourg, Rosa 176, 180
Lyashchenko, P. 100

Machine Tractor Stations (MTS) 93, 97, 98, 100
machinery
  agricultural 96–7
  prices 267–70, 334–7
  production 279–80, 320–1
Magna Carta 116
Maiminas, E. 240
Makarov, V. 87
Makhaisky, J. 202
Malafayev, A. 83
Malenkov, Georgi 104, 105
Malthus, Thomas 35
Mandel, Ernest 71, 198, 233, 234, 235
Maoism 191
Marcovic, Mikhailo 215
marginal utility theory 31–3
markets 144–52
  Friedman 153–63
  planning and 222–31
Markus, C. 204, 205, 211, 343, 348
Marshall, Alfred 259
Marx, Karl 154, 171n
  abstractions 245
  Marxism in Russia 192–3
  planning 27, 71, 78, 132; anarchy of capitalism 131; information 341
  utopian 233
  value 32, 347
Marxism 171–221
  Eurocommunism and neo-Marxism 200–7
  key elements 172–4
  'Left' critique 191–200
  Stalinism 179–91
  Tugan-Baranovsky and 31–6 *passim*
Matskevich, V. 297, 299
Mayakovsky, V. 178
McCauley, M. 215
McCulloch, J. 11
Medawar, Sir Peter 312
Medvedev, Roy 187
Medvedev, V. 336
Mellman, Seymour 160
Menger, G. 25, 31
Mensheviks 43, 57, 180, 183, 203
methodological individualism 241–2
Mikhailovsky, N. 192
military opposition to reform 349–50
Mill, John Stuart 25, 26
Mises, L. von 132, 140, 236, 250, 362
Mitterrand, François 236
mixed economy proposals 226–31

modernization 114–25
Molotov, V. 213
monetarism
  criticised 222–4
  naive 144, 146–8
money 6–7, 16–17
  elimination of 173
  mixed economy 229
monopolies, natural 149, 51, 168, 228
Mordvinov, N. S. 3, 18–22
Morgenstern, O. 267
Mozhaev, B. 88

naive monetarism 144, 146–8
Napoleon 118
nationalization 57
NATO military expenditure 333
natural monopolies 149–51, 168, 228
Nemchinov, V. 112
neoclassical economics, and reforms 244–61
New Economic Policy (NEP) 48, 118, 138, 178
  end of 80–9
  Lenin and 53, 56–70, 72, 81, 178
  transition to 56–60
  Trotsky's view of 72–6 *passim*
New Left Review 233
New Right extremism 222–4
New York Times 75, 162
Nicholas I, Tsar 11, 18, 19, 22, 116
Nicholas II, Tsar 118
Nicholson, J. L. 275, 277, 283
Nikonov, A. 87, 304
NKVD 93, 97, 184
Nogi, General 55, 56
nomenklatura 179, 185–6, 208–9
Novack, Michael 169
Novakovsky, Yu. 83
Nove, Alec 172, 237
  defence expenditures 328
  localism 108
  NEP 82
  nomenklatura 186
  prices 270
  producers 161, 230
Novikov, O. 269, 336
Novozhilov, V. 74, 82, 105, 112, 347
Novyi Mir 95, 186, 305, 307
Nuikin, A. 87
Nutter, W. 265

Obolensky, V. V. 59
Observer 167
Ogonyok 358
Olsevich, Y. 172
'one-dimensional' marginalism 252–4
one-party state 44, 179–83, 184–5
Oxford University Institute of Statistics *Bulletin* 270
oriental despotism 203–5

Palterovich, D. 336
Parkinson, Cecil 168
Pashukanis, E. 123
peasantry
  Lenin's view of during NEP 62–4
  Second World War 90–103
  see also agriculture
Perevedentsev, V. 303
Perlamutrov, V. 336
personality, cult of 186
Pervukhin, M. 106
Peter the Great, Tsar 19, 186, 192, 207
  factories 29, 30
  modernization 114–15, 121
  Stalin and 118
Petrakov, N. 364
planning 129–43
  Friedman 153–63
  key element in Marxism 174
  markets and 222–31
  problems in reform 344
Plekhanov, G. 176, 203, 204
Podkaminer, R. 286
Pogrebinsky, M. 95
Poincaré, Raymond 84
Pokrovsky, M. 192
Poland 218, 232, 240, 283, 286, 358

planning model 138
Popov, G. 363
Popov, V. 244
Posevkomy 57
Pososhkov, I. 19
Pravda 315, 353
kolkhozy 294
Kronstadt rising 59
privileges 358
waste 343–4
Preobrazhensky, E. A. 63, 68, 71, 84–5, 177, 178
money 46
'primitive socialist accumulation' 73, 130, 193
state capitalism 60
and Trotsky 75, 85
prices
consumer goods 270–5
critique of neoclassical theory 257–8
machinery 267–70, 334–7
unreliability of indices 265–76
wages and 283–4
private plots 99, 294–5, 308–9
Proudhon, Pierre Joseph 25
Prychitko, David 248
'public choice' theories 256
public goods 257
public services 130, 227–8
efficiency 167–8, 169
Pushkin, Alexander 3, 115, 116

Quesnay, F. 35

Radical Philosophy 225
Rakovsky, R. 186, 200, 209
RAPO (*raion* agro-industrial association) 306, 307, 310
rational expectations 144, 147, 148, 222
Reagan, President Ronald 332
Red Army 46, 47
reforms
modernization 114–25
neoclassical economics and 244–61
opposition to 240, 347, 349–50, 356–9, 363
progress of economic 355–65
within-system 340–54
Reisner, M. 123
Ribbentrop, Joachim von 213
Ricardo, David 4, 15, 26, 32
Richardson, G. B. 250
investment 131, 151, 156, 248, 249
Rigby, T. H. 206
Robbins, Lord 260
Romania 218, 232
Rosefielde, S. 316, 317, 333, 334
defence expenditure estimates 327, 329
ruling class 209–11, 216
Russian American Company 18
Rybakov, Anatoli 80, 81, 84, 86
Rykov, A. I. 44, 62, 75, 85, 186
kulaks 84
Stalin 80

Sakharov, Andrei 201
Samuelson, P. 255
Sargent, T. 247
Say, J.-B. 4, 11, 13, 26
Schapiro, Leonard 115–16
Schiller, Otto 90–1
Schlözer, August-Ludwig von 4
Schroeder, G. 271, 343
Schumpeter, J. 11, 34, 224, 250
Scotland 157–8
Scotsman 167
Selden, Arthur 236
Selskaya zhizn 310
Selucky, R. 205
Selyunin, V. 337, 356
Semyonov, Yu. 203
serfdom 17–18, 19–20, 116, 117, 156–7
Sergeyev, Professor A. 244
Serpell report 149
Seton, F. 265, 266
Severin, B. 271
Shackle, G. L. S. 150, 246, 249
Shcherbakov, A. S. 99
Shironin, V. 239
Shletser, Christian 4–10, 259
Shmelev, G. 88
Shmelev, N. 87, 363

shortages 245–6
Shtorkh, Alexander Karlovich 10–18, 19, 20, 21, 259
Shturman, Dora 205
Shubik, M. 250
Sik, O. 226
Simon, H. 250, 256
Sintaksis 201
Sismondi, S. de 26
Skvortsova, V. 310
Smith, Adam 3, 4, 19, 20, 28, 357
  infrastructure 257
  Shtorkh and 11, 13–14, 17
Sochor, Lubomir 189, 190
social services 228–9
Social Research 233
socialism
  feasible 230, 232–43
  Lenin and economics of 66–7
  'really existing' and Marxism 171–221
Sokol'nikov, G. 67, 72
'Solidarity' 218
Solow, R. 247
Solzhenitsyn, Alexander 184, 187, 215
South Korea 131, 142
sovkhozy (state-farms) 295, 296, 299, 302n, 309
sovnarkhozy 106, 108–9
St Petersburg 114
'Stakhanovist' campaigns 185
Stalin, Josef 48, 104, 129, 201, 203–4, 325
  basic law of socialism 190
  centralized planned economy 183
  coercion 183
  collectivization drive 88, 186
  false claims 187–8
  NEP 74, 75; abolished 80, 86, 87; 'left turn' 82, 85
  'revolution from above' 118
  'socialism in one country' 178
  warning to economists 105
'Stalin constitution' 187–8
Stalinism
  modernization 118–21
  nature of 179–91
state, withering away of 174
state capitalism 194–6
state-farms (*sovkhozy*) 295, 296, 299, 302n, 309
Steinberg, D. 331, 334
  defence expenditure estimates 329–30, 332
Stockholm International Peace Research Institute (SIPRI) 327, 333
Stolypin, Piotr Arkadevich 117
Strumilin, S. G. 328
Struve, Peter B. 34, 35
surplus value 34–5
Suslov, M. 188
Sutela, P. 175
Sverdlik, Sh. S. 271, 274
Szamuely, L. 46
Szelenyi, I. 200, 202, 205

talent, rent of 14–15
Taussig, F. 33
technology, imported 312–24
terror, Stalin's use of 179, 183–4, 199, 202, 204
Thatcher, Margaret 16, 130, 222, 228, 242, 323
  enterprise culture 241
  society 255
Thatcherism 240, 241–3
Ticktin, H. 198
Tinbergen, J. 139
Toda, Yasushi 316
Tolstoy, Leo 117
totalitarianism 206, 216
trade 9, 17
trade cycle 28
transitional society 196–9
transport subsidies 166–7
Trotsky, Leon 54, 71–80, 178, 186
  belief in investment 74–5, 85
  critique of Stalinism 192, 193, 194, 199
  Lenin and 'substitutionism' 180
  militarization of labour 46, 88, 182–3
  private trade 57
  transitional epoch 224

views on the party 78–9, 181–2
trudodni (workday units) 92, 93, 94, 97, 100
Trzeciakowski, W. 318
Tsipko, A. 80n
Tugan-Baranovsky, M. I. 24–39, 64

under-consumption theories 26–8
unemployment 229
Utechin, Sergei 188

Vainshtein, Albert L. 82, 84
Val'tukh, K. 268, 335
value
  Shtorkh's theory 11–12
  surplus 34–5
Varga, E. 105
Vavilov, N. I. 201
Vernadsky, G. 10, 11
Vestnik finansov 74, 82
Vestnik Statistiki 334
Voloshin, M. 118
Voltaire, F. de 115
Voprosy ekonomiki 244, 245, 347, 349, 352, 356
Voprosy istorii 352
Vorontsov, Vasily 26
Voslensky, M. 205, 208, 214
Vosnesensky, N. 91, 98, 105

wages system, elimination of 173
Walras, L. 25, 31, 251
Walters, Alan 259
war communism 43–9, 88, 177–8
  Lenin and *see* Lenin
Ward, B. 159, 291
waste 344
Weitzman, Martin 316, 317
welfare measurement 282–3
Wells, H. G. 58
Westernization 114–17
Wiener, Norbert 260
Wieser, F. 33
Wiles, P. 275, 326, 328, 329, 331
Williamson, O. E. 151, 169, 228n, 250–1, 252
Wittfogel, K. 203
Wrangel, General 47
WTO military expenditure 333
Wu, Henry 246

XYZ 210

Yudenich, General 46
Yugoslavia 232, 240
  planning/self management combination 138–9, 158, 159, 218, 291
Yuridicheski Vestnik 25
Yurovsky, L. N. 88

Zaslavskaya, T. 120, 191, 341, 347, 349
  reform 343, 351; agriculture leading 309; obstacles to 345, 348, 359
Zasulich, Vera 174, 192
Zauberman, A. 328
Zelenin, V. 96, 101
Zhuravlev, S. 334, 336
Zinoviev, Alexander 215
Zinoviev, Grigory 74, 85, 178, 186